To Vera, Mary, Richard, and James,
without whom this book would not have been possible.

Mastering the Standard C++ Classes

An Essential Reference

Cameron Hughes
Tracey Hughes

Wiley Computer Publishing

John Wiley & Sons, Inc.

NEW YORK • ⬛⬛⬛⬛⬛ SBANE • SINGAPORE • TORONTO

Publisher: Robert Ipsen

Editor: Marjorie Spencer

Assistant Editor: Margaret Hendrey

Managing Editor: Marnie Wielage

Electronic Products, Associate Editor: Mike Sosa

Text Design & Composition: North Market Street Graphics

Designations used by companies to distinguish their products are often claimed as trademarks. In all instances where John Wiley & Sons, Inc., is aware of a claim, the product names appear in initial capital or ALL CAPITAL LETTERS. Readers, however, should contact the appropriate companies for more complete information regarding trademarks and registration.

This book is printed on acid-free paper. ∞

Published by John Wiley & Sons, Inc.

Published simultaneously in Canada.

This publication is designed to provide accurate and authoritative information in regard to the subject matter covered. It is sold with the understanding that the publisher is not engaged in professional services. If professional advice or other expert assistance is required, the services of a competent professional person should be sought.

Library of Congress Cataloging-in-Publication Data:
   Hughes, Cameron, 1960–
      Mastering the standard C++ classes : an essential reference /
   Cameron Hughes, Tracey Hughes.
       p.   cm.
   Includes bibliographical references.
   ISBN 0-471-32893-6 (pbk./CD-ROM : alk. paper)
    1. C++ (Computer program language)   I. Hughes, Tracey.
   II. Title.
   QA76.73.C153H837   1999
   005.13'3—dc21   99-25757
                                    CIP

Printed in the United Sates of America.

10 9 8 7 6 5 4 3 2 1

CONTENTS

C++ is a general-purpose programming language. It has complete support for three of the most important approaches to programming in use today:

- Structured programming
- Object-oriented programming
- Parameterized (generic) programming

The support for these three programming paradigms makes C++ one of the most flexible, powerful, and complete languages available. Any general discussion of C++ can be divided into two important parts: the expressive and comprehensive language and a large library of reusable software components. The second part is called the standard C++ library. It consists of a vast collection of functions, objects, and algorithms. In this book, we focus on two important sets of components in the standard C++ library:

- Standard C++ classes
- Standard C++ algorithms

While there is no shortage of books that describe the C++ language and how to program in C++, there are very few books that attempt to explain the standard C++ library. There are even fewer books that attempt to describe and explain all the object-oriented and parameterized components available in the standard C++ library. Some books describe only certain components of the standard C++ classes, such as the iostreams or the Standard Template Library, while others provide only brief general overviews. At the time of this writing, there is a shortage of material aimed at giving the C++ programmer and software developer a comprehensive understanding of the ANSI/ISO C++ classes and algorithms. It is the goal of this book, *Mastering the Standard C++ Classes,* to provide the C++ programmer and software developer with a complete tutorial and reference on the object-oriented components and algorithms in the new ANSI/ISO C++ standard.

The Standard C++ Classes and Algorithms

The standard C++ classes and algorithms cover a lot of territory. They provide the C++ developer with:

An object oriented approach to input/output

Parameterized (generic) programming support

An object-oriented approach to exception handling

An object-oriented approach to internationalization

Object-oriented data structures

An object-oriented approach to computer memory models

The standard classes and algorithms give the C++ programmer a collection of reliable *ready-made, ready-to-use* (and in most cases *easy-to-use*) software components. These classes provide the developer with object-oriented versions of string processing, exception handling, object-oriented data input and output, runtime type manipulation, memory management, data management, object-oriented super-computing support, hardware control, internationalization, and much more.

In *Mastering the Standard C++ Classes,* we give a detailed explanation of the standard C++ classes and algorithm components. We describe the inner workings of each class and the services that each class offers. This book also contains a tutorial for the entire collection of standard C++ classes, each including a simple, easy-to-understand discussion of how to use the class along with an explanation of system requirements and performance issues. This book also serves as a comprehensive reference for each class and every member function included in the C++ standard class library.

What's So Important about the Standard C++ Classes and Algorithms?

The American National Standards Institute (ANSI) and the International Standards Organization (ISO) have accepted and approved a standard for the C++ language and C++ library. This means that any C++ implementation that is ANSI/ISO-compliant will support the classes and algorithms that we discuss in this book. It also means that the reader can develop a single set of software components that can be used both nationally and internationally. The fact that the C++ library classes and algorithms are now standardized means that the C++ programmer and software developer can implement C++ components in one environment and then compile them in another. For instance, C++ standard components in a Unix environment will work with C++ standard components in a Macintosh environment. Standard classes and algorithms implemented on PC workstations can also work on supercomputers.

Robust, Generic, and Predictable Components

The standard C++ classes and algorithms are important to the developer because they have already been tested. They represent robust software units ready to be put to work immediately. They can be treated as a solid foundation of software building blocks used to build larger object-oriented programs, class libraries, application frameworks, and large-scale software systems.

The performance and the efficiency of the standard C++ algorithms are documented and will be described in this book. Knowing the performance of the standard C++ algorithms in advance means there are no performance surprises for the developer. If a sorting program uses the standard C++ classes and algorithms, we can know exactly how long it will take to sort a large list of objects. We can know exactly how long it will take a search to determine whether a particular object is in a file, list, or some other container. Since the standard components support parameterized (generic) programming, we can solve a problem once, and use the solution over again in many different contexts. Thus, the standard C++ classes and algorithms are designed to increase programmer productivity and software reusability. Simply put, they are designed to make your job easier.

Who Is This Book For?

This book provides an introduction to the standard C++ classes and algorithms, and can therefore be used by novices and advanced programmers alike. A brief acquaintance with the C++ programming language is assumed. Many of the basic concepts of object-oriented programming and parameterized programming are reviewed so that the uninitiated or forgetful will find this book easy to read and informative. Further, Java programmers who have a need to integrate Java programs with C++ will find a thorough discussion and documentation of the standard C++ classes, their attributes, and methods.

Chapter 13 specifically addresses how to access Java classes from C++ classes. C++ programmers who need to learn how to embed the Java Virtual Machine (JVM) into a C++ program will also find this book useful. And because this book is both a tutorial and a reference, professional C++ programmers will find the class descriptions and member function explanations in the reference portion of this book a welcome addition to the documentation that comes with most C++ compilers. Designers of object-oriented application frameworks and CORBA classes will find the discussion of the architecture and interfaces of the standard C++ classes timely and appropriate.

Compiler Environments

The examples and sample applications in this book have been designed using the ANSI/ISO standard for the C++ language. Therefore, any C++ implementation supporting the new ANSI/ISO standard can compile all the examples in this book. It does not mean, however, that if the reader doesn't have the latest compiler technology the book will not be useful. It is important to note that at the time of this writing virtually none of the compiler vendors were 100 percent compliant with the new standard, so we have attempted to keep the code examples within the limits of most commercial C++ implementations. More than 90 percent of the code examples in this book were successfully compiled with little or no changes under:

Sun's Visual Workshop C++ 3.0

GNU C++ 2.7.2 and 2.8

Inprise (Borland) 5.0

Inprise (Borland) C++ Builder 3.0

Inprise (Borland) C++ Builder 4.0

Microsoft Visual C++ 5.0

Microsoft Visual C++ 6.0

IBM's Visual Age 4.0

Portland Group's C++ Workstation

Some compilers that we tested did not support valarray < > and templatized iostreams.

Chapter Organization and Code Examples

Each chapter consists of practical discussions and examples. Diagrams and tables are used to aid in explaining and organizing difficult topics. Some of the chapters contain ancillary information to encourage a more advanced understanding of the foundations behind the algorithms, exception handling, and the container classes. This information is displayed in sidebars, and so can be skipped without missing the important points in the chapter. The code examples have been designed to be simple and easy to understand; we made no attempt to present optimized or highly efficient code. Our goal was to present the concepts demonstrated in the code examples in a straightforward manner.

C++ Class Reference

An electronic document containing the reference sections of this book is contained on the CD-ROM that accompanies this book. The reference document offers complete coverage of the C++ classes and algorithms, using Microsoft's Internet Explorer 3.0 and 4.0.

Testing and Code Reliability

We tested all the examples and applications in this book to ensure correctness, but we offer no warranties that the programs contained in this book are free of defects or error, are consistent with any particular standard of merchantability, or will meet you requirement for a particular application. They should not be relied on for solving a problem whose incorrect solution could result in injury to a person or loss of property. The authors and publishers disclaim all liability for direct or consequential damages resulting from your use of the examples or applications presented in this book and contained on the CD-ROM accompanying this book.

ACKNOWLEDGMENTS

We would like to give a warm thanks to our editors Marjorie Spencer and Margaret Hendrey at Wiley who endured our many, many restarts and missed deadlines. We would like to thank Isabelle Mauny from IBM/Toronto, and the folks from Inprise for the state-of-the-art C++ compilers that were donated to this project for testing. We would also like to thank Professor Raoul Hewitt III for his help with the German translation, collating sequences, and locale programming. Finally, we would like to thank our many friends and colleagues from Youngstown State University who allowed us to bring out notebook computers to lunch.

CHAPTER 1

Introduction to the C++ Class Library

"We are generalists.... You can't draw neat lines around plane-wide problems"

—KYNES
DUNE

The standard C++ class library is an extremely flexible and extensible set of reusable software building blocks. It offers complete support for object-oriented software construction. It also contains full support for implementing generic software frameworks. The components in the C++ class library can be used in software development efforts of all sizes, ranging from low-level operating systems or compiler-type design to high-level real-world modeling and event simulation. We have seen these components at work in object-oriented software that include areas as diverse as:

Emergency room simulation	High-speed locomotives control
Hydroponic gardens	Chemical structure analysis
Playground modeling	Movie theater automation
Cartoon character animation	Global position locators
Satellite tracking	Cookie baking
All-terrain vehicles control	Software clocks
Calendars	Virtual answering machines
Android nervous systems	Weight-loss simulations
Operating systems	Compilers
Software calculators	Internet financial transaction processing
Wedding dress selection	

Although most of the standard C++ classes represent lower-level foundation objects, the majority of components in the C++ class library can be used as-is or be extended using object-oriented programming or genericity (parameterized) programming techniques. The C++ standard class library equips the software developer and software designer with one of the most powerful and useful set of software components available.

It is important to note that these components are multipurpose. They are very different from some of the popular commercially available single-purpose or restricted-purpose class libraries. For example, some class libraries are designed to handle only graphical user interfaces. Others are designed to handle only database manipulation; still others handle only numerical computation. There are application frameworks that focus specifically on serial communications and networking. This is not the case with the standard C++ classes; more general in purpose, they are not dedicated to any particular problem-solving domain. They can be used as building blocks to help form the structural foundation for higher-level classes, class libraries, and application frameworks; they can be used as software mortar, or glue, to help hold together more complex object-oriented architectures. There are many ways to categorize, organize, and view the classes and software components in the class library, but in this book, we will consider the standard classes and components from three points of view:

- Functional
- Architectural
- Interface

The *functional view* shows how the classes are divided into different areas of functionality; that is, which classes are used for input/output, which classes are used for memory management, which classes are used for error handling and so forth. The *architectural view* shows how the classes fit together and what their class relationships are. We'll answer, for instance, which classes are related to other classes and how? Or how are the memory management classes used in conjunction with the error-handling classes? The architectural view also shows how object orientation and genericity are used to build the standard C++ class library, and how the standard C++ algorithms work with the iterators and containers to form generic object-oriented data structures. The *interface view* shows how software designers and developers must design and develop software components if they are to properly interface with the C++ standard class library. After all, the primary objective of sound parameterized programming and object-oriented programming is to obtain clean, meaningful, and well-designed software interfaces.

The C++ Standard Classes: A Functional View

The standard C++ classes and components fit logically into six categories:

- Input/output
- Containers and ADTs
- Memory management
- Algorithms
- Error handling
- Runtime environment support

Although there are other logical categories into which the standard C++ classes and components can be placed (and often are!), these six categories represent the basic areas of functionality into which the components fall. These six categories and the components that belong to them are shown in Table 1.1, which represents the functional view of the standard C++ classes and components.

NOTE:

We include the standard algorithms, function objects, and predicates in our discussion of the C++ classes because of the relationship between these components and the standard classes. Although these components can be used in other ways, their primary function is to work in conjunction with the standard C++ classes and other user-defined classes.

Object-Oriented Input/Output

The iostream classes present an object-oriented model of input and output (I/O). This means data accepted as input or generated as output is done through the use of services the iostream objects offer. The iostream classes provide the C++ programmer with the complete range of I/O services. Data that needs to be read from the keyboard, internal memory, external storage, or other devices connected to the computer can be processed using input objects based on the iostream classes. Data that needs to be sent to internal memory buffers, files in external storage, the console, printers, or any other output devices can be processed using output objects based on the iostream classes. If some input device or output device is not immediately supported by the iostream class library, then that support can be added because the iostream library is open and extensible through the use of inheritance, overriding, and overloading methods, iterators, and templates. The C++ iostream class library is one of the most powerful and flexible input/output facilities available.

The C++ language borrows the concept of the input and the output stream from Unix and the C language, but the streams in the C language are not object-oriented, whereas the iostream model is. There are 15 core classes in the iostream class library. Table 1.2 lists the functional categories into which the 15 classes are divided. The 15 classes fall into three basic categories:

- Buffer
- State/formatting
- Translation

Buffer Components (Bytes in Transition)

There are three basic buffer components:

basic_filebuf< >   (filebuf)

basic_stringbuf< >   (stringbuf)

basic_streambuf< >   (streambuf)

Table 1.1   Functional Categories of Standard C++ Classes and Components

MEMORY MANAGEMENT		
allocator	auto_ptr	
INPUT/OUTPUT		
ios_base	basic_iostream	basic_stringstream
fpos	basic_ostream	basic_filebuf
basic_ios	basic_stringbuf	basic_ifstream
basic_streambuf	basic_istringstream	basic_ofstream
basic_istream	basic_ostringstream	basic_fstream
CONTAINERS/ADTs		
deque	vector	string
queue	map	iterator
priority_queue	multimap	valarray
list	set	complex
stack	multiset	
RUNTIME ENVIRONMENT SUPPORT		
RT Object Identification	*RT Execution Environment*	
type_info	char_traits	
bad_cast	numeric_limits	
bad_typeid		
RT Country/Language Domain		
locale	numpunct	time_put_byname
ctype	numpunct_byname	money_get
ctype_byname	collate	moneypunct
codecvt_byname	time_get	moneypunct_byname
num_get	time_get_byname	messages
num_put	time_put	messages_byname
money_put		
ALGORITHMS	**ERROR HANDLING**	
searching	*Runtime Error*	*Logic Error*
sorting	length_error	range_error
statistical information	domain_error	overflow_error
set operations	out_of_range	underflow_error
numeric operations	invalid_argument	
heap operations		
comparison operations		
container management		

Table 1.2 Functional Class Categories

BUFFER CLASSES		
basic_streambuf	basic_filebuf	basic_stringbuf
TRANSLATOR CLASSES		
basic_iostream	basic_istream	basic_ostream
basic_fstream	basic_ifstream	basic_ofstream
basic_stringstream	basic_istringstream	basic_ostringstream
FORMAT CLASSES		
ios_base	basic_ios	

The buffer components act as temporary holding bays for sequences of bytes. These components encapsulate the blocks of memory where the input and output data are temporarily stored while they are in transit from their input sources or their output destinations. Figure 1.1 shows how an object might travel from some external input device to a temporary buffer component to its final destination in memory.

There are three basic types of buffer classes in the iostream class library:

File buffers	basic_filebuf< >
Device buffers	basic_streambuf< >
In memory buffers	basic_stringnbuf< >

The kind of input/output that is needed in the program determines which buffer(s) will be used. Each buffer class is associated with a different translator class. Table 1.3 lists the buffer classes and their associated translator classes, and we will discuss their association further when we explore the architectural view of the C++ standard classes.

Stream State and Format Control Components

In addition to the components that represent temporary storage, the iostream classes contain two basic classes that encapsulate and maintain the state that the input or output stream is in:

- ios_base< >
- basic_ios< >

There are many possible states that a stream can be in during the execution of a program. A stream may be in a *good* state, meaning that the stream is ready to either have data inserted or extracted. A stream may be in *failed* state, meaning that unless the stream is reset in some fashion, further operations on the stream will not be successful. A stream may be in a *bad* state, meaning that all bets are off (a bad state is often shorthand for "it's time to throw an exception!"). The stream can be put into user-defined states. States assigned by the programmer can be somewhere between a good state and a bad state. For instance, a *device not ready* state is not the same as a bad or a failed state. However, until the device becomes ready, any further insertion or extraction opera-

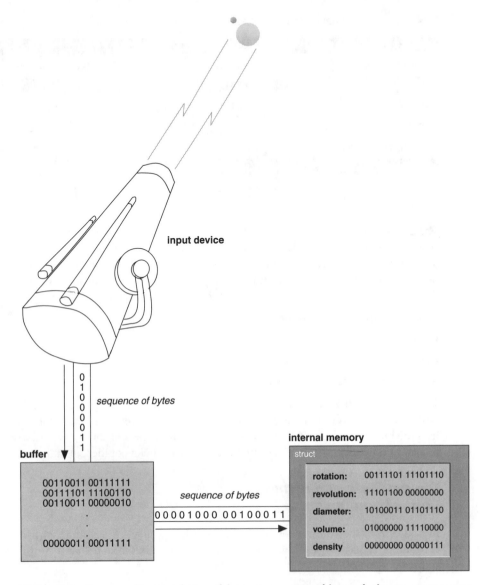

Figure 1.1 How an object might travel from some external input device to a temporary buffer component to its final destination in memory.

tions performed on a stream representing that device will not be successful. In addition to good, fail, and bad states, there is the *end-of-file* (EOF) state, which is also somewhere between a good and a fail state, because until the stream is rewound or repositioned in some fashion, further insertion or extraction operations on the stream will not be successful.

In addition to state information, the ios components maintain formatting information. The state control components are responsible for encapsulating the buffer state and the format state of the data that is being input or output. This formatting of the stream

Table 1.3 Buffer Classes and Their Associated Translator Classes

BUFFER CLASS	TRANSLATOR CLASS
basic_streambuf	basic_iostream
	basic_istream
	basic_ostream
basic_stringbuf	basic_stringstream
	basic_istringstream
	basic_ostringstream
basic_filebuf	basic_fstream
	basic_ifstream
	basic_ofstream

determines whether numbers will be represented as floating point or fixed and whether strings will be left- or right-justified when they are output. The formatting also can be used to determine whether a decimal point will appear in a numeric value, to determine the width of a string to print, or the fill character to be used for blanks that occur within a string. The ios components also have formatting states that maintain whether a numeric value will be represented as decimal, hexadecimal, or octal. Uppercase or lowercase are also state designations that can be maintained by the ios components.

The buffer components give the iostream objects temporay holding areas for input or output data. The state/formatting components maintain the state the stream objects are in and how they will be represented upon input into or output from the stream.

Device-Independent Streams

One of the advances of I/O devices in modern programming languages is the notion of device independence. Many programming languages still in use have different language statements for different devices. This means that entirely different language statements may be used depending on the device being accessed. This device-dependent programming results in programs that are not portable and that are difficult to maintain. In contrast, the C++ object-oriented model of input and output is based on the notion of *streams*. A stream simultaneously represents two ideas. The first is that the stream is a generic sequence of bytes proceeding to some input device or from some output device. The second idea is that the stream is a generic device. When we are dealing with the stream in its purest form, our only concern is whether the stream is open for reading a generic sequence of bytes or for writing a generic sequence of bytes or both. We do not build specific data structures or file control blocks for specific devices. We do not have one set of program statements for devices, such as tape drives, and another set of program statements for devices, such as direct access disk drives. We do not have special commands representing differences between character-oriented devices and block-oriented devices.

No matter what the input or the output device is, the interface to the stream is the same. The iostream class has nine basic stream classes. Table 1.4 lists the categories these nine streams belong to. These streams are sometimes referred to as *stream translation* or *stream conversion* classes, because two of the primary jobs of these translator classes are to convert complex objects into simple input streams and extract complex objects from simple output streams. Since objects can have a variety of sizes and shapes, inputting and outputting objects can be difficult. For instance, if our program contains a cafeteria object, how do we write that object to disk? Or, if our program is modeling a playground, and we need a new jungle gym object, how do we read the object into the computer program?

Inputting and outputting complex or user-defined objects is especially troublesome if we are attempting to achieve the stream model of input and output. As just stated, it is a primary function of the translator classes to transform objects into generic sequences of bytes that can be inserted into or extracted from a stream. Whether the objects represent complex user-defined classes or simple built-in types, one or more of the nine stream classes will be used to translate these objects into simple sequences. This translation or conversion is a two-way process: the input stream classes read generic sequences of bytes and convert those bytes into the appropriate user-defined or built-in objects; the output stream classes take user-defined or built-in objects and translates them into generic sequences of byes. The buffer components, the state/formatting components, and the translation combined present an object-oriented, device-independent model of input/output in a C++ program.

Containers and Abstract Data Types

Object-oriented programming in C++ is primarily concerned with software construction, modeling, event simulation, and system building, using software components and building blocks. The component and building block approach is important because it improves programmer productivity. We use the following ten items to measure programmer productivity:

- The time it takes to organize a software approach to a task or a solution to a problem.

- The time it takes to deliver a software system, subsystem, or component.

- The performance of the software component in terms of the efficient use of system resources.

Table 1.4   Basic Stream Classes

STREAM CLASSES		
Console	*In-memory*	*File*
basic_iostream	basic_stringstream	basic_fstream
basic_istream	basic_istringstream	basic_ifstream
basic_ostream	basic_ostringstream	basic_ofstream

- The programmer's confidence that the software component is robust and fault-tolerant.

- The maintainability factor of the software component.

- The clarity of architecture of the software component.

- The programmer's ability to communicate and explain the software component's function.

- The completeness of the software component delivered.

- The correctness of the software component delivered.

- The amount of reuse employed in constructing the system, subsystem, or software component.

The C++ language delivers support for the building block approach through its object-oriented facilities. Not only do these facilities give C++ programmers the tools to build object-oriented software components, some of the most useful aspects of the language are the software components that are built in the language. The C++ standard class library provides a wealth of *ready-made* fundamental software building blocks, a large number of which are part of the iostream classes, and an even larger number of which are part of the standard C++ container classes and abstract data types (ADTs).

What Are Containers?

Containers are objects designed to hold, or contain, groups or collections of objects. In the same fashion that a box can contain a set of books or a bag can hold a collection of pencils, a C++ container can contain an object or collection of objects. Containers act as *generic holders.* Containers in C++ may hold mixed contents. This means they may contain collections of different kinds of objects or objects of the same type. When a container holds a group of mixed objects, it is called a *heterogenous* container. When the container holds a group of same objects, it is called a *homogenous* container. Containers get their name from their function, and once we have containers to store objects in and retrieve objects from, we can think about the kinds of operations that we can perform on objects that are stored or associated with containers.

Next to inputting a piece of data into the computer or outputting a piece of data to a device connected to the computer, no activity is more commonly performed in computer programming than these operations: searching, sorting, adding, retrieving, and storing data. In fact, directing a computer to perform this type of data manipulation can be considered inherent to the definition of computer programming. The container classes in C++ are used to help institute these basic operations.

Sorting, searching, adding, subtracting, storing, and other data manipulation operations usually require specific data types and data structures before they can be employed. In nonobject-oriented programming languages such as C, Fortran, Pascal, and Cobol, computer programs are divided into data types, data structures, and the operations and algorithms that perform work on those data structures. Table 1.5 lists some of the commonly used data structures and ADTs.

Table 1.5   Commonly Used Data Structures and ADTs

CONTAINERS	ABSTRACT DATA TYPES
stack	strings
queue	valarray
array	complex numbers
list	iterators

These data structures and data types are used to store information in a computer during program execution. While the computer program is performing data operations such as searching, sorting, adding and subtracting, storing, retrieving, and manipulating, the data normally has to be stored in some kind of memory within the computer. That memory is organized in some fashion that makes the operations easy or efficient to perform. The organization of the data within memory is called its *data structure*. The operations or well-defined procedures that perform work on this organized data are often called *algorithms.*

The problem with many programming languages is that the programmer has to define these algorithms and data structures each time a program is written; they are not supplied as a part of the programming language. For instance, in C, if a programmer needs to sort a list made up of a variable number of integers or strings, he or she must first construct some kind of memory organization that will hold the integers or strings (data structure), then define a sequence of steps that will process that data in such a way that the data will be sorted. For every data type the programmer intends to sort, he or she must figure out how to organize memory (data structure). For example, to sort a list of strings would require a data structure that could hold a list of strings; to sort a list of floating point numbers would require a data structure that could hold a list of floating point numbers. Each data structure would have to be built from scratch by the programmer. This is not the case in C++, because the C++ standard classes provide the programmer with these data structures in the form of *containers*. These built-in containers give the programmer ready-made object-oriented versions of the data structures that have to be built from scratch in C, Pascal, Cobol, or Fortran. The containers and algorithms that work with the containers represent two of the most important components of the standard C++ class library.

There are ten core container classes and five basic ADTs supplied with the standard C++ class library. Table 1.6 lists the containers and ADTs and their categories. There are two basic container categories: sequence and associative.

Sequence containers are used to store objects logically in a linear arrangement. Objects that are stored in sequence containers are usually processed based on their position within the sequence. For example, we may want to specify the object at the beginning of a list or at the end of a list. We may want to specify an object that is in the middle of a vector or an object that is the second object stored in a vector, and so forth. The stack class presents only the top of the stack to the user. The queue class presents either the first object in the queue or the last object in the queue. This is in contrast to associative containers that present another logical view of the container. They store objects in the container based on their relationships to other objects within the con-

Table 1.6 Containers and ADTs and Their Categories

CONTAINERS	
Sequence	*Associative*
vector	map
deque	multimap
stack	set
queue	multiset
list	
priority queue	
ADT's	
Numeric	*Nonnumeric*
valarray	string
complex number	bitset

tainer. With associative containers, storage and retrieval is based on keys and relationships between objects, as opposed to storage and retrieval based on sequences.

For example, we may have a map class called OurMap that is set up like this:

```
OurMap["purple"] = "barney";
OurMap["yellow"] = '"tweetie bird'";
OurMap["green"] = "hornet";
OurMap["blue"] = "smurf";
```

The class OurMap is a container that holds string objects. The string objects are:

barney

tweetie bird

hornet

smurf

We are not concerned with the position of these objects within the OurMap container. Whenever we wish to access a specific string object, we specify the key for that string object. OurMap container has four keys:

purple

yellow

green

blue

When we specify a specific key, we are able to access the corresponding object. For instance:

```
X = OurMap["purple"];
```

stores the object *barney* into the variable X. Access to objects within the associative containers are based on keys. Access to objects within the sequence containers are based on position of the object within some sequence. For example, if we have a vector object called OurVector, then:

```
X = OurVector[5];
```

assigns X to the object at the sixth position within the OurVector container—based on the fact that vectors and arrays in C++ start at position 0. If we were to specify:

```
X = OurVector[0];
```

this would assign to X the first object in the OurVector container. To access objects in sequence containers, we specify *positions.* To access objects in associative containers, we specify *keys.*

The container classes provide object-oriented versions of some of the fundamental data structures. The container objects can be used to store either built-in or user defined objects. Once objects are placed into containers, they can be sorted, searched, or manipulated in the same fashion nonobject-oriented data types are processed within the classic data structures.

In addition to the functional division of the containers into the sequence and associative categories as listed in Table 1.6, we can separate certain of the containers into a category called *adaptors.* Table 1.7 lists the adaptor classes along with the classes that are not adaptors.

What Are Adaptors?

Adaptor classes are interface classes, created by providing new interfaces to existing classes. Adaptors classes modify or adjust the interface of other classes in order to simplify, restrict, make safe, disguise, or change the view of the set of services that the modified class is providing. When a class is used for the sole purpose of changing the interface of another class, it is called an adaptor, or an interface class (see Stroustrup, 1991, p. 457). For example, the stack class is created by providing a new interface to one of the nonadaptor classes, that is, vector, list, or deque. Figure 1.2 illustrates how a stack class is used to adapt a vector class to give the user a new kind of interface. (We discuss interface classes in more detail in Chapter 2.)

Table 1.7 Adaptor and Nonadaptor Classes

NONADAPTOR CLASSES	ADAPTOR CLASSES
vector	stack
list	queue
deque	priority queue
map/multimap	
set/multiset	

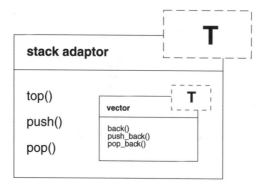

Figure 1.2 How a stack class is used to adapt a vector class to give the user a new kind of interface.

Object Visitation in the Container Classes

There must be a mechanism that allows the user to access each object in a container. Some containers have this mechanism specified as part of their definitions. For instance, for the pop operation of a stack object, the user can access every object that has been stored in the stack. Another example of an access mechanism specified as part of the definition of an object is the [ ] operator of the vector. With the [ ] subscript operator, the user can access every object that has been stored in a vector or matrix. However, there are container definitions that don't specify anything about object access. For example, the notion of a set specifies requirements about set membership, set intersection, set union, subset, set complements, and so forth, but there is no mention about visiting each member in the set. For the set class, the designer must specify some sort of access mechanism that allows total object visitation. The standard C++ class library provides a generic method that allows total object visitation of any of the containers in the class library. This method involves a class of generic pointers called *iterators*. Object visitation in containers is accomplished by two methods:

- Member functions
- Iterators

What Are Iterators?

Iterators are best described as object-oriented, polymorphic, generalized pointers. An iterator can be a data member of the container and can be implemented with *friend* member function and other similar techniques. However, the standard C++ class library implements the iterator as a separate but cooperating class with the container class it is designed for. The iterator provides a method to perform sequential or, in some cases, direct access to any object in a given container. The iterator acts as a kind of cursor or position locator in a container of objects. Once the iterator has reached the required object, it can be used to access the object. In the same way that a pointer in C++ is dereferenced to access the data to which the pointer is pointing, the iterator is dereferenced to allow the user to access the object to which the iterator is pointing. Whereas pointers refer to the location objects within computer memory, iterators refer to the location of objects within containers. There are five basic categories of iterators listed in Table 1.8 along with their distinguishing characteristics.

These iterators enable us to move around within a container as well as to access and manipulate particular objects in a container. Some iterators are read-only. They prevent the user from modifying the object to which it refers. Other iterators, such as the bidirectional iterators, allow us to move forward or backward within a container, and give us the ability to change the object to which it is referring.

Important New ADTs

Most commercial C++ compilers have always had some sort of string class, though implemented a little differently. They also offer different services, and the member functions have different names (or have the same names but different purposes). This leads to portability problems. The ANSI standard committee recently signed off on the final draft of a standard for the C++ language. It includes some very useful classes and object-oriented versions of a number of traditional ADTs. The string class is one of the new standard editions to the C++ language.

The New String Standard

The string class completely encapsulates the most commonly used functions found in string processing and raw text manipulation. Table 1.9 lists the basic services available for the new standard string class.

The new string class now has a clean interface to the iostream classes, the container classes, the iterator classes, the allocator classes, and the C++ exception-handling mechanism; it also supports wide characters. This support is possible because the new string class has been implemented as a template:

```
basic_string<X, Y, Z>
```

where X is the type of wide, narrow, or other character the string class will contain. Y is a set of character traits defining how some of the fundamental operations are per-

Table 1.8 Categories of Iterators and Their Distinguishing Characteristics

ITERATOR	READ	WRITE	ACCESS	ITERATION	COMPARISON
Input	= *p		* ->	++	== !=
Output		*p =	*	++	
Forward	= *p	*p =	* ->	++	== !=
Bidirectional	= *p	*p =	* ->	++ --	== !=
Random Access	= *p	*p =	* ->	++ -- +	== != <
				+= -- -=	<= > >=

What Is an ADT?

The C++ class is an object-oriented version of the traditional notion of the *abstract data type* (ADT). The abstract data type describes the properties and the available services provided by the structure to the outside world. Classes can be used to represent abstract data types (ADT and the C++ class are often used interchangeably). A data type is a collection of values and a set of operations that manipulate those values. An ADT defines the basic concepts of the data type. Both built-in and user-defined data types have this level of abstraction. There are four C++ ADTs or classes that are more or less standalone classes and do not easily fit into the functional categories that we have discussed so far.

formed on character type X, and Z is an allocator class responsible for some of the memory management for basic_string. A typedef is usually created to supply the basic_string template with some default parameters. It looks something like this:

```
typedef basic_string<char,char_traits<char>,allocator<char>> string;
```

This typedef provides a default definition and a string declaration, to allow the programmer to use the string class in its most common form. When the basic_string template is specialized using the char type, it is often referred to as the *narrow string class*, as opposed to the *wide string class* defined by using a wchar_t object to the basic_string template. When a wide string class is defined as a typedef, it often looks like:

```
typedef basic_string<wchar_t> wstring;
```

Although the typedefs string and wstring are different because of the char and wchar_t specifications, the services provided for string are identical to those provided for wstring. The templatizing of the string class allows the C++ programmer to design more support for internationalization within a program. The multiple language character sets can now be supported in a standard fashion within a C++ program.

The New Standard Complex Number Class

Prior to the adoption of the recent standard for the C++ language, most C++ compiler producers provided their own complex number class. Those of us who needed to use C++ for portable serious number crunching were at the mercy of the compiler writers. Although the names of some of the member functions were the same, the functions would often have subtle differences in behavior. Some compilers supported complex conjugation, but most did not. Consequently, the applications of basic complex number algebra among different compiler implementations was often unpredictable, and legitimate support for the transcendental functions or basic hyperbolic function support was sketchy. There was no standard or complete set of services offered that covered the complex number classes by the commercial compiler vendors. This changed with the advent of the new ANSI/ISO standard for the complex number class. Now, for those interested in trajectories in the complex plane, phasor diagrams, analytic continuation, and so on, there standard core support for complex number and the funda-

Table 1.9 String Data Type Services

METHODS	DESCRIPTION
Element Access	
[], at( )	Returns the character at the given position.
Element Access via Iterator	
begin( )	Returns an iterator that points to the first character.
end( )	Returns an iterator that points to past-the-end value.
rbegin( )	Returns reverse_iterator(end( )).
rend( )	Returns reverse_iterator(begin( )).
Data Component Access	
c_str( )	Returns a pointer to the first element of the array whose last element is a null character.
data( )	Returns a pointer to the first element of the array.
Assignment	
assign( )	Assigns a string, a character, a substring to another string.
=	Assigns a string or a character to another string.
Comparisons	
compare( )	Compares a string to another string or array of characters.
Insertion/Append	
insert( )	Inserts a character, characters, subsequence, or string at a given position.
+=	Appends a character or string to another string.
append( )	Appends a character, characters, subsequence, or string to another string.
Concatenation	
+	Constructs a new string by putting one string after another.
Search	
find( )	Variations of this function will find and return the starting position of a subsequence.
Replace/Erase/Clear	
replace( )	Can replace a specific character or substring of a string.
erase( )	Removes a character or characters from a string.
clear( )	Erases all the characters in the string.
empty( )	Returns size( ) == 0.

Table 1.9 (*Continued*)

METHODS	DESCRIPTION
Substring Operations	
substr( )	Returns a substring of a string.
Statistical	
size( )	Returns the number of characters in the string.
length( )	Returns size( ).
max_size( )	Returns the maximum size of the string.
resize( )	Changes the length of the string to the given size.
reserve( )	Informs the string object of a future size change.
Input/Output	
<<, >>	Insertion and extraction operators.
getline( )	Reads a line of characters terminated by the EOL to a string.
Copy/Swap	
swap( )	Swaps the contents of two strings.
copy( )	Copies a string to another string.

mental operations on the complex number. The operations and functions provided for the standard complex class are listed in Table 1.10.

The complex number class has a clean interface to the iostream classes through the << inserter operator and the >> extractor operator. It has basic support for complex number algebra, the trigonometric functions, hyperbolic functions, and polar coordinate manipulation. We now have a complex number data type that is pretty much on par with the other numeric data types in C++.

Valarray: A Numeric-Intensive Array

Another important class in the standard C++ class library for number crunching is valarray. This class encapsulates the mathematical idea of a one-dimensional array of numeric values, and is meant to provide efficient highly optimized mathematical operations on an array of numeric values. In fact, valarray<T>, along with its associate classes slice_array<T>, gslice_array<T>, indirect_array<T>, and mask_array<T>, go a long way to helping the C++ programmer in the war of words of us against the Fortran folks. Traditionally, Fortran has been the *lingua franca* between scientists, engineers, and the computer, because the Fortran community boasts many robust mathematical and numeric libraries. Libraries such as LINPACK, LAPACK, and the Basic Linear Algebra Subprograms (BLAS) form the foundations of some of the most significant scientific number crunching done on computers, ranging from workstation to supercomputer. The libraries are used to perform heavy-duty parallel vector, matrix, and other

Table 1.10 Standard Complex Number Data Operations and Functions Type

METHODS	DESCRIPTION
Arithmetic Operators	
+, +=	Complex number addition
−, −=	Complex number subtraction
/, /=	Complex number division
*, *=	Complex number multiplication
Comparison Operators	
==, !=	Complex number equality and inequality
Assignment Operator	
=	Complex number assignment
Functions	
real( )	Returns the real part of the complex number
imag( )	Returns the imaginary part of the complex number
GLOBAL FUNCTIONS AND OPERATIONS	
Trigonometric Functions	
sin( )	Sine of complex number
sinh( )	Hyperbolic sine of complex number
cos( )	Cosine of complex number
cosh( )	Hyperbolic cosine of complex number
tan( )	Tangent of complex number
tanh( )	Hyperbolic tangent of complex number
Exponentiation, Power, and Logarithmic Functions	
pow( )	Complex number raised to a power
exp( )	Base e exponential of complex number
log( )	Base e logarithm of complex number
log10( )	Base 10 logarithm of complex number
Other Mathematical Functions	
abs( )	Magnitude of complex number
arg( )	Phase angle of complex number
norm( )	Squared magnitude of complex number
conj( )	Conjugate of complex number
polar( )	Value corresponding to a complex number
sqrt( )	Square root of complex number
Input/Output Operators	
>>	Extract complex number from input stream
<<	Insert complex number to output stream

NOTE: There is a global counterpart for all bolded member functions and operators.

linear algebra computations. The valarray<T> family of classes gives the C++ community some of the important building blocks that will enable us to play catch up!

The valarray class and its associates are designed with high performance and possible parallelization in mind. Table 1.11 lists the core services available for objects of type valarray.

Many of the operations on valarray would be by N rows, so the potential for parallel execution exists for those environments that support such processing. For example, take the three valarrays X, Y, Z:

$$X[0] = 1 \qquad Y[0] = 4 \qquad Z[10] = 10$$
$$X[1] = 2 \qquad Y[1] = 5 \qquad Z[11] = 10$$
$$X[2] = 3 \qquad Y[2] = 6 \qquad Z[12] = 10$$

Table 1.11 Valarray Core Services

METHODS	DESCRIPTION
Assignment	
=	The elements of one valarray are assigned to another valarray. An assignment assigns a scalar value to each element in the array.
=	A subset of type slice_array, gslice_array, mask_array, or indirect_array (specified by operator[ ]) of the valarray is replaced.
Element Access	
[ ]	Returns the value at the given position.
Subset Operations	
[ ]	Returns a subset of the array of type: valarray, slice_array, gslice_array, mask_array, or indirect_array.
Unary Operators	
+, −, ~, !	Returns a valarray in which the operator has been applied to each element.
Member Functions	
size( )	Returns the number of elements in the array.
shift( ), cshift( )	Shifts the elements in the array a given number of positions.
apply( )	Applies a function to every element in the array.
resize( )	Changes the size of the array to a given size.
sum( )	Returns the sum of all the elements in the array.
GLOBAL FUNCTIONS	
min( )	Returns the smallest value in the array.
max( )	Returns the largest value in the array.

Then the operation

$$A = X * Y * Z$$

may be done in parallel if the environment supports parallelism, thanks to the way the fundamental operations are implemented for the valarray class (ADT). These three valarrays will be multiplied and stored in valarray A, as follows:

$$A[0] = 1 * 4 * 10$$

$$A[1] = 2 * 5 * 10$$

$$A[2] = 3 * 6 * 10$$

That is, the operation X * Y * Z will be multiplied by rows and can therefore be multiplied in parallel. Thus, the value of A[0] can be calculated independently of the value of A[1] and A[2]; the value of A[0] is not dependent on A[1] or A[2] and the value for A[1] is not dependent on the value of A[0] or A[2] and so on.

There are many applications in which parallel optimization of this sort would be very useful—for example, many graphic applications that require solid modeling, ray tracing, geometric translation, rotation, or other types of transformation. There are numerous mathematic, scientific, and engineering applications that can take advantage of scalar arithmetic on highly optimized single-dimensioned arrays. Table 1.12 lists some of the basic arithmetic operations available on a valarray object.

It is important to note that any special optimizations that would available for the valarray type would be done by the compiler implementor, and as such are compiler-specific. Nevertheless, the interface remains standard across any implementation of the valarray class. So, while the implementation details may differ—that is, how one compiler implementor optimizes versus how another optimizes—the user interface to the valarray class will be the same. And because the valarray class has the core set of arithmetic operations defined, it is almost on par with the built-in mathematical types of the C++ language.

Masks, Flags, and Binary Digits

The standard library provides a wide range of useful classes, from high-level ADTs such as maps, stacks, and deques, down to low-level classes such as bitset<N>. The bitset class represents a sequence of binary digits (bits) that can have the value of either 0 or 1, and provides the classic list of services for bit processing (see Table 1.13). The available operations on bitset classes should satisfy even the most demanding hardware-level abstractions. One of the advantages of the C++ language is support for both high-level modeling and low-level programming in the same package.

Traditionally, bitmasks are used to contain device states, condition flags, hardware registers, signal statuses, and so on. The char and int types are usually used to store the bit values and bitmasks. The bits are manipulated using the C++ shift operators <<, >>, &, |. The bitset<N> set class improves on the classic bitmask by applying the concepts of object orientation to the notion of a sequence of bits. The to_ulong( ), and to_string( ) methods allow the programmer to export values that have been appropriately manip-

Table 1.12 Valarray Object Arithmetic Operations

ARITHMETIC OPERATIONS	DESCRIPTION
Computed Assignment	
+=	Addition
−=	Subtraction
%=	Modulus
*=	Multiplication
/=	Division
Global Operators	
sin( )	Sine
sinh( )	Hyperbolic sine
asin( )	Arcsine
cos( )	Cosine
cosh( )	Hyperbolic cosine
acos( )	Arccosine
tan( )	Tangent
tanh( )	Hyperbolic tangent
atan( )	Arctangent
atan2( )	Arctangent of x[i] / y[i]
pow( )	Raised to a power
exp( )	Base e exponential
log( )	Base e logarithm
log10( )	Base 10 logarithm
abs( )	Magnitude
sqrt( )	Square root

NOTE: There is a global nonassignment counterpart for all bolded member operators.

ulated. These values can be used in the normal fashion—for example, with device drivers, operating system components, and so on.

Memory Management

There are two classes that fit nicely into the memory management category. They are:

- allocator<T>
- auto_ptr<T>

Although these classes do not manage memory directly, they are involved in encapsulating and "putting an object-oriented face" on many of the issues of memory directly

Table 1.13 Bitset Core Services

METHODS	DESCRIPTION
Operators	
&=	Clears each bit in a bitset for which the corresponding bit in another bitset is clear.
|=	Sets each bit in a bitset for which the corresponding bit in another bitset is set.
^=	Toggles each bit in a bitset for which the corresponding bit in another bitset is set.
~	Flips the bit.
<<=, >>=	Bit replacement.
Functions	
set( )	Sets all bits or a specific bit.
reset( )	Resets all bits or a specific bit.
flip( )	Toggles all bits or a specific bit.
to_ulong( )	Returns the sum of the bit values in the bit sequence.
to_string( )	Returns a string object with a string value initialized with the bit sequence.
count( )	Returns a count of the number of bits set in the sequence.
size( )	Returns the length of the bit sequence.
any( )	Returns true if any bit in sequence is 1.
none( )	Returns true if there is no bit in the sequence that is 1.
test( )	Returns true if the bit at the given position is 1.
Access Methods	
[]	Returns the bit at the given position.
Equality and Inequality	
==, !=	Equality or inequality between two bitset objects; each bit is compared.
GLOBAL OPERATORS	
&	Clears each bit in a bitset for which the corresponding bit in another bitset is cleared.
|	Sets each bit in a bitset for which the corresponding bit in another bitset is set.
^	Toggles each bit in a bitset for which the corresponding bit in another bitset is set.
Input/Output	
<<, >>	Insertion and extraction.

involved with resource initialization, memory models, pointer types, pointer difference information, and certain aspects of allocating and deallocating an object of type T.

Little Portable Memory Models

The allocator class is an object-oriented and parameterized component that helps to support portable memory model programming. It is used to provide a platform-independent view of memory to most of the classes in the standard C++ library. The allocator has a liberating effect on the classes in the library because most of the classes have been templatized, and one of the arguments the template definitions require is an allocator object.

Since the allocator object encapsulates the memory model of the computing environment, we can support multiple memory models by supporting multiple allocators. Figure 1.3 shows the relationships between standard C++ classes, allocators, and diverse machine memory models. In the figure, we have a Cray J932 supercomputer, a Digital Alpha Axp, and a Macintosh PowerBook, each with a C++ compiler. However, each computer has a radically different memory model, word size, pointer stride, and approach to allocating and deallocating objects. The size of a pointer on the Cray J932 is certainly different from an equivalent pointer on a Macintosh PowerBook. How are these differences accounted for when allocating storage for container objects, string objects, iostream objects, or valarray objects? The allocator class encapsulates these differences and provides data hiding and abstraction for the classes in the C++ standard library that use allocator objects. This means a container object can be specialized to a particular environment simply by changing the allocator class that is associated with

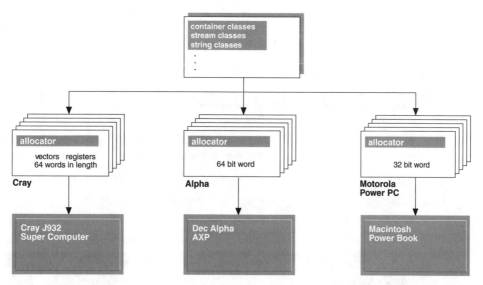

Figure 1.3 Relationships between standard C++ classes, allocators, and diverse machine memory models.

the container. Table 1.14 lists the core aspects of the memory model that the allocator class encapsulates.

The allocator classes can also be extended through inheritance and user-defined specifications. This means that users can define special-purpose allocators. For instance, if we have a container object that is physically distributed over more than one computer, via a network, then specialized allocators and iterators are in order. The allocator would be responsible for encapsulating the memory models of the network operating systems and network machines, and the iterators would be responsible for providing a method to visit each object in the container, regardless of its location on the network. Furthermore, as machines with multiple processors become more accessible, the *pram* (parallel random access machine) memory model and its derivatives will become increasingly important. By using the allocator class as a memory model helper, the C++ programmer can move much further along the path of platform-independent software development.

auto_ptr

The auto_ptr class is another memory management helper class. It is initialized by a pointer; from that point, it is used as a regular pointer with a number of differences. First, auto_ptr is a parameterized object. After an object of type auto_ptr is initialized, it will always point to the object of the correct type. Normally, nonobject-oriented pointers can be easily abused and misued. The programmer can initialize a regular pointer to point to one kind of object and then assign it to another kind of object that happens to have a different size. What happens when pointer arithmetic is performed? The auto_ptr class prevents this kind of problem, and the memory it references is also automatically released when the auto_ptr object goes out of scope.

The auto_ptr class is more of a convenience than a necessity in the standard class library. Most of the work done by the auto_ptr object can be accomplished by properly designed destructors. However, the auto_ptr class does have the virtue of automatic

Table 1.14 Allocator Class Encapsulations

MEMBER FUNCTIONS	DESCRIPTION
address( )	Returns a reference to an object.
allocate( )	Returns a pointer to the initial element of an array of storage.
construct( )	Constructs an object by using new( ).
deallocate( )	Deallocates the storage of an object.
destroy( )	Destroys an object.
max_size( )	Returns the largest value for which allocate( ) succeeds.
GLOBAL OPERATORS	
Equality and Inequality	
==, !=	Returns true or false.

memory release for the object to which it points. The automatic release of object memory is the beginning of a garbage collection mechanism.

Data-Independent Problem Solvers

The standard algorithms are a collection of procedural solutions to some of the classic problems in computer programming. There are 60 (counting variations) algorithms in the standard, and they cover a lot of software turf, everything from searching and sorting containers to object permutation generation. Table 1.15 lists the categories to which the standard algorithms belong. These algorithms can be considered the software work horses of the standard C++ library. They come ready to use; the programmer only has to put them to work. What makes the standard algorithms so powerful is that they are designed to work with any container class that supports the notion of the iterator. Figure 1.4 shows the functional view of the standard C++ classes. The algorithm components are the only components that are not classes, but we include them in our discussion of the functional view of the standard class library because they are designed to work closely with the container and the iterator classes. In fact, certain of the container classes are most useful when they are used in conjunction with the algorithm components.

Traditionally, an algorithm is described as a detailed, step-by-step, well-defined solution to a problem. For a procedural solution to be called an algorithm, it must provide the correct result each time it is presented with acceptable data. Furthermore, the steps of the solution must be unambiguous. The solution must be able to be implemented in software and executed on a computer.

In theory, the algorithmic solution does not concern itself with data types. However, once the algorithm is implemented in a computer language, a data type must be specified. For example, we can specify a selection sort algorithm as follows:

```
selection
begin
    I := 1 to N
        begin
            min = I
            for J := I + 1 to N
            begin
                if a[J] < a[min] then
                    min := J
            end
            t := a[min]
            a := a[I]
            a[I] := t
        end
end
```

In this algorithm, we have a number of variables: I, N, min, J, a[ ], and t. We can talk about the correctness, efficiency, or appropriateness of this algorithm without worrying about the type of data the algorithm is sorting.

Table 1.15 Categories of Standard Algorithms

ALGORITHM TYPE	ALGORITHMS	
sorting	sort( )	stable_sort( )
	partial_sort( )	partial_sort_copy( )
	merge( )	inplace_merge( )
searching	find( )	find_if( )
	find_end( )	find_first_of( )
	adjacent_find( )	search( )
	search_n( )	binary_search( )
	nth_element( )	lower_bound( )
	upper_bound( )	equal_range( )
set operations	set_union( )	set_difference( )
	set_intersection( )	set_symmetric_difference( )
	includes( )	
numeric operations	next_permutation( )	prev_permutation( )
	accumulate( )	partial_sum( )
	inner_product( )	adjacent_difference( )
heap operations	push_heap( )	pop_heap( )
	make_heap( )	sort_heap( )
statistical information	min( )	max( )
	min_element( )	max_element( )
	count( )	count_if( )
comparison operations	equal( )	lexicographical_compare( )
container management	copy( )	copy_backward( )
	replace( )	replace_if( )
	replace_copy( )	replace_copy_if( )
	reverse( )	reverse_copy( )
	mismatch( )	swap( )
	swap_ranges( )	iter_swap( )
	transform( )	fill( )
	fill_n( )	remove( )
	remove_if( )	remove_copy( )
	remove_copy_if( )	unique( )
	unique_copy( )	rotate( )

Table 1.15 *(Continued)*

ALGORITHM TYPE	ALGORITHMS	
	rotate_copy( )	random_shuffle( )
	partition( )	stable_partition( )
	generate( )	generate_n( )
	for_each( )	

But once the decision is made to implement this algorithm in a language such as C, Fortran, Cobol, or Pascal, we must specify what the algorithm is sorting. We must specify whether the algorithm is sorting floating-point numbers, integers, strings, characters, or some other data type. The problem occurs once we have chosen the data type the algorithm sorts. Once we declare a[ ] to be an array of strings, our selection algorithm will sort only strings. If we declare a[ ] to be an array of floating-point values, our sort will sort only floating-point values. If we have to sort floating-point values, strings, integers, characters, and so on, all in the same program, then we have to implement the algorithm for each type that it needs to sort.

The standard C++ library solves this problem by using object orientation and parameterized types. The container classes are designed to be able to hold any kind of object. The algorithms are designed, basically, to work with any kind of container that supports

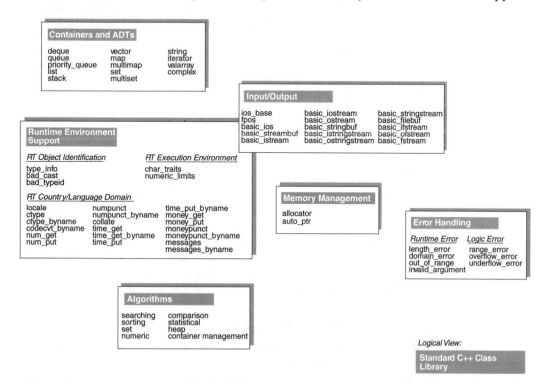

Figure 1.4 The logical view of the standard C++ classes.

the appropriate iterators. Since the algorithms manipulate iterators and not data types, the algorithms can perform their work without needing to know the type of object they are working on. The *algorithm-iterator-container* connection is a very powerful mechanism for data-independent programming, and we will discuss it in more detail later in this chapter.

It is important to note that the containers and algorithms provided in the C++ standard class library provide generic object-oriented implementations to many important classic algorithms and data structures. In many languages, these algorithms and data structures have to be implemented by hand again and again, each time they are required for a different data type. In C++, these components come tested, debugged, ready to use, and available to any kind of object, built-in or user-defined.

Fault Tolerance and Robust Software

The primary goal of testing is to identify any software defects or software anomalies; the primary goal of debugging is to remove those software defects and software anomalies. Once a piece of software has been tested and debugged, its fate (hopefully) is to be executed on a computer so it can perform some useful work. That said, even the most thorough testing and debugging cannot guarantee that an executing piece of software will not encounter an abnormal execution environment, abnormal data, unexpected conditions, or abnormal user direction. Bizarre and unusual runtime situations occur. Fortunately, the C++ language and serveral useful software components found in the standard library give the programmer tools with which to deal with such runtime anomalies.

C++ supports the notion of *exception handling*. Put simply, exception handling gives a piece of software some *appropriate* action to take when all else fails. We emphasize *appropriate* here for a reason. Take for example a piece of a program that opens a file, reads its contents, then closes the file:

```
ifstream Fin("Myfile");

while(!Fin.eof())
{
    Fin >> Mydata
}
Fin.close();
```

There are dozens of ways for this code to fail: If Myfile has already been opened by exclusive use by another process, there is a problem. If Myfile does not exist, there is a problem. What if Myfile is empty? Does this piece code do what the programmer expects? This piece of code could have been designed more carefully to handle each of these very possible conditions. After all, a program that is performing I/O should anticipate these obvious conditions. Missing files, empty files, sharing violations are normal for any code that does file input/output.

But, what if Myfile exists but its contents have been changed maliciously by a virus to include nasty control character sequences or operating system jump codes? What if Myfile has been truncated halfway through the file and so has no EOF? In most installations, rampant viruses and truncated files would not constitute the normal state of affairs, but would be considered unusual runtime anomalies. Clearly, we need tools to use and we need to know the appropriate action to take when our software encounters abnormal or unexpected conditions. The tools are the C++ constructs *try, throw, catch*, and the *exception classes*. The basic approach is:

1. Try some operation.

2. If the operation fails for abnormal reasons, throw an exception object of some type.

3. The exception handler catches the exception object.

4. The exception object and the exception handler together work out the appropriate action to take next.

The action to take is specified in part by the exception object and in part by the exception handler. When software can recover from an operation that has failed due to abnormal circumstances, we say the software is *fault-tolerant*, and that it has a *robust* architecture. The standard classes provide us with two basic groups of exception classes, listed in Table 1.16, along with the kind of exceptions they are used to report.

We should use these classes as foundation classes for a fault-tolerance strategy, and in addition to testing and debugging a piece of software, we should design it to be robust and give it fault-tolerant facilities. The nine exception classes are a good place to start. The two groups of exception classes represent two basic areas of program error: logic errors and runtime errors.

Though there are differing approaches to object-oriented exception handling, there is a growing consensus that exception class hierarchies should be built and that polymorphism should be used to categorize the widest possible range of potential exceptions. The runtime errors are usually represented by the classic case of abnormal condition. The logic errors usually represent errors that can be anticipated but not necessarily avoided. Whether the exception is runtime or logic, the C++ standard class library provides a family of exception classes as base classes to build exception class libraries.

Runtime Type/Runtime Execution Support

The last group of classes we will look at in the functional view comprise the *runtime support classes*. This is a mixed bag of classes, which includes the runtime type information classes, as well as char_traits, locale, and the numerics classes. We include them

Table 1.16 Exception Class Groups and Exceptions They Report

RUNTIME_ERROR	LOGIC_ERROR
length_error	range_error
domain_error	overflow_error
out_of_range_error	underflow_error
invalid_argument	

in the runtime support classes because they can be used as helper classes in managing the physical runtime execution environment differences, operating system differences, country and language differences, and character set differences. Thus, a properly designed piece of software can use these runtime classes to improve the software's portability at many levels.

We divide runtime support into three levels:

- Runtime object identification
- Runtime execution environment
- Runtime country/language domain

Table 1.17 lists the three runtime support categories and the classes assigned to each. There are other classes, such as the allocator class, that could play dual roles and be put in the runtime as well as another category, we have left those classes out. In practice, some of the classes switch functional categories depending on how they are used. In this chapter, our goal is to present three simple logical views of the standard C++ classes:

- Functional view
- Architectural view
- Interface view

Note that these three views are not the only logical categorizations of the standard C++ classes. The standard C++ library includes not only classes but other kinds of components such as free-standing functions, constants, and macros. The ANSI standards committee has divided the entire library into a group of functional categories. Although the

Table 1.17 Runtime Support Categories and Their Classes

RUNTIME ENVIRONMENT SUPPORT		
RT Object Identification	*RT Execution Environment*	
type_info	char_traits	
bad_cast	numeric_limits	
bad_typeid		
RT Country/Language Domain		
locale	numpunct	money_get
ctype	numpunct_byname	money_put
ctype_byname	collate	moneypunct
codecvt	time_get	moneypunctbyname
codecvt_byname	time_get_byname	messages
num_get	time_put	messages_byname
num_put	time_put_byname	

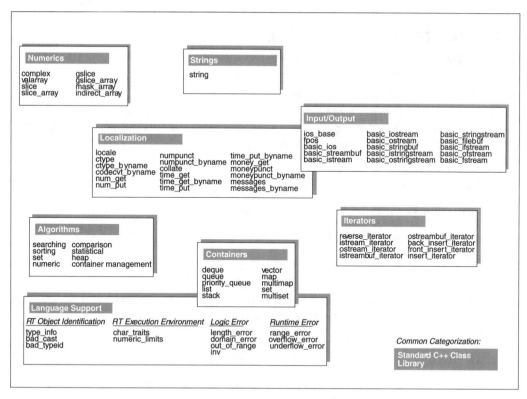

Figure 1.5 One of the common categorizations of the standard C++ library.

names of some of the categories and some of the category candidates have changed during the standardization process, the basic functional breakdown has remained the same. Figure 1.5 shows one of the common categorizations of the standard C++ library.

These categorizations incorporate all the functionality in the standard library, including both object-oriented components and nonobject-oriented components. Our categorization differs for two basic reasons. First, we have chosen a simplified version to make the standard class library more accessible and easier to learn and remember. Second, because this book only covers the standard classes and algorithms, a complete discussion of all the categories is not necessary. Furthermore, an object-oriented emphasis requires a clarification of some of the categories. We will provide this clarification by looking at the standard classes through two additional views:

- Architectural view

- Interface view

When we combine an architectural view, an interface view, and a functional view of the standard class library, we get a more complete picture of what the library has to offer and how to use it.

The Architectural View of the Standard C++ Class Library

The standard C++ class library universe is full of interesting types of components. We have negators, streams, binders, predicates, algorithms, iterators, containers, allocators, sentries, function objects, adaptors, auto_ptrs, and char_traits. The functional view of the standard classes answers the questions:

- What are they?
- What are the classes used for?

The architectural view of the standard classes answers the questions:

- How are all of these different components related?
- How do they fit together?
- What structure do they cause the class library to have?

In addition to the interesting types of components found in the standard class library, it supports two major programming paradigms:

- Object-oriented programming
- Generic programming (parameterized programming)

These two powerful paradigms are woven throughout the standard class library and form the foundational and conceptual basis for its architecture. Figure 1.6 is a block diagram that shows the compound architectural view of the standard class library. There are three primary reasons that the C++ library has a compound architecture:

- Except for the algorithms component in Figure 1.6, each component represents a C++ class or collection of classes.
- Most of the classes are template classes.
- The algorithm components only access the container components through generic iterators.

The object-oriented component of the architecture is enforced by the C++ class construct. The genericity component of the architecture is enforced by iterators and templates.

What Is the Object-Oriented Paradigm?

The object-oriented paradigm is an approach to software construction whereby the software designer and software developer are concerned with representing all aspects of a software system or subsystem as a collection of interacting objects. The goal of the interacting objects is to model some person, place, thing, or idea. Almost everything we come in contact with can be understood as an object. For instance:

automobiles   restaurants

shopping malls   automatic teller machines

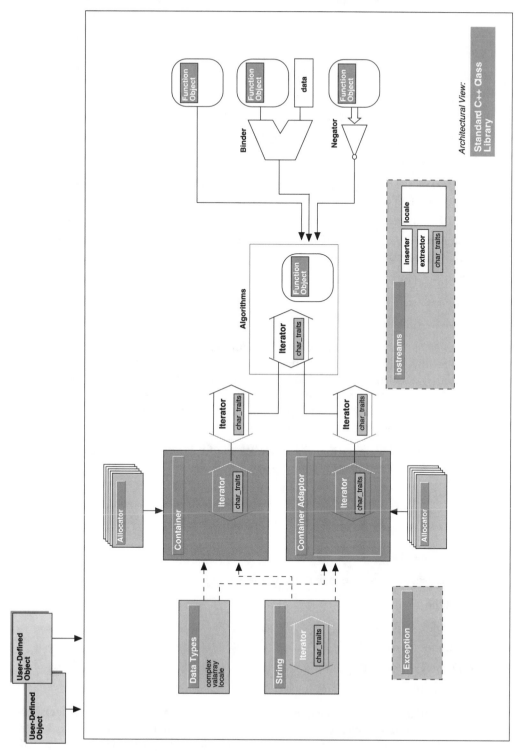

Figure 1.6 A block diagram that shows the compound architectural view of the standard class library.

can openers	cash register clerk
currency	time
date	molecule
family physician	supernova
golfing	cooking
chemical explosion	table and chair

Gulliver's Travels

These examples of people, places, things, or ideas can be modeled as objects in C++. The notion of an object covers the notion of processes and actions as well.

Object-oriented programming is an approach to programming whereby the *object* is the fundamental unit of modularity. Any object-oriented programming environment must support at least the following basic concepts:

- Encapsulation
- Inheritance
- Polymorphism

Encapsulation is a method that combines operations and data into one unit or software package. In order for the combination of data and operations to be truly object-oriented, it must support the notion of *information hiding*. The unit of data is encapsulated, which means there is only restricted access to it, unless special circumstances dictate otherwise (which should happen rarely). The data, together with the operations that work with the data, are called an *object*.

Take, for example, the notion of a clock. We could divide the data components of a clock into four pieces of data:

- Hours
- Minutes
- Seconds
- Clock hands

There are several operations that we might want to perform on our clock data:

- Set the hours.
- Display the hours.
- Set the seconds.
- Display the seconds.
- Move the clock hands (and so on).

To encapsulate our simple clock representation in C++, we would bind our clock data components with the operations we would like to be able to perform on the clock data. We could use the C++ class or struct mechanism to accomplish this, to end up with something that looks like:

```
class clock{
protected:
    int Hours;
    int Seconds;
    int Minutes;
    struct ClockHands;
public:
    virtual void setTheHours(int X);
    virtual int hours();
    virtual void setTheMinutes(int X);
    virtual int minutes();
    ...
};
```

Having encapsulated our clock data with our clock operations, we have a single unit. The runtime version of this unit is called an object. The only operations that may manipulate our clock's hours, seconds, minutes, or clock hands are the operations defined by the clock class. This provides the information hiding that we need; it allows only those operations defined by the clock class to be aware of the clock's data components, and it allows only the clock's defined operations to manipulate those components. This type of encapsulation is necessary to support object-oriented design and programming.

Inheritance is a mechanism that enables the creation of new classes using existing classes. The new class contains all of the functionality of the existing class either with some new methods or data added. The new class defines the qualities that make it distinctive, while it reuses the qualities that it "inherited" from the existing class or classes. Instead of re-creating all methods or data from scratch, inheritance is used. The existing class is traditionally called the *ancestor* or *base* class. The new class that inherits the qualities of the ancestor or base class is called the *descendant* or *derived* class.

Taking our clock example a little further, let's say we want to extend our clock class to make a new kind of time-keeping class. We could create a digital hourglass using inheritance. In C++, this is accomplished using syntax that looks like:

```
class hour_glass : public clock{};
```

This declaration states that hour_glass will inherit clock's data component and operations. When an object of type hour_glass is created, it will have all of the capability of clock, along with any capabilities added that specifically applies to hourglass.

Polymorphism allows the same name to be used for different implementations of a task. In an inheritance hierarchy, polymorphism allows derived classes to redefine a task found in the base. The name of the task in the base class and the derived class will be the same; however, the implementation of the task will be different. The difference may be minor or significant.

If we use polymorphism in our clock example, the functions in hour_glass can be redefined:

```
class hour_glass : public clock{
protected:
```

```
    int SandDensity;
    int SandAmount;
public:
    hour_glass();
    void setTheHours(int X);
    int hours();
};
```

Although the method names setTheHours( ) and hours( ) in the hour_glass class are the same as those in the base class clock, the fact that time is set up and displayed differently in an hourglass than in a clock means the methods of each will behave differently. Note that even though the methods behave differently, they have the same basic meaning. This is an important feature of polymorphism: it allows the syntax and semantics to remain the same while the implementation can be different.

The object-oriented paradigm is completely supported in the C++ standard class library through the use of the class, inheritance, virtual functions, operator overloading, and function overriding.

Genericity

"*Genericity* is the ability to define parameterized modules. Such a module, called a generic module, is not directly usable; rather, it is a module pattern. In the most common case, the parameters (called *formal generic parameters*) stand for types. Actual modules, called *instances* of the generic module, are obtained by providing actual types (*actual generic parameters*) for each of the formal generic parameters" (Meyer, 1998, p. 37).

For example, we might have a generic parameterized module that performs some standard sequence of actions, such as:

1. Put object X into Y.
2. Turn Y up to Z degrees.
3. Heat X at Z degrees until object X is done.
4. Remove X from Y.

This is an example of a generic module. We have a sense of the operations it performs, but unless we specify what the parameters X, Y, and Z are, we cannot tell specifically what the module is doing. For instance, X may be frankfurters, Y may be an oven, and Z may be the best temperature at which to cook frankfurters. On the other hand, X might be a sculpture, Y might be a kiln, and Z might be the temperature to heat the sculpture until its glaze becomes hardened. The important point here is that the sequence of operations is sufficiently general because of the parameters X, Y, Z. Thus, this sequence of actions can be used by cooks, chemists, bomb makers, sculptors, hairdressers, toy manufacturers, and so on.

The power of generic programming comes from identifying a sufficiently generic but useful sequence of actions or set of characteristics, which can then be used over again in many applications, under many different conditions, and in many different ways, without changing any code. Simply by providing the necessary parameters, the generic module becomes an instance of some specific module.

Support for genericity in the standard C++ classes library architecture is found in the extensive use of template classes, template functions, and iterators. These C++ components are used to specify *skeleton modules* that take on meaning only when they are supplied with the proper parameters. The modules are generic and have some generic pattern. The generic pattern will represent either some generic sequence of work that needs to be done or some generic characteristic that a module can have. The generic pattern becomes a specific pattern once the proper parameters are supplied.

In addition to supporting genericity through templates, the C++ class library employs genericity through the use of iterators. The class library has several important components that depend on iterators, listed in Table 1.18 along with the classes of iterators they require. The iterators are generic pointers, so the algorithms, iostreams, and containers are all shielded from data type-specific manipulation. Using iterators with the primary C++ classes allows the programmer to specify algorithms, containers, and user-defined objects in the most general of ways. If we can specify some useful construct, object behavior, or algorithm in a generic way, we increase its reusability. And as stated, code reuse is an extremely important goal in many programming and software development situations.

Object-Oriented Programming and Generic Programming

Be aware that generic programming is *not* part of the object-oriented paradigm. Generic programming has its own set of tools and techniques separate from the object-oriented approach. In some cases, the rules of good generic programming may violate

Table 1.18   C++ Classes That Depend on Iterators and Their Required Classes

CLASSES	ITERATOR	CLASSES	ITERATOR
Containers/ADTs			
deque	Random Access	queue	Random Access
priority_queue	Random Access	list	Bidirectional
stack	Random Access	vector	Random Access
map	Bidirectional	multimap	Bidirectional
set	Bidirectional	multiset	Bidirectional
sting	Random Access		
RT Country/Language Domain			
money_get	Input	money_put	Output
time_get	Input	time_put	Output
time_get_byname	Input	time_put_byname	Output
num_get	Input	num_put	Output

some of the rules of good object-oriented programming, and vice versa. The standard C++ class library contains components that are the result of object-oriented design and programming as well as the result of generic programming. It is the object-oriented approach and the generic approach to the standard components that give the C++ class library its *compound*, or *dual*, nature.

Now that we have seen the basic foundations of the C++ class library architecture, let's look at how some of the various pieces of the framework of the class library fit together. Figure 1.6 shows how the core component types of the C++ class library fit together. This figure represents an architectural view of the class library: The iostreams provide the I/O; the containers provide the object storage; the allocators and auto_ptrs provide the memory management; the negators, binders, predicates, and function objects work with algorithms and help to modify containers.

Because the class library supports object orientation, the programmer may use the objects in the library as-is, or specialize many of the objects in the class library through inheritance, by overriding and overloading functions. And because the class library supports genericity, the components in the library can be used over again with any built-in data type, as well as with any user-defined type, as long as the proper protocols and interfaces are followed. This takes us to the discussion of the third view of the C++ class library: the *interface view*.

The Interfaces

The interface view gives us the means to actually *use* the classes in the library, and in fact is our only means of interacting with the standard classes. It is through the interface view that we create objects, destroy objects, assign objects, access objects, specialize objects, and so on. Without an interface view, the C++ programmer could not use any of the classes in the standard library. Table 1.19 lists the core interfaces to the C++ standard class library and their uses.

There are several fundamental services of the standard C++ class library with which every user of the class library must interact, so it is important to understand the interfaces to these services, which are:

Table 1.19   C++ Standard Class Library Core Interfaces and Their Uses

CORE INTERFACES	DESCRIPTION
constructor	Creates an object.
copy constructor	Makes a copy of an object.
destructor	Destroys an object.
<<, >>	Insertion and extraction operators; inserts or extracts objects or values to and from a stream.
get( ), put( )	Used to input or output values or objects.
=, = =, !=	Assignment, equality, inequality operators.

- Object creation
- Object destruction
- Object assignment
- Object access
- Object specialization
- Object I/O
- Exception handling
- Required methods

The methods that perform these services present the most used interface to the standard C++ class library. To use any object in the class library, we must be familiar with two primary interfaces: public and protected.

Moreover, there are four facets to an interface that we should focus on when we look at the interface for a class, class library, or application framework:

- Available services/functionality
- Interface syntax
- Interface symantics
- Protocol

Available Services/Functionality

Questions about an object's capability can be posed in two ways:

What services does this object offer?

What functionality does this object have?

The distinction is made from the two basic approaches to designing an object. An object can be thought of as an abstract data type that has a list of services to offer, or it can be thought of as a model for some real-world person, place, thing, or idea. If the object is looked upon as a model or simulation, then the question is: What functionality does the object have?

The standard C++ class library has both types of objects. For instance, the basic_string< > class represents an ADT that offers a list of services. On the other hand, the iostream classes present an object-oriented view of the notion of an I/O stream. How the objects will be used determines whether to use the *functionality* or *list of services* terminology. Regardless which approach is chosen, the interface to that object is the only way the programmer can interact with the object. Therefore, before we can use the object in any productive manner, we need to know what functionality it has or what services it has to offer. In C++, we determine functionality or list of services by looking at the protected or public data members and member functions of an object. For example, Listing 1.1 contains a declaration for the basic_string class of the standard C++ library. Notice that the class has many public members.

Listing 1.1   Declaration of basic_string Class

```
1 template<class charT, class traits = char_traits<charT>,
2 class Allocator = allocator<charT> >
3 class basic_string {
4 public:
5     typedef traits traits_type;
6     typedef typename traits::char_type value_type;
7     typedef Allocator allocator_type;
8     typedef typename Allocator::size_type size_type;
9     typedef typename Allocator::difference_type difference_type;
10    typedef typename Allocator::reference reference;
11    typedef typename Allocator::const_reference const_reference;
12    typedef typename Allocator::pointer pointer;
13    typedef typename Allocator::const_pointer const_pointer;
14    typedef std::reverse_iterator<iterator> reverse_iterator;
15    typedef std::reverse_iterator<const_iterator> const_reverse_iterator;
16    static const size_type npos = 1;
17    explicit basic_string(const Allocator& a = Allocator());
18    basic_string(const basic_string& str, size_type pos = 0,
19    size_type n = npos, const Allocator& a = Allocator());
20    basic_string(const charT* s, size_type n,
21                  const Allocator& a = Allocator());
22    basic_string(const charT* s, const Allocator& a = Allocator());
23    basic_string(size_type n, charT c, const Allocator& a = Allocator());
24    template<class InputIterator>
25    basic_string(InputIterator begin, InputIterator end,
26    const Allocator& a = Allocator());
27    ~basic_string();
28    basic_string& operator=(const basic_string& str);
29    basic_string& operator=(const charT* s);
30    basic_string& operator=(charT c);
31    iterator begin();
32    const_iterator begin() const;
33    iterator end();
34    const_iterator end() const;
35    reverse_iterator rbegin();
36    const_reverse_iterator rbegin() const;
37    reverse_iterator rend();
38    const_reverse_iterator rend() const;
39    size_type size() const;
40    size_type length() const;
41    size_type max_size() const;
42    void resize(size_type n, charT c);
43    void resize(size_type n);
44    size_type capacity() const;
45    void reserve(size_type res_arg = 0);
46    void clear();
47    bool empty() const;
48    const_reference operator[](size_type pos) const;
```

Listing 1.1 (*Continued*)

```
49      reference operator[](size_type pos);
50      const_reference at(size_type n) const;
51      reference at(size_type n);
52      basic_string& operator+=(const basic_string& str);
53      basic_string& operator+=(const charT* s);
54      basic_string& operator+=(charT c);
55      basic_string& append(const basic_string& str);
56      basic_string& append(const basic_string& str,
57                          size_type pos,size_type n);
58      basic_string& append(const charT* s, size_type n);
59      basic_string& append(const charT* s);
60      basic_string& append(size_type n, charT c);
61      template<class InputIterator>
62      basic_string& append(InputIterator first, InputIterator last);
63      basic_string& assign(const basic_string&);
64      basic_string& assign(const basic_string& str,
65                          size_type pos,size_type n);
66      basic_string& assign(const charT* s, size_type n);
67      basic_string& assign(const charT* s);
68      basic_string& assign(size_type n, charT c);
69      template<class InputIterator>
70      basic_string& assign(InputIterator first, InputIterator last);
71      basic_string& insert(size_type pos1, const basic_string& str,
72      basic_string& insert(size_type pos1, const basic_string& str);
73                          size_type ps2,size_type n);
74      basic_string& insert(size_type pos, const charT* s, size_type n);
75      basic_string& insert(size_type pos, const charT* s);
76      basic_string& insert(size_type pos, size_type n, charT c);
77      iterator insert(iterator p, charT c = charT());
78      void insert(iterator p, size_type n, charT c);
79      template<class InputIterator>
80      void insert(iterator p, InputIterator first, InputIterator last);
81      basic_string& erase(size_type pos = 0, size_type n = npos);
82      iterator erase(iterator position);
83      iterator erase(iterator first, iterator last);
84      basic_string& replace(size_type pos1, size_type n1,
85                          const basic_string& r);
86      basic_string& replace(size_type pos1, size_type n1,
87                          const basic_string& str,
88                          size_type pos2, size_type n2);
89      basic_string& replace(size_type pos, size_type n1,
90                          const charT* s, size_type n2);
91      basic_string& replace(size_type pos, size_type n1, const charT* s);
92      basic_string& replace(size_type pos, size_type n1,
93                          size_type n2, charT c);
94      basic_string& replace(iterator i1, iterator i2,
95                          const basic_string& str);
96      basic_string& replace(iterator i1, iterator i2,
```

Continues

Listing 1.1 Declaration of basic_string Class (*Continued*)

```
97                                 const charT* s, size_type n);
98        basic_string& replace(iterator i1, iterator i2, const charT* s);
99        basic_string& replace(iterator i1, iterator i2, size_type n, charT c);
100       template<class InputIterator> basic_string& replace(iterator i1,
101                                                           iterator i2,
102                                                           InputIterator j1,
103                                                           InputIterator j2);
104       size_type copy(charT* s, size_type n, size_type pos = 0) const;
105       void swap(basic_string<charT,traits,Allocator>&);
106       const charT* c_str() const; // explicit
107       const charT* data() const;
108       allocator_type get_allocator() const;
109       size_type find (const basic_string& str, size_type pos = 0) const;
110       size_type find (const charT* s, size_type pos, size_type n) const;
111       size_type find (const charT* s, size_type pos = 0) const;
112       size_type find (charT c, size_type pos = 0) const;
113       size_type rfind(const basic_string& str, size_type pos = npos) const;
114       size_type rfind(const charT* s, size_type pos, size_type n)
115       size_type rfind(const charT* s, size_type pos = npos) const;
116       size_type rfind(charT c, size_type pos = npos) const;
117       size_type find_first_of(const basic_string& str,
118                               size_type pos = 0) const;
119       size_type find_first_of(const charT* s, size_type pos,
120                               size_type n) const;
121       size_type find_first_of(const charT* s, size_type pos = 0) const;
122       size_type find_first_of(charT c, size_type pos = 0) const;
123       size_type find_last_of (const basic_string& str,
124                               size_type pos = npos) const;
125       size_type find_last_of (const charT* s, size_type pos,
126                               size_type n) const;
127       size_type find_last_of (const charT* s, size_type pos = npos) const;
128       size_type find_last_of (charT c, size_type pos = npos) const;
129       size_type find_first_not_of(const basic_string& str,
130                                   size_type pos = 0) const;
131       size_type find_first_not_of(const charT* s, size_type pos,
132                                   size_type n) const;
133       size_type find_first_not_of(const charT* s, size_type pos = 0) const;
134       size_type find_first_not_of(charT c, size_type pos = 0) const;
135       size_type find_last_not_of (const basic_string& str,
136                                   size_type pos = npos) const;
137       size_type find_last_not_of (const charT* s, size_type pos,
138                                   size_type n) const;
139       size_type find_last_not_of (const charT* s,
140                                   size_type pos = npos) const;
141       size_type find_last_not_of (charT c, size_type pos = npos) const;
142       basic_string substr(size_type pos = 0, size_type n = npos) const;
143       int compare(const basic_string& str) const;
144       int compare(size_type pos1, size_type n1,
```

Listing 1.1 (*Continued*)

```
145              const basic_string& str) const;
146    int compare(size_type pos1, size_type n1,
147    const basic_string& str,size_type pos2, size_type n2) const;
148    int compare(const charT* s) const;
149    int compare(size_type pos1, size_type n1,
150              const charT* s, size_type n2 = npos) const;
151    };
```

The only way a user can interface with this class is through the protected and public member functions. We can refer to the functional view or architectural view of the string class, but if we want to use the string, then we must interact with it through the interface view. Derived classes have access to both the protected and public member functions of their parent classes. Users other than derived classes can access only public members. There are several common types of methods that all classes should offer. These are listed in Table 1.20 with their uses. These method types form the primary ways that the user of the class can interact with the class.

The Interface Syntax

After we determine the services or functionality an object has to offer, we have to determine how to syntactically invoke the object's capabilities. The object will have one or

Table 1.20 Common Types of Methods and Their Uses

TYPES OF METHODS	USAGE
Accessor	Used to access (but not to change) one or more of the class attributes.
Modifier	Used to modify one or more of the class attributes; examples of modifiers are: insert, erase, assign, etc.
Creator/Initializers	Used to construct a new class and perform the initializations of variables, opening of files, preparing of devices for use, etc.
Destroyer/Finalizers	Used to delete or destruct an existing class and perform any clean-up such as closing files, devices, etc.
Statistical	Information generators; they generate information about the class such as size, capacity, location, etc.
Input/Output	Used to perform the input and output of the class, such as the overloading of the insertion and extraction operators.
Operators	Performs operator overloading for the class for operators, such as: =, = =, !=, <, >, +, −, *, /, etc.

more member functions, which will require certain arguments and generate certain return types. For example:

```
iterator erase(iterator first, iterator last);
```

The member function erase( ) requires two iterator types and returns an iterator. If we are to use the string object's erase( ) method, we must obey the syntax aspect of the object's interface. The compiler will help us to follow syntax requirements.

The Interface Protocol

Once we understand the syntax for interacting with the object, we must obey the protocols of the object. An object's protocol may include the order in which particular methods must be invoked, or exception-handling policies. Protocol may require that a user of the class first define certain methods; for instance to use many of the containers completely, the user has to define certain operators or methods. Specifically, the user may be required to define:

operator =

operator < >, !=

operator <<

operator >>

copy constructors, function objects, and so on

An object's protocol refers to the rules the user must obey in order to use the object correctly. If a class is a pure abstract virtual function, then the user must define implementations for the function before the object can be put to use. Proper constructor values are also part of an object's protocol.

To get the most out of the C++ standard library, the user must be aware of the list of services available and the syntax and protocol requirements of the different functional groups within the library. In addition to the list of services, syntax and protocol, the user of the class library must also be aware of the *interface semantics* of the class methods and classes within the library.

Class Interface Semantics

The semantics of a class, its methods, and attributes refer to the meaning that those items have when used in their proper context. Class semantics are of interest when class inheritance, function overloading, or function overriding are used.

In this book, we present the standard C++ classes from three views:

- Functional view
- Architectural view
- Interface view

The standard classes are best understood if approached by all three views.

C++ and Standard Software Lego

Now that the ANSI/ISO standard for C++ is complete we have standard interfaces and protocols for important classes such as string, vector, list, set, complex, and so forth. The iostream classes now have a set of consistent interfaces. The template implementations of the container classes have been worked out. The valarray class has been added and will be an important tool for building engineering and scientific libraries. Finally, there is a set of classes in C++ that can be used as standard building blocks allowing the C++ programmer to build class libraries, frameworks, and applications faster and more reliably. The C++ classes can be used as foundations of class libraries. The class libraries can be used as foundations of application frameworks. And application frameworks can be used as *software legos* to build complex and powerful applications of all kinds and sizes.

CHAPTER 2

Introduction: Anatomy of a Class

"This means of course that one's model of the Universe is smaller—lesser, in some sense—than the reality. But that's not such a bad thing. Models by definition are lesser than the reality they represent, and for models of the Universe this constraint obviously must be particularly stringent . . ."

—TIMOTHY FERRIS
UNIVERSE AND EYE:
MAKING SENSE OF THE NEW SCIENCE

The notion of a class is the most fundamental idea in object-oriented programming. It is also the basis for object-oriented analysis and design. A class is what distinguishes object-oriented programming from structured programming, functional programming, logic programming, and other programming techniques. There are two interpretations of the class concept in object-oriented programming. The first views a class as an abstract data type (ADT). "Fundamentally, a data type is a collection of values and a set of operations on those values. That collection and those operations form a mathematical construct that may be implemented using a particular hardware or software data structure. The term abstract data type refers to the basic mathematical concept that defines the type" (Tenebaum et al., 1992, pp. 13–14). The C++ language provides implementations for several commonly used ADTs; they are:

- Integers
- Characters
- Floating-point numbers

C++ implements these ADTs and institutes the basic operations on them. For example, the int data type in C++ supports the operations of addition, multiplication, subtraction, division, modulo, integer comparison and so on. When using these types, we are not necessarily concerned with their implementations, rather with the list of services or operations available to the data type. According to Tenebaum et al.:

In defining an abstract data type as a mathematical concept, we are not concerned with space or time efficiency. Those are implementation issues. In fact, the definition of an ADT is not concerned with implementation details at all. It may not even be possible to implement a particular ADT on a particular piece of hardware or using a particular software system.

The ADT view of a class and its corresponding object is simply as a list of services or available operations. Most of the classes in the standard C++ library can be viewed as realizations of ADTs. Classes implemented by standard C++ such as:

- basic_string
- complex
- valarray
- set and multiset
- list
- deque
- map and multimap
- vector
- stack
- queue

are classic examples of some commonly found data types and data structures in computer programming. Through the ADT view, we can see each of these classes as a data component and list of operations.

The second, widest, view of a class is as a *model* of some person, place, thing, or idea. It includes the ADT interpretation. In the model interpretation, classes are used to create software models, of which there are two fundamental types, and C++ can be used to create both. The first type of model is a scaled representation of some process, concept, or idea. This type of model is usually used for the sake of simulation or event modeling, which is then used for analysis, decision making, or experimentation. For example, we could use the C++ class concept to build a model of a movie concession stand. Our goal might be to simulate the customers' selections of frankfurters, popcorn, and hot pretzels. To that end, we might want to find out how best to balance the cooking and rewarming of these items based on how customers purchase them. We could examine the temperatures necessary, based on the ratio at which popcorn is sold in comparison to frankfurters and hot pretzels. We might also want to simulate purchases during the week versus during the weekend. We could then design C++ models of frankfurters, popcorn, pretzels, cashiers, money, patrons, check-out lines, popcorn poppers, ovens, and so on. With this type of modeling, we are concerned with how the objects interact with each other. The simulation and event processing are simply means to an end. The modeling process allows us to evaluate behaviors and characteristics of the objects involved.

The second type of software model is a *software reproduction* of some real-world task, process, or idea. The purpose of this model is to function as its real-world counterpart, as a part of some system or application. The software model is not used for decision making or analysis; it takes the place of some manual component in a system or subsystem; it is actually a software replacement for some thing, process, or idea. For example, we could use the object-oriented capabilities of C++ to model a desktop calculator, using the class construct to declare the components of a software calculator used to replace the desktop calculator. This type of object-oriented modeling produces software for production, as opposed to analysis, or decision making. Here, the class calculator duplicates all of the functional characteristics of the desktop calculator.

Note the difference between the class as an implementation of an ADT and the class as a model. Usually, the data type is used to support the programming effort. A programmer may use floats, ints, chars, bools, rationals, and so on as the nails to hold some software framework together. When the C++ class is used as a model, the class is usually the framework! It is more than just a data type or data structure; the modeled class serves as a virtual stand-in. That is, the software model captures the essence of the real thing. The ADT interpretation of the class focuses on the list of services or operations available on the data component of the class, whereas the model interpretation focuses on the behavior, characteristics, and attributes of the class. Under the ADT interpretation, we ask the question: What services or operations are available? Under the model interpretation, we ask these questions: How does this object behave? What are its characteristics, capabilities, and attributes? The C++ class supports both the model interpretation and the ADT interpretation.

Now that we know the two basic approaches to the class concept in C++, let's look at 10 important types of classes in C++.

Standard C++ Class Library Classes

There are two uses of the word class in C++. The first refers to the C++ language construct represented by the *class* keyword. The second refers to the logical notion of a set of behaviors and attributes encapsulated to form an object. Classes can serve many different functions within the development of an object-oriented application or class library. We can talk about different types of classes based on how those classes are used in an object-oriented development effort. Some are useful only as blueprint classes that provide recommended interface policies for other classes. Others should be used only as ancestor, or base, classes. Still other classes do not make good base classes and, therefore, should not be used in inheritance hierarchies. Here are the 10 important class types in the standard library:

- Concrete
- Abstract
- Interface (Adaptor)
- Node
- Support
- Utility
- Container
- Iterator
- Allocator
- Parameterized

Most object-oriented development efforts will use some or all of these basic kinds of classes. Keep in mind that they do not represent any particular language constructs. C++ does not have a *concrete* keyword that describes a concrete class, or an *allocator* keyword that describes an allocator class. These 10 types represent classes that have very specific functionality, used for specific purposes and representing techniques for implementing classes, as opposed to built-in types supported by specific keywords. Each has a unique function within an object-oriented architecture. Table 2.1 describes the ten class types.

Concrete Classes

Many classes in C++ are designed as potential candidates for base or ancestor classes, but the concrete class is designed and implemented as a *finished* class. Usually, concrete classes are standalone classes; they represent the end of an ancestor descendant lin-

Table 2.1   Ten Common C++ Class Types

TYPES OF CLASS	DESCRIPTION
Concrete	A complete class whose implementation is defined. Instances of the class can be declared; it is not intended to be a base class.
Abstract	Supplies the interface for derived classes; used as the blueprint for the construction of other classes. It can only be used as the base class.
Interface (Adaptor)	Used to modify or enhance the interface of another class or set of classes. The modification can make the class easier to use, more functional, safer, or semantically correct.
Node	Contains no pure abstract virtual functions; supplies virtual member functions that can be overridden in derived classes. Provides protected data members and member functions that can be inherited by derived classes that specialize the node classes through polymorphism and inheritance.
Support/Utility	Constructed regardless of a domain; a utility class is useful within different applications.
Container	Used to hold objects in memory or external storage. Containers are objects that act as "generic holders" for other groups of objects. They can be designed to hold multiple types of objects.
Iterator	Acts as an object-oriented version of pointers. Provides a generic method for selecting or accessing each object that belongs to an object-oriented container or sequence.
Allocator	Acts as an object-oriented portable memory model. Used to encapsulate memory management issues within a class; provides a *system-independent* method of allocating memory for any class that accepts the allocator type as an argument in the constructor.
Parameterized	Contains generic code to manipulate any type; an actual type is the template parameter passed to the code body.

eage. "Typically, concrete types are not fitted into a general system of related classes. Each concrete type can be understood in isolation without reference to other classes" (Stroustrup, 1991). Although a concrete class may be built on other classes, it acts as a termination point for further inheritance. In most cases, it simply does not make sense to use a concrete class, a base class, or ancestor. For example, the stack class shown in Listing 2.1 is from the standard C++ library.

As a concrete class, there is not much reason to specialize a stack class. Every normal use of a stack is encapsulated by this class, therefore, it is meant to be used as-is. It is a standalone class. Usually this stack class would not make a good base class. It was not designed as a generalization of anything other than a stack, so attempting to use it as a base class would be awkward. Naturally, there is always the possibility that some application would require some exotic descendant of a stack class, but this reflects the exception not the rule. Once concrete classes are implemented, they are not specialized later in some descendant class. The concrete class can be optimized in its implementation, because there is no need to worry about the functionality in derived classes (Stroustrup, 1991, pp. 431–435).

Concrete classes are often easier to use than other types of classes because it does not require the user to implement member functions before it can be used, whereas container classes, for example, require the user to implement comparison operators, assignment operators, and so on. The concrete class comes complete, ready to use, and at a performance level on par with built-in data types in terms of efficiency. Concrete classes attempt to reduce dependency on other classes. They can have base classes but only where necessary.

Listing 2.1 Stack Class

```
1// Listing 2.1 This is a declaration of the STL stack class.
2  template <class Container>
3     class stack {
4         friend bool operator==(const stack<Container>& x,
5                                const stack<Container>& y);
6         friend bool operator<(const stack<Container>& x,
7                                const stack<Container>& y);
8     public:
9         typedef Container::value_type value_type;
10        typedef Container::size_type size_type;
11    protected:
12        Container c;
13    public:
14        bool empty() const { return c.empty(); }
15        size_type size() const { return c.size(); }
16        value_type& top() { return c.back(); }
17        const value_type& top() const { return c.back(); }
18        void push(const value_type& x) { c.push_back(x); }
19        void pop() { c.pop_back(); }
20  };
```

Abstract Class

An abstract class supplies a blueprint for all its descendants. In fact, an abstract class is *only* a blueprint. The user cannot declare an object of an abstract class; to use the abstract class, the user must first derive a new class from the base class and provide actual definitions for any pure virtual functions declared in the abstract class. By default, an abstract class must have at least one descendant to be useful. This is in sharp contrast to the concrete class. Whereas the concrete class does not support descendants, the abstract class *requires* descendants to be usable. The concrete class type is not a particular language construct; it is a technique and policy for designing a logical class. And though the abstract class is not a language construct either, it is supported by a C++ language construct. For a class to be abstract, it must have at least one pure virtual function, which has the form:

```
virtual return type function( ) = 0;
```

For example, class device has two pure virtual member functions, start( ) and stop( ), and a virtual destructor:

```
class device{
public:
    virtual void start (void ) = 0;
    virtual void stop(void ) = 0;
    virtual ~device(void);
};
```

Initializing the start( ) and stop( ) functions to 0 causes them to become pure virtual functions. Without the 0 initializer, they are just virtual functions. Class device does not actually define these functions; it only declares them. Any class that has a pure virtual function cannot be used to create a runtime object; therefore, to use the class, the user must derive a class from the abstract class and provide function definitions for every virtual function declared by the abstract base class. For instance, popcorn_popper is derived from device and provides definitions for the two pure virtual functions:

```
class popcorn_popper : public device{
protected:
    int Duration
public:
    popcorn_popper(void);
    ~popcorn_popper(void);
    virtual void start(void) { pop() ;}
    virtual void stop(void) { butter();}
};
```

The declaration:

```
device Popper; // illegal
```

cannot be made because device is an abstract class. Runtime objects cannot be created from abstract classes. In contrast, the declaration:

```
popcorn_popper Popper; // legal
```

can be made because class popcorn_popper has implemented the two pure virtual functions start( ) and stop( ) by making calls to the pop( ) and butter( ) functions. If class popcorn_popper had only implemented one of the pure virtual functions, then class popcorn_popper would also be considered an abstract class because it would still contain one pure virtual function.

The pure virtual functions act as implementation policies, requiring any user of the abstract class to implement the pure virtual functions for the abstract class to be used. Ideally, the semantics of the pure virtual functions would be maintained in the implementation of the descendant classes; that is, the user would define functions start( ) and stop( ) that had some reasonable interpretation of locking. The user should not define start( ) and stop( ) in a way that does not make sense; for example, defining start( ) and stop( ) as addition and subtraction functions would violate the semantics of the notions of starting and stopping.

Abstract classes are useful for establishing patterns, blueprints, and guidelines for descendant classes to follow. If the semantics of the blueprints are followed, the descendant classes are likely to behave as expected by both the supplier and user of the abstract class. By using abstract classes, the C++ programmer can provide specifications for a C++ component that will guide the implementor of that component in its construction.

Interface (Adaptor) Class

An interface, or adaptor, class is used to modify or enhance the interface of another class or set of classes. The modification can make the class easier to use, more functional, safer, or semantically correct. An interface class adjusts or fine-tunes the interface to make it more useful or more efficient. Some examples of interface adjustments are: changing a function or a data member name, a data type, return type, argument list, and so on. Good examples of interface classes are the stack, queue, and priority_queue container adaptors. These adaptors (interface classes) provide a new public interface for the list, vector, and deque containers. The stack class in Listing 2.2, for example, is used as an interface class to modify the interface of a vector class.

By the declaration:

```
stack < vector< T> > Stack;
```

The stack class gives the user a semantically correct class. The formal notions of a stack refer to the operations of popping and pushing the stack. The stack is said to be a LIFO (last-in-first-out) data structure, meaning that the last piece of data pushed on the stack will be the first piece of data popped off the stack. The top operation returns the next item to be popped off the stack. Note on lines 16, 17, 18, and 19 in Listing 2.2, the top( ), push( ), and pop( ) operations simply call other member functions, such as c.pop_back( ), c.push_back( ), and c.back( ). The stack class presents operations that have names more familiar to the user by adjusting the names provided by class c. Class c in this case is a vector container. Ultimately, this modification of the vector's public interface will make the code that uses the stack adaptor easier to understand, maintain, or debug.

Listing 2.2 Stack Used as Interface Class of a Vector

```
1 // Listing 2.2 This is a definition of the STL stack class.
2  template <class Container>
3     class stack {
4         friend bool operator==(const stack<Container>& x,
5                                const stack<Container>& y);
6         friend bool operator<(const stack<Container>& x,
7                                const stack<Container>& y);
8     public:
9         typedef Container::value_type value_type;
10        typedef Container::size_type size_type;
11    protected:
12        Container c;
13    public:
14        bool empty() const { return c.empty(); }
15        size_type size() const { return c.size(); }
16        value_type& top() { return c.back(); }
17        const value_type& top() const { return c.back(); }
18        void push(const value_type& x) { c.push_back(x); }
19        void pop() { c.pop_back(); }
20  };
```

Listing 2.2 also demonstrates that interface classes are lean, sometimes using inline functions. The interface class inherits or contains the class, then defines the adjustments that are to be made. On line 11, c is the class whose interface is being intercepted and renamed by the stack class.

The interface class may also act as a wrapper around a function that is not a member of any class. This use of the interface will come in handy when we want to provide an object-oriented interface to a piece of software that is not object-oriented. We can either wrap a nonobject-oriented function in an object-oriented interface; or we might want to wrap a piece of data, encapsulate it, and give it an object-oriented interface. For example, if we wanted to extend the basic_string class by giving it a toUpper( ) method, we could use the nonobject-oriented toUpper( ) character function in an interface class. Listing 2.3 demonstrates this technique.

The class mystring acts as an interface class for the built-in C++ function toUpper( ), which takes a single character as an argument and returns the uppercase version. We have wrapped this function in the toUpper( ) method of the mystring class. Now we can interact with this function through the object-oriented interface of the mystring class.

Node Class

Perhaps the most powerful kind of class used in C++ programming is the node class. It supplies the foundations for inheritance and polymorphism. Like the abstract base class, the node class is designed to be inherited, and unlike the abstract base class, the

Listing 2.3 An Extension of the String Class

```
1  //Listing 2.3 extends a string class by adding a toUpper() method.
2  #include <string>
3  #include <iostream.h>
4
5  class mystring : public string{
6  public:
7      mystring(char *X);
8      void toUpper(void);
9  };
10
11
12
13  mystring::mystring(char *X) : string(X)
14  {
15  }
16
17  void mystring::toUpper(void)
18  {
19      char *X;
20      int N = length();
21      int Index;
22      X = new char[length() + 1];
23      strcpy(X,data());
24      for(Index = 0;Index < N;Index++)
25      {
26          X[Index] = toupper(X[Index]);
27      }
28      replace(0,N,X,N);
29      delete [] X;
30  }
31
32
33  void main(void)
34  {
35      mystring X("started in lower case");
36      X.toUpper();
37      cout << X;
38  }
```

node class contains no pure abstract virtual functions. The node class is immediately usable, yet is designed with an eye toward the future; that is, it is designed to be reusable. It supplies virtual member functions that can be overridden in derived classes. It provides protected data members and member functions that can be inherited by derived classes. It uses pointers to base classes to allow for manipulation of member functions in descendant classes. The user can specialize node classes through polymorphism and inheritance. Furthermore, the node class can be both a base class and a derived class, and provides the substance of a class hierarchy.

The exception classes (listed in Table 2.2) are examples of node classes defined by the standard library. Though these classes can be used as-is, they are not very useful unless they are specialized through inheritance. These classes best serve the user when used as base classes for user-defined exception classes. The exception classes should contain methods that help the exception handlers recover the error that has occurred, but the exception classes in the standard library do not contain such logic. At best, they generate simple messages and can be used with the runtime identification facilities to identify base classes involved. This is where the node class comes in handy. Remember, we can extend a node class through inheritance. Let's take, for example, the logic_error class. We could extend this class to have more functionality during an exception. For example, the class update_error:

```
class update_error : public logic_error{
public:
    update_error(string &WhatError);
    save_update(void);
    ...
};
```

extends the logic_error node class. The update_error class is thrown when certain types of file-updating errors occur. In a distributed or networked file processing situation with multiple users of the same file, occasionally, file-updating problems arise. For example, more than one user may attempt to update the same location in a file. This type of situation is normally handled with file locking, semaphores, mutexes, or some other protection mechanism. But when all protection devices fail, we need to throw an exception. Our update_error class can report the kind of exception that has occurred. Furthermore, because we have specialized it with our save_update( ) method, the update error_class can save its updates to a temporary file. This type of exception handling would prevent the user from losing a valuable file update. The information is stored in a temporary file with the save_update( ) method, so the user can go back and update the file later. The update_error class has logic_error as its base class, and therefore has all of the functionality of the logic_error class. The node class concept relies on inheritance and specialization.

Support/Utility Class

Support/utility classes are constructed regardless of a domain; they are used across domains. A utility class is very useful in different applications. For example, a utility

Table 2.2 Standard Library Exception Classes

RUNTIME_ERROR	LOGIC_ERROR
length_error	range_error
domain_error	overflow_error
out_of_range_error	underflow_error
invalid_argument	

class can be a date class, a time/clock class, or a meter class that determines how long it takes for an operation or task to perform. This type of functionality is used during the installation of software, the downloading or uploading of files, and so on. Another type of support/utility class can be a user interface class, such as a list box class or a scrollbar class. Examples of standard C++ classes that fit this category are the type_info class and the locale class. The type_info class helps the programmer identify types of objects at runtime. When multiple inheritance or polymorphism is used, the type_info class helps the programmer identify the object's type. The locale class encapsulates components for internalization; for instance, money formats, time formats, and character-set collating sequence information.

Container Classes

Containers are objects that act as "generic holders" for other groups of objects. A C++ container can be designed to hold multiple types of objects in the same way that a box can hold a collection of balls, blocks, hats, tools, or chocolates. We are concerned with putting objects in, accessing the objects, and getting objects out of containers. Container classes may be only a part of a class library, or a class library may consist only of container classes.

Although application frameworks normally utilize containers, containers are not application frameworks. Containers are general-purpose grouping structures. The developer or designer can use collections and containers to manipulate groups of heterogeneous or homogeneous objects. Containers can also be used to manage a group of objects in the same way that traditional arrays or lists are used to manage traditional data types such as integers or characters.

Because containers are objects, the benefits of inheritance, polymorphism, and encapsulation can all be applied to collections and containers. Many of these structures are object-oriented versions of:

Stacks	Lists
Queues	Associative arrays
Deques	Graphs
Sets	Trees
Multisets	Tables

However, the possibilities for collections and container design go far beyond these traditional data structures. Collection and container classes can be used to implement domain classes. We've come across:

Garages	Vehicles
Banks	Rings
Cells	Paragraphs
Crowds	Cabinets
Transfinite sets	Warehouses

Rooms   Tubes

Groups   Fields

The standard C++ class library contains the most commonly used containers, and those not included can be easily added through inheritance and interface classes.

Iterator Classes

Iterator classes are object-oriented versions of pointers. They provide a generic method for selecting or accessing each object that belongs to an object-oriented container or object-oriented sequence. Many container and sequence classes provide member functions like current( ) that return either pointers or references to the objects to which the iterator is referring. Like a pointer, the iterator can be moved sequentially through the container by calling member functions such as next( ) or previous( ). The current( ), next( ), and previous( ) type member functions allow the user to visit or access every object in the container or sequence, that is, to *iterate* through the container.

Iterators can also be implemented as operators, meaning the ++, −−, +=, or *= notation can be used to navigate through a group of objects. When iterators are implemented as methods or operators, they are usually part of the class they will be accessing; they are implemented as methods of the container or sequence class. However, iterators can also be implemented as separate classes. The standard C++ library uses both techniques to implement iterators. When implemented as separate classes, more than one iterator can be associated with a collection or container object simultaneously. We could declare two iterators, and use one iterator to move forward through the container and one iterator to move backward through the container. Listing 2.4 uses two iterators: one named Forward and one named Backward.

Table 2.3 shows the output from the program in this listing. Separating iterators from the container they are iterating means that several types of iteration may be applied to the collection and container at once, giving the programmer extremely flexible object visitation capabilities.

Allocator Classes

Allocator classes are object-oriented portable memory models. They are used to encapsulate memory management issues within a class. They provide a *system-independent* method of allocating memory for any class that accepts the allocator type as an argument in the constructor. Allocator objects encapsulate pointer types, reference types, pointer difference types, address information, maximum size information, and so on.

Parameterized (Template) Classes

One of the most important features of C++ is its support of code reuse. The goal of code reuse is to be able to implement the code for a class, structure, function, and so on once and be able to use that code repeatedly, and in different ways. For code to be reusable,

Listing 2.4 Use of Forward and Backward Iterator Classes

```
1   // Listing 2.4
2   // This program demonstrates multiple iterators at work
3   #include <list>
4   #include <string>
5
6   using namespace std;
7   void main(void)
8   {
9
10
11      list<string> WordList;
12      WordList.push_back("These");
13      WordList.push_back("Are");
14      WordList.push_back("The");
15      WordList.push_back("Voyages");
16      list<string>::iterator Forward = WordList.begin();
17      list<string>::reverse_iterator Backward = WordList.rbegin();
18      while((Forward != WordList.end()) && (Backward != WordList.rend()))
19      {
20          cout << *Forward << '\t' << '\t' << *Backward << endl;
21          Forward++;
22          Backward++;
23      }
24  }
25
26
27
```

it should be *generic*. The implementation of generic code should be unaffected by the data type the construct uses or manipulates; it has the same form whatever the data type. This makes generic code very reusable. In most cases, the more generic the code, the more reusable it is. This type of programming is called *parameterized programming*, whereby new software modules can be constructed using a parameterized type called a *template*.

A template is a parameterized construct containing generic code that can use or manipulate any data type. It is called parameterized because it accepts as a parameter the

Table 2.3 Listing 2.4 Output

These	Voyages
Are	The
The	Are
Voyages	These

type of data that it will use. The template is a specification of how a group of related classes or functions can be constructed. Templates are used to achieve *parametric polymorphism,* also called *horizontal genericity.* It is called horizontal because the genericity is across different types of classes in a horizontal fashion, in contrast to polymorphism achieved by using virtual methods called *vertical genericity,* where the genericity is within one lineage of classes. In vertical genericity, polymorphism is achieved through inheritance, operation overloading, and method overriding. Figure 2.1 contrasts the type of polymorphism that occurs with virtual methods and templates. Templates can be used to construct a family of classes called *class templates* and a family of functions called *function templates.*

To create a template, the keyword *template* is followed by the argument that will be used in the declaration of the template class or template function. The argument is bracketed as follows:

```
template<class Type>
```

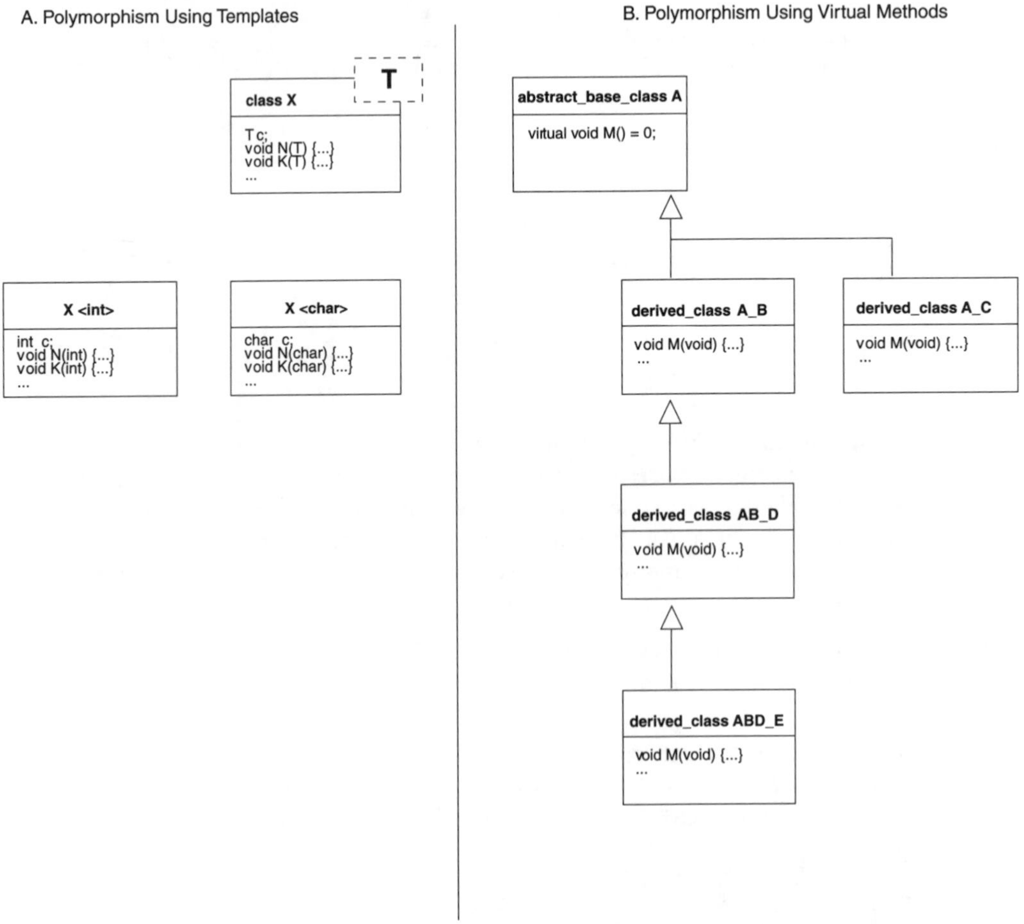

A. Polymorphism Using Templates

B. Polymorphism Using Virtual Methods

Figure 2.1 Contrasting the polymorphism that occurs with virtual methods and templates.

The class or function declaration follows. The argument Type represents any type passed to the template. Type can represent a built-in data type or a user-defined class. Throughout the declaration and definition of the template, the value Type is used like other built-in data types or user-defined data types. Once the template has been declared, objects of the template class or function can be instantiated. The instantiation of the template is the passing of a specific type to the template and the declaration of a variable. For example, the C++ standard vector template is a container that can hold types assessed directly by using an index. A vector template class can hold any built-in data type, such as integers, floats, char, and so on. They can also hold user-defined objects. The data type the vector will contain will depend on the data type passed as a parameter during the declaration of the vector. Listing 2.5 is class template declaration for a vector that can hold any type.

Note that template<class T> is placed before a rather usual class declaration. Type T represents the type passed to the template. T will be used in the declaration and the definition whenever the reference to the type is needed. For example, the protected data member Data is of type T. Data of type T is a vector element. The subscript operator is overloaded. It will return an element of type T in position Index of the vector.

The class template must be assigned a unique name; it cannot be the name of some other class, template, function, object, value, or type within the scope of the template. Other than the prefix and the use of type T, the class template declaration is the same as a nontemplate class declaration.

Function Template

A function template specifies the form of a family of functions. The individual function constructed from a function template is called a *template function*. The function template is generic so that the implementation of the function is not dependent on a specific data type. The template function generated can manipulate or use the data type passed as the template's parameters. The template function is referred to by a variable name.

Listing 2.5 Template Declaration for Simplified Vector

```
1  // Listing 2.5 is a template declaration for a simplified vector.
2
3  template<class T> class vector{
4  protected:
5      T *Data;
6      unsigned int Size;
7  public:
8      vector(int Size);
9      ~vector();
10     T& operator[](int Index);
11     // other required member functions
12
13 }
```

A selection sort function can be declared as a function template. A selection sort sorts values in descending order. Listing 2.6 is a function template for a selection sort of any type.

Here, template<class T> is placed before the implementation of a selection sort function. Type T represents the type passed to the function that will be sorted. The selection sort will sort in descending order any type passed to the template's parameters. For the sort to work with user-defined types, the class must define the member functions for comparison and an assignment operator.

The function template is used with a function call. The formal parameters will pass the type and all other information needed to the function template. Listing 2.7 shows an example of a function call to the function template selection_sort.

In this listing, a vector of binary_number objects and the size of the vector are passed to the function. The selection_sort function will sort the vector of binary_number objects in descending order. Note that a user-defined class such as binary_number must define comparison and assignment operations in order for the selection sort to perform.

Member Functions of the Class Template

Member functions of a class template are function templates. The definitions of the member functions must handle arbitrary types. Data members that represent elements of the class have to be of type T. The prototypes of the member functions are structured

Listing 2.6 Selection Sort Function Template

```
1// Listing 2.6 is a function template for a selection sort.
2
3   template<class T> void selection_sort(T A[], int Size)
4   {
5       int i,j,index;
6       T large;
7
8       for(i = Size - 1; i > 0; i--){
9           large = A[0];
10          index = 0;
11          for(j = 1; j <= i; j++){
12              if(A[j] > large){
13                  large = A[j];
14                  index = j;
15              }
16              A[index] = A[i];
17              A[i] = large;
18          }
19      }
20  }
```

Listing 2.7   Function Call to selection_sort

```
// Listing 2.7 demonstrates a function call to the election_sort function
// template. It is used to sort a vector of binary_number objects.

void Test(binary_number ABinNum[20], int Size = 20)
{
    selection_sort(ABinNum, Size);
}
```

in the same way as the prototypes for nontemplate classes. The member function name is preceded by the name of the class and a colon. This will include the template<class T> prefix. For example, Listing 2.8 is the member function definition of the subscript operator of the class template vector.

Note that following the template<class T>, the prototype has the same structure as any class member prototype. The return type is succeeded by the class name, the scope resolution operator, then the member function name and its argument list.

Creating an Object from a Class Template

When creating an object from a class template, the name of the template class is followed by the type, in brackets, and the variable name of the instantiated class. For example:

```
vector <binary_number>ABin(6);
```

declares a template class vector of six binary_number objects. The variable name for this class template is ABin, which can be used like any other class name object.

A type definition can be used to create a synonym for a template of a specific parameterized type. For example:

```
typedef vector<binary_number>ABin;
typedef vector<network_adapter_card>ANetCards;

ABin(10);
ANetCards(3);
```

Listing 2.8   Member Function Definition

```
// Listing 2.8 is the member function for the subscript operator for the
// class template vector.

template<class T> T& vector<T>::operator[](int Index)
{
return(Data[Index]);
  }
```

are two type definitions. The first defines a template class vector of binary_number objects using the identifier ABin. The second type defines a template class vector of network_adapter_card objects using the identifier ANetCards. The identifiers ABin and ANetCards are synonyms of the template class declarations vector<binary_number> and vector<network_adapter_card>, respectively.

Template Arguments

Template arguments do not have to be user-defined classes; they can be built-in data types. There can also be multiple arguments, all of which appear within the angle brackets. To instantiate objects of a template, the supplied arguments have to match the required objects. For example, if a template were declared as follows:

```
template<class T, int M> class X{..}
```

and if a template class were declared:

```
X<binary_number, char > TestClass; // this is not correct
```

this would generate a compile error because of a type mismatch. The class template accepts an arbitrary type and an int, not a char. This would be the legal declaration:

```
X<binary_number, int M> TestClass;
```

If the class template requires two different arbitrary types, using two of the same type will not cause a compile error. For example, if a template were declared as follows:

```
template<class T, class P> class X{..}
```

and a template class were declared:

```
X<binary_number, binary_number> TestClass; //this is correct
```

a compile error would not occur.

Domain Classes

Although the standard class library does not contain domain classes, we mention them here because a domain class is the most important type used in most object-oriented development efforts. A domain class is created to simulate some entity within a specific domain. The meaning of the class is specific to that domain. The domain class models some aspect of reality; it captures rules, assertions, and behaviors of some real-world process or concept. Thus, the domain classes are the application or system-specific classes. For instance, in a tax application, individual classes relative to that domain would be constructed like a 1040 tax form class or a W-2 form class. In a space flight simulator, rocket classes, fuel classes, weather classes, and pilot classes would be among the domain classes.

Unless the domain is system programming, domain classes are totally separate from programming support classes, user interface classes, or database classes. Domain classes may be abstract base classes, concrete classes, or node classes. An object-oriented application will have a hierarchy of domain classes that represent the core of the application. For example, in creating an application that will be used to calculate taxes, a 1040_tax_form class may inherit a base class called tax_form and contain a class called deductible. The class types in the standard C++ library are generally domain-independent classes.

Now that we have explained what classes are and the types of classes that are commonly found in the C++ programming environment, let's take a closer look at the anatomy of the typical class in the standard C++ library.

Attributes, Characteristics, and Methods

Each class in the standard C++ library will have one or more members. The members can be a combination of data members (also called attributes or characteristics) and member functions (also called methods). The characteristics are declarations of variables and types such as:

```
int   Size;
typedef  set<string>:: iterator I;
int Capacity;
char *P;

class Container;
```

The methods are functions such as:

```
int size(void);
void capacity(int N);
char *data(void);

virtual bool open(void);
```

Most C++ implementations organize the class declarations by attribute type and method type. For example, the declaration of the set class in Listing 2.9 shows how a class might be divided.

Notice how the typedefs are listed together beginning at line 5. The set class defines the *allocation* and *deallocation* methods after the typedefs. The *accessor* methods follow the allocation and deallocation methods. The *modifier* methods follow the accessor methods, and so on. The basic idea is that the attributes and methods of a class are divided into functional categories, shown in Table 2.4. The methods can also be grouped into the following functional categories:

Object creators (constructors)

Object destroyers (destructors)

Object accessors

Object modifiers (insert, erase, assignment, etc.)

Object reporters (size, capacity, location, etc.)

Listing 2.9 Set Class Declaration

```
1    // Listing 2.9
2    template <class Key, class Compare>
3    class set {
4    public:
5    // typedefs:
6
7        typedef Key key_type;
8        typedef Key value_type;
9        typedef Compare key_compare;
10       typedef Compare value_compare;
11   private:
12       typedef rb_tree<key_type, value_type,
13                       ident<value_type,key_type>,key_compare> rep_type;
14       rep_type t; // red-black tree representing set
15   public:
16       typedef rep_type::const_reference reference;
17       typedef rep_type::const_reference const_reference;
18       typedef rep_type::const_iterator iterator;
19       typedef rep_type::const_iterator const_iterator;
20       typedef rep_type::const_reverse_iterator reverse_iterator;
21       typedef rep_type::const_reverse_iterator const_reverse_iterator;
22       typedef rep_type::size_type size_type;
23       typedef rep_type::difference_type difference_type;
24
25   // allocation/deallocation
26
27       set(const Compare& comp = Compare()) : t(comp, false) {}
28       set(const value_type* first, const value_type* last,
29           const Compare& comp = Compare()) : t(comp, false) {
30           for (const value_type* i = first; i != last; ++i)
31               t.insert(*i);
32           }
33       set(const set<Key, Compare>& x) : t(x.t, false) {}
34       set<Key, Compare>& operator=(const set<Key, Compare>& x) {
35           t = x.t;
36           return *this;
37       }
38
39   // accessors:
40
41       key_compare key_comp() const { return t.key_comp(); }
42       value_compare value_comp() const { return t.key_comp(); }
43       iterator begin() const { return t.begin(); }
44       iterator end() const { return t.end(); }
45       reverse_iterator rbegin() const { return t.rbegin(); }
46       reverse_iterator rend() const { return t.rend(); }
47       bool empty() const { return t.empty(); }
```

Listing 2.9 (*Continued*)

```
48        size_type size() const { return t.size(); }
49        size_type max_size() const { return t.max_size(); }
50        void swap(set<Key, Compare>& x) { t.swap(x.t); }
51
52    // insert/erase
53        typedef pair<iterator, bool> pair_iterator_bool;
54        // typedef done to get around compiler bug
55        pair_iterator_bool insert(const value_type& x) {
56            pair<rep_type::iterator, bool> p = t.insert(x);
57            return pair<iterator, bool>(p.first, p.second);
58        }
59        iterator insert(iterator position, const value_type& x) {
60            return t.insert((rep_type::iterator&)position, x);
61        }
62        void insert(const value_type* first, const value_type* last) {
63            for (const value_type* i = first; i != last; ++i)
64                t.insert(*i);
65        }
66        void erase(iterator position) {
67            t.erase((rep_type::iterator&)position);
68        }
69        size_type erase(const key_type& x) {
70            return t.erase(x);
71        }
72        void erase(iterator first, iterator last) {
73            t.erase((rep_type::iterator&)first,
74                    (rep_type::iterator&)last);
75        }
76
77    // set operations:
78
79        iterator find(const key_type& x) const { return t.find(x); }
80        size_type count(const key_type& x) const { return t.count(x); }
81        iterator lower_bound(const key_type& x) const {
82            return t.lower_bound(x);
83        }
84        iterator upper_bound(const key_type& x) const {
85            return t.upper_bound(x);
86        }
87        typedef pair<iterator, iterator> pair_iterator_iterator;
88        // typedef done to get around compiler bug
89        pair_iterator_iterator equal_range(const key_type& x) const {
90            return t.equal_range(x);
91        }
92    };
93
94    template <class Key, class Compare>
```

Continues

Listing 2.9 Set Class Declaration (*Continued*)

```
95    inline bool operator==(const set<Key, Compare>& x,
96                           const set<Key, Compare>& y) {
97        return x.size() == y.size() && equal(x.begin(), x.end(),
98                                             y.begin());
99    }
100
101   template <class Key, class Compare>
102   inline bool operator<(const set<Key, Compare>& x,
103                          const set<Key, Compare>& y) {
104       return lexicographical_compare(x.begin(), x.end(), y.begin(),
105                                      y.end());
106   }
```

Object I/O (inserters, extractors, read, write, etc.)

Object operators (=!, < >, +, −, *, /, etc.)

Table 2.5 shows the functional categories that methods can be divided into and the basic function of each category. Most object methods will fall into one of these categories, and nearly all of the methods in the standard C++ classes fall into one of the categories in Table 2.5. The categories represent part of the interface to the standard C++ class libraries, presented here in simplified form. In practice, many of the categories can be subdivided. For example, the modifier methods can be further divided into:

Insertion methods

Deletion methods

Replacement methods

Swap methods

Transformation methods

Summation methods

Assignment methods

We call these modifier methods because they will modify some characteristic or attribute of the object to which they are applied. The accessor methods generally do not modify

Table 2.4 Functional Categorization of Attributes

TYPES OF ATTRIBUTES	USAGE
Data Structures	Structures used by the class.
Statistical	Contains statistical information about the class such as size, capacity, location, etc.
Typedefs	Type definitions.

Table 2.5 Functional Categorization of Methods

TYPES OF METHODS	USAGE
Accessor	Used to access (but not change) one or more of the class attributes.
Modifier	Used to modify one or more of the class attributes; Examples of modifiers are insert, erase, assign, etc.
Creator/Initializers	Used to construct a new class and perform the initializations of variables, opening of files, preparing of devices for use, etc.
Destroyer/Finalizers	Used to delete or destruct an existing class and perform any clean-up such as closing files, devices, etc.
Statistical	Information generators; generates information about the class such as size, capacity, location, etc.
Input/Output	Used to perform the input and output of the class, such as the overloading of the insertion and extraction operators.
Operators	Used to manage operator overloading for the class for operators such as: $=$, $==$, $!=$, $<>$, $+$, $-$, $*$, $/$, etc.

the object they are accessing. The *creator* methods create new objects, and the *destroyer* methods remove existing objects from memory and return the unused memory to the system. The *reporter* methods generally return information about the object, as opposed to returning some data component of the object. For example, the capacity( ) method may return the number of objects that a container is capable of holding. This type of object access is different from, say, returning one of the objects or some part of one of the objects that a container is holding. The reporter method gives information about the object.

We found that every object will have one or more attributes and one or more methods, and that the attributes and methods can be organized into functional categories. Next, we will see that all attributes and methods in a class have an access policy, and that the interface to every object in the standard C++ library has an access policy. The access policy determines which attributes and methods a user can access and which attributes and methods a derived class can access. The C++ class concept supports three levels of access:

- Private
- Protected
- Public

Every attribute and method that is a part of a class will have one of these three levels of access.

The Private Policy

When attributes and methods are declared private, they are accessible only by methods of the immediate class. This means that private data members and member functions cannot be accessed by any function that is not a member of the class. This restricted access extends to descendants of the class. For instance, here:

```
class A{
private:
    char *Data;

};

class B : public A{ };
```

class B has inherited class A. However, class B does not have access to the Data attribute of class A. This data member has been declared private and so is not part of class A's interface. The private access policy says that private attributes and methods are not accessible to derived classes and are, therefore, not a part of the derived class's interface.

Members-Only Access

Attributes and methods of a class can be declared protected, meaning they can be accessed by immediate members of the class and any descendants of the class. Contrary to private policy, members declared protected can be accessed by any descendant classes. The data members and member functions that are accessible only to the immediate class and descendants of the class are called the class's *protected interface.* Although the descendants of a class may have access, functions that are not in the class hierarchy cannot have access. For instance:

```
class A{
protected:
    char *Data;
public:

    A(void);

};

void main(void)
{
    A Temp;
    cout << Temp.Data // illegal call to protected data member
}
```

Temp is declared an object of type A. A has Data as a protected data member. Although Temp is an object of type A, the main( ) function cannot access the Data attribute because Data is protected, and access is restricted to only family functions.

Open to the Public

A class may declare attributes and methods as public, which means they can be accessed by anyone, whether they are members of the class or not. These data members and member functions make up the public interface of a class.

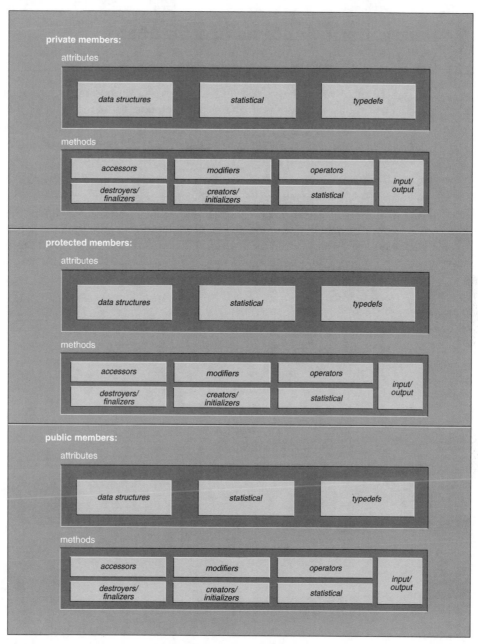

Figure 2.2 Skeleton of the basic anatomy of a standard C++ class.

Summary: Basic Anatomy of a Standard C++ Class

To get the most out of the standard C++ classes, it is important to understand their basic anatomy. Every class has attributes and methods. Those methods will be divided into several functional categories. Most classes have creators, destroyers, accessors, modifiers, and reporters. The members in every class have an access policy. C++ supports three primary access policies: private, protected, and public.

Figure 2.2 shows a skeleton of the basic anatomy of a standard C++ class. All members in a class fit somewhere in this skeleton. Therefore, it is recommended to become familiar with these categories and how the methods and attributes are set up in source code. Most compiler vendors organize the class declarations so that similar attributes are declared together and so that methods of the same purpose are declared together. This is a good practice, and helps to document a class. Understanding the anatomy of a class will help you to understand the class's protocol.

CHAPTER 3

The Iostreams

"In a robot, likewise input-peripherals feed into the internal computations, which lead eventually to changes in the output peripherals. In between, the program causes a host of things to happen inside the system itself."

—MARGARET A. BODEN
ANDROID EPISTEMOLOGY

The iostreams are a set of C++ classes used to implement an object-oriented model of input and output. The iostream facilities are packaged as a standard component with all C++ compilers is an object-oriented input/output facility providing access to un-buffered (low-level) and buffered I/O operations. If for some reason these iostream facilities are not sufficient for the job at hand, the programmer can improve them through inheritance, polymorphism, encapsulation, and specialization. The I/O facilities in C++ are not restricted to a specific set of keywords. The class implementation of I/O adds extensibility and complete flexibility to the output capabilities of the C++ environment. Although the stream is a powerful programming construct, enabling the programmer to meet extremely challenging I/O demands, the object-oriented iostream is the proverbial silver bullet. A complete I/O library in a computer environment will cover the entire spectrum between physical devices and logical objects. It will serve the needs of system programmers (those who write device drivers, operating systems, interrupt handlers, and such) as well as the needs of application programmers (those who normally deal with higher-level constructs). In Figure 3.1, the hardware devices at the left of the spectrum represent traditional system-level programming requirements and concerns. Faced with programming I/O at this end of the spectrum, we have to deal with myriad characteristics and attributes from a wide range of devices such as:

Keyboards	Modems	Monitors	Printers	Bar-code readers
Tape drives	Fax cards	Disk drives	Serial ports	Parallel ports
Sound cards	Disk controllers	Data acquisition	Joysticks	Video capture
Pointing	Pen input	adapters	NTSC	boards
devices	devices	Scanners	adapters	Memory chips

and more.

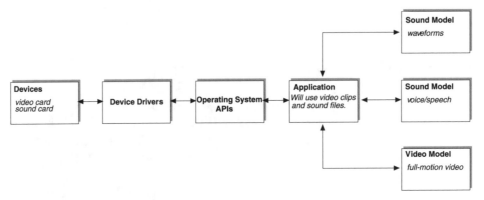

Figure 3.1 Hardware devices at the left end of the spectrum represent traditional system-level programming requirements and concerns.

These devices traditionally have come in two flavors: *block devices* or *character devices*. Table 3.1 lists the primary features of block and character devices.

A block device accesses multiple bytes at one time, usually in a direct manner. A block device does not need to access data sequentially; it can retrieve or place multiple bytes at a specific address or location. A disk drive is a good example. A disk drive can access data in chunks of 128, 256, 512, 1024, 32768 bytes at a time. In contrast, a character device accesses one character at a time in a sequential fashion. Character devices are normally associated with queues, stacks, or some derivative. A keyboard is a good example. It processes its input in a serial mode, one keypress at a time.

A complete I/O facility will give the programmer the means to effectively program block devices, character devices, or any combination thereof. At the other end of the

Table 3.1 Primary Features of Block and Character Devices

BLOCK DEVICES	CHARACTER DEVICES
Stores information in a fixed size called *blocks*.	Delivers or accepts a stream of *characters* without regard to block structure.
Does not need to access data sequentially.	Accesses data sequentially.
Can access a block independently from another, and performs seek operations.	Does not have seek operations.
Data files can be accessed by common system calls (read, write, etc.).	Data files can be accessed by common system calls (read, write, etc.).
Can retrieve or place multiple bytes at a specific address or location.	Accesses one character at a time in a stream; not addressable.
Files are mapped by a directory file.	Operates using a queuing process.
Example of block device is a *disk*.	Examples of character devices are *printers, screens,* and *mice*.

input-output spectrum shown in Figure 3.1 dwell the logical entities: the objects that are input into the computer and/or its peripheral devices and the objects that are output from the computer and/or its peripheral devices. These objects take the form of numbers, characters, text, sounds, speech, printed text, graphics, full-motion video, voice activation, and so on.

Along with access to physical devices, efficient access to higher-level logical entities, structures, and data types represent the entire gamut that a programmer may face when implementing any given component of software. The iostream facility in C++ is a complete I/O library. The iostreams take the traditional concept of I/O programming to a higher level by adding the object-oriented model. The object-oriented model in C++ captures the idea of an input/output device as a stream, with each stream representing a different type of I/O: streams that represent files, streams that represent the console, streams that represent blocks of memory, and streams that represent devices.

Classes and the iostreams

The iostreams are made of three fundamental types of classes:

- Stream state components
- Buffer components
- Conversion or translation components

The block diagram in Figure 3.2 shows the functional relationship among the three types of components. The stream state classes contain the condition of a stream at any given point or time. The buffer components are temporary holding areas for bytes in transit. The conversion components are responsible for converting objects to sequences of bytes and sequences of bytes to objects.

Stream State Components

The stream state components contain specifications that represent the format of how data should be interpreted coming into or going out of the stream. For instance, data may need to be read into a hexadecimal, binary, or double-precision format; or the data may need to be sent to the output in scientific notation. The state component of the stream maintains information that determines the format of the bytes in the stream. The stream class also holds information that represents the condition the stream is in.

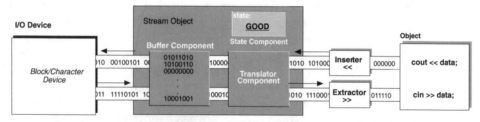

Figure 3.2 The functional relationship among the three types of components.

As input and output operations are performed on the stream, the condition of the stream can change. At any given time, the stream has an associated *state.* The stream may be in a *good* state, signaling that the previous operation on the stream was successful and that the next operation on the stream can be attempted. The stream may be in a *fail* or *bad* state, signaling that the previous operations failed, and unless action is taken any subsequent operations will fail. The stream may also be in an *eof* state, meaning that the source of data has been exhausted.

Buffer Components

The iostreams buffer components specify a generic holding area for the data while it is in transit from an input device or to an output device. The buffer classes also contain the specifications for the operations that can be performed on the data in the generic holding area. The buffer classes specify position designators that determine where the next character in the holding area will be read from, or where in the holding area the next character will be written.

Conversion Components

The iostreams conversion components either convert the data types to an anonymous sequence of bytes on the output stream or translate an anonymous sequence of bytes from the input stream into either user-defined data types or built-in data types. The conversion classes are largely responsible for giving the programmer the device-independent "look and feel" that the iostreams have.

These classes are interconnected through inheritance, aggregation, and containment. Figure 3.3 is a general class relationship diagram that shows the inheritance and containment relationships among the major types of components found in the iostreams. The conversion classes are usually descendants of a stream state class. The stream state class may possess a buffer class. The buffer class may have buffer ancestors, and so on. Because the iostreams are a set of classes (not functions!), all the concepts and advantages of object orientation can be applied.

Through inheritance, the programmer may combine the data members and member functions of a class designed to model input with a class designed to model output, the result of which is a class suitable for both input and output. In this way, a buffer class can be combined with a printer class to produce a buffered printer class. Likewise, using inheritance, the programmer can specialize or modify the functionality of any of the iostream classes, through function overloading or function overriding. Through polymorphism, the programmer can maintain a single input/output interface to multiple device types. This moves the program in the direction of device independence. When the technique of polymorphism is properly applied, code reuse and modularity follow. Through encapsulation, the programmer can combine I/O channels with the proper operations on the I/O channels, ensuring that the channel is accessed only through or by "intelligent" type safe member functions, preventing unauthorized access by rogue device drivers and the like.

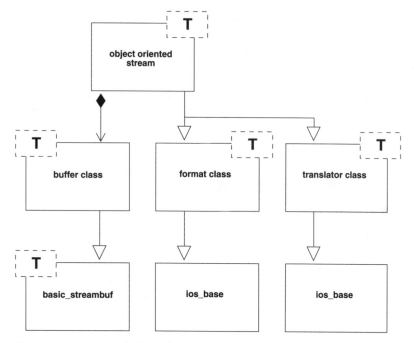

Figure 3.3 A general class relationship diagram illustrating the inheritance and containment relationships among the major types of components found in the iostreams.

Stream State Classes: ios_base<T> and basic_ios<T>

The stream state component is represented by ios_base<T> and basic_ios<T>. The stream state class basic_ios<T> forms an important base class for the conversion classes, while the basic_ios class contains information about how the stream has been opened. For instance, it answers, has the stream been opened in the append mode, or can the stream be read from and written to? Some streams are read-only, others are write-only; still others can be opened for both read and write operations. The basic_ios class holds the information that designates the attached stream as a binary stream or a text stream. This class also controls the information that determines the base to which integers will be formatted when being inserted into or extracted from a stream. That is, determining whether the integers will be formatted as decimal, hexadecimal, or octal and whether the floating point numbers will be formatted as scientific notation or in a fixed decimal format. Finally, the basic_ios class controls precision information for numbers entering or exiting a stream.

Buffer Classes: basic_streambuf, basic_filebuf, basic_stringbuf

The buffer components that act as temporary holding areas for bytes in transit from devices to memory or from memory to devices are basic_streambuf, basic_filebuf, basic_stringbuf. The buffer classes process generic sequences of bytes. The basic_streambuf class is the base class for basic_filebuf and basic_stringbuf. The basic_streambuf class has methods that get bytes, put bytes, skip bytes, put bytes back, and so on. The basic_streambuf class has the functionality that controls what happens with stream overflow or underflow conditions. The basic_streambuf class is contained as a data member of one of the other iostream classes; for instance, the basic_ios class usually contains a basic_streambuf data member. Positioning is another responsibility of the basic_streambuf class. It controls the movement of a get pointer and put pointer. The get pointer identifies the next byte to be read, assigned, or viewed; the put pointer points to the next byte to be written, assigned, or viewed.

Conversion Classes: basic_istream and basic_ostream

Six conversion classes form the foundation of data translation and the iostream class hierarchy: *basic_istream, basic_ostream, basic_istringstream, basic_ostringstream, basic_ifstream, basic_ofstream.* The basic_istream class models an input stream. The basic_ostream class models an output stream. Both basic_istream and basic_ostream have basic_ios as a base class. Both basic_istream and basic_ostream have access to a basic_streambuf class. The basic_istream and basic_ostream classes encapsulate the primary object-oriented representation of a sink (output) and a source. The basic_istream and basic_ostream classes provide the C++ programming environment with the notion of the object-oriented stream. The basic_istream has member functions that accept into the stream generic sequences of data, and convert them to built-in types, user-defined types, or user-defined structures. The basic_ostream accepts built-in types, user-defined types, or user-defined structures, and converts them to generic sequences of bytes that can be sent to the output (sink).

Together, the basic_istream and basic_ostream classes summarize the base functionality of the entire family of iostream classes. They are base classes for most of the other classes in the iostream hierarchy. Standard iostream implementations have used multiple inheritance to derive a single class called basic_iostream derived from basic_istream and basic_ostream.

NOTE:
Do not confuse the iostream class with the iostream family of classes. The iostream class is a single entity derived from a basic_istream class and a basic_ostream class. The iostream classes represent the entire object-oriented network of classes in the C++ environment, which includes the ios class, basic_streambuf family, basic_ostream family, basic_istream family, and the manipulators.

Packaging the I/O facilities as a set of classes allows the programmer to custom shape and mold the input and output exactly to fit the requirements of even the most demanding system. Classes provide the foundations for modeling I/O events, processes, devices, and operations. The notion of the class adds extensibility to I/O in C++. We cannot predict the types of devices that will be connected to a computer at any given time in the future, nor can we modify the language every time a new peripheral is introduced. However, with the concept of classes and the iostreams our ability to process I/O can evolve to adapt to whatever the current prevailing environment is.

Object-Oriented Input/Output

Taking an object-oriented approach to the block and character devices gives the programmer the ability to implement designs that match these devices in form and function—although in many applications it is desirable to program independently of the structure of the devices that will be accessed. In some systems-level work, it is not only desirable but necessary to consider the structure in order to take full and efficient advantage of the specific capabilities of the device being accessed. Device drivers and interrupt handlers are examples of software components that usually require specific knowledge of the physical and logical structure of some I/O device.

An object-oriented I/O facility gives the programmer the power to model physical and logical characteristics of any device connected to or accessed by the computer. Modeling and simulations are natural activities in an object-oriented environment, and the programmer has the option of programming at a high level, ignoring the underlying structure, or of emulating the actual device he or she is programming to achieve maximum performance.

Using an object-oriented approach to input and output, the programmer can implement the input/output data structures directly from an I/O model. For example, the programmer might implement a voice object that accepts text input and sends speech output. If the programmer needs to access a character device for input and output—perhaps a high-resolution video adapter—the programmer can simulate the attributes and functionality of the video adapter using object-oriented techniques. Any I/O facility that provides the low-level access, the stream paradigm, and object orientation gives the programmer a complete picture of input and output in a computer environment. The standard C++ iostreams library offers the programmer a complete toolkit of building blocks to construct whatever kind of I/O interface is necessary. The library supports user-defined streams and contains eight predefined streams, listed in Table 3.2, along with their types and function.

Table 3.2 Eight Predefined Streams

PREDEFINED STREAMS	CLASS	C EQUIVALENT	CHARACTER TYPE	FUNCTION
cin	basic_istream	stdin	char	input stream
wcin	basic_istream	stdin	wchar_t	wide character input
cout	basic_ostream	stdout	char	output stream
wcout	basic_ostream	stdout	wchar_t	wide character output
cerr	basic_ostream	stderr	char	error output
wcerr	basic_ostream	stderr	wchar_t	wide character error output
clog	basic_ostream	stderr	char	error output (nonbuffered)
wclog	basic_ostream	stderr	wchar_t	wide character error (nonbuffered)

The eight streams can accept input and output from the standard input (stdin), the standard output (stdout), and standard error (stderr). The standard streams have two forms: *narrow* and *wide.* The wide form supports multibyte characters; the narrow form represents single-byte character sets. The narrow form uses the char data type for its byte size, and the wide form uses the wchar_t data type for its default byte size.

Extractors

The basic_istream class models an input stream in C++. When data is taken from a stream of type basic_ostream and stored in a variable, it is called an *extraction.* The data is extracted from a stream in order to be input to a variable. The right-shift (>>) operator is called the extraction operator. The right-shift operator is overloaded to perform input operations on built-in and user-defined data types.

The cin and wcin objects are instances of the basic_istream class linked to the console. They and the extraction operator (>>) can be used to extract built-in data types as well as a user-defined object. The wcin object is a basic_istream<wchar_t> adapted for use with wide characters. In order for the extraction object to work with user-defined objects, the >> operator must be defined for the user-defined object. Listing 3.1 is an example of a program that uses cin and the extraction operators to input to a char, float, double, integer, and string.

cout, wcout, and inserters

The basic_ostream class models an output stream in C++. When data is sent to a stream of type basic_ostream, it is called an *insertion.* The data is inserted to a stream in order

Listing 3.1   Using Extraction Operator and cin

```
// This program demonstrates the use of the cin object and
// extraction operator.
#include <iostream>
#include <cmath>
#include <string>

void main(void)
{
    char PI;
    float pi;
    double Pi;
    int pI;
    string Pie;

    cin >> PI;
    cin >> pi;
    cin >> Pi;
    cin >> pI;
    cin >> Pie;
}
```

to output it to an external device. The left-shift operator (<<) is called the insertion operator. The left-shift operator is overloaded to perform output operations on built-in and user-defined data types.

The cout and wcout objects found in standard iostream implementations are instances of the basic_ostream class linked to the console. The cout object and the insertion operator (<<) can be used to output built-in data types. The wcout object is a basic_ostream<wchar_t> adapted for use with wide characters. Listing 3.2 is an example of a program that uses cout and the insertion operators to output char, float, double, integer, and string built-in data types.

The insertion operator can be overloaded to output user-defined data types. It is declared as a *friend function* in the header file of the user-defined type. The friend function returns a reference to an object of type basic_ostream. It also accepts a reference to an object of type basic_ostream and the object of the user-defined class.

The iostreams in C++ give the programmer a complete I/O facility. From systems programming to multimedia-level programming, the iostreams can be used to model I/O devices and I/O data structures. Because the stream classes are implemented as templates, they can be used with different character sizes. The char and wchar_t data types represent different byte sizes, thereby allowing the iostream classes to deal with different character sets and unicode. The stream components also contain locale objects to add to their flexibility. Locale objects are responsible for character set conversion and encapsulation of cultural and internationalization formatting. The combination of the multibyte capability and the embedded locale objects makes the standard C++ iostreams one of the most powerful input/output facilities available. Now let's take a detailed look at the iostreams class hierarchy.

Listing 3.2   Using Insertion with cout

```
// This program demonstrates how the insertion operator can be
// used with cout.
#include <iostream>
#include <cmath>
#include <string>
void main(void)
{
    char PI = 227;
    float pi = 3.1416;
    double Pi = M_PI;
    int pI = 3.1416 * 10000;
    string Pie("Pie in the sky");
    cout << PI << endl;
    cout << pi << endl;
    cout << Pi << endl;
    cout << pI << endl;
    cout << Pie << endl;
}
```

The iostream Class Hierarchy: Relationship Overview

The iostream class hierarchy is a network of interrelated and interdependent classes; it implements the object-oriented stream. Object-oriented input, output, and memory formatting can all be accomplished through the use and specialization of the iostreams. The basic structure of the iostream hierarchy can be seen in the class relationship diagram in Figure 3.4. It shows the fundamental structure and relationships between the primary classes in the iostream family.

The input classes basic_istream, basic_ifstream, and basic_istringstream are related through the inheritance mechanism. The ultimate base class for the basic_istream family is basic_ios. The output classes basic_ostream, basic_ofstream, and basic_ostringstream are also related through the inheritance mechanism. The ultimate base class for the basic_ostream family is also basic_ios. Standard iostream implementations will also contain a basic_iostream class derived from basic_istream and basic_ostream, a stringstream class derived from basic_istringstream and basic_ostringstream, and a basic_fstream class derived from basic_ifstream and basic_ofstream.

The basic_istream and basic_ostream family of classes will also have a possession relationship with basic_streambuf or one of its derivatives. The basic_istream and basic_ostream family of classes do not inherit the basic_streambuf or its derivatives. Instead, they contain a basic_streambuf or basic_streambuf derivative as a data member. The fundamental basic_streambuf derivatives are:

- basic_filebuf
- basic_stringbuf

The basic_ios, basic_istream classes, basic_ostream classes, and basic_streambuf classes make up the foundation for the iostream input and output facilities in C++. Table 3.3 lists the entire set of classes for the iostreams and their categories. The first class in the hierarchy that we will explore is basic_streambuf.

The iostream typedefs

Standard implementations of the C++ library will provide typedef declarations for the template classes of the iostream components:

```
typedef basic_ios<char> ios;
typedef basic_ios<wchar_t> wios;
typedef basic_streambuf<char> streambuf;
typedef basic_istream<char> istream;
typedef basic_ostream<char> ostream;
typedef basic_iostream<char> iostream;
typedef basic_stringbuf<char> stringbuf;
typedef basic_istringstream<char> istringstream;
typedef basic_ostringstream<char> ostringstream;
typedef basic_stringstream<char> stringstream;
```

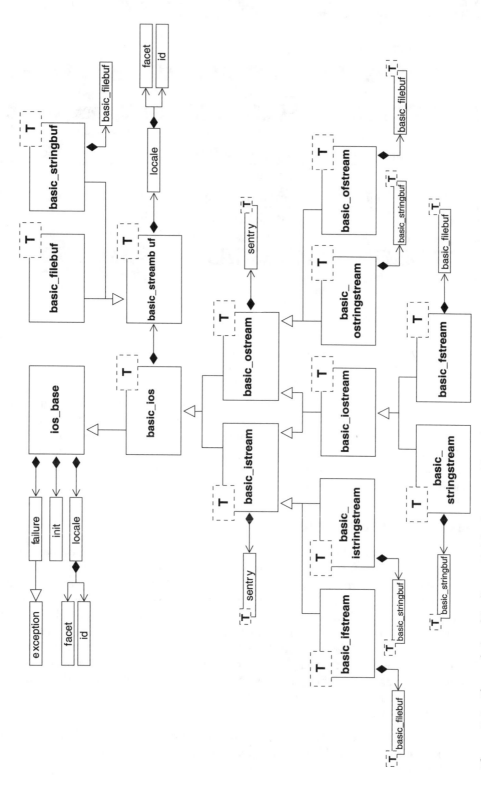

Figure 3.4 Class relationship diagram of the iostream hierarchy.

Table 3.3 iostream Class Set

BUFFER CLASSES		
basic_streambuf	basic_filebuf	basic_stringbuf
TRANSLATOR CLASSES		
basic_iostream	basic_istream	basic_ostream
(input/output stream: stdin/stdout)	(input stream: stdin)	(output stream: stdout)
basic_fstream	basic_ifstream	basic_ofstream
(input/output file stream)	(input file stream)	(output file stream)
basic_stringstream	basic_istringstream	basic_ostringstream
(input/output internal memory)	(input internal memory)	(output internal memory)
FORMAT CLASSES		
ios_base	basic_ios	

```
typedef basic_filebuf<char> filebuf;
typedef basic_ifstream<char> ifstream;
typedef basic_ofstream<char> ofstream;
typedef basic_fstream<char> fstream;
```

The typedefs make the iostream classes easier to use. They relieve the programmer from some of the drudgery of lengthy class declarations. They also preserve some compatibility between the standard implementations of the iostream classes and older non-standard implementations. The template versions of the iostreams are new. To maintain compatibility between the new iostreams and the older nontemplate versions, the typedefs are made in a header file, usually iosfwd.

The basic_streambuf Class

The basic_streambuf class can be divided into two levels: the buffer abstraction and the protected members that act on the buffer, and the virtual methods used to permit specialization of any derived class. The basic_streambuf class defines a buffer abstraction for iostreams. As a base class, it contains only the basic members to act on characters in a buffer. The abstract buffer permits a persistent and, theoretically, unlimited storage or retrieval of sequential data. This abstraction requires one or two pointers that define the position in the buffer at which characters are being inserted or extracted. Queuing buffers, such as basic_stringbuf, require both a put and a get pointer. Input and output buffers, such as basic_filebuf, may have one or two pointers; the number depends on describing the buffer as performing puts and gets to the same pointer or having two pointers tied together.

The implemented buffer is an extension of an I/O device. Because of the nature of block versus character or block versus block I/O devices, some buffering must occur in core memory.

Structure of a basic_streambuf

The basic_streambuf class can be physically described as a set of memory areas with a number of protected methods that define the behavior of the memory areas. Three areas that make up the buffer are reserve, put, and get. The reserve area is normally a fixed block of memory used as a memory resource by the other areas. The other two areas overlap (partially or fully) the reserve area, but never "meet" each other. The get area may be divided into two areas: get and put back. At least two flags indicate whether the reserve area exists and whether it is owned by basic_streambuf. The get and put areas are managed by a set of pointers. Each area is assigned three pointers. Figure 3.5 shows the basic structure of a streambuf object.

The locale object, get area, put area, reserve area, and the six get and put pointers are private to the basic_streambuf. The minimum number of pointers is determined by the protected member functions that examine and set the state of the buffer. Usually, two pointers define the reserve area base and end. The get and put areas are assigned three pointers each. Each area has a pointer that points to the beginning of the area, to the end of the area, and to the current position where a character will either be read or put. For the get area, the three pointers are returned by:

```
eback()    // start of get area
gptr()     // current location for next character to be read
egptr()    // One past the end of the get area
```

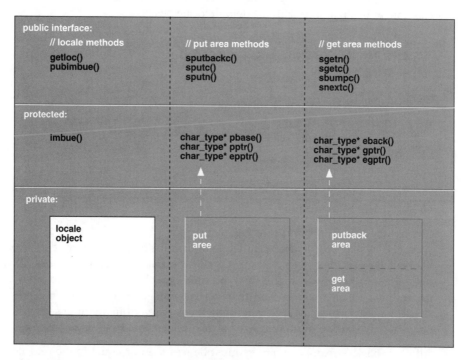

Figure 3.5 Basic structure of a streambuf object.

For the put area, the three pointers are returned by:

```
pbase()    // start of put area
pptr()     // current location for next character to be placed
eppt()     // one past the end of the put area
```

The gptr( ) and pptr( ) methods indicate the next insertion or extraction point within a buffer. The value of these pointers (to adhere to the return values of the protected methods) must always fall between the base and end of their respective areas. The value of the base must be less than or equal to the end pointer value. Methods to examine the streambuf's pointers are nonvirtual and protected. They are used only for implementing derived buffer classes. Conceptually, pointers are between characters; however, in implementation, they must point to characters. As a convention, all pointers should be viewed as pointing to just in front of the character at which they really point. This convention will be followed when describing streambuf's methods.

Constructing the streambuf Class

The basic_streambuf( ) constructor with no arguments creates an empty buffer with all pointers and flags set to null. This means that a buffer can be allocated when needed. Since this constructor is *protected*, only a derived class uses this constructor. This is a change from previous nonstandard versions of the streambuf class where the constructor was public. To use this class, it must be a part of a derived class. In addition to initializing the buffer pointers, the streambuf( ) constructor also initializes the locale component of streambuf with the default locale object.

Accessing streambuf: The Protected Accessors

The streambuf object has eight protected accessors used to access the get and put areas:

GET AREA	PUT AREA
eback( )	pbase( )
gptr( )	pptr( )
egptr( )	epptr( )
gbump(int n)	pbump(int n)

Because these accessors are protected, they can only be accessed in a class derived from streambuf. The eback( ) member function returns the beginning of the get area. The difference between the get pointer, gptr( ), and the eback( ) member function is the current size of the putback area. On putting data back into an input stream, the programmer must make certain that the current get pointer does not precede the eback( ) member function. When refilling the get area from an input source, it may be necessary to ensure a minimum size for the putback area.

All other basic_streambuf pointers must be less than or equal to the returned value. The gptr( ) member function returns a pointer to the next byte to be read in the get area. All consumable characters will be between gptr and egptr member functions. Though the gptr member function is less than egptr( ), the next character to be fetched will be *gptr( ). Otherwise, the next character must come from an input source. The epptr( ) member function returns a pointer to the byte following the last byte of the put area. The gbump( ) member function adjusts gptr (get pointer) by the specified integer value, which is either positive or negative. No check is made to ensure that the resulting value is within eback( ) and egptr( ).

The pbase( ) member function returns a pointer to the first byte of the put base. Characters between pbase and pptr member functions are buffered for output consumption. Unlike the putback area, characters in this area should be viewed as inaccessible. The pptr( ) member function returns a pointer to the next byte of the put area. The space between pptr and epptr member functions is available for buffering when the pptr member function is less than epptr( ); otherwise, the output device must consume all data between pbase( ) and epptr( ) before any additional characters can be buffered. The pbump( ) member function adjusts pptr (put pointer) by the specified integer value, which is either positive or negative. No check is made to ensure that the resulting value is within pbase( ) and epptr( ). The pbackfail( ) member function normally returns eof. If it is redefined in a derived class, then, on success, the supplied character "c" is returned, or eof on failure.

The seekoff( ) member function repositions the get and/or put pointers of the stream by the specified byte offset. The direction of the seek is from the beginning, current, or end of the stream. The offset may be negative. The pointers updated are specified by the third parameter. If the derived class does not support file positioning, then eof is returned. The seekpos( ) member function returns seekoff (streampos (pos), ios_base::beg, mode), making it necessary to overload only the seekoff (void) method.

Accessing streambuf: The Public Accessors

The streambuf class has 8 public accessors that can be used to access the get and put areas:

GET AREA	PUT AREA
snextc( )	sputbackc(char_type c)
sbumpc( )	sungetc( )
sgetc( )	sputc(char_type c)
sgetn(char_type* s, streamsize n)	sputn(const char_type* s, streamsize n);

These 8 accessor methods work either with one character at a time or with a block of characters.

Accessing the Get Area

The sgetc( ) member function peeks at the first character after the get pointer—that is, it gets the next character in the input area. The sgetn( ) member function retrieves *n* characters and places them in the supplied buffer, *s*. If there are fewer than *n* characters in the get area, the sgetn member function will request additional input from the source. This is normally done through a call to the underflow( ) method. Depending on the implementation of the underflow( ) method, it may go to the physical media that the source is connected to looking for more bytes. If the sgetn( ) can get characters, it will then reposition the get pointer and return the actual number of characters retrieved.

Many implementations occasionally use an "undocumented virtual" method to refill the get area when it is empty. The snextc( ) member function increments the get pointer and returns the character to which it is pointing. It will return eof if it is already at the end of the get area or if the end of the buffer is reached after the increment at which it is point-ing. The sbumpc( ) member function returns the character at which the get pointer is cur-rently pointing, then increments the get pointer. If the get pointer is at the end of the get area, then eof is returned. All methods, except the sgetn( ) method, work with a single character at a time. Each of the get methods also indirectly calls upon one or more of the protected members that access the get area. Figure 3.6 illustrates what happens when the get area (buffer) does not have enough characters to fill a get request. An undeflow( ) method is called that attempts to fetch more characters from the input device (source).

Accessing the Put Area

The public methods used to access the put area also consist of three methods that work with one character at a time, and one method that can put a block of characters into the output stream. The sputbackc( ) member function decrements the get pointer by one position and assigns the supply character, *c*, to the get area. The sputc( ) member func-tion stores the *c* character at the current position referenced by the put pointer, then increments the put pointer. It returns overflow( ) on any failure. If the put pointer is at the end of the put area, then the virtual method overflow( ) is called to clear out as much of the put area as possible. If this occurs, it returns the result from overflow( ). The sputn( ) member function stores *n* characters from the buffer *s* into the put area. It

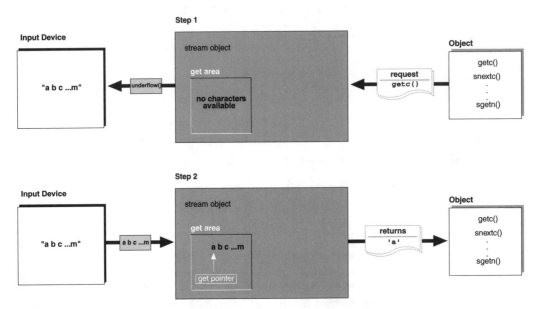

Figure 3.6   The flow of a get request when the buffer does not have enough characters to fulfill that request.

then repositions the put pointer and returns the number of characters inserted. Figure 3.7 illustrates what happens when the put area (buffer) is full. An overflow( ) method is called that will attempt to flush the buffer to the output device.

Getting Information about Available Bytes

The in_avail( ) member function returns the number of characters that are available in the get area. It is equivalent to egptr( ) - gptr( ); however, it guarantees that a nonnegative value will be returned.

Underflow and Overflow in the basic_streambuf Class

If the programmer creates a derived class from basic_streambuf, this method should be overloaded. The overflow( ) member function is used to transfer data from a stream's put area to an output device. It is usually called when the put area is full, but it can be called at other times, for instance by a stream flush call. The supplied character should be saved within the method, after which the following default behavior occurs:

1. All characters between pbase( ) and pptr( ) are sent to the output device.
2. The setp( ) method is called to update the put area.
3. Generally, the put pointer is set to pbase( ), and the end of put area is left alone.
4. The supplied character, c, if not eof, is placed in the restored put area, and the put pointer is updated.
5. The overflow( ) member function will return a 0, on success, or eof, on failure.

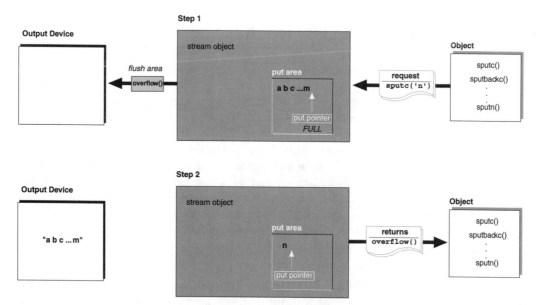

Figure 3.7 The flow of a put request when the buffer is full and cannot receive any more characters.

Just like the overflow method, underflow( ) should be overloaded in any class derived from basic_streambuf. The underflow( ) member function is called when data is requested from the stream and there is no information in the get area. If it is called when the get area is not empty, it returns the character at the get pointer. Otherwise, it resets the get area (set gptr( ) to eback( ), plus an implementation-defined putback size) and fills the get area with any available data from the input device. Reducing or enlarging the get area within the reserve area, according to the size of data most efficient for the input device, is not unusual.

The sync( ) Member Function

The sync( ) method tells the derived basic_streambuf to check its internal pointers, compare them with any external devices, and update the internal pointers as necessary. The normal behavior of this method is to write out any waiting characters in the put and, if possible, get areas. When the sync member function returns the put area, it is empty. In other words, pbase( ) and pptr( ) are equal, and eof is returned on failure. The sync( ) method is protected, and therefore, can only be used inside derived classes.

Implementation Considerations: Virtual and Additional Methods

Virtual methods, protected with noted exceptions, are used to customize any class derived from basic_streambuf. The programmer is free to overload these methods as seen fit, but their interface and the semantics of their return values must be followed explicitly. Also, if a derived class does not support the virtual method's default behavior, its specified error value should be returned. Not doing so may cause the public methods of basic_streambuf to behave unexpectedly.

The Ultimate Base Class: ios_base

By calling the ios_base class the ultimate base class of the entire iostream family, we mean that every major class in the iostream class hierarchy (except for basic_streambuf) has an ios component. The stream classes get the ios_base class because they inherit basic_ios; basic_ios is derived from ios_base. Together, the ios_base and basic_ios classes make up the ios component. Therefore, all of the protected and public data members and member functions of ios are accessible to all of the derived iostream classes. The ios class supplies the stream classes with their state and formatting capabilities. The immediate derived classes of basic_ios are basic_istream and basic_ostream. The class relationship diagram in Figure 3.8 shows the relationships among ios_base, basic_ios, basic_istream, basic_ostream, and basic_streambuf. The basic_istream and basic_ostream classes form the base classes for the remainder of the iostream hierarchy.

The ios class is the *state* component of the iostream class hierarchy. All classes derived from ios have three states associated with them: open, buffer, and format. These states are encapsulated within the ios_base class. The *open state* designates how the stream has been opened—for reading, writing, or appending. The open state can specify that a new file be created or existing file used; it can describe a stream as either binary or text. Table 3.4 shows the possible open modes and their meanings.

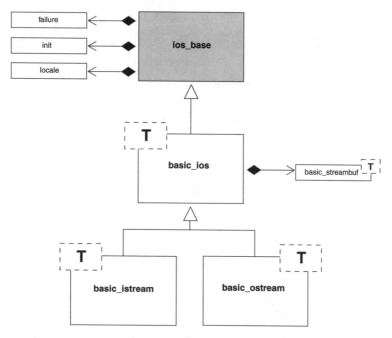

Figure 3.8 Class relationships among ios_base, basic_ios, basic_istream, basic_ostream, and basic_streambuf.

The *format state* determines which type of conversion takes place when objects are inserted into the stream or when objects are extracted from the stream. For example, 4 bytes may be extracted from the stream and interpreted as hexadecimal during the input process and written as right-justified during the output process. The format state also describes whether objects are left-justified or right-justified as they are inserted into a stream, and how integers are represented as they are inserted to or extracted from a stream. The base of the integers can be decimal, hexadecimal, or octal. The floats and doubles can be formatted as fixed floating-point or in scientific notation. Finally, the format state describes the fill character that will be used for padding during stream operations. Table 3.5 shows the format flags that can be set and unset using the setf( ) and unsetf( ) member functions of the basic_ios class. The format flags can also be set and unset using the manipulators.

Table 3.4 Open Modes and Their Meanings

OPEN MODES	DESCRIPTION
ios_base:: app	Open in append.
ios_base:: ate	Create the file.
ios_base:: binary	Open as a binary file.
ios_base:: in	Open file for input.
ios_base:: out	Open file for output.
ios_base:: trunc	Truncate file on input.

Table 3.5 Format Flags Used with setf( ) and unsetf( )

FORMAT FLAGS	DESCRIPTION
boolalpha	Inserts and extracts bool type in an alphabetic format.
fixed	Generates floating-point output in fixed-point notation.
internal	Adds fill characters at a designated internal point in certain generated output; or identical to *right* if no such point is designated.
left	Adds fill characters on the right (final positions) of certain generated output.
right	Adds fill characters on the left (initial positions) of certain generated output.
dec	Converts integer input or generates integer output in decimal base.
hex	Converts integer input or generates integer output in hexadecimal base.
oct	Converts integer input or generates integer output in octal base.
scientific	Generates floating-point output in scientific notation.
showbase	Generates a prefix indicating the numeric base of generated integer output.
showpoint	Generates a decimal point character unconditionally in generated floating-point output.
showpos	Generates a plus sign (+) in nonnegative-generated numeric output.
skipws	Skips leading white space before certain input operations.
unibuf	Flushes output after each output operation.
uppercase	Replaces certain lowercase letters with their uppercase equivalents in generated output.

Constructing the basic_ios (ios) Object

The default constructor for the ios class is protected. This means that you cannot use it as a standalone class unless you specify a streambuf component for it to use. The public constructor for the basic_ios class requires a streambuf object. The basic_ios class holds the buffer component for the basic_istream and basic_ostream family of classes. This buffer is a basic_streambuf class. The basic_streambuf, basic_filebuf, basic_stringbuf have an associated state called the *buffer state*. Table 3.6 shows the four buffer states and their interpretations.

These buffer classes can be in a good state, an eof state, or an error state. If the buffer is in a good state, the next insertion or extraction operation can be attempted; if the

Table 3.6 Four Buffer States and Their Interpretations

BUFFER STATE	DESCRIPTION
good	Buffer is usable.
bad	Buffer is unusable.
eof	No additional characters are available from the associated streambuf; or, an attempt to output characters failed because streambuf could not accept them.
fail	A requested operation has failed.

buffer is in an error state, the next insertion or extraction operation will be ignored. Because the basic_ios class is the ultimate base class for the iostream classes, every iostream object has an internal state that can be accessed through the member functions of the basic_ios class. The basic_ios class diagram in Figure 3.9 shows the relationship among the ios_base, basic_ios, locale, and the basic_streambuf classes, with their containment relationships. The basic_ios class does not inherit the basic_streambuf or the locale class; instead, the ios class contains a pointer to a basic_streambuf and to a locale class. This means that the ios class and its derived classes can access only the get and put areas of the basic_streambuf through the streambuf's public member functions.

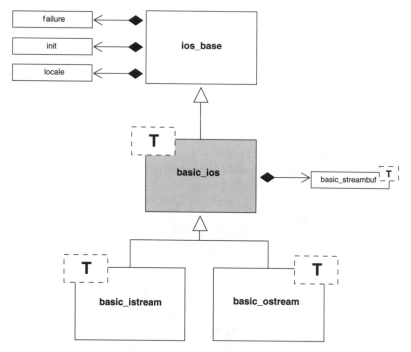

Figure 3.9 Relationship of the basic_ios class to the ios_base, basic_ios, locale, and the basic_streambuf classes, with their containment relationships.

Open Modes

Table 3.7 lists the open modes supported by the ios component. The open modes are not necessarily restricted to the file streams. They can be used in certain circumstances with the stringstream objects—ios_base::ate, and ios_base::app. The open modes are specified in either the declaration of a stream, for example:

```
fstream Out("Myfile", ios_base::out);
```

or during a call to the open( ) member function, for example:

```
fstream Out;
Out.open("Myfile",ios_base::in | ios_base::out);
```

These modes specify the manner in which the stream is treated upon opening, reading, and writing. The *in* mode specifies that the stream is opened for reading. If a stream has been opened only for reading, the programmer cannot send output to this stream. The *out* mode specifies that the stream is opened for writing. If a stream has been opened only for writing, the programmer cannot extract data from this stream. A stream can be opened for reading and writing by *ORing* these two modes together. The ORing operation is signified with the pipe( ) symbol, as shown in this code fragment:

```
fstream Device;
Device.open("Myfile",ios_base::in | ios_base::out);
```

The *ate* mode specifies that the position pointer should be set to the end of the file upon initial open. The *app* mode specifies that the stream should always be appended. The ate, app, and *trunc* modes can also be used with ostringstream and stringstream constructors, for example:

```
char Buffer[80];
stringstream Memory(Buffer,79,ios_base::app);
ostringstream Memory(Buffer,79,ios_base::ate);
stringstream Memory(Buffer,79,ios_base::trunc);
```

When ate and app modes are used, the position pointer is moved to the NULL value in the character array upon construction of these objects. The trunc mode is basically a start-from-scratch mode. If the stream's object already exists, and the stream is opened in trunc mode, the contents of the stream's object are destroyed. The *nocre-*

Table 3.7   Open Modes Supported by the ios Component

OPEN MODES	DESCRIPTION
ios_base:: app	Opens in append.
ios_base:: ate	Creates the file.
ios_base:: binary	Opens as a binary file.
ios_base:: in	Opens file for input.
ios_base:: out	Opens file for output.
ios_base:: trunc	Truncates file on input.

ate mode specifies that the file should be opened only if it already exists. If the file does not exist, the open( ) member function fails. The *noreplace* mode specifies that the file can only be appended to; or, when opened, the position pointer must move to the end of the stream's object. This is accomplished by specifying either the app or ate mode.

The *binary* mode specifies that the stream be opened for raw binary processing, as opposed to text or ASCII processing. This mode affects how the n is handled. When a stream is in *text* mode, the n new-line character is converted into two characters—the carriage-return character and a line-feed character—upon output. The carriage-return and line feed pair (crlf) are converted to an n upon input. This is in contrast to processing on a binary stream. When a stream is opened in binary mode, the \n is written as \n character on output and read as \n on input; furthermore, numbers are written in binary form upon output and read as binary upon input. Conversely, when a stream is opened in text mode, numbers are written to the output using their ASCII representation; that is, numbers are written as characters, as opposed to absolute binary bytes. The same is true upon input in text mode: Numbers are translated from ASCII to their input targets.

NOTE:
The *text open* mode is not applicable to Unix environments.

Buffer Component of the ios Class

The ios component has a streambuf object. The streambuf component provides the ios family of classes with a buffer area in which to store characters. The basic_streambuf object specifies a generic holding area for the data while it is in transit from an input source or to an output destination. The source or destination may be a block of memory, a file, or an I/O device. Through the pointer to the basic_streambuf object, the basic_ios class and any of its derived classes have access to all of the functionality of the basic_streambuf object. This pointer can be accessed through the rdbuf( ) member function. This function takes no arguments and returns the basic_streambuf pointer contained in the ios_base class.

Buffer State Component of the ios Class

The ios class maintains a state variable that describes the associated buffer at any given time. The state variable is normally represented by an int data type, which is then further divided into bits, with specific combinations of bits representing the state of the buffer. These bits are set (turned on) or unset (turned off), and are normally declared as enumerations with certain values (bitmasks):

```
enum iostate{
            goodbite = 0x00,
            eofbit = 0x01,
            failbit = 0x02,
            badbit = 0x04,
```

These bits represent four basic states that the basic_streambuf component can be in: good, eof, fail, bad.

Keep in mind that some implementation may include more buffer states, but these are the standard states available in any ANSI/ISO-compliant implementation. We refer to these states as the *buffer state,* although sometimes they are referred to as *error states.* But only two of these conditions are strictly error conditions, so we prefer to say "buffer states" when referring to the condition of the buffer component. If the buffer is in a good state, no bits are set in the state variable. The good( ) member function returns a nonzero value if the buffer component is in a good state. If the buffer is in an eof state, then the eof bit is set (turned on) within the state variable. The eof( ) member function returns a nonzero value if the eof bit is set. If the buffer is in a bad state, the badbit is turned on; the badbit is set when some operation on the basic_streambuf object has failed. The bad( ) member function will return a nonzero value if the badbit is set. If failbit or badbit is set within the state variable, the buffer is said to be in a fail state. The fail( ) member function returns a nonzero value if either the badbit or the failbit is set.

It is important to understand the difference between the fail state and the bad state. If a buffer is in a bad state, it is also in a fail state; however, a buffer can be in a fail state but not be in a bad state. For example, if an operation tries to read past end-of-file, the operation will fail; this puts the stream in a fail state, but does not necessarily mean that the stream is unusable. When a stream is in a bad state, this normally signals that the stream is unusable. The value of the state variable is returned by the rdstate( ) member function. The state of the buffer is propagated through the operations on that buffer, meaning that all of the operations that access the buffer are aware of the buffer state. If the buffer is in a good state, insertion and extraction operations can be attempted, whereas if the buffer is in a bad state, all insertion and extraction operations will be ignored. The clear( ) member function must be called in this circumstance. The buffer is unusable unless the clear( ) member function is called.

The clear( ) member function serves two primary functions: first, to clear the error state of a buffer associated with an ios_base class; second, to set bits within the state variable. The clear( ) member function takes an int data type as an argument and returns a void. If the clear( ) member function is called with an argument of zero, the state variable for the buffer is reset to zero. If the clear( ) member function is called with the value of a state the buffer may be in—for instance:

```
ios_base Object;
Object.clear(ios_base::failbit | Object.rdstate());
```

the failbit is set in the state variable. Notice that the technique for doing this involves a *bitwise ORing* of the state variable with the desired bit to be set.

NOTE:

In addition to calling clear( ) to reset a stream, it may also be necessary to call seekg(0), seekp(0) to get the desired results. These member functions are from the stream classes and are used to reposition—or in some cases, reset—the starting get and put location within a stream.

Format State Component of the ios Class

The *format state* determines the type of conversion that will take place when objects are inserted to or extracted from the stream. Some of the attributes of the ios_base class that relate to the format state are listed in Table 3.8. These attributes represent the primary formats and states that the ios component controls. The ios_base class contains the format flag attributes, which are typically represented by a bit pattern. Each bit in the format state represents a format flag. The flags( ) member functions can return or set the format flag state, and is used to access the format attributes. This flags( ) member function takes no arguments and returns a fmtflags object. The overload of the flags( ) member function will set format state to that specified in its argument and return the previous value. The argument is a fmtflags object.

Each format flag controls a specific way the information is formatted. In general, the effect of setting any of these format flags is persistent. The width( ) formatting control is not persistent; it is reset to zero after every use. The remainder of the format flags remain in effect until they are explicitly changed. We divide the fmtflags objects into these four categories:

- Integer formatting
- Real number formatting
- Object justification
- Character control

Table 3.8   Format State Attributes of the ios_base Class

FMTFLAGS		
boolalpha	oct	skipws
dec	right	unitbuf
fixed	scientific	uppercase
hex	showbase	adjustfield
internal	showpoint	basefield
left	showpos	floatfield
IOSTATE		
app	binary	out
ate	in	trunc
SEEKDIR		
beg	cur	end
OTHER		
precision	width	locale

Integer Formatting

Keep in mind that the integers are the set of negative and positive counting numbers, including zero. Integers do not include decimal points (fractions). The hex (hexadecimal), oct (octal), or dec (decimal) format flags are used to format integers according to a specific numeric base. If the dec format flag is set, integers will be represented in the decimal base, or *base 10*. If the hex format flag is set, integers will be represented in the hexadecimal base, or *base 16*. An integer formatted for hexadecimal output can only contain the characters 0, 1, 2, 3, 4, 5, 6, 7, 8, 9, a, b, c, d, e, f. If the oct format flag is set, integers will be represented in the octal *base 8*. An integer formatted for the octal base can only contain the characters 0, 1, 2, 3, 4, 5, 6, 7. By default, integers are printed in base 10 unless there is a different cultural convention in effect. The basefield data member contains the values of the dec, oct, and hex format flags.

When the showbase format flag is set, the format state of the stream specifies that numeric data will display its base convention for output. The default is numeric data *absent* of the base conventions. The base convention for hexadecimal numbers is 0x, and the base convention for octal numbers is 0, placed before the number. The formatting for integers can be set easily using the setf( ) function. For instance:

```
cout.setf(ios_base::hex);
cout << '10 in hexadecimal is ' << 10;
```

will display:

```
10 in hexadecimal is a
```

Real Number Formatting

Real numbers include the integers and numbers with decimals (fractions). In C++, real numbers are often referred to as *floating-point numbers,* which can be formatted in scientific (*e-notation*) or fixed notation by setting the scientific or fixed format flags. When a floating-point value is inserted into some output stream, it will have a decimal point. If the showpoint flag has been set, then that decimal point will appear in the output. The floating-point number will appear in either fixed decimal format, with the decimal point in the same place for each floating-point number sent to the output, or the number will appear in an e-notation (or scientific) format, where the location of the decimal point depends on the size of the number, precision, and significant digits.

The floatfield data member contains the values of scientific and fixed-format flags. If the scientific format flag is set, the format state of the stream will represent floating-point data in e-notation, which expresses floating-point numbers with the decimal placed after the first digit. The "e" represents exponentiation of 10 to a power. Floating-point data will be represented in scientific notation if the exponent after the conversion is less than –4 or greater than or equal to the current precision. When the fixed format flag is set, the format state of the stream specifies that floating-point numbers will be displayed in decimal notation with a set number of digits after the decimal. The number of digits after the decimal is determined by the precision currently set. Fixed and scientific flags can be set easily with the setf( ) function:

```
cout.setf(ios_base::scientific | ios_base::showpoint);
cout << 0.8038;
```

will print:

```
8.0379e-01
```

Setting a showpoint format flag describes the format state of the stream in which floating-point numbers will display a decimal point and trailing zeros for output. The decimal point and trailing zeros will be displayed only with a floating-point number with precision greater than zero. There will be as many trailing zeros as needed to meet precision. If this flag is set, and precision is zero, there will be no decimal point or trailing zeros. The showpos format flag, when set, specifies a format state of the stream that displays a plus sign for positive integers for output. Negative integers will automatically display a minus sign, despite the setting of this flag.

Setting the precision of a floating-point number is done through a call to the precision( ) member function. The precision( ) member function takes no arguments and returns an integer, which is the value stored in the precision variable. The precision format controls how many numbers appear after the decimal point. For example, if we set precision(2), then:

```
cout.setf(ios_base::showpoint | ios_base::fixed);
cout << 3.456;
```

will print:

```
3.46
```

The default precision is 6. The precision affects both the e-notation (scientific) and fixed formats for real numbers.

Object Justification

When the left format flag is set, the format state of the stream specifies that padding, used to meet a field width, be placed after the actual data value; when the right format flag is set, the padding used to meet a field width is placed before the actual data value. A set internal format flag describes a format state of the stream that pads a field width between any sign type (base information or integer sign) and the actual data value. The data will be right-justified. By default, the right format flag is set. The adjustfield data member contains the values of right, left, and internal format flags.

Character Control

When the skipws flag is set, the format state of the stream specifies that white-space characters will be ignored for input; when the flag is not set, white-space characters will not be ignored. White-space characters include spaces, tabs, and new-line characters. If an attempt is made to extract numeric data preceded by a white space, and the skipws flag is not set, the failbit flag would be set and extraction would stop until the failbit flag was cleared. When set, the uppercase format flag specifies a format state in which numeric data represented with hexadecimal digits will display the hex base indicator (when the showbase format flag is set) and hexadecimal digits a–f in uppercase. Floating-point numbers represented in scientific notation will display an uppercase *E* for output. The default is lowercase. Setting the unitbuf format flag causes the format state of the stream to specify that output be flushed after each output operation. The fill( ) member function returns the fill character and takes no arguments. The fill character is used to pad a field in which the data takes less space than the field width specifies. The field will be padded according to the setting of the adjustfield bits. The default fill character is a space. The overload fill( ) member function will set the fill character to the character passed in its argument, and return the previous fill character.

The width of the field specifies the amount of space that will be used for data, string, or numeric characters. A call to the width( ) member function will return the value of width as an int. If the data inserted is less than the field width, the data will be padded, right-justified, left-justified, or internal to the format, depending on the value of adjustfield. If the data to be inserted or extracted is more than the field width, the data will be expressed completely, not truncated. This means that the width formatter can never be used to truncate; it can only be used to format an object with equal or larger space. The default width is zero, which means the width will be the length necessary to express the object completely. The width member function is set only for the immediate input or output operation; it is reset for each subsequent operation. The width( ) formatter is the only formatting that is not persistent. If the output needs to be padded, it will be padded based on the last call to the fill( ) method. If the fill( ) method has not been called, the object will be padded with blanks.

Setting and Unsetting Format Flags

The ios_base class provides a number of member functions to set format flags. The flags( ) member function can set all the format flags at one time to the fmtflags object supplied by its argument. The setf( ) member function is used to set an individual flag, and will set the format flag specified by its argument and return the previous format flag. Setting a flag has the effect of *turning on* a particular formatting feature. Here is an example of the setting of a format flag:

```
fmtflags prevflag;
prevflag = cout.setf(ios_base::scientific,ios_base::floatfield);
```

This will set the scientific format flag. The member function returns the previous format flags (the value stored in the format flag variable) as a fmtflags object. This value can be used or discarded; flag(0) will reset the format flags to their default values.

The overload of setf( ) will clear a collection of flags and set an individual flag to that specified in one of its two arguments: the individual flag to be set, and the group of flags to be cleared, specified by adjustfield, basefield, or floatfield. Both arguments are of type fmtflags. The setf( ) member function will clear the flags specified by the second argument, then set the individual flag (one of the collection) specified by the first argument. Next, the member function will return the previous value of the format state variable as a long int. The following is an example of the use of this member function:

```
fmtflags prevflag;

prevflag = cout.setf(ios_base::scientific, ios_base::floatfield);
```

This will clear the floatfield flags, scientific and fixed, then set the scientific format flag. Then it will return the previous value of the format state variable.

The unsetf( ) member function is used to clear an individual format flag, which is specified in unsetf( ) argument as a long int. This member function will return the previous value of the format flag state variable, also as a long int. For example, this code sample will clear the scientific format flag:

```
fmtflags prevflag;

prevflag = cout.unsetf(ios_base::scientific);
```

Format flags can be ORed together in a single message to combine numerous settings of different flags, to be used to set or unset format flags. This is an example of setting and clearing format flags using this technique:

```
cout.unsetf(ios_base::scientific |ios_base::uppercase);
cout.setf(ios_base::fixed | ios_base::showpoint);
```

The program in Listing 3.3 demonstrates how flags are set and cleared, how they affect integer values and floating-point values, and how flags that are set in combination with other flags affect output.

This program accepts a directory name as an argument, and determines the size of the directory. The program then calculates the percent each file is to the total directory size. On the standard output, the program prints the file name, file size, file size in hexadecimal, percentage to directory size, and the last date the file was modified. The output is formatted using the format flags and format methods from the ios_base, basic_ios components.

As stated, all of the formatting is persistent except the width( ) formatter. This means that all flags and the fill( ) and precision( ) member functions will remain in effect for all processing until the flags are cleared or reset to their default values. The width( ) member function has to be set before the value that it is to affect. The adjustfield, basefield, and floatfield flags are mutually exclusive, meaning only one flag from each group should be set at a time. If more than one flag from a group is set, it will have no affect on the output; for example, if the right and left adjustfields are set, only one of them will affect the output, or if the octal and hexadecimal basefield flags are set, only one flag will be recognized.

Flags for integer values will have no affect on floating-point values, and flags for floating-point values will have no affect on integer values. Some flags work with other flags; for example, if the width( ) member function is not set to a value that is larger than the field the output occupies, the fill( ) member function will have no affect on the output. On the other hand, if the length of the output is less than the value specified by the last call to the fill( ) method, then the value specified by fill( ) will be used to pad the output; and the value of adjustfield will cause the output to be left-justified, right-justified, or internally justified. If the showbase flag is set for a dec-

Listing 3.3 Use of Format Flags

```
1   // Listing 3.3
2   // This program demonstrates the use of the format flags, and
3   // formatting capabilities of the ios_base component
4
5   #include <iostream>
6   #include <sys/stat.h>
7   #include <dirent.h>          // Requires POSIX compatibility
8   #include <string.h>
9   #include <dir.h>
10  #include <time.h>
11
12  using namespace std;
13
14  int main(int Argc,char *Argv[])
15  {
16   if(Argc == 2){
17      DIR *Directory;
18      Directory = opendir(Argv[1]);
19      chdir(Argv[1]);
20      if(!Directory == NULL){
21         float DirectorySize = 0;
22         struct dirent *Entry;
23         struct stat Buffer;
24         Entry = readdir(Directory);
25         while(Entry != NULL)
26         {
27             if (stat(Entry->d_name,&Buffer) == 0){
28                DirectorySize = DirectorySize + Buffer.st_size;
29             }
30             else{
31                    cerr << "could not stat " << Entry->d_name
32                         << endl;
33             }
34             Entry = readdir(Directory);
35         }
36         rewinddir(Directory);
37         cout << "\f";
38         cout.precision(4);
39         Entry = readdir(Directory);
40         while(Entry != NULL)
41         {
42             cout.setf(ios::left | ios::fixed);
43             cout.fill('*');
44             cout.width(20);
45             stat(Entry->d_name,&Buffer);
46             cout << Entry->d_name << "\t";
47             cout.width(12);
48             cout.setf(ios::right);
```

Listing 3.3 *(Continued)*

```
49                 cout.fill(' ');
50                 cout.setf(ios::dec);
51                 cout << Buffer.st_size << "\t ";
52                 cout.width(12);
53                 cout.setf(ios::right);
54                 cout.fill(' ');
55                 cout.setf(ios::hex);
56                 cout << Buffer.st_size << "\t";
57                 cout.width(9);
58                 cout.setf(ios::right | ios::showpoint);
59                 cout.fill(' ');
60                 cout << (Buffer.st_size/DirectorySize * 100)
61                     << '%' << "\t";
62                 cout.width(9);
63                 cout.setf(ios::right);
64                 cout.setf(ios::scientific);
65                 cout.fill(' ');
66                 cout << (Buffer.st_size/DirectorySize * 100)
67                     << '%' << "\t";
68                 cout.width(12);
69                 cout.setf(ios::left);
70                 cout << ctime(&Buffer.st_atime) << endl;
71                 Entry = readdir(Directory);
72             }
73          cout.precision(0);
74          cout.setf(ios::oct | ios::fixed);
75          cout << "Directory Size: " << DirectorySize << endl;
76      }
77      else{
78              cerr << "could not open " << Argv[1] << endl;
79      }
80      closedir(Directory);
81      return(1);
82  }
83  return(0);
84
85  }
```

imal value, this will have no affect on the output. If the uppercase flag is set for numeric values that are not in scientific notation or does not display a character for its base, this will have no affect on the output.

Tying the Streams

A basic_ostream object can be tied to basic_istream object for purposes of *buffer flushing*. Buffer flushing sends output immediately to an output device. This can be useful for a calling insertion operation immediately following extraction operations, or an extraction operation immediately following an insertion operation. For example:

```
#include <iostream>
using namespace std;
void main(void)
{
    double PI;
    double Speed;
    double AvNum;
    cout << " What is the value of pi ? " << endl;
    cin >> PI;
    cout << "What is the speed of light ? " << endl;
    cin >> Speed;
    cout << "What is Avogadro's number ?" << endl;
    cin >> AvNum;
    .
    .
    .
}
```

When consecutive insertions and extractions are intermixed without explicitly flushing the buffer, the prompts may not be displayed on the console until *after* the input is extracted from the stream. Buffers are implicitly flushed when they are full or some other buffer-flushing condition has occurred. If the buffer is not full and no other buffer-flushing condition has occurred, then data may remain in the buffer and not be sent to the output until explicitly flushed. The predefined stream cin is tied to cout by default to prevent this subtle problem during intermixing insertions and extractions.

A basic_ostream object is tied to a basic_istream object using the tie( ) member function. In a user-extended basic_istream, there may be no basic_ostream tied to it. Tying is not mandatory. However, if the buffers are not flushed properly, output to a device may occur in an unnatural sequence. The tie( ) member function has two forms: first, basic_ostream *tie( ) returns a pointer to the stream that has been tied; second, tie(*basic_ostream) accepts a pointer to a basic_ostream. The basic_istream is then tied to a basic_ostream through this pointer.

When two streams are tied and one stream is processed, the other is affected. For example when a cin object is getting ready to extract some characters from the stream, and a basic_ostream object is tied to it, the basic_ostream will be flushed first, after which the extraction will take place. Calling the tie( ) member function with an argument of zero separates the object from its tied stream, if there was one.

An Object-Oriented Model of Input

The basic_istream class is a twin of the basic_ostream class. What the basic_ostream class is to output, the basic_istream class is to input. The basic_istream class is the foundation for the object-oriented input stream in the C++ environment. It encapsulates the input model in the C++ environment; in fact, it is the object-oriented equivalent of the input stream concept. The basic_istream class is derived from the basic_ios class. This means that the characteristics and attributes contained in the basic_ios class are also contained in the basic_istream class and its derived classes. All the member functions that are callable from some basic_ios class are also callable from a basic_istream class. All the protected and public data members contained in the ios class are contained in the basic_istream class.

The basic_ios class contains a pointer to a basic_streambuf class. The basic_istream class inherits this pointer to the basic_streambuf class; thus, the basic_istream class has full access to the functionality of the basic_streambuf class and the services it provides. The basic_istream class also has access to a locale object through the ios_base class. Figure 3.10 shows the relationships among the basic_istream class, basic_ios class, ios_base class, locale class, and the basic_streambuf class. The relationship between basic_istream and basic_ios is one of inheritance. The figure also shows that basic_istream will contain a basic_streambuf component, meaning that the basic_istream class can only access the functionality of the basic_streambuf class through its public members.

Through encapsulation and inheritance, the basic_ios class and basic_streambuf class form the basic_istream class. The basic_istream class implements the notion of the object-oriented input stream, which may be a binary stream or a text stream. Because the iostreams are template classes, the basic_istream can represent both single-byte and multibyte character sets. Similarly, the basic_istream class has facilities to process single characters or blocks of characters. When characters or blocks of characters are taken from a basic_istream object, the operation is referred to as extraction. Data is extracted from an input stream and stored in some data object or data structure. The object-oriented stream can be buffered or unbuffered. A basic_istream object can be tied to input devices such as keyboards, disk drives, and CD-ROMs. A C++ program can contain multiple basic_istream objects; there may be a separate basic_istream

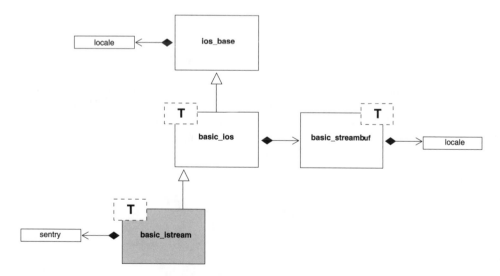

Figure 3.10   Relationships among the basic_istream class, basic_ios class, ios_base class, locale class, and the basic_streambuf class.

object for every input device and input file in the program. This gives the programmer maximum flexibility in I/O design.

The basic_istream class is the fundamental base class for the basic_ifstream class and the istringstream class. These two classes are a specialization of basic_istream that deal with files and memory areas, respectively. Familiarity with the structure and operations of the basic_istream and basic_ostream classes are necessary for a good understanding of the iostream class hierarchy.

Constructing an istream Object

To create an istream object, you must specify a buffer object, as shown here:

```
explicit basic_istream(basic_streambuf<charT, traits>* sb);
```

A stream is useless without a buffer component. The buffer component is actually tied to the I/O device; therefore, without a buffer component, a stream does not have anywhere to read bytes from or to write bytes to. The stream classes help to provide the device-independent interface to I/O devices.

The istream Accessors: Stream Extraction and Object Translation

Objects are *inserted* into the output stream and *extracted* from the input stream. For an object to be extracted from the input stream, an object representing the input stream must first exist. A good and much used input stream object example is the predefined objects cin or wcin (wide characters), which are specific instances of the class basic_istream. The declaration:

```
basic_istream<char> cin; // (simplified declaration)
basic_istream<wchar_t> wcin; // (simplified declaration)
```

has been made for the C++ programmer. The cin instance of basic_istream is an object, not a function or a keyword! Because cin is an object, it has a data component and operations that interact with its data component. In fact, the cin object has a basic_ios object and a basic_streambuf object encapsulated within its own structure. This means that everything that basic_ios is and has the cin object is and has. The basic_istream class relation diagram is identical to the object relationship diagram for the cin object; therefore, all the applicable basic_istream data members and member functions can be accessed by a cin object. For instance:

```
cin.rdstate();
cin.rdbuf();
cin.width();
cin.flags();
cin.open("keyb",ios_base::in);
cin.rdbuf()->sgetn();
// etc.
```

The cin and wcin objects are predefined, so the C++ programmer is at liberty to define as many basic_istream objects as are necessary.

The Extraction Operator

The >> operator is defined in C++ as the right bitwise shift operator. Normally, this operator takes two arguments and shifts bits in one argument the number of times indicated in the second argument. This operator has been overloaded in the iostream classes so that it can be used for input operations. The operator takes on additional meaning when it is overloaded. While the >> operator retains its original meaning relative to bit shifting, it also has new responsibilities when used with a basic_istream object. Although the semantics of the operator are enhanced during overloading, the syntax of the operator's usage must remain the same. When the >> operator is overloaded in the iostream classes, it is called the *extraction operator*. It no longer only performs right bit shifts; it also extracts data objects from a data stream. The data stream may be connected to any input device connected to the computer. The cin basic_istream object is connected to the console and is normally associated with standard-in (stdin).

The >> extraction operator gives the basic_istream class its appearance of genericity and device independence. This is accomplished through polymorphism. Because the >> operator has been overloaded for all the built-in data types, the programmer can extract any built-in data type from a basic_istream object using the same syntax. For example, the program in Listing 3.4 uses the same >> operator to extract eight different types of objects from the cin and wcin streams.

Listing 3.4   Use of the >> Operator for Extraction

```
// Listing 3.4
// This program demonstrates the use of the >> operator
// with different built-in data types.
#include <iostream>
#include <string>
using namespace std;
void main(void)
{
    wstring WideString;
    string NarrowString;
    double Num1;
    long Num2;
    long double Num3;
    int Num4;
    char CharacterArray[100];
    char Character;
    cin >> NarrowString;
    wcin >> WideString;
    cin >> Num1;
    cin >> Num2;
    cin >> Num3;
    cin >> Num4;
    cin >> CharacterArray;
    cin >> Character;
}
```

The >> insertion operator is a good example of single-interface multiple implementation.

Extraction Translation and Conversion

The extraction operator does more than just extract objects from a stream (technically, the basic_streambuf component does the extraction). The extraction operator also calls a function that does data conversion or translation. Operators in C++ are really just function names that invoke functions. When the programmer specifies:

```
cin >> object; // form 1
```

it is the equivalent of calling the function:

```
>>(cin,object); // form 2
```

The function name is in *infix notation* in the first form. In the second form, the function name is in *prefix notation*. The prefix function notation has the name >>, and it is passed by two arguments, a basic_istream object and object. The function's purpose is to take a generic stream of bytes and convert it into the specified data type during extraction. Put more simply, the >> function converts a generic stream of bytes into an object. The basic_istream class uses its locale's numeric (num_get) facets and code conversion (ctype) facets to help with the formatting. This conversion process is sometimes called *translation*. The >> operator or function is said to translate a stream of bytes into a built-in or user-defined object. It is this facility that gives the C++ environment the capability to easily handle user-defined data types and data structures. If the >> operator is defined for the user-defined data type or data structure, the >> operator is responsible for translating the generic stream of bytes into the user-defined object. This is how the stream concept is connected to object orientation. The combination of parameterized char_traits, the locale objects, and the iostream object-oriented model makes the iostream I/O facility one of the most powerful and flexible input/output systems available.

Formatted stream extraction begins to achieve its goal through polymorphism—that is, by defining the >> operator for all fundamental built-in data types and allowing the operator to be defined for user-defined data types. Second, formatted stream extraction obtains (translates) objects from generic streams of bytes. Figure 3.11 illustrates the flow of bytes during an iostream extraction.

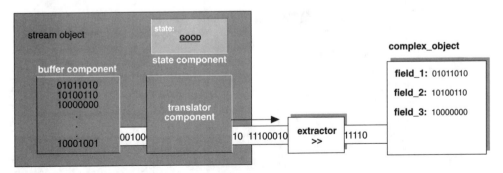

Figure 3.11 Sequence of bytes moving through the extraction operator to an object format.

Unformatted Extractions

The >> operator performs formatted extractions. The objects extracted from the basic_istream class originate as a generic sequence of bytes. They are converted from simpler data types into more complex data objects during the translation and conversion process. In many circumstances, however, extracting the data from the input stream without formatting or translation is desirable. For example, it may be preferable to read in items such as bitmaps, disk images, sound files, video files, compressed files, and so on from external storage into a memory block in RAM. In most cases, multimedia file formats such as Xpm, Fig, Bmp, Jpg, Mpeg, Avi, Au, and Wav, which are stored in a binary format, are *nonprintable*. (We use the term binary here to distinguish between character sets such as ASCII or Unicode and the binary 01s or hexadecimal characters that are meant to be machine-readable only.)

In addition to reading files in raw binary format, we may want to read in raw bytes from a serial or parallel port. The basic_istream class has several member functions that extract information from the stream without performing a text mode translation. These member functions are get( ), getline( ), and read( )s.

The basic_istream Class Accessors

In addition to the >> extraction accessor method, the istream class has three accessor methods used to access the bytes stored within a stream object. The get( ) member function has been overloaded, and can be used to get data from the attached basic_streambuf type and store it into input objects. The get( ) member function takes on five basic forms.

```
basic_istream<charT,traits>& get(charT& c);
basic_istream<charT,traits>& get(charT* s, streamsize n);
basic_istream<charT,traits>& get(charT* s, streamsize n,charT delim);
basic_istream<charT,traits>& get(basic_streambuf<charT,traits>& sb);
basic_istream<charT,traits>& get(basic_streambuf<charT,traits>& sb,
                                 charT delim);
```

The first get( ) form extracts a single character from the stream and stores it in c. This member function will take a character from an input stream. Since the iostreams are template classes, the type character extracted from the input stream will be charT, based on the instantiation for the basic_istream. A reference to the basic_istream object will be returned. It will perform no translation or conversion on the character; the character will be taken from a stream of type basic_istream and stored into a variable.

The second two get( ) member function forms will extract characters from the attached buffer until either *n* number of characters has been extracted, the delim is reached, or some error condition is caused, whichever happens first. The error condition could be the get( ) member function trying to extract beyond the EOF. The streamsize *n* is the most characters that will be extracted from the input stream. The delim is a character that will cause the extraction process to terminate. Obviously, if the extraction process does not encounter the delim, it will attempt to extract *n* characters. An error condition occurs when the source of the extraction does not contain *n* characters. This form of the get( ) member function will leave delim in the stream; it will not extract delim and store it in destination. This means that, in some cases,

ASCII versus Binary

Technically speaking, everything is stored on disk as a series of zeros and ones (01011111...) Certain formats are considered printable, such as ASCII and Unicode, whereas other formats are considered only machine-readable. Let's take, for example, the number:

255

In ASCII, each character is represented by 1 byte. The number 255 consists of 3 bytes in ASCII code:

001100011   00110101   00110101

As a regular binary number, 255 can be represented with a single byte as:

11111111

When the iostreams are opened in a text mode, they will interpret the input stream based on whichever character set is in effect. If the text mode in effect is ASCII, then the sequence:

00110010   00110101   00110101
| | |
32h   35h   35h
| | |
2   5   5

will be read one byte at a time and decoded according to ASCII character codes. Notice that 255 in binary:

11111111

(which means)

$$1^{128} + 1^{64} + 1^{32} + 1^{16} + 1^{8} + 1^{4} + 1^{2} + 1^{1}$$

requires only 1 byte, and 255 in ASCII requires 3 bytes. If we were using another character set, 2 5 5 might require more bytes. For instance, in Unicode, each character is represented by 2 bytes; therefore, the number 255 would require 6 bytes in text mode. Pure binary files will be smaller than their text mode equivalents. Bitmaps, sound files, movie images, database formats, and compressed files rarely use ASCII, Unicode, or other printable text mode formatting.

there will be an unwanted character in the input stream that must be dealt with. The basic_istream& ignore(int n, int delim); member function can solve this problem. The ignore( ) member function discards *n* number of characters or up to the delim, whichever comes first.

The third get( ) member function form:

```
basic_istream<charT,traits>& get(basic_streambuf<char_type,traits>& sb);
basic_istream<charT,traits>& get(basic_streambuf<char_type,traits>& sb,
                                 char_type delim);
```

extracts a number of characters from a basic_streambuf and stores them into another basic_streambuf. The first form extracted characters from a basic_streambuf and stored them into a character array. The second form goes from basic_streambuf to basic_stream-buf. However, the second form does not specify how many characters to extract. It will extract characters until delim or EOF is reached or until an error condition occurs.

The getline( ) is a member function of the basic_istream class. It will take a sequence of characters and store them in a variable. This is the prototype for getline( ):

```
basic_istream<charT,traits>& getline(charT* s, streamsize n);
basic_istream<charT,traits>& getline(charT* s, streamsize n,
                                     char_type delim);
```

It will accept a pointer to charT. The charT type is whatever object the basic_istream is instantiated with. The pointer to the charT is the destination where the sequence of characters will be stored. The member function will accept characters up to length *n* or to the delimiter, depending on which is encountered first. The getline( ) member function extracts a number of characters from the attached buffer and stores those characters into a character array pointed to by s. The getline( ) member function will extract characters from the attached buffer until either *n* number of characters has been extracted, the delim is reached, or some error condition is caused, whichever happens first. The error condition could be the getline( ) member function trying to extract beyond EOF. The streamsize *n* is the most characters that will be extracted from the input stream. The delim is a character that will cause the extraction process to terminate. If the source of the extraction does not contain *n* characters, then an error condition occurs.

Whereas the get( ) member function did not extract the delimiter from the stream, the getline( ) member function does. Neither member function stores the delimiter in the destination. The read( ) is a member function of the basic_istream class. It will read a block of binary data from an input stream. Here is the read( ) prototype:

```
basic_istream<charT,traits>& read (charT* s, streamsize n);
```

This member function will accept an array or a pointer to a charT and the number of bytes to be read. The pointer to a buffer or an array will store the block of characters. It points to a buffer of charT. The read( ) member function has been overloaded, and can be used to extract data from the attached stream buffer and store it into a character array. Listing 3.5 shows an example of a program using the read( ) member function on built-in data types.

Listing 3.5 Using read( ) and write( ) Member Functions

```
1    // Listing 3.5
2    // Demonstrates how to write out a built-in type using
3    // the binary mode
4
5    #include <iostream>
6    #include <fstream>
7
8    using namespace std;
9
10   void main(void)
11   {
12
13       float Number = 345678932.23;
14       float Number2;
15       ofstream Out("out.dat",ios::binary);
16       Out.write((const char *)&Number,sizeof(double));
17       Out.close();
18       ifstream In("out.dat",ios::binary);
19       In.read((char *) &Number2,sizeof(double));
20       cout << Number2 << endl;
21       cin.get();
22       In.close();
23   }
```

This program first writes out a float in a binary format to a file called out.dat. It then uses the read( ) member function of the ifstream object to extract a number from the file. Opening the file for reading in the same mode that it was opened for writing is important. In this case, we wrote the file in binary mode, so it should be opened for reading in binary mode. In Listing 3.6, a string of characters is assigned to a strstreambuf.

The program in this listing sends:

```
Th

These are the voyages...
Thes
```

to the console. It uses the get( ) member function to get characters from the Input-stream, one character at a time.

The peek( ) and putback( ) Accessor Methods

The peek( ) method returns the next character in the stream without extracting the character from the stream. Calling the peek( ) method has no affect on the get pointer.

The putback( ) member function takes a char argument:

```
basic_istream & putback(char Character);
```

Listing 3.6 Using the get( ) Member Function

```
1    // Listing 3.6
2    // This program demonstrates the use of get() member function.
3    // The program also shows how to declare a basic_istream object
4    // and its associated buffer.
5
6    #include <iostream>
7    #include <sstream>
8    #include <string>
9
10   using namespace std;
11
12   void main(void)
13   {
14       string Source("These are the voyages....");
15       char Dest[81] = "";
16       stringbuf Buffer(Source);
17       istream InputStream(&Buffer);
18       if(!InputStream){
19           cerr << "Error Setting up stream";
20       }
21       InputStream.get(Dest,81,'e');
22       cout << Dest << endl;
23       InputStream.seekg(0,ios_base::beg);
24       InputStream.get(Dest,InputStream.rdbuf()->in_avail(),'\n');
25       cout << Dest << endl;
26       InputStream.seekg(0,ios_base::beg);
27       InputStream.get(Dest,5,'\n');
28       cout << Dest << endl;
29   }
```

It attempts to put this character back into the stream. The character must equal the character that the get pointer is at. If Character does not equal the character the get pointer is at, the putback function fails.

Accessor Methods for the Stream State

The gcount( ) member function returns the number of bytes extracted for the last unformatted extraction performed. The gcount( ) member function can be used immediately after the get( ), getline( ), and read( ) member functions to determine how many characters were extracted. Although the gcount( ) member function is useful for counting characters, the buffer state functions:

```
good()

bad()
fail()
eof()
```

should be used constantly while working with the iostreams. These member functions give the programmer a snapshot of the stream state at any given point.

The Sentry Object and the ipfx( ) and isfx( ) Prefix and Suffix Methods

One of the components of an istream object is a sentry object, used to make sure that important housekeeping functions are called, such as flushing buffers, throwing exceptions, releasing file locks, and freeing semaphores. The sentry object accomplishes its housekeeping duties by calling two functions: ipfx( ) and isfx( ). These two functions perform pre- and postcondition processing for the >> extraction operator and precondition processing for some of the unformatted extraction member functions. The constructor for the sentry object calls the precondition ipfx( ) method and the destructor for the sentry calls the postcondition isfx( ) method.

The prefix or precondition member function will have a slightly different behavior, dependent on whether the operation is dealing with formatted or unformatted extraction. The ipfx( ) and isfx( ) member functions can also have implementation-specific processing responsibilities, such as resetting printer fonts back to their original settings or restoring a modem back to its original mode. The precondition ipfx( ) function checks the buffer state of the attached basic_streambuf object. If the buffer is in an error state, the precondition ipfx( ) function returns a zero. If this function returns a zero, the insertion operation will fail. Nothing can be extracted from the stream until the error state is cleared. If the buffer is not in an error state, the ipfx( ) member function will flush the attached buffer and return a nonzero value.

The sentry object uses the ipfx( ) and isfx( ) methods as part of an object-oriented mechanism that helps to propagate errors throughout the iostream class hierarchy. With a sentry object in place, once a stream enters an error state, it remains in that error state in a do-nothing mode until the error state is cleared. The error state can be cleared by calling the clear( ) member function.

The basic_ostream Class: An Object-Oriented Model of Output

The basic_ostream class is the foundation for the object-oriented output stream in the C++ environment. The object-oriented facilities in the C++ language bring the added power of I/O modeling, user-defined I/O structures, and uniformity of expression to the stream concept. The basic_ostream class is derived from the basic_ios class, meaning that the power of expression and representation contained in the ios class is also contained in the basic_ostream class and its derived classes. All the member functions that are callable from an basic_ios class are callable from a basic_ostream class, and all the protected and public data members that are contained in the ios class are contained in the basic_ostream class.

The basic_ios class contains a pointer to a basic_streambuf class. The basic_ostream class inherits this pointer, giving it full access to the functionality of the basic_stream-buf class and the services it provides. Figure 3.12 shows the relationship among the basic_ostream class, basic_ios class, and the basic_streambuf class. The relationship between basic_ostream and basic_ios is one of inheritance, meaning that ios is a subset of the basic_ostream class. The figure also shows that basic_ostream will contain a pointer to a basic_streambuf class. This means that the basic_ostream class can only access the functionality of the basic_streambuf class through its public members.

The basic_ostream class implements the notion of the object-oriented output stream, which can be a binary or text stream and buffered or unbuffered. The basic_ostream class has facilities to process single characters or blocks of characters. When characters or blocks of characters are sent to a basic_ostream object, the operation is referred to as *insertion.* A C++ program can contain multiple basic_ostream objects. There can be a basic_ostream object for every output device and output file in the program, giving the programmer maximum flexibility in I/O design.

The basic_ostream class is the fundamental base class for the basic_ofstream class and the basic_ostringstream class. These two classes are a specialization of basic_ostream that deal with files and memory areas, respectively. Familiarity with the structure and operations of the basic_ostream class will shed light on the entire iostream class hierarchy. The cout and wcout objects are examples of basic_ostream objects predefined. The C++ programmer is at liberty to define as many basic_ostream objects as are necessary.

Construction of an ostream Object

To create an ostream object, you must specify a buffer object, as shown here:

```
explicit basic_ostream(basic_streambuf<charT,traits>* sb);
```

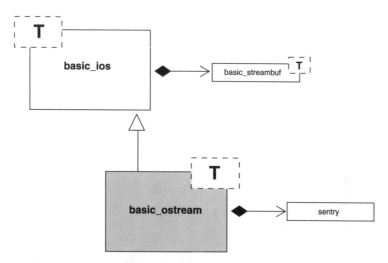

Figure 3.12 Relationships among the basic_ostream class, basic_ios class, and the basic_streambuf class.

A stream is useless without a buffer component. The buffer component is actually tied to the I/O device; therefore, without a buffer component, a stream does not have anywhere to read bytes from or write bytes to. The stream classes help to provide the device-independent interface to I/O devices.

The Insertion Operator

The << operator is defined in C++ as the left bitwise shift operator. This operator has been overloaded in the iostream classes so that it can be used for output operations. When the << operator is overloaded in the iostream classes, it is called the insertion operator. It no longer performs only left bit shifts; it also inserts objects into a data stream. The data stream may be connected to any output device connected to the computer. The cout basic_ostream object is connected to the console. When objects are inserted into the cout basic_ostream object, they are sent to the console (monitor). For example, the program in Listing 3.7 sends a string to the console.

The << insertion operator gives the basic_ostream class its appearance of genericity and device independence, accomplished through polymorphism. Because the << operator has been overloaded for all the built-in data types, the programmer can insert any built-in data type to a basic_ostream object using the same syntax. For example, the program in Listing 3.8 uses the << insertion operator with four different data types.

The << insertion operator is a good example of single-interface multiple implementation.

Insertion Translation and Conversion

The insertion operator does more than just insert objects into a stream. It is really a function written as an infix operator. The << operator can be thought of as a function name, which simply invokes either a built-in or user-defined function. When the programmer specifies:

```
cout << object;
```

it is equivalent to calling the function:

```
<<(cout,object);
```

Listing 3.7 Inserting a String with cout

```
// Listing 3.7
// This program demonstrates the insertion of a string into the
// cout object.

#include <iostream>
void main(void)
{
    cout << "These are the voyages.... ";
}
```

Listing 3.8   Using the Insertion Operator with Different Data Types

```
// Listing 3.8
// This program demonstrates the usage of << operator with
// different built in data types.

#include <iostream>

void main(void)
{
    float AFamousNumber = 3.1459;
    double ALargeNumber = 6.023E23;
    int LightSpeed = 3.00E8;
    string AString("The Standard C++ Library");
    cout << Astring << endl;
    cout << ALargeNumber << endl;
    cout << LightSpeed << endl;
    cout << AfamousNumber << endl;
}
```

In the first form, the function name is in infix notation. In the second form the function name is in prefix notation. The prefix function notation has the name <<, and it is passed two arguments, an basic_ostream object and object. The function's purpose is to take the object and convert it into a stream of bytes that will be inserted into the stream and inevitably sent to the output device connected to the stream. Put more simply, the << function converts objects into a generic sequence of bytes. This conversion process is sometimes called *translation*. The << operator or function is said to translate an object into a stream of bytes. It is this facility that gives the C++ environment the capability to easily handle user-defined data types and data structures. If the << operator is defined for the user-defined data type or data structure, the << operator is responsible for translating the user's object into a generic stream of bytes. This is how the stream concept is connected to object orientation.

Formatted stream insertion begins to achieve its goal through polymorphism; that is, by defining the << operator for all the built-in data types and allowing the operator to be defined for user-defined data types. The second step in achieving its goal is to convert (translate) objects into generic streams of bytes.

Unformatted Insertions

The << operator performs formatted insertions. The objects inserted into the basic_ostream class are not sent to the output as they are. They are first translated into simpler data types (sequences of bytes). In many circumstances, inserting the data into the stream without formatting or translation is desirable, for example, when writing bitmaps such as BMPs, JPGs, FIGs, and GIFs to file. These images are stored in memory and we would like to write them to the file without any further translation. Memory blocks containing multimedia data such as sound images (WAV, AU), and video images (MOV, AVI) are also candidates for unformatted output to files. The basic_ostream class has two member functions that send information to the stream without further translation: first, put( ) inserts either a character, unsigned character, or signed character into the output stream, as shown in Listing 3.9.

This program sends the character *A* to the output.

The second member function, write( ), inserts from one character to a block of characters into the output stream. (See the ASCII versus Binary sidebar earlier in this chapter.)

```
basic_ostream<charT,traits>& write(const char_type* s, streamsize n);
```

This member function does not do any translation. It is used to write unformatted binary blocks to files and output devices. It takes a pointer to a const char_type, along with the number of bytes to write as an argument, then sends the data to its stream, as shown in Listing 3.10.

When the program in Listing 3.10 is executed, it will write the value of LightSpeed in its unformatted form to the stream to which the cout object is connected. The cout stream is connected to the console, therefore a series of bytes appears on the console that represent an unformatted double. Notice that the address of the double is being cast to an unsigned char* pointer. This is necessary so that the data can be inserted into the stream as a sequence of generic bytes.

The basic_ostream Class Accessor Methods

The ostream object has two basic methods that access the output stream: put( ) sends one character at a time to the output stream, and write( ) can write bitmaps, records, generic bytes, and other types of objects to the output stream. The put( ) method will place a character into an output stream, and because the streams are templates and can accept different character sizes or types, the character can be a signed or unsigned, char or char of any other type that is a legitimate char_type. This is the prototype for put( ):

```
basic_ostream<charT,traits>& put(char_type c);
```

A reference to the basic_ostream object will be returned. It will perform no translation or conversion on the character; instead, the character will be sent to the external device to which the basic_ostream object is linked. The write( ) function is a member of the basic_ostream class. It will write a block of binary data to the output stream linked to an external device. This is the prototype for write( ):

Listing 3.9   Using put( ) Member Function

```
// Listing 3.9
// This program show how the put() member function is called by
// a basic_ostream object.
#include <iostream.h>
void main(void)
{
    cout.put('A');
}
```

Listing 3.10   Using the write( ) Member Function

```
// Listing 3.10
// This program uses the write() member function to insert
// a double into the basic_streambuf of the cout object.
#include <iostream>
using namespace std;
void main(void)
{
    double LightSpeed = 3.00E8;
    cout.write((unsigned char*)&LightSpeed,sizeof(double));
}
```

```
basic_ostream<charT,traits>& write(const char_type* s, streamsize n);
```

This member function will accept an array or a pointer to a buffer and the number of bytes to be written. The pointer stores the block of characters. It can write any object of type char_type.

iostream Class = basic_istream + basic_ostream

The iostream class is derived from the basic_istream and the basic_ostream classes. Figure 3.13 shows the relationship as one of inheritance. As depicted there, it is multiple inheritance. The iostream class has a basic_istream component and a basic_ostream component, so it can be used for input and output modeling.

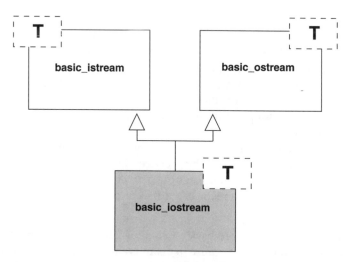

Figure 3.13 Class relationship of the basic_iostream class, showing the multiple inheritance of basic_istream and basic_ostream by the basic_iostream class.

The protected and public data members and member functions contained in basic_istream and basic_ostream are components of the iostream class.

The Sentry Object and the opfx( ) and osfx( ) Prefix and Suffix Methods

One of the components of an ostream object is a sentry object, used to make sure that important housekeeping functions are called, such as flushing buffers, throwing exceptions, releasing file locks, and freeing mutexes and semaphores. The sentry object for the ostream class accomplishes its housekeeping duties by calling the opfx( ) and osfx( ) methods. These two methods perform pre- and postcondition processing, and are called during the construction and destruction of the sentry object that is part of the ostream class. The sentry object's constructor calls the precondition opfx( ) function and the sentry object's destructor calls the postcondition osfx( ) method. The precondition opfx( ) function checks the buffer state of the attached basic_streambuf object. If the buffer is in an error state, the precondition opfx( ) function returns a zero, and the insertion operation will fail. Nothing can be inserted into the stream until the error state is cleared. If the buffer is not in an error state, the opfx( ) member function will flush the attached buffer and return a nonzero value.

The sentry object uses the opfx( ) and osfx( ) methods as part of the object-oriented mechanism that helps to propagate errors throughout the iostream class hierarchy. With the sentry object in place, once a stream enters an error state, it remains in that error state in a do-nothing mode until the error state is cleared. The error state can be cleared by calling the clear( ) member function.

The ifstream Class

The ifstream class is derived from the basic_istream class and is a specialized basic_istream class. The ifstream class models the input file stream. Whereas the basic_istream class focuses on an input stream normally attached to the console, the ifstream focuses on a stream normally attached to a file. The ifstream class is important in the operating system environments that implement devices as files, including Unix, Linux, NT, and OS/2. In these operating system environments, ifstream classes can be used to access any device recognized as a file by the operating system. The ifstream class adds member functions and important data members specifically designed to deal with files. Figure 3.14 shows the relationship between ifstream and the basic_istream class, one of inheritance. Figure 3.15 compares the ifstream class and the basic_istream class. Notice in Figure 3.15 that ifstream has a filebuf component, as opposed to a basic_streambuf component.

The filebuf component is a specialized basic_streambuf. Through this component, the ifstream class has access to the file. Because ifstream is a descendant of basic_istream, it has the same capacity to deal with formatted and unformatted operations. Any protected or public member function that can be called in a basic_istream class can be

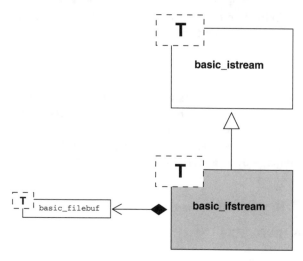

Figure 3.14   The class relationship between ifstream class and basic_istream class.

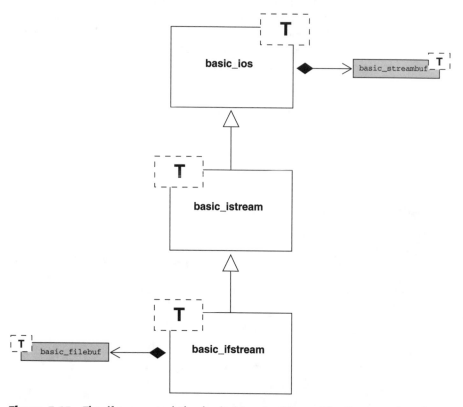

Figure 3.15   The ifstream and the basic_istream classes. The ifstream class has a filebuf component, as opposed to a basic_streambuf component.

called in an ifstream class. Extraction has basically the same semantics in an ifstream class. The ifstream class is said to extend the services of the basic_istream class to include files.

NOTE:

The ANSI/ISO standard for the iostreams does not support the concept of a file descriptor. Older implementations of the iostreams often included file descriptor access through the filebuf class and some type of fd( ) method. This type of access is no longer supported. If file descriptor access is needed, you must design your own interface or take advantage of a vendor-specific interface, if one is available.

Constructing an ifstream Object

An ifstream object has two public constructors:

```
basic_ifstream();
explicit basic_ifstream(const char* s,
                    ios_base::openmode mode = ios_base::in);
```

The first constructs a stream that is not connected to any file or device; the second constructs a stream that will be connected to the device named by s. The device or file will be opened in the mode specified by mode. The constructor opens the file specified by s; if the file cannot be opened, the buffer state will contain the error condition. If the ifstream was constructed with the first constructor, then the open( ) method will be called to connect the stream with a file or device.

```
open(const char *FileName, int OpenMode);
```

This member function can be called after the ifstream object has been declared, as shown in Listing 3.11.

The close( ) member function closes the file attached to the ifstream class.

Listing 3.11   Opening a File for Binary Input

```
// Listing 3.11
// This program creates an ifstream object and opens a file for binary
// input.
#include <fstream>
void main(void)
{
    unsigned char Byte;
    ifstream Source;
    Source.open("myfile.dat",ios_base::in | ios_base::binary);
    Source >> Byte;
    Source.close();
}
```

Accessor Methods for the ifstream Class Buffer

The ifstream class declares two member functions that handle buffers: rdbuf( ), and set-buf( ). The rdbuf( ) member function returns a pointer to the filebuf component that the ifstream class contains. This is a powerful and often-overlooked facility in the iostreams. Through the pointer to ifstream's filebuf, the ifstream class has access to all the functionality of a filebuf (basic_streambuf) class. This means that given the declaration:

```
ifstream Source("File1.txt);
```

the filebuf component member functions may be accessed as follows:

```
Source.rdbuf()->sgetn();
Source.rdbuf()->sbumpc();
Source.rdbuf()->snextc();
Source.rdbuf()->sgetc();
Source.rdbuf()->in_avail();
Source.rdbuf()->sungetc();
Source.rdbuf()->sputbackc();
      etc.
```

This gives the C++ programmer total control of the buffer area connected to the ifstream class object. The setbuf( ) member function allows the programmer to specify both the size of the buffer attached to the filebuf object and the position in the buffer where the extraction will start. The setbuf( ) member function should be called before a file is assigned to the ifstream class.

Using an ifstream Object

The iostream class hierarchy is built on inheritance, encapsulation, and polymorphism. In order for the C++ programmer to get the maximum benefit from the iostream classes, the programmer must be constantly aware of the hierarchy and components of all the iostream classes. In object-oriented programming, the emphasis is on relationships between classes and objects. Knowing what a class contains makes it possible to determine which member functions can be called. Remember, an object is considered as a type in the C++ environment, and so can be used in expressions, put in array declarations, written to files, sorted, added, printed, read, created, destroyed, and more. The program in Listing 3.12 creates an array of ifstream objects, two of which are connected to text files that will be extracted from the input stream. This program extracts numeric values from the two files (List1.txt and List2.txt) and performs a merge-sort on the values. As the program is performing the merge-sort, it inserts the values into the predefined cout stream. Listing 3.12 is an example of using multiple streams within one program.

Notice that the program in Listing 3.12 contains four streams. The first and second are ifstreams that have been attached to List1.txt and List2.txt, respectively. The third and fourth streams, cerr and cout, are ostreams, predefined streams. Error messages can be inserted into the cerr object. Notice that the ifstream objects are contained within the array named Stream. This is another advantage of object-oriented I/O: The streams are objects

Listing 3.12 Using Multiple Streams in One Program

```
1    // Listing 3.12
2    // This program reads in two sorted files and performs a merge
3    // sort to the predefined stream cout. It demonstrates that
4    // the programmer can declare an array of stream objects.
5
6    #include <fstream>
7    #include <stdlib.h>
8
9    ifstream Stream[2];
10
11
12   void main(void)
13
14   {
15
16       double Object[2];
17       Stream[0].open("list1.txt");
18       if(!Stream[0].good()){
19           cerr << "could Not open file 1";
20           exit(0);
21       }
22       Stream[1].open("list2.txt");
23       if(!Stream[1].good()){
24           cerr << "could not open file 2 ";
25           exit(0);
26       }
27       Stream[0] >> Object[0];
28       Stream[1] >> Object[1];
29       while(!Stream[0].eof() && !Stream[0].fail() &&
30             !Stream[1].eof() && !Stream[1].fail())
31       {
32
33           if(Object[0] < Object[1]){
34               cout << Object[0] << endl;
35               Stream[0] >> Object[0];
36           }
37           else
38               if(Object[1] < Object[0]){
39                   cout << Object[1] << endl;
40                   Stream[1] >> Object[1];
41               }
42               else{
43                   cout << Object[0] << endl
44                        << Object[1] << endl;
45                   Stream[0] >> Object[0];
46                   Stream[1] >> Object[1];
47               }
48
```

Listing 3.12 *(Continued)*

```
49            }
50            while(!Stream[0].eof() && !Stream[0].fail())
51            {
52                 Stream[0] >> Object[0];
53                 cout << Object[0] << endl;
54
55            }
56            while(!Stream[1].eof() && !Stream[1].fail())
57            {
58
59                 Stream[1] >> Object[1];
60                 cout << Object[1] << endl;
61
62            }
63            Stream[0].close();
64            Stream[1].close();
65
66    }
```

just like any other object in the C++ environment and can be used in expressions, array declarations, and so on. Notice also that this program does not do any serious error checking; the good( ), fail( ), and eof( ) member functions are called only for demonstration purposes.

The ofstream Class of the Object-Oriented Output File

The ofstream class is derived from the basic_ostream class and is a specialized basic_ostream class. The ofstream class models the output file stream, and can be used whenever the C++ programmer has to deal with files. Whereas the cout basic_ostream class focuses on an output stream that is normally attached to the console, the ofstream focuses on a stream that is normally attached to a file. Some operating systems such as Unix, Windows NT, and OS/2 see devices as specialized files. In these OS environments, ofstream classes can be used to access any device recognized as a file. The ofstream class adds member functions and important data members specifically designed to deal with files. Figure 3.16 shows the relationship between the ofstream and the basic_ostream classes; it is one of inheritance. Figure 3.17 compares the ofstream class and the basic_ostream class; notice that ofstream has a filebuf component, as opposed to a basic_streambuf component.

The filebuf class is derived from the basic_streambuf class. It is the filebuf class that is ultimately connected to the device or file opened. The inheritance relationship shown in Figure 3.16 shows that the entire basic_ostream class is a component of the ofstream class. This means that any protected or public members in basic_ostream are accessible in an ofstream class. The ofstream class has formatted and unformatted extraction functionality. The ofstream class indirectly inherits the basic_ios class through the

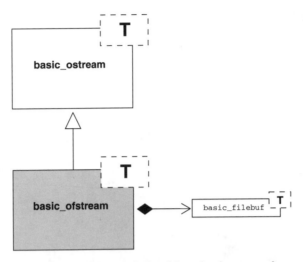

Figure 3.16 Class relationship of ofstream class indicating it inherits the basic_ostream class.

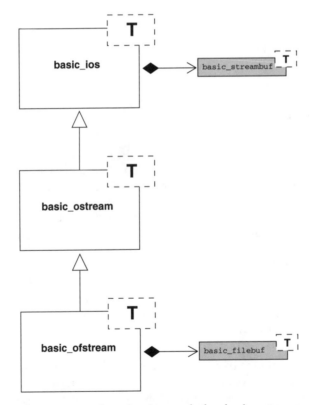

Figure 3.17 The ofstream and the basic_ostream classes. The ofstream has a filebuf component, as opposed to a basic_streambuf component.

basic_ostream class. This gives the ofstream class a format state, a buffer state, and an open state. The ofstream class extends the capabilities of the basic_ostream class to deal with output files.

Constructing an ofstream Object

An ofstream object has two constructors:

```
basic_ofstream();
explicit basic_ofstream(const char* s,
                        ios_base::openmode mode = ios_base::out);
```

The first constructor builds an ofstream object that is not connected to any file or device. The second constructor builds an ostream object connected to a device or file named by s. The device or file is opened in openmode, mode. If the first constructor is used, the open( ) method must be used to attach the stream to a device or file.

```
ofstream(const char * FileName ,int OpenMode);
```

An ofstream object can be declared, and the file to be attached to the object can be specified in the constructor, as follows:

```
ofstream Source("myfile.dat",ios_base::out | ios_base::app);
```

The constructor opens the file specified by s. If the file cannot be opened, the buffer state will contain the error condition. Files are opened through the constructor method or through calling the open( ) method, as shown here:

```
open(const char *FileName, int OpenMode);
```

This member function can be called after the ofstream object has been declared as in Listing 3.13.

The close( ) member function closes the file attached to the ifstream class.

Listing 3.13 Demonstrating open( ) and close( )

```
// Listing 3.13
// This program demonstrates the open() and close()
// member functions
#include <fstream>
using namespace std;
void main(void)
{
    unsigned char Byte;
    ofstream Destination;
    Destination.open("myfile.dat",
                     ios_base::noreplace | ios_base::binary);
    Destination << Byte;
    Destination.close();
}
```

The state of the buffer can be checked by calling:

```
bad()
good()
fail()
eof()
```

Once the file is attached, the ofstream class object can use the file as if it originally opened the file.

Accessor Methods for the ofstream Class Buffer

The ofstream class declares two member functions that handle buffers: rdbuf( ) and setbuf( ). The rdbuf( ) member function returns a pointer to the filebuf component that the ofstream class contains. This is a powerful and often-overlooked facility in the iostreams. Through the pointer to ofstream's filebuf, the ofstream class has access to all the functionality of a filebuf (basic_streambuf) class. This means that given the declaration:

```
ofstream Destination("File1.txt");
```

the filebuf component member functions may be accessed as follows:

```
Destination.rdbuf()->sputn();

Destination.rdbuf()->sbumpc();
Destination.rdbuf()->snextc();
Destination.rdbuf()->sputc();
Destination.rdbuf()->out_waiting();
Destination.rdbuf()->showmanyc();
//etc.
```

This gives the C++ programmer total control of the buffer area connected to the ofstream class object. The setbuf( ) member function allows the programmer to specify both the size of the buffer attached to the filebuf object and the position in the buffer where the insertion will start. The setbuf( ) member function should be called before a file is assigned to the ofstream class.

fstream class = ifstream + ofstream

Like the iostream class, the fstream class is an input and output class. When the programmer needs to do simultaneous input and output to a file or a device opened as a file, the programmer can declare an object of type fstream. The fstream object will have all of the combined protected and public data members and member functions of the ifstream and ofstream classes. Figure 3.18 shows the components that make up the fstream class. Keep in mind the notion of inheritance. The fstream class will contain ios_base, basic_ios, locale, sentry, basic_istream, basic_ostream, ifstream, ofstream, streambuf, and filebuf classes. The fstream class represents a culmination of most of the entire iostream hierarchy.

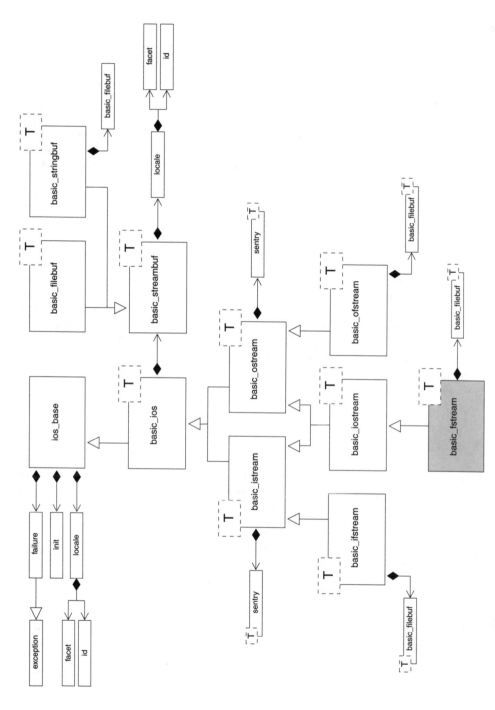

Figure 3.18 Class relationship of the fstream class, showing its components.

Files

A file is a logical abstraction for any type of external device. A file is opened and associated with a stream in order for data to be exchanged to and/or from the program. The iostream class library works with two primary types of files: binary and text. The text files will contain information encoded in ASCII, Unicode, EBCDIC, UCS, or UTF format. Binary files can contain multimedia data such as sound files, video files, bitmap images, or compressed data. Binary files may also be used to store database records, sequential data, or other types of external data structures such as B-trees. (For more information on test files versus binary files, see the ASCII versus Binary sidebar earlier in this chapter.) The iostream classes can be used to write and read data from both types of files. To do file input and output, the <fstream> must be included in the program header file.

Opening and Closing Files

To read or write to a binary or text file, the file has to be opened. But before the file is opened, an associated stream object must be declared. Files and streams can be prepared as write-only, read-only, and read/write. There are two basic ways to declare a stream and open a file. The first uses separate statements, one to declare a stream object and the other to open the file. For an input stream, an object of class ifstream is declared; for an output stream, an object of class ofstream is declared; for a stream capable of both input and output, an object of class fstream is declared. The associated files for the declared stream are opened.

A file can be opened using the open( ) member function of the ifstream, ofstream, and fstream classes. This is the prototype for the open( ) member function:

```
void open(const char* s, openmode mode = in);
```

Here, *s* is the name of the file to be opened, which may include a path name and mode that specifies how the file will be opened and accessed. The mode values, their meanings, and their *stdio equivalents* are listed in Table 3.9. The mode can be one or more of the values combined by ORing two or more together.

The ifstream and ofstream classes have a default mode. The ifstream class default value for mode is ios_base::in; the ofstream class default value for mode is ios_base::out. If the default values for mode are to be used, specifying them in the parameters for open is not necessary( ). To declare a stream capable of both input and output, both ios_base::in and ios_base::out must be specified in the parameter list. The constructor member functions of the ofstream, ifstream, and fstream classes can also be used to open a file and associate a stream for that file. The constructors will automatically open a file of that class type with the default parameters. For example, to declare a stream capable of both input and output, and to open a normal file for that stream, could be accomplished this way:

```
fstream <name of stream>("filename",ios::in | ios::out);
```

To close a file, use the close( ) member function of the ifstream, ofstream, and fstream classes. The close( ) function has no return value or parameters.

Table 3.9 Mode Values, Their Meanings, and stdio Equivalents

OPEN ACCESS MODES	C EQUIVALENTS	DESCRIPTION
ios_base::in	r	Opens an existing file for input.
ios_base::out	w	Creates a new file for output.
ios_base::out|trunc	w	Truncates an existing file for output.
ios_base::out|app	a	Appends an existing file for output.
ios_base:in|out	r+	Opens an existing file for updating, starting at the beginning of the file for input and output.
ios_base:in|out|trunc	w+	Truncates an existing file for updating for input and output.
ios_base::binary|in	rb	Opens an existing binary file for input.
ios_base::binary|out	wb	Creates a new binary file for output.
ios_base::binary|out|trunc	wb	Truncates an existing binary file for output.
ios_base::binary|out|app	ab	Appends an existing binary file for output.
ios_base:binary|in|out	r+b	Opens an existing binary file for updating starting at the beginning of the file for input and output.
ios_base:binary|in|out|trunc	w+b	Truncates an existing binary file for updating for input and output.

Writing to a Text File

Insertors can be used to send built-in data types to text and user-defined objects to an external device. The program in Listing 3.14 uses an ofstream object to create an HTML text file.

Reading from a Text File

The extraction operator can be used to read built-in data types from a text file. The data is read from the input file and stored into the appropriate variables. So, given a text file that contains the line:

What is 500 * 44.4 = to?

An ifstream object can extract this information into built-in data types as shown in Listing 3.15.

This listing shows char, int, float, and string data types read from a text file using a combination of the get( ) method and the >> extraction operator. The get( ) method is used to read the words "What is" from the file because we want the variable Array to include the space that is between "What" and "is". The rest of the line uses the >> extraction operator because we would like to ignore the spaces.

Listing 3.14   Using ofstream to Create an HTML File

```cpp
// Listing 3.14
// This program uses the ofstream class to
// generate a simple HTML skeleton
// that can be opened with a web browser.
#include <iostream>
#include <fstream>
using namespace std;
void main(void)
{
    ofstream Internet("WebPage.html");
    Internet << "<html>" << endl << "<head>" << endl;
    Internet << "<title>C++ Standard Class Library</title>" << endl;
    Internet << "</head>" << endl << "<body>" << endl;
    Internet << "<h3>Object Oriented I/O</h3>" << endl;
    Internet << "The iostreams can be used to generate HTML files!"
            << endl;
    Internet << "and Web pages" <<endl;
    Internet << "</body>" << endl << "</html>" << endl;
    Internet.close();
}
```

Listing 3.15   Reading Built-in Data Types from Text File

```cpp
// Listing 3.15
// This program demonstrates how easily built-in data types
// can be read from a text file.
#include <fstream>
#include <iostream>
using namespace std;
void main(void)
{
    char Array[9];
    int Num1;
    char Character;
    float Num2;
    char Character2;
    string Word;
    ifstream In("test.asc");
    In.get(Array,7,'5');
    In >> Num1 >> Character >> Num2 >> Character2 >> Word;
    In.close();
}
```

Writing to a Binary File

The put( ) member function is used to write a byte or character to a binary file. The write( ) member function will write a block of binary data to the binary file, then return a stream of basic_ostream type. Just like the text files, a stream has to be declared and a file associated with the stream has to be opened. The put( ) and write( ) member functions are used to write built-in data types to a binary file. Recall that a binary mode writes out characters as a sequence of bytes, without translation. To write an object to a stream in binary mode, the object must be cast to char*. Two common techniques are used. First, if we have an object User of type user_defined, then the method:

```
write(reinterpret_cast<char *>(&User),sizeof(user_defined);
```

or, second:

```
write((char *)&User,sizeof(user_defined);
```

will write the object User to a binary stream.

Reading from a Binary File

The get( ) and getline( ) member functions are used to read a character and a sequence of characters from a binary file. The read( ) member function will read a block of binary data from the binary file, then return a stream of basic_istream type. The get( ), getline( ), and read( ) member functions are used to read built-in data types from a binary file. Keep in mind that a binary file does not store the characters in ASCII or Unicode type character code; the information is stored as a series of generic bytes in the file. Therefore, we must cast those bytes to the type that we are attempting to read. Two common casting techniques are used. First, if we have an object User of type user_defined, then the method:

```
read(reinterpret_cast<char *>(&User),sizeof(user_defined));
```

or, second:

```
read((char *)&User,sizeof(user_defined));
```

will read an object from a binary file into the object User.

Writing Objects to and Reading Objects from a Binary File

The write( ) and read( ) member functions can be used to write or read a user-defined data type to and from a binary file. These functions accept a pointer to a signed or unsigned char and the number of bytes to be written or read. The address of the user-defined type has to be converted to an address of a signed or unsigned char. The size of the built-in data type or user-defined type must be supplied to the read( ) and write( ) methods. The sizeof operator can be used to determine the size of the object to be read or written. Keep in mind that the size objects that contain dynamically allocated data must calculate the real size of the data on a heap when calculating the object size. The program

Listing 3.16   Using Casting to Read and Write Objects

```cpp
// Listing 3.16
// This program demonstrates how to use
// casting to read and write objects to a
// file opened in binary mode.
#include <fstream>
#include <string>
#include <iostream>
using namespace std;
class user_defined{
public:
    double Num1;
    char X[1024];
    char Character;
};
void main(void)
{
    fstream Object("user.dat",ios::binary |ios::out);
    user_defined User;
    User.Num1 = 3.1459;
    strcpy(User.X,"These Are The Voyages...");
    User.Character = '@';
    Object.write(reinterpret_cast<char *>(&User),
             sizeof(user_defined));
    Object.close();
    Object.open("user.dat",ios::binary | ios::in);
    Object.read(reinterpret_cast<char *>(&User),sizeof(user_defined));
    Object.close();
}
```

in Listing 3.16 shows how the read( ) and write( ) methods are used to read in user-defined objects.

This program also demonstrates how the same object stream can be used for both input and output.

The istringstream Class (Memory Devices)

The istringstream class implements the functionality of an object-oriented input memory device. Whereas the cin type basic_istream object is normally tied to the console, and the ifstream class is connected to a file or a device recognized as a file, the istringstream class is connected to a block of memory or a character array. The istringstream class is a model of a character or byte array.

The istringstream class is derived from the basic_istream class. Figure 3.19 shows the inheritance relationship between the istringstream class and the basic_istream class.

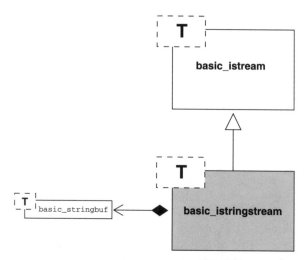

Figure 3.19 Inheritance relationship between the istringstream and basic_istream classes.

This means that the protected and public data members and member functions of basic_istream are all inherited and accessible by the istringstream class.

In contrast to the basic_istream class, which has a basic_streambuf component, and the ifstream, which has a filebuf component, the istringstream class has a stringbuf component, which is a specialized basic_streambuf derived from basic_streambuf. The stringbuf component is connected to a character array, as opposed to a file. The source of a stringbuf is intended to be a memory device. The programmer can have direct access to the istringstream memory device through the stringbuf component. The stringbuf component can be reached via the rdbuf( ) member function.

In the nonobject-oriented standard library, the C++ programmer has access to memory buffers and a set of functions that manipulate character arrays and strings. However, these facilities do not offer the advantages of object orientation. The istringstream class brings object orientation to the character array or memory block. The memory block or memory object can represent buffered or unbuffered data and formatted or unformatted data.

Constructing istringstream Objects

Following are the constructors for istringstream class:

```
explicit basic_istringstream(ios_base::openmode which = ios_base::in);
explicit basic_istringstream(const basic_string<charT,traits,
                      Allocator>& str,
                      ios_base::openmode which = ios_base::in);
```

The istringstream object can be constructed with the default stringbuf buffer component, or the programmer may specify a string to initialize the buffer component of the istringstream.

Accessors for the istringstream Class

The inheritance relationship allows the istringstream class to apply the extraction >> operator to a memory device. The programmer can use the read( ) and the get( ) member functions to extract characters from the block of memory to which the istringstream class object is connected. Because the istringstream class is derived from basic_istream, it also is indirectly derived from the ios class. This means that istringstream has a format state, buffer state, and open state!

The ostringstream Class

The ostringstream class implements the functionality of an object-oriented output memory device. Normally, the cout type basic_ostream object is tied to the console, and the ofstream class is connected to a file or a device recognized as a file. In contrast, the ostringstream class is connected to a block of memory or a character array. The ostringstream class is a model of a character or byte array.

The ostringstream class is derived from the basic_ostream class. Figure 3.20 shows the inheritance relationship between the ostringstream class and the basic_ostream class. This means that the protected and public data members and member functions of basic_ostream are all inherited and accessible by the ostringstream class. The inheritance relationship allows the ostringstream class to apply the insertion << operators to a memory device. The programmer can use the write( ) member function to insert characters into the block of memory to which the ostringstream class object is connected. Because the ostringstream class is derived from basic_ostream, it is also indirectly derived from the ios class. This means that ostringstream has a format state, buffer state, and open state!

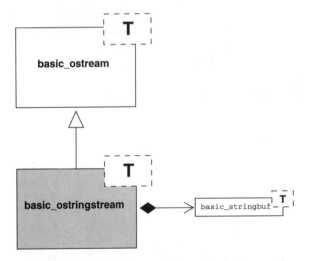

Figure 3.20 Inheritance relationship between the ostringstream and the basic_ostream classes.

Whereas the basic_ostream class has a basic_streambuf component, and the ofstream has a filebuf component, the ostringstream class has a stringbuf component, which is a specialized basic_streambuf derived from basic_streambuf. The stringbuf component is connected to a character array, as opposed to a file. The source and target of a stringbuf is intended to be a memory device. The programmer can have direct access to the ostringstream memory device through the stringbuf component. The stringbuf component can be reached via the rdbuf( ) member function.

The C++ program has access to memory buffers and a set of functions that manipulate character arrays and strings in the nonobject-oriented standard library, but these facilities do not offer the advantages of object orientation. The ostringstream class brings object orientation to the character array or memory block, both of which can represent buffered or unbuffered data, formatted or unformatted data.

The Buffer Component of ostringstream

The ostringstream buffer component is accessed by the rdbuf( ) member function, which returns a pointer to the stringbuf component of the ostringstream class. Through this component, the C++ programmer has access to all of the public member functions of the stringbuf class.

Constructing ostringstream Objects

The reserved area used by the stringbuf component either can be dynamically allocated by the system or provided by the programmer. The constructor used with the ostringstream object will determine whether the ostringstream object is attached to a string. The ostringstream constructor that takes one argument:

```
explicit basic_ostringstream(ios_base::openmode which = ios_base::out);
```

will designate a dynamically allocated buffer for the ostringstream class.

The ostringstream constructor:

```
explicit basic_ostringstream(const basic_string<charT,traits,
                             Allocator>& str,
                             ios_base::openmode which = ios_base::out);
```

will cause the ostringstream class object to be constructed and connected to a string as a buffer.

Accessing the ostringstream Buffer

The character string attached to the ostringstream object can be accessed using the str( ) member function. The str( ) member function returns a copy of the string that the ostringstream object is using. The ostringstream object will be attached to a user-declared string, or the ostringstream object will be attached to a dynamically allocated string that the ostringstream allocates. It is the responsibility of the ostringstream destructor to take care of the space that has been dynamically allocated if the str( ) member function has not been called.

Accessors for the ostringstream Class

The inheritance relationship allows the ostringstream class to apply the insertion << operators to a memory device. The programmer can use the write( ) member function to insert characters into the block of memory to which the ostringstream class object is connected. Because the ostringstream class is derived from basic_ostream, it is also indirectly derived from the ios class. This means that ostringstream has a format state, buffer state, and open state!

stringstream class = istringstream + ostringstream

The stringstream class is another bidirectional (input/output) class. Figure 3.21 shows the components that make up the stringstream class. The stringstream object will have a character array or character string as the source and target of its operations. Though the stringstream class is often overlooked, it is one of the most important classes for tying the iostream family of classes to graphical user interface environments, such as Windows and the Macintosh. Because the stringstream class and its base classes are models of a memory device, insertion and extraction can take place in a device-independent manner. The program in Listing 3.17 shows how the stringstream class is used.

This program implements a simple parenthesis balancer, with the objective of insuring that left and right parentheses are balanced and in the correct order. The program accepts an expression on the command line, then checks this expression for balanced parentheses.

Manipulators

Manipulators are functions or objects that are inserted to or extracted from a stream and affect the format state of the stream. The format state of the stream is represented by the ios component of the stream object under consideration. The ios component has a state variable that specifies the base in which numeric objects are represented—decimal, octal, or hexadecimal. The ios component has width, precision, and fill character components. Manipulators can change the state of these components.

All the state components of the ios class have member functions that can set, unset, or instantiate them, so technically, manipulators are not necessary. However, they help make a program more readable. They provide a level of convenience and expressional elegance. The syntax of manipulators allows them to be inserted into a stream just like any other object in the C++ environment. Table 3.10 lists the 30 predefined manipulators.

The New-Line Manipulator: endl

The endl manipulator is inserted into an ostream class object or one of its derived classes. It causes a new-line character, n, to be inserted into the output stream. The endl manipulator also flushes the stream after \n has been inserted. It is used only on output streams.

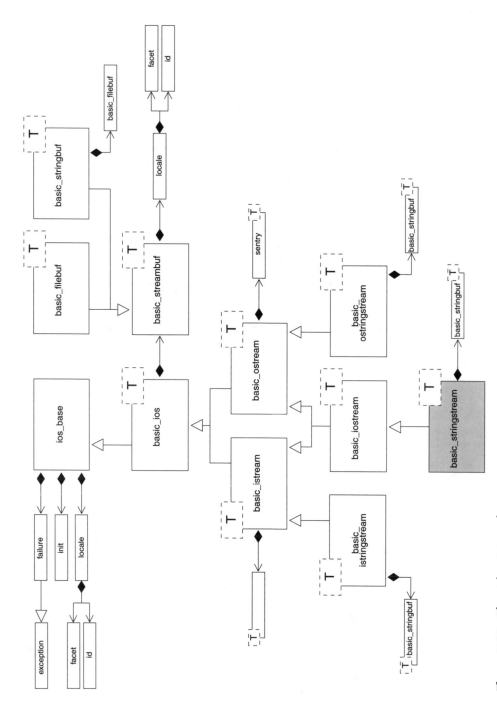

Figure 3.21 The stringstream class components.

Listing 3.17 Using stringstream

```
1    // Listing 3.17
2    // This program shows how manipulators are used with the iostreams
3
4
5
6    #include <iostream>
7    #include <sys/stat.h>
8    #include <dirent.h>           // Requires POSIX compatibility
9    #include <string.h>
10   #include <dir.h>
11   #include <time.h>
12   #include <iomanip.h>
13
14   int main(int Argc,char *Argv[])
15   {
16       if(Argc == 2){
17           DIR *Directory;
18           Directory = opendir(Argv[1]);
19           chdir(Argv[1]);
20           if(!Directory == NULL){
21               float DirectorySize = 0;
22               struct dirent *Entry;
23               struct stat Buffer;
24               Entry = readdir(Directory);
25               while(Entry != NULL)
26               {
27                   if (stat(Entry->d_name,&Buffer) == 0){
28                       DirectorySize = DirectorySize + Buffer.st_size;
29                   }
30                   else{
31                       cerr << "could not stat " << Entry->d_name
32                           << endl;
33                   }
34                   Entry = readdir(Directory);
35               }
36               rewinddir(Directory);
37               cout << "\f";
38               cout.precision(4);
39               Entry = readdir(Directory);
40               while(Entry != NULL)
41               {
42                   cout<< setiosflags(ios_base::left | os_base::fixed);
43                   cout << setfill('*') << setw(20);
44                   stat(Entry->d_name,&Buffer);
45                   cout << Entry->d_name << "\t" << setw(12);
46                   cout << setiosflags(ios::right) << setfill(' ');
47                   cout << dec << Buffer.st_size << "\t "
48                       << setw(12);
```

Listing 3.17 *(Continued)*

```
49                      cout << setiosflags(ios::right) << setfill(' ');
50                  cout << hex << Buffer.st_size << "\t" << setw(9);
51                  cout << setiosflags(ios::right) << showpoint
52                          << setfill(' ');
53                  cout << (Buffer.st_size / DirectorySize * 100)
54                          << '%' << "\t";
55                  cout << setw(9) << setiosflags(ios_base::right)
56                          << scientific;
57                 cout << setfill(' ')
58                          << (Buffer.st_size / DirectorySize * 100)
59                          << '%' << "\t";
60                  cout << setw(12) << setiosflags(ios_base::left);
61                  cout << ctime(&Buffer.st_atime) << endl;
62                  Entry = readdir(Directory);
63              }
64          cout << setprecision(0);
65          cout << setiosflags(ios_base::oct | ios_base::fixed);
66          cout << "Directory Size: " << DirectorySize << endl;
67      }
68      else{
69              cerr << "could not open " << Argv[1] << endl;
70      }
71      closedir(Directory);
72      return(1);
73  }
74  return(0);
75
76 }
```

The Null Manipulator: ends

The ends manipulator causes a NULL to be inserted into an ostream class object or one of its derived classes. This manipulator can be used to convert character arrays to character strings upon insertion to an output stream; it is used only with an output stream. The output stream used with the ends manipulator is usually of the family from the stringstream class. The manipulator can be inserted into the stream like any other object:

```
cout << CharacterArray << ends;
```

Flushing a Stream

The flush manipulator is inserted to an ostream object or one its derived objects. It will flush the buffer component of the ostream object, and affects the stream as if setf(ios::unitbuf) had been called prior to inserting values into the stream.

Table 3.10 Predefined Manipulators

MANIPULATORS	DESCRIPTION
Integer Formatting	
boolalpha(ios_base&)	Extracts or Inserts symbolic representation of true and false, rather than numeric values.
noboolalpha(ios_base&)	Extracts or inserts numeric values.
oct(ios_base&)	Extracts or inserts integer values in octal format.
dec(ios_base&)	Extracts or inserts integer values in decimal format.
hex(ios_base&)	Extracts or inserts integer values in hexadecimal format.
showpos(ios_base&)	Inserts a plus sign in a nonnegative-generated numeric field.
noshowpos(ios_base&)	Removes a plus sign from a nonnegative-generated numeric field.
showbase(ios_base&)	Inserts a prefix that represents the base of the generated integer field: 0 for octal and 0x for hexadecimal.
noshowbase(ios_base&)	Removes the prefix that represents the base of the generated integer field.
setbase(int)	Inserts integers in the specified base.
uppercase(ios_base&)	Inserts X instead of x.
nouppercase(ios_base&)	Inserts x instead of X.
internal(ios_base&)	Inserts fill characters between the sign and the value; pads to the field width.
setfill(int)	Sets the fill character to int.
Real-number Formatting	
showpoint(ios_base&)	Inserts a decimal point into a generated floating-point field.
noshowpoint(ios_base&)	Removes the decimal point of a generated floating-point field.
showpos(ios_base&)	Inserts a plus sign in a nonnegative-generated numeric field.
noshowpos(ios_base&)	Removes a plus sign from a nonnegative-generated numeric field.
uppercase(ios_base&)	Inserts E instead of e.
nouppercase(ios_base&)	Inserts e instead of E.
setprecision(int n)	Sets *n* digits after the decimal point.

Numeric Formatting Manipulators

The manipulators that change the format state of numeric bases have member function counterparts in the ios class. The hex manipulator sets the format state to translate numbers inserted or extracted to the hexadecimal base. The oct manipulator sets the format state to translate numbers inserted or extracted to the octal or base 8. The dec manipulator sets the format state to translate numbers to base 10. These manipulators are mutually exclusive; if they are inserted or extracted from the stream at the same time, the results are unpredictable. The setbase( ) member function takes an int argument and must be 0, 8, 10, or 16. The setbase(int X) member function changes the state of the format stream to represent numbers in base X.

Skipping White Spaces

The ws manipulator skips leading white space characters on input by extracting them from the input stream. White spaces are tabs, spaces, and new-line characters. The ws manipulator is used only with an istream class object or one of its derived classes. The same skipping effect can be achieved by calling the setf(ios::skipws) member function.

Flag Manipulators

The setiosflags( ) and resetiosflags( ) manipulators change the format state variable of the ios component. The flags that these manipulators can turn on and off are the same flags that the ios::setf( ) and ios::unseat( ) member functions access. When flags are passed to the setiosflags( ) and resetiosflags( ) manipulators, they use the full scope resolved name. For example, ios::showpoint would be passed to setiosflags( ) using the following syntax: setiosflags(ios::showpoint) or setioflags(basic_ios::showpoint). Through the use of these manipulators, the programmer can control the format state of the stream.

When the skipws flag is set, the format state of the stream specifies that white space characters will be ignored for input. When the left format flag is set, the format state of the stream specifies that padding used to meet a field width is placed after the actual data value. If the right format flag is set, the format state of the stream specifies that padding used to meet a field width is placed before the actual data value. A set internal format flag describes a format state of the stream, which pads a field width between any sign type (base information or integer sign) and the actual data value. The data will be right-justified. By default, the right format flag is set.

When the showbase format flag is set, the format state of the stream specifies that numeric data will display its base convention for output. The default is numeric data absent of the base conventions. The base convention for hexadecimal numbers is 0x, and the base convention for octal numbers is 0 placed before the number. There is no base convention for decimal numbers. Setting a showpoint format flag describes the format state of the stream in which floating-point numbers will display a decimal point and trailing zeros for output. The decimal point and trailing zeros will be displayed only with a floating-point number with precision greater than zero. As many trailing zeros as needed to meet precision will be used. If this flag is set, and precision is zero, there will be no decimal point or trailing zeros. The showpos format flag, when set, specifies a format state of the stream that displays a plus sign for positive integers for output. Negative integers automatically display a minus sign, regardless of the setting of this flag. The other bases are unsigned. The uppercase format flag, when set, specifies a format state in which numeric data represented with hexadecimal digits will display the hex base indicator (when the showbase format flag is set) and hexadecimal digits A–F in uppercase. The floating point numbers represented in scientific notation will display an uppercase E for output. The default is lowercase.

The hex, oct, or dec format flags can be set so that integer data inserted to or extracted from the stream can be represented in these various bases. If the dec format flag is set, integers will be represented in the decimal base. If the hex format flag is set, integers will be represented in the hexadecimal base. If the oct format flag is set, integers will be represented in the octal base. By default, numeric values retain their original base.

Floating-point numbers can be represented in scientific or fixed notation by setting the scientific or fixed format flags. If the scientific format flag is set, the format state of the stream will represent floating-point data in scientific notation. Scientific notation expresses floating-point numbers with the decimal placed after the first digit. As noted earlier, scientific notation is also calle e-notation. The "e" represents exponentiation of 10 to a power. Floating-point data will be represented in scientific notation if the exponent after the conversion is less than –4 or greater than or equal to the current precision. When the fixed format flag is set, the format state of the stream specifies that floating-point numbers will be displayed in decimal notation with a set number of digits following the decimal, determined by the precision currently set.

The setiosflags( ) method turns the flags specified in its argument on. The programmer can specify a single flag or a combination of flags to be turned on. If more than one flag is specified in the setiosflags( ) argument list, they must be ORed together, for example:

```
setiosflags(ios::scientific | ios::showpoint | ios::unitbuf);
```

The resetiosflags( ) manipulator turns off whichever flag bit is specified. The argument to resetiosflags( ) may be a single flag or a combination of flags ORed together.

Padding and Fill Manipulators

The setw( ) manipulator sets the width of positions that will be inserted to or extracted from a stream. It takes an int argument, which represents the field width size to pad the object with on insertion. The setw( ) manipulator cannot reduce the required size of an object. For instance, if:

```
char CharacterArray[80];
```

is declared, then specifying setw(60) will not truncate the CharacterArray when it is inserted to the output stream. Instead, all of the characters necessary to represent the CharacterArray will be inserted to the output stream. The setw( ) manipulator can increase only the field width of the object to be inserted.

The setfill( ) manipulator accepts an int that represents a character to be used in padding the output. If the actual field width of the object is less than the x_width data member specifies, the remaining positions will be padded with the character passed to the setfill( ) manipulator, and will either be left- or right-justified. The program in Listing 3.18 demonstrates how to use the manipulators in a C++ program.

Listing 3.18 Using Manipulators

```
1    // Listing 3.18 demonstrates how to use manipulators.
2
3    #include <iostream>
4    #include <string>
5    #include <sstream>
6
7    using namespace std;
8
9
10   int main(int argc, char *argv[])
11   {
12       char Character;
13       int LeftParen = 0;
14       int RightParen = 0;
15       int ValidExpression = 1;
16       int Count = 1;
17       stringstream Mystream;
18       for(Count = 1;Count < argc;Count++)
19       {
20           Mystream << argv[Count];
21       }
22       Mystream << ends;
23       if(Mystream.peek() == ')') {
24           ValidExpression = 0;
25       }
26       Mystream.seekg(0,ios::end);
27       Mystream.unget();
28       if(Mystream.peek() == '('){
29           ValidExpression = 0;
30       }
31       Mystream.seekg(0,ios::beg);
32       while(ValidExpression && Mystream.good())
33       {
34
35           Mystream.get(Character);
36           if (Mystream.good() && !Mystream.eof()){
37               cout.put(Character);
38               if(Character == ')'){
39                   RightParen++;
40               }
41               if(Character == '('){
42                   LeftParen++;
43               }
44               if(RightParen > LeftParen){
45                   ValidExpression = 0;
46               }
47           }
48       }
49       if(RightParen != LeftParen){
```

Continues

Listing 3.18   Using Manipulators *(Continued)*

```
50          ValidExpression = 0;
51      }
52      if(!ValidExpression){
53          cerr << "Unbalanced Parenthesis" << endl;
54      }
55      return(ValidExpression);
56
57  }
```

This program accepts a directory name as an argument, and determines the size of the directory, then calculates the percent each file is to the total directory size. Finally, the program prints on the standard output the file name, file size, file size in hexadecimal, percentage to directory size, and the last date that the file was modified. The output is formatted using the format flags and format methods from the ios_base, basic_ios components.

Summary

The C++ iostreams are among the most powerful object-oriented I/O facilities available. The iostreams provide an object-oriented interface to input and output within a C++ program. The iostreams provide object-oriented interfaces to disk access, memory access, and printer access. The iostreams can also be used to access devices such as network cards, tape drives, cdroms, and other I/O peripherals. One of the important features of the iostreams is that they are extensible. The iostreams allow the programmer to add support to I/O support for a device that is not currently supported. The iostreams can be extended to work with interprocess communication and pipes. The iostreams can also be used as is. They provide the programmer with ready-made I/O components that can be used directly. They also provide the programmer with I/O building blocks that can be used to design more complex I/O facilities.

CHAPTER 4

String Classes

"Serious inquiry begins when we are willing to be suprised by the simple . . ."

—NOAM CHOMSKY
LANGUAGE AND THOUGHT

The String Concept

Besides numeric values, strings are the most commonly used data type in a program. In computer parlance, a string is a sequence of characters. Take, for example, the sequences:

twinkle little star

000111001000

yabadabadoo

007

They are all examples of strings. The characters of a string can be numbers, text characters, or special symbols, as long as they exist in the character set in use. A string can be a word, a sentence, or the contents of a file. A subset of consecutive characters of the sequence is called a *substring*. In the sequences just given, "little" or "star" are examples of substrings of the string "twinkle little star." Likewise, "000" or "111001" are examples of substrings of the string "000111001000."

An individual character, a substring, numerous substrings or strings can be the focus of an operation that manipulates a character sequence within the string. There are several operations that manipulate the content of a string or strings. Some of the more common operations are:

- Appending the string.
- Prepending the string.

- Inserting a substring.

- Retrieving a substring.

- Concatenating two or more strings.

An individual character or a substring can be the focus of a search. Determining if a character occurs in a string or the number of times it occurs in a string can be the purpose of a search. Consider the following string:

Jane hid my limb

In this string, i and m occur twice; d, l, j, b, e, n, a, h, and y occur once. After it has been determined that a character is in the string, each occurrence of the character can be replaced with a different character, creating a new string. If all the i's were replaced with a's, the original string would be altered to read:

Jane had my lamb

New characters or strings can be inserted into a string:

Jane had my cloned lamb

A string can be prepended onto an existing string. In this example:

Dr. Jane had my cloned lamb

"Dr." has been prepended to our string. A string can be concatenated onto an existing string, creating a new string. Concatenation simply means "add together." When strings are concatenated, neither string is altered, but a new string is created. The new string will consist of the characters of the first string followed by the characters of the second string. In the following example, the string "in the house." has been added to our string:

Dr.Jane had my cloned lamb + in the house. = Dr.Jane had my cloned lamb in the house.

A search for a sequence of characters or substring can be performed on a string. In the same string, a search for the substring "had my cloned" obviously occurs in the string:

string: Dr.Jane <u>had my cloned</u> lamb in the house.

But the substring "lab" does not occur in the string. The substring "house." can be replaced with the substring "lab." in the next example:

string: Dr.Jane had my cloned lamb in the lab.

A comparison can be made between two strings. Say that a comparison between string1 and string2 is to be performed:

string1: Dr.Jane had my cloned lamb in the house.

string2: Dr.Jane hid my cloned limb in the house.

These strings differ in two places. Comparisons of characters are performed by evaluating each character and continuing to a position where the characters differ. Once a difference is detected, the operation stops. Other operations, such as deleting characters and substrings, determining string length, and copying strings can also be performed on strings. The commonly used string manipulation operations are listed in Table 4.1.

Table 4.1 Common String Manipulation Operations

STRING OPERATIONS	DESCRIPTION
search	Searches a string for a particular character.
append	Adds characters to the end of a string.
concatenate	Adds characters or a string to the end of another.
assign	Assigns a string or a sequence of characters to another string.
copy	Copies one string to another string.
erase	Removes a character from a string.
insert	Places a character in a string.
substring operation	Performs operations on a sequence that is a subset of a string.

Representing Strings

The C++ language supplies many built-in data types. Integer, floating-point, and character are the three standard data types. There are four different kinds of integer data types, three different kinds of floating-point data types, and two different kinds of character data types, all of which are part of the C++ language and declared with a C++ keyword, listed here.

INTEGER	FLOATING POINT	CHARACTER
int	float	char
unsigned int	double	unsigned char
long	long double	
unsigned long		

Although C++ has support for many built-in types, there is no built-in string data type. Instead, the string is represented as an array of characters. Each cell of the array contains a single character, as depicted in Figure 4.1.

For the sequence of characters to be considered a string, and not an arbitrary sequence of characters, a null terminator is placed in the last cell, as shown in the figure. A null terminator appears as /0, the null character, which signifies the end of the string. A string or an array element can be initialized or assigned a null character by using a set of double quotation marks (" "). The null character is placed at the end of the string by the compiler when the array is initialized with a string constant or string literal. This

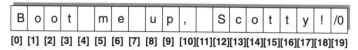

B	o	o	t		m	e		u	p	,		S	c	o	t	t	y	!	/0
[0]	[1]	[2]	[3]	[4]	[5]	[6]	[7]	[8]	[9]	[10]	[11]	[12]	[13]	[14]	[15]	[16]	[17]	[18]	[19]

Figure 4.1 Each cell of the array contains a single character.

null character will extend the length of the string by one. A string literal is a string surrounded by double quotes:

"Boot me up, Scotty!"

"The man from \n U.N.C.L.E. \t"

"\" 7 7 7 - 9 3 1 1 \"

All of these are valid string literals. String literals can contain numerical and special characters, such as:

- linefeeds \n
- tab \t
- carriage return \r
- form feed \f
- backspace \b

The double quotes do not become a part of the string. If double quotes are to be a part of the string, a backslash character used before the quotes (\") distinguishes them from the double quotes encapsulating the string literal. The backslash is used if a backslash (\\) or single quotes (\') are to be a part of the string literal as well.

Once a string is initialized with a string literal, its size is fixed. If a string is initialized with the literal:

"The man from \n U.N.C.L.E. \t"

the length of the character string constant is 28. There are 27 characters between the double quotes, including the spaces and the special characters. The null character makes 28.

An array of characters may simply be a sequence of characters, not a string, stored in an array. The sequence as a single construct may have no meaning, and therefore will not be treated as string with a null terminator. The sequence has a size but no *sentinel*, signifying the end of the sequence. For example, an array can hold the states of multiple circuits, 1 meaning the circuit is open and 0 meaning the circuit is closed. Let's say the following are the states of the eight circuits:

0 1 1 0 0 0 0 1

The states are stored in an array where each element of the array represents the state of a circuit and the index corresponds to the circuit label, as illustrated in Figure 4.2. This is not a string, but this same sequence with a null character placed at the end can be considered a string representing the ASCII code for lowercase a.

The C++ library supplies functions that manipulate the null-terminated character arrays and functions that manipulate a sequence of characters. They are listed in Table 4.2. All

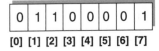

Figure 4.2 The states of a circuit can be stored as a sequence of characters. The index corresponds to the circuit label. This is not a null-terminated string.

of these functions are declared in <string.h>. Functions that manipulate a sequence of characters begin with *mem*. One of the parameters points to the beginning of the string, and another is the number of elements. The functions that manipulate null-terminated character arrays begin with *strn* and *str*. Functions that begin the *strn* also have a parameter that indicates the beginning of the string and the number of elements. In their operations, the number of elements or the null character is used to terminate processing, whichever occurs first. Functions that begin with *str* have parameters that indicate the beginning of the string. In general, their operations use the null character to terminate processing.

The String Class

The C++ standard class library adds to the C++ language the notion of an object-oriented string. The string class encapsulates the attributes of a string and supplies a list of services that allow access to those attributes. The attributes or data component of the class includes:

- Sequence of characters
- Size or length of the sequence of characters
- Type of character in the sequence
- Character traits
- Size of a character
- Allocator
- Iterators

The string class also describes a myriad of services for string manipulation that include:

- Search
- Assign
- Concatenate
- Append

Some of the services are listed by category in Table 4.3.

The string class enables the programmer to manage the storage of strings and character sequences not supplied by the nonobject-oriented string functions. Traditionally, once the size of the string has been allocated, its size is fixed. For example:

```
char Message[] = "hello Janeway";
```

shows that a string has been created that has a size of 14, including the null character. This is the same as allocating a string in this way:

```
char Message[14];
```

The size of this string is static and therefore cannot exceed this size.

Copying a sequence larger than the amount of storage allocated corrupts memory. For example, copying this literal into Message will prove disastrous:

Table 4.2 String Manipulation Functions

STRING FUNCTIONS	DESCRIPTION
Null-Terminated	
strcpy( )	Copies a source string, including the null character, into a destination string.
strcat( )	Appends a copy of the source string, including the null character, to the end of a destination string.
strcmp( )	Compares a source string to a destination string.
strchr( )	Locates the first occurrence of a char in a string.
strrchr( )	Locates the last occurrence of a char in a string.
strspn( )	Computes the length of the maximum initial segment of a string that consists entirely of characters from another string.
strstr( )	Locates the first occurrence of a substring in a string.
strtok( )	Breaks a string into a sequence of tokens. Each token is delimited by characters of another string that serve as separators.
strerror( )	Maps the error number in *errnum* to an error message string.
strlen( )	Computes the length of a string.
strcspn( )	Computes the length of the minimum initial segment of a string that consists of characters not contained in another string.
strpbrk( )	Locates the first occurrence in a string of any character from another string.
strxfrm( )	Transforms a string and places the resulting string into an array.
strncmp( )	Compares not more than *n* characters of a source string to a destination string. Characters that follow the null character are not compared.
strncat( )	Appends a copy of not more than n characters of the source string, including the null character, to the end of a destination string.
strncpy( )	Copies not more than *n* characters (excluding all characters that follow the null character) from a source string to a destination string.
Sequence of Characters	
memcpy( )	Copies *n* characters from the source sequence into the destination sequence.
memove( )	Copies *n* characters from a source sequence into a temporary array of *n* characters, then copies *n* characters to the destination sequence.
memcmp( )	Compares the first *n* characters of the source sequence to the first *n* characters of the destination sequence.
memchr( )	Locates the first occurrence of a character in the first *n* characters of the source sequence.
memset( )	Copies a value into the each of the first *n* characters of the destination.

Table 4.3 String Manipulation Services by Category

METHODS	DESCRIPTION
Element Access	
[], at( )	Returns the character at the given position.
Element Access via Iterator	
begin( )	Returns an iterator that points to the first character.
end( )	Returns an iterator that points past-the-end value.
rbegin( )	Returns reverse_iterator(end( )).
rend( )	Returns reverse_iterator(begin( )).
Data Component Access	
c_str( )	Returns a pointer to the first element of the array whose last element is a null character.
data( )	Returns a pointer to the first element of the array.
Assignment	
assign( )	Assigns a string, a character, a substring to another string.
=	Assigns a string or a character to another string.
Comparisons	
compare( )	Compares a string to another string or array of characters.
Insertion/Append	
insert( )	Inserts a character, characters, subsequence or string at a given position.
+=	Appends a character or string to another string.
append( )	Appends a character, characters, subsequence or string string to another string.
Concatenation	
+	Constructs a new string by putting one string after another.
Search	
find( )	Variations of this function will find and return the starting position of a subsequence.
Replace/Erase/Clear	
replace( )	Can replace a specific character or substring of a string.
erase( )	Removes a character or characters from a string.
clear( )	Erases all the characters in the string.
empty( )	Returns size( ) == 0.
Substring Operations	
substr( )	Returns a substring of a string.

Continues

Table 4.3   String Manipulation Services by Category (*Continued*)

METHODS	DESCRIPTION
Statistical	
size( )	Returns the number of characters in the string.
length( )	Returns size( ).
max_size( )	Returns the maximum size of the string.
resize( )	Changes the length of the string to the given size.
reserve( )	Informs the string object of a future size change.
Input/Output	
<<, >>	Insertion and extraction operators.
getline( )	Reads a line of characters terminated by the eol to a string.
Copy/Swap	
swap( )	Swaps the contents of two strings.
copy( )	Copies a string to another string.

```
strcpy(Message, "Boot me up Scotty!");
```

because this literal contains 18 characters. However, the character sequence of the string class is dynamic. A sequence of a longer length can be assigned without restraint:

```
string Message("hello Janeway");
Message = "Boot me up Scotty!";
```

because memory can be reserved, allocated, and deallocated automatically. The length of the sequence at initialization was 13, and with the new assignment has grown to 18 characters. Because the string object does not utilize the null character, the length of the sequence is precisely the number of characters in the literal.

Prior to the introduction of the standard C++ string class, multiple versions of a string class existed. Every C++ compiler had its own version of the string class. Some versions offered certain functionality, while other versions did not. Some implementations offered the same functionality but differed in their implementation. This altered the performance and behavior of the service. Sometimes there was inconsistency in the interface or in what the services were called; the same service might have different names from one implementation to another. This type of inconsistency demanded that there be some type of standard implementation of the string class.

Basic String Class

The standard C++ string class is basic_string defined in <string>. This class is not composed of any other class, nor does it inherit any classes, it has no hierarchical structure. Figure 4.3 shows the class relationship diagram for the string class. The basic_string class is a class template, and has three classes to which it is associated, the template parameters: charT is the character type contained in the string, traits represents the

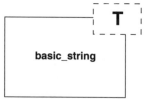

Figure 4.3 String class relationship.

character traits, and Allocator represents the encapsulation of information about the memory model.

Basic String Class Template Parameters

This code snippet is the beginning of the class template declaration for basic_string:

```
namespace std{
   template <class charT,
            class traits = char_traits<charT>,
            class Allocator = allocator<charT> >
      class basic_string{
      public:
        ...
      };
   }
```

The second parameter, traits, and the third parameter, Allocator, have default values of char_traits and allocator respectively; char_traits and allocator are themselves class templates. Their template parameter is charT.

Because basic_string is a class template, the programmer can determine the character type the string will contain. Note, it may be necessary to use other character types contained in another character set. The most commonly used characters are contained in the ASCII set, which has 256 characters consisting of the upper- and lowercase letters, digits, special characters, symbols, and control codes. The programmer may use a different set of characters if he or she finds the ASCII character set deficient. If the programmer needs to manipulate other languages not easily represented by the ASCII code, or is programming in a domain that uses special characters not found in the ASCII code, another character set can be used by the string class. One such character set is Unicode, a 16-character encoding scheme established by the Unicode Consortium. It contains more than 65,000 distinct characters, and was designed to support the interchange, display, and processing of written text of several languages.

Associated with the character type are the *character traits*. The character traits are encapsulated in the char_traits class. This class declares the types and functions needed to manipulate the character type. The functions define comparisons, equality, assignment, and so on among characters. The actual definition of the char_traits class is totally dependent on the character type being used by the string; that is, each character type will have its own definition of this class. These functions and types are used by other classes, such as the string class and iostream classes. For example, when two strings are compared for equality, the characters of one string are compared with the characters of another string. This string comparison operation calls the comparison operation of the char_traits class defined for that particular character type. Thus, the character traits must be specialized for the specific character type in use.

An allocator is the third template parameter. The allocator class encapsulates information about the characteristics of the memory model in use. Stack and heap, flat, or segmented memory models will affect the size and behavior of pointers, specifically, iterators that are widely used by many of the classes in the standard C++ class library.

Two important typedefs involving basic_string will be found in any standard implementation of C++:

```
typedef basic_string<char> string;
typedef basic_string<wchar_t> wstring;
```

The first type definition declares a string class in which the character type is the built-in type char. This type definition will allow for conventional declaration of objects of type string instead of basic_string. The second type definition declares a wstring class in which the character type is wchar_t, which t is called a *wide character* because it is represented by 16 bits as opposed to the built-in char that is a *narrow character* represented by 8 bits. Wide characters can be 2 or more bytes, such as the characters in the Unicode character set. The character traits of wide characters are declared in struct char_traits<wchar_T> and already defined. Once the string class has been instantiated, a string object can be constructed.

String Class Services

Some of the most commonly used services of the basic_string class are:

- Constructors
- Destructors
- Assignment functions and operators
- Accessors
- Copiers

String Object Construction

The basic_string class has six constructors:

```
explicit basic_string (const Allocator& a = Allocator());
basic_string(const basic_string& str, size_type pos = 0,
             size_type n = npos, const Allocator& a = Allocator());
basic_string(const charT* s, size_type n,
             const Allocator& a = Allocator());
basic_string(const charT* s, const Allocator& a = Allocator());
basic_string(size_type n, charT c,
             const Allocator& a = Allocator());
template <class InputIterator>
   basic_string(InputIterator begin, InputIterator end,
               const Allocator& a = Allocator());
```

First here is explicit, a constructor with a single parameter that is explicitly called. This means that the constructor is invoked only when the argument type matches the parameter type exactly. The compiler will not perform any type conversion. For example, a constructor can expect an int, but a char can be implicitly converted to an int when called:

```
class ThisClass{
public:
    ThisClass(int x){intType = x;}
    ...
};

void main(void)
{
    char letter = 'b';
    ThisClass t(letter);
    ...
}
```

In this case, the character is implicitly converted to its numeric representation. If a constructor is explicit, then the constructor has to be invoked explicitly. In this case, an error will occur if the constructor is called with int:

```
class ThisClass{
public:
    explicit ThisClass(int x){intType = x;}
    ...
};

void main(void)
{
    char letter = 'b';
    ThisClass t(letter); // an error
    ...
}
```

Another constructor is a template function. Actually, all member functions of a template class are template functions, but some member functions may require an additional template parameter in addition to those defined for the class.

Each constructor requires an allocator object, which has a default value. The default value is normally adequate, but for special applications or computers with unusual word sizes, it may be necessary to define a new allocator. If the default values were used, then:

```
string Name;
```

would invoke the explicit constructor.

A basic_string object can be initialized:

- As empty
- With a null-terminated string or substring
- With another string object

- With a substring of a string object

- With a sequence of characters

When a string object is constructed, it affects the string data, the size of the string, and the capacity of the string. A string object can be initialized as empty by calling the explicit constructor using the default value for the allocator, as in the example just given. There the string object Name has been initialized as empty. The length or size of the data is 0. The string object can be initialized with a null-terminated string or substring. As mentioned earlier, a null-terminated string is an array of characters with a null character in the last cell of the array. An array of characters can be declared with an array or with a pointer. The following declares arrays of 13 and 14 characters, and initializes them with string literals using both methods:

```
char Arr[14] = "hello scotty!";
char *Ptr = new char(13);
Ptr = "hello spock!";
```

String objects can now be constructed using character arrays:

```
string Str1(Arr, 13);
string Str2(Ptr);
```

The constructors accept pointer constants. In the first string construction, Str1, the name of an array written without the indexes is interpreted as a pointer constant. The size of the literal is specified. The size is the number of characters in the literal; null characters are not utilized. The pointer constant or the actual string literal, which is a const char pointer, can be used:

```
string Str1("hello scotty!", 13);
string Str2("hello spock!");
```

A string object can be initialized with another string object:

```
string Str3(Str1);
```

This construction utilizes the copy constructor. It takes four arguments; the last three have default values.

There are two constructors that can be used to initialize a string object with an arbitrary sequence. One will initialize a string object with multiple copies of the character type:

```
char Letter = 'A';
string Str4(12,Letter);
```

In this example, a string object, Str4, is initialized with 12 copies of A. The other constructor is a template function. The template parameters for this constructor are input iterators. Any class that has input iterators can be used to initialize the string object. For example:

```
wstring WStr1(Str1.begin(), Str1.end());
```

initializes a wide character string object with a sequence of narrow characters. The size of the string object will be Str1.begin( ) - Str1.end( ).

Constructing String Objects with Substrings

The characters of the string are numbered, starting at the index 0 and ending at index size( ) - 1. Therefore, substrings are conveyed as a character position, plus a number of characters. A substring of a string object can be used to initialize another string object. The copy constructor has three parameters that contain default values:

```
basic_string(const basic_string& str, size_type pos = 0,
             size_type n = npos,
             const Allocator& a = Allocator());
```

Note that pos has a default value of 0, meaning the copy will start at index 0; n has a default value of npos and is initialized to the largest possible value. All of the characters of the basic_string object are copied by default. To copy a substring of the object, pos and/or n are given new values. Consider the following:

```
string Str5(Str1, 3, 7);
```

The string stored in the Str1 is "hello scotty!" Str5 is initialized with a substring of this string starting at index 3 then adding 7 additional characters. Str5 string now contains:

"lo scot"

Figure 4.4 shows how the Str5 string object is initialized with a substring of Str1.

Substrings of null-terminated strings can be used to initialize string objects by invoking this constructor:

```
basic_string(const charT* s, size_type n,
             const Allocator& a = Allocator());
```

In this example:

```
string Str6(Ptr,5);
```

Str6 is initialized with the substring "hello." Ptr is the base address, or index 0, and there are 5 additional characters in the substring. Pointer arithmetic can be used to offset the starting position. In the following example:

```
string Str7(Ptr+3,8);
```

Str7 is initialized with the substring "lo spock." The substring is copied starting from position 3 then adds 8 characters.

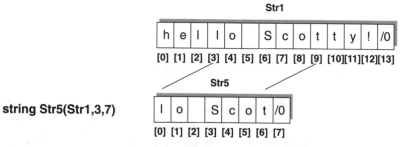

Figure 4.4 The Str5 string object is initialized with a substring of Str1.

String Assignment

Assignment of strings is performed with operators and functions:

```
basic_string& assign(const basic_string&);
basic_string& assign(const basic_string& str,size_type pos,size_type n);
basic_string& assign(const charT* s, size_type n);
basic_string& assign(const charT* s);
basic_string& assign(size_type n, charT c);
template<class InputIterator>
  basic_string& assign(InputIterator first,InputIterator last);

basic_string& operator=(const basic_string& str);
basic_string& operator=(const charT* s);
basic_string& operator=(charT c);
```

As in construction, we can assign to a string object, a string literal, a substring of another string object, a string object, or a null-terminated character array to a string object. When using assign( ), the parameters are very similar:

```
Str1.assign(Str2);       // Str1 is assign Str2
Str3.assign(Str4,0,12); // Str3 is assign Str4 starting at index 0 and
                         // ending at index 11
Str3.assign(Str4,3,7);   // Str3 is assigned a substring of Str4
                         // starting at index 3 and ending at index 9
Str5.assign(Ptr,12);     // Str5 is assigned Ptr starting at index 0
                         // and ending at index 11
Str5.assign(Ptr+3,6);    // Str5 is assigned Ptr starting at index 3
                         // and ending at index 8
Str6.assign(Arr);        // Str6 is assigned Arr
Str7.assign(Str6.begin(), Str6.end()); // Str7 is assigned Str6 using
                         // input iterators
```

With the assignment operators, string objects can be assigned other string objects and character arrays:

```
Str3 = Str1;
Str4 = Ptr;
Str5 = "hello janeway!";
```

Although string objects cannot be initialized during construction with the char type, a single character can be assigned:

```
Str4 = letter;
Str4 = 's';
Str4 = "s";
```

Assignment to References

The basic_string class supports subscripting. Subscript operations return a reference to a value, in this case, a reference to a character type. This operation can be used on the left side of an assignment expression:

```
Str4 = Ptr;
Str4[9] = 'o';
```

In this example, a new character is assigned to a specific position in the string. This changes Str4 from "hello spock!" to "hello spook!"

Accessing the String Data Component

The accessors of the string class return the value of a particular attribute. The most commonly used accessors of the string class return:

- The sequence of characters
- The size or length of the sequence
- A particular character from that sequence
- The allocator

It is important to note that the data component of a string class consists of more than simply a sequence of characters. The class has iterators, size attributes, char_trait attributes, as well as a sequence of character attributes. When we refer to the string class or the data component of the string class, we are referring to *all* of its attributes. The accessor methods for the string class return various attributes of the data component.

Accessing the Character Sequence

The manner in which the character sequence is actually stored in the string object is hidden from the user. It is probably not stored in an array, but there are two string operations that return pointers to a buffer or array where the character sequence is stored. Figure 4.5 shows the relationship among the const pointer, the array, and the actual storage of the character sequence. The array is allocated by the string object and used by these accessors:

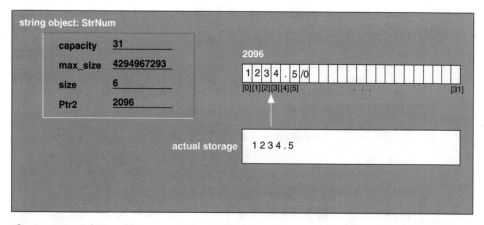

Figure 4.5 Relationship among the const pointer, the array, and the actual storage of the character sequence.

```
const charT* c_str() const;
const charT* data() const;
```

For a string object, c_str( ) will return a const pointer to a null-terminated array of characters. The size of the array will be the number of characters in the string, plus the null character. Also, for a string object, data( ) will return a const pointer to an array of characters in which the size is the exact number of elements in the string. Use c_str( ) when further manipulation of the sequence requires the string functions or functions that utilize the null terminator. For example, in:

```
string StrNum("1234.5");
const char *Ptr2;
double Number;
Ptr2 = StrNum.c_str();
Number = atof(Ptr2);
```

the return value of StrNum.c_str( ) is assigned to a const pointer, Ptr2. The Ptr2 value is converted to a double and stored in Number. It may be necessary to use functions outside of the string class to perform operations that are not supplied by the string class. This is one way for these functions to operate on the character sequence of the string object; but to keep the object-oriented paradigm, the services or operations can be added to the string class by extending the class. This will be discussed later in this chapter.

Accessing a Substring

The following accessor will return a basic_string object in which the character sequence is a substring of the sequence of the const string object:

```
basic_string substr(size_type pos = 0,size_type n = npos) const;
```

The beginning of the substring will start at n; n–pos characters are copied to the new string object. For example:

```
string NewStr();
NewStr = Str1.substr(0,11);
```

Str1 contains the character sequence "hello scotty!" and NewStr will contain the substring "hello scott".

Accessing Elements of the Character Sequence

Subscripting is one way to access individual elements of the character sequence:

```
const_reference operator[](size_type pos) const;
reference operator[]( size_type pos);
```

In the example demonstrating assignment to a reference, the subscript operation was on the left side of the assignment and a non-const string was being indexed. The statement returned a reference. But when a const string is being indexed, as in this example, the operator returns a const reference. When the subscript operation is on the right side of the assignment operator, the const reference returned can only be used as a value:

```
Letter = Str5[1];
```

Str4[3] returns "e" that is assigned to Letter. Letter now contains "e."

Another method used to access individual elements of the character sequence is the at( ) member functions:

```
const_reference at(size_type n) const;
reference at(size_type n);
```

These member functions perform similarly to the subscript operations. The following example demonstrates subscript operations using at( ) member functions:

```
Letter = Str5.at(1);
Str4.at(9) = 'o';
```

Accessing Elements of the Character Sequence Using Iterators

The string class includes eight iterator declarations, all random-access iterators:

```
iterator begin() const;
const_iterator begin() const;
iterator end();
const_iterator end() const;
reverse_iterator rbegin();
const_reverse_iterator rbegin() const;
reverse_iterator rend();
const_reverse_iterator rend() const;
```

The iterators point to elements in the string object. The dereferencing of an iterator using the * operator returns the element to which the iterator points. Therefore, iterators can be used to move sequentially through the characters in the sequence by incrementing or decrementing the iterators. The begin( ) method returns an iterator (a const_iterator for a const string object), which points to the first character of the sequence. The end( ) method returns an iterator pointing to one past the last character in the sequence. The rbegin( ) and rend( ) methods both return reverse_iterators (const_reverse_iterators for const string objects), which point to the last and the first character in the sequence, respectively. You can look at rbegin( ) as the equivalent of reverse_iterator(end( )), and rend( ) as equivalent to reverse_iterator(begin( )). The rbegin( ) and rend( ) methods can be used to traverse through the character sequence in reverse order. Listing 4.1 demonstrates how begin( ), end( ), rbegin( ), and rend( ) can be used to traverse a character sequence.

Because all of the iterators are random-access, they can directly access any character in the sequence by using pointer arithmetic. Consider lines 10 through 14 from Listing 4.1:

```
10        string NewStr("explore new worlds..");
11        string::iterator F;
12        F = NewStr.begin();
13        string::reverse_iterator R;
14        R = NewStr.rbegin();
```

The following code:

```
cout << *(P + 3) << *(R + 4) ;
```

Listing 4.1 Traversing a Character Sequence

```
1    Listing 4.1
2    #include <string>
3    #include <iostream>
4    #include <string.h>
5
6    using namespace std;
7
8    void main(void)
9    {
10       string NewStr("explore new worlds..");
11       string::iterator F;
12       F = NewStr.begin();
13       string::reverse_iterator R;
14       R = NewStr.rbegin();
15
16       while(F != NewStr.end())
17       {
18            cout << *F;
19            F++;
20       }
21       cout << endl;
22
23       while(R != NewStr.rend())
24       {
25            cout << *R ;
26            R++;
27       }
28       cout << endl;
29
30   }
31
```

would output "ll". In this line, *(P + 3) accesses the first "l" in the sequence, and *(R + 4) accesses the last "l" in the sequence. Table 4.4 shows the output from Listing 4.1.

Accessing Information about the String Object

These accessors return information concerning the storage of a const string object:

```
size_type size() const;
size_type length() const;
size_type max_size() const;
size_type capacity() const;
bool empty() const;
```

On the surface, it looks as if length() would return the length of the character sequence, and size() would report the size of the string object. However, length() and size() both return the number of characters in the sequence.

Table 4.4 Output from Listing 4.1

explore new worlds..
..sdlrow wen erolpxe

The max_size( ) method returns the largest number of characters that can be placed in the string object. The max_size( ) calculation is memory-model-dependent. For instance, the max_size( ) method will return the number of characters that take up no more than 64K in an MS-DOS or 16-bit Windows environment. Likewise, the member function will return a much larger number of characters in virtual paging operating system environments like Unix, VMS, or OS/2. The reason max_size( ) returns a larger possible number of characters in these environments is due to the virtual memory management capabilities and flat memory models of these operating systems. They do not have 64K segment limits, so all available RAM can be used to store the characters. Furthermore, because they are virtual paging operating systems, the operating system can use disk space as an internal memory supplement. Of course, the maximum amount of virtual space that can be allocated for a string is a theoretical number, and doesn't always mean that such an allocation can be practically made.

The capacity( ) method reports the largest number of characters that can be stored without reallocating more memory. Whereas the max_size( ) member function returns the largest possible number of characters that can be stored in the string object, the capacity( ) member function reports only how many characters can be stored before more memory has to be reallocated. Because the string object has automatic memory management, it increases the amount of memory that it needs as necessary. As the user inserts characters into the sequence, and the string object does not have enough memory available for those additional characters, more memory is allocated. How much memory does the string object allocate? This is dependent upon the operating system environment. The size( ) – capacity( ) indicates the number of characters that can be added to the sequence without reallocating more storage. The empty( ) method returns the Boolean value to the expression size( ) == 0.

This accessor:

```
allocator_type get_allocator() const;
```

will return the allocator of a const string object. The size( ) and capacity( ) services report back to the user information about the storage of the object.

Memory Management of the String Object

Other services provided by the basic_string class allow the user to alter or change the size of the sequence. Since the string object's size is dynamic, whenever a new character sequence of a different length is assigned to the object, the size of the sequence is changed automatically. These services allow the user to explicitly change the size of the sequence, as shown here:

```
void resize(size_type n, charT c);
void resize(size_type n);
void reserve(size_type res_arg = 0);
```

The resize( ) method changes the size of the character sequence by creating a replacement sequence of the size specified by n. If n is less than or equal to size( ), a new character sequence is created that is the same as the original sequence reduced by size( )–n. If n is larger than size( ), the sequence is padded by n–size( ) of the specified character c; and if no character is given, the sequence is padded with the null character. The size( ) method will return n, which has to be less than or equal to max_size( ). Say that the original character sequence is "hello janeway!" of the string object Str5; size( ) will return a value of 14. If the message:

```
Str5.resize(9);
```

were sent, the sequence would be reduced by four characters, and the new sequence would be "hello jan". The size( ) method would return 9. If these messages:

```
Str5.resize(14);
Str5.resize(17, 'e');
```

were sent, in the first case, the sequence would be extended by five null characters, and the new sequence would be "hello jan   ". The size( ) method would return 14. In the second case, the sequence would be extended by three e characters, and the new sequence would be "hello jan   eee". The size( ) would return 17.

The reserve( ) method sets aside memory of the size specified by the argument for the character sequence:

```
void reserve(size_type res_arg = 0);
```

It ensures that capacity( ) will return a value equal to or greater than res_arg. The resize( ) and reserve( ) methods cause memory to be reallocated. The resize( ) method is used when the size of the sequence is not large enough or is too large to accommodate the characters. With resize( ), the size of the sequence can be increased or decreased. If the new size is less than the capacity, then no reallocation will take place. If the new size is larger than the capacity, more storage is reallocated and capacity will be equal to or greater than the new size. Figure 4.6 shows when resize( ) affects the size and the capacity of a string object.

The reserve( ) method affects capacity. If the argument for reserve( ) is greater than the value of capacity( ), reserve( ) causes the capacity to be increased to that value or greater. It does not affect size( ). When anticipating the size of a sequence, reserve( ) can be called to assure that enough storage has been allocated to accommodate the sequence. This is done to prevent reallocation when any type of resizing of storage is performed. Figure 4.7 shows how reserve( ) affects the capacity of the string object. Reallocation of storage affects the validation of pointers, references, and iterators of the sequence of characters.

Copying and Swapping

The character sequence of a string object can be copied to a buffer located outside the string object:

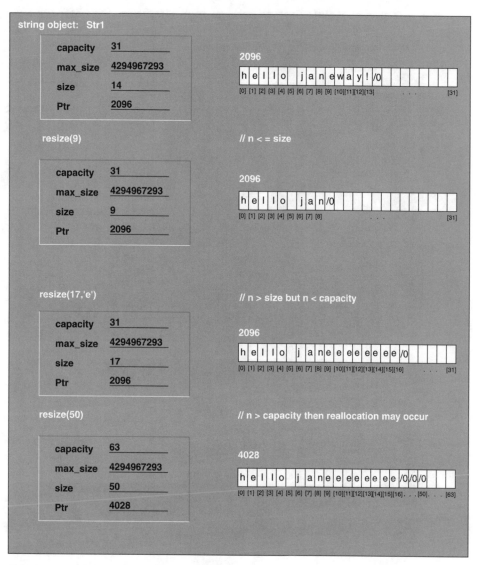

Figure 4.6 When resize( ) affects the size and the capacity of a string object.

```
size_type copy(charT* s, size_type n, size_type pos = 0) const;
```

Starting at position pos, n characters are copied from the const string object's character sequence to the buffer pointed to by s; pos has to be less than or equal to the size of the sequence. The number of characters copied is determined by whichever value is less: n or size( )–pos. The number of characters copied is returned. The buffer must be a size equal to or greater than that number. In the following example, "hello scotty!" from the string object Str1 is copied to the Message array:

```
int Size;
char *Message;
```

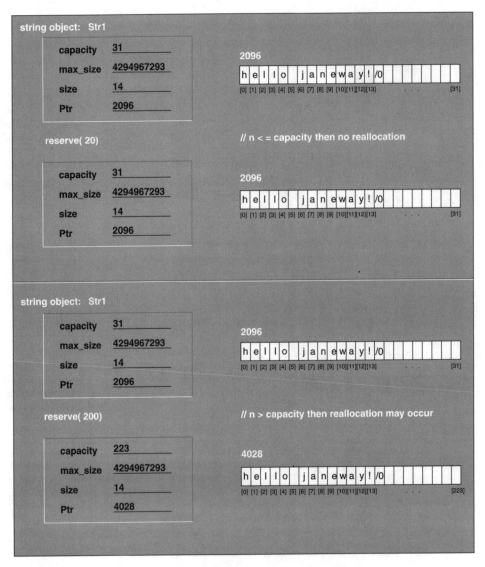

Figure 4.7 How reserve( ) affects the capacity of the string object.

```
Message = new char(Str1.size());
Size = Str1.copy(Message, Message.size(), 0);
```

A substring can also be copied by specifying the range of the substring indicated by the last two parameters:

```
Size = Str1.copy(Message,7, 6);
```

This copies the substring "scotty!" to the array.

The swap( ) method copies the sequence of the string object with the sequence of the string object:

```
void swap(basic_string<charT, traits, Allocator>& s);
```

If the size of one character sequence is larger than the size and/or capacity of the other, the capacity and size will be increased to accommodate the new assignment. Conversely, the size of the string object that now contains the smaller sequence will be reduced in size and capacity.

Exception Handling

The errors that occur most commonly when manipulating the string object are made when writing or reading beyond the end of the character sequence or creating a string object sequence that is too large. This can happen when assigning or initializing a string object with a sequence whose size exceeds max_size( ) or the largest possible number of elements controllable by the string object. If a string object is assigned the contents of a file, this can easily occur.

If such a value is used as a parameter for a service, out_of_range and length_error exception objects are thrown. These exceptions can also be thrown if an operation that accesses a position in the sequence exceeds the size of the sequence. These logical errors can be easily avoided by using the size( ), length( ), and/or max_size( ) methods, which return the size of the current sequence and the maximum size of a sequence, respectively, prior to the call to the operation. This would void the exception, for example:

```
string Str;
...

FileSize = filelength(InFile.rdbuf()->fd());
if(FileSize > Str.max_size()){
   // do something
}
```

The size of the file is checked to determine if it is larger than the maximum size of a character sequence. To prevent accessing a position in the sequence that exceeds the length of the sequence, call the size( ) or length( ) member functions:

```
     ...
if(SeqPos > Str.size()){
   // do something
}
```

Once this is done, a sequence can be assigned, appended, or inserted to the string object without the fear of an exception being thrown. Nevertheless, to handle an exception, an exception handler must be created. This is the general structure of an exception handler for a string object:

```
try{
     // code here
}
catch(length_error X){
     // exception handling code for length_error object
}
catch(out_of_range Y){
     // exception handling code for out_of_range object
}
```

Exceptions also can be thrown when attempting to construct string objects. A length_error object is thrown when attempting to construct a string object and initializing it with npos copies of a given character. An npos value is a static value that represents the largest value possible for size_type. The length of a sequence should always be less than npos. An out_of_range object is thrown when attempting to construct a string object and initializing it with an array of characters with a length equal to npos. Attempting to copy one string object to another when the starting position of the sequence, pos, is greater than the size of the sequence will also cause an out_of_range object to be thrown. All of the following will generate the exceptions described:

```
char P1[19] = "the final frontier";
string S1("no man has gone");
string S3(string::npos,'o');    // length_error - n==npos
string S2(P,string::npos);      // out_of_range - n==npos
string S4(S1,20);               // out_of_range - pos > S1.size()
```

Other operations, such as assign( ), copy( ), and substr( ), will all generate exception objects if the position is greater than the size of the sequence. This is a type of *range checking.* The number of characters copied or assigned can be larger than the size of the sequence. This will not generate an exception. Such a value, even if it is string::npos, will be interpreted by the compiler as the rest of the characters in the sequence. The at( ) method also throws an exception if the position is greater than the size( ), but the subscript operator does not throw an exception. The following are examples of local errors that would cause an exception to be thrown:

```
char P2[22] = "these are the voyages";
string S3(P2);
string S5;
S2.assign(S1, 20, 20);          // out_of_range - pos > S1.size()
S2.copy(S5, string::npos, 3);   // out_of_range - pos > S1.size()
S3.substr(30, string::npos);    // out_of_range - pos > S1.size()
Letter = S5.at(3);              // out_of_range - pos > S1.size()
Letter = S5[2];                 // exception not thrown
```

The resize( ) method will throw a length_error if n is greater than max_size( ).

Extending the String Class

The mystring class introduced in Chapter 2 is an example of extending the string class by inheritance. In Listing 4.2, mystring inherits basic_string, creating a new string class that can convert lowercase to uppercase and remove all the white spaces from a sequence.

The mystring class acts as an interface class for the built-in C++ function toUpper( ). It is wrapped in the member function toUpper( ). The removeWhitespace( ) member function calls the find( ) and erase( ) methods of the basic_string class. The find( ) method searches the character sequence for an occurrence of a white space. If it finds one, it returns the position in the sequence of the white space. The erase( ) method removes the character, replacing it with nothing. The size of the sequence is reduced, and all charac-

Listing 4.2 Extending the String Class

```
1     Listing 4.2
2     #include <string>
3     #include <iostream>
4     #include <string.h>
5
6     using namespace std;
7
8     class mystring : public string{
9     public:
10        mystring(char *X);
11        void toUpper(void);
12        void removeWhitespace(void);
13    };
14
15
16    mystring::mystring(char *X) : string(X)
17    {
18    }
19
20    void mystring::toUpper(void)
21    {
22
23        char *X;
24        int N = length();
25        int Index;
26        X = new char[length() + 1];
27        strcpy(X,data());
28        for(Index = 0;Index < N;Index++)
29        {
30                X[Index] = toupper(X[Index]);
31        }
32        replace(0,N,X,N);
33
34    }
35
36    void mystring::removeWhitespace(void)
37    {
38
39        int N;
40
41        while(N != string::npos)
42        {
43                N = find(" ");
44                if(N != string::npos){
45                    erase(N,1);
46                }
47        }
48
```

Continues

Listing 4.2 Extending the String Class (*Continued*)

```
49    }
50
51
52    void main(void)
53    {
54        mystring X("started in lower case");
55        X.toUpper();
56        X.removeWhitespace();
57        cout << X;
58
59    }
60
```

ters after the removed space are shifted. Once all of the white spaces have been removed, find( ) returns string::npos, which indicates there are no longer any white spaces contained in the sequence. Table 4.5 shows the output of the driver in Listing 4.2.

Summary

A string can be a word, a sentence, or the contents of a file. A substring is a subset of consecutive characters. A string can be represented as an array of characters. Those characters can be an arbitrary sequence which, as a single construct, has no meaning; or those characters can be a sequence of characters with a null character in the last cell. The null character is placed at the end of the sequence if the string is initialized or assigned a *string literal*, which is is surrounded with double quotes.

The basic_string class is an object-oriented string that encapsulates the attributes of a string and supplies a list of services that allow access to those attributes. The class is defined in <string>. It is a template class with three template parameters: charT, traits, Allocator. The traits and Allocator parameters have default values of char_traits and allocator. The char_traits class declares types and functions needed to manipulate the character type. The character type charT can be a wide or narrow character. The string and wstring are type definitions in which the basic_string character types are char and wchar, respectively.

A basic_string object can be constructed and initialized as empty, with a null-terminated string or substring, with another string object, with a substring of a string object, or with a sequence of characters. A string object cannot be *constructed* with a single character, but it can be *assigned* a single character. The sequence of characters can be accessed with the c_str( ) or data( ) methods. A substring of the sequence can be

Table 4.5 Output from Listing 4.2

STARTEDINLOWERCASE

accessed by the substr( ) method. Individual characters can be accessed by the subscript operator or with iterators.

The size, length, and capacity of the object can be accessed with the size( ), length( ) and capacity( ) methods. The sequence can be resized with the resize( ) method, which concatenates or pads the sequence. The reserve( ) method can be called to assure that enough storage has been allocated to accommodate the sequence. This prevents reallocation of storage when resizing is performed.

The basic_string object's sequence can be copied to a buffer outside the object, or the sequence can be swapped with another basic_string object's sequence. The basic_string class can be extended by inheritance.

CHAPTER 5

The Exception Classes

"The nature of the model required to describe a system depends on the nature of the apparatus it is interacting with."

—ALASTAIR RAE
QUANTUM PHYSICS ILLUSION OR REALITY

The exception classes are designed to help the programmer deal with software component failure. In this case, the software components are objects in the standard C++ class library. If, while the user is putting one of these objects to work and an error occurs, the object is designed to throw some type of exception to let the user know that the object cannot continue to function properly, the user can take corrective action, if possible, or exit the software subsystem in an orderly manner. This type of response to software failure is often referred to as *fault tolerance*. A fault-tolerant system is one that either corrects or survives *software faults*.

> A fault-tolerant computer system is one that continues to operate even after some of its components fail (Borg, 1987).

> Fault-tolerant systems provide for graceful degradation; a fault-tolerant system with failed components provides service, but at reduced levels. Fault-tolerant systems are designed so that a failed component can be taken off-line, repaired, and placed back on-line all while the system provides uninterrupted service (Deitel, 1990).

> Fault-tolerant systems include design features that counter the effects of hardware or software faults. . . . A fault-tolerant system is a system that is insensitive to defects (Musa, 1987).

The exception classes in the standard C++ class library are designed to help the developer deal with faults, exceptions, failures, and errors. To get the most out of the exception classes and the C++ exception-handling mechanism, it is important to make a distinction between faults, exceptions, failures, and errors. Therefore, some definitions are in order.

What Is a Software Error?

There is no shortage of definitions of what a software error is, many of them are different. Chapters, indeed, entire books, have been written in attempts to describe what a software error is or is not. We will spare the reader most of the philosophical debate; but to reach a common understanding of how to use the exception classes properly, we must lay some ground rules concerning errors and software defects. A simplified definition for software error is that the software performs in a way that violates the software's specification or fails to perform according to its specification.

Software Specifications

A software specification is the measuring stick that we use to decide whether a piece of software has defects. We cannot determine a piece of software's correctness without some sort of specification. The specification contains the description and requirements of what a piece of software is supposed to do and what it is not supposed to do. It is true that producing accurate software specifications is a tall order! Complete, thorough, and accurate specifications are notoriously difficult to produce. Specifications typically fall between two extremes: The spec may come as a set of formal documents and requirements compiled by end users, analysts, user interface engineers, domain specialists, and others; or the spec may only have been a set of goals and loosely defined objectives verbally communicated to the software designers and developers.

Whichever the case, specifications are the starting point when discussing what is and what is not an error. The higher quality the specification, the easier it is to define what an error is. When a project's specification is vague, elements are poorly defined, and the requirements are not definitive, the definition of software error for that particular project is a moving target. Under those conditions, we cannot say whether the software is in error or not! Vaguely defined specifications lead to vaguely defined errors. (For a more complete discussion of software errors see Kamer, 1988; Musa et al., 1987; and Kan, 1995.)

In general, software errors and defects should be detected and corrected during the various testing phases, specifically, during:

- Review of the specifications
- Testing of the design phase (object-oriented walk-through)
- Unit testing
- Black-box testing
- White-box testing
- Integration testing
- Regression testing
- Acceptance testing

The point here is, using the exception classes and the C++ exception-handling mechanism to catch basic software errors is a *misuse* of that facility. The exception classes and the C++ exception-handling mechanism are appropriately used to *recover from* or *survive* software failures and faults. Table 5.1 contrasts the traits of error-handling methods and objects with exception-handling methods and objects.

Software Failures and Exceptions

"A software failure is the inability of a software element to satisfy its purpose" (Meyer, 1988, pp. 147–148). Software failures are caused by exceptions (also called faults). Meyer continues: "An exception is the occurrence of an abnormal condition during the execution of a software element." Let's take a closer look at the difference between an error condition and an exception. Let's use for an example a database object that has the usual services:

```
class database{
private:
    datafile Data;
public:
    open();
    search();
    sort();
    close();
    ...
};
```

If we request the database object to open a nonexistent file, then we have an error. The nonexistence of files in database environments should be *anticipated*, and the appropriate logic coded. If, on the other hand, we request the database object to open a file and return some records, and it does so, but the records have been corrupted by a virus,

Table 5.1 Traits of Error-Handling Methods and Objects

TRAITS OF ERROR HANDLING	TRAITS OF EXCEPTION HANDLING
Errors are discovered during design and testing.	Errors are unknown until runtime.
Normal flow of control is maintained.	Normal flow of control is disrupted (non-local gotos).
Correct programs don't contain errors.	Correct programs can encounter exceptions.
Program logic is designed to anticipate and correct specific errors and classes of errors.	Program logic is designed to recover from or or survive unexpected conditions, software and hardware anomalies.
Performed by the producer of the code.	Performed by the consumer of the code.
Specific errors and error types are mentioned in the software specification and requirements.	Exceptions and anomalies not covered by the software specification and requirements.
Program continues to execute when the error condition is encountered.	Program may continue to execute but might have to gracefully degrade.

then we have an *exception*. Although we might anticipate corrupted records, viruses present a different set of issues. Usually, file-handling objects have logic to deal with missing, empty, or locked files, and so on, but not the logic to deal with the particulars of some new virus. During the testing phase, we can observe how our database behaves when a request to open a missing file is made. We can then add the code so that the object behaves appropriately when such a condition arises.

But because it is impossible to have access to every possible software virus, we cannot deal with unknown virus types during the testing phase. The introduction of viruses at runtime presents the program with exceptions (faults) that can cause software failure. Again, the exception-handling mechanism is best used as a combatant against faults. After a software system or subsystem has been thoroughly tested, the errors have been identified, and the appropriate logic has been added, only "true" exceptions should remain. Thus, exception handling should be viewed as the last bastion against software failure. When the testing process can yield no more errors, then and only then should exception-handling machinery be put in place.

Defining Testing, Debugging, and Exception Handling

Testing in this context is the process of comparing a piece of software against specifications and identifying any software defects. *Debugging* is the process of removing all software defects discovered during the various testing phases. *Exception handling* is the process of dealing with negative software or hardware anomalies that were not planned for in the software requirement specification. As a rule, *error handling* is done during the debugging sessions, and *exception handling* is done at execution time.

Now that we have stated the general rule and (hopefully) convinced you to use exception handling only as a last resort, it must be noted that the C++ exception-handling mechanism is often used to handle common logic errors under certain regular conditions. To understand why, we will look at some typical approaches to error handling within a program.

Common Approaches to Error Handling

The C++ Programming Language (Stroustrup, 1991) lists four basic alternative actions that a program can take when it encounters an error. According to Stroustrup, upon detecting a problem that cannot be handled locally, the program could:

1. Terminate the program.
2. Return a value representing "error."
3. Return a legal value and leave the program in an illegal state.
4. Call a function supplied to be called in case of error.

These four alternatives are generally seen in producer/consumer relationships. The producer is typically a piece of code that implements a library function, class, class library, or application framework. The consumer is typically a piece of code that calls a library function, class, class library, or application framework. The consumer makes a request. The producer encounters an error in attempting to fulfill the request, and the four alternatives immediately become applicable. The problem with these four alternatives is that none of them is applicable in every situation. In fact, when we are faced with producer/consumer relationships, these alternatives are not applicable in most situations.

If the goal is to develop fault-tolerant and reliable software, then terminating the program when an error occurs is not acceptable. Many software systems must be continuously available and cannot tolerate system halts. Alternative 2 is applicable only where acceptable error return values are possible. Take, for example, a vector class that defines the operator [ ]. If we have a vector X of ints, and the following assignment to Y is made:

```
int Y;
vector<int> X(10);
Y = X[23];
```

then what error value do we place into Y? X may contain both positive and negative numbers. Since X has only 10 elements, an attempt to access element 23 is an error. Clearly, alternative 2 will not satisfy this common condition. Likewise, alternative 3 is not foolproof because many programmers and developers simply do not check global error or state variables. If we had set an error variable for assignment to Y, the unwitting programmer may use whatever is stored in Y as the correct value. Alternative 4 is good, *if* there is some way that the consumer can make the producer aware of such a function. Usually, giving the producer access to an error-handling function is not practical. (For a complete discussion of these error handling alternatives see Stroustrup, 1997.)

The C++ exception-handling mechanism and the exception classes provide a fifth alternative to the producer and consumer. Errors encountered in a class library method that cannot be handled locally will cause an exception to be thrown because the producer of the class library method does not know what the consumer of the class library method wants to do about the error. For example:

```
list<int> X(MAX_SIZE + 10);
```

This requests a list object containing 10 more int than the list can hold. The class producer could have decided to only return a list of MAX_SIZE length instead of throwing an exception, but this would be misleading to the consumer of the list who would be under the impression that X has a size of MAX_SIZE + 10 once it is constructed. The producer could set some global error value such as errno and not construct the list at all. The consumer would then have to check the global error value after every construction to see if the construction was successful. Finally, the producer could have terminated the program once it encountered this illegal request. None of these options is satisfactory where fault-tolerant programs are required. Throwing an exception in this case is a valid option, and this is the approach that the standard C++ class library takes to handling errors at runtime.

Instead of setting global error values, terminating the program, or returning mysterious error numbers, the standard C++ classes are designed to throw exceptions when a runtime error is encountered. Although exception handling is not recommended for basic logic errors encountered during runtime, in the case of class library producers throwing exceptions, it is a legitimate alternative.

The Exception Class Hierarchy

The standard C++ class library has nine exception classes divided into two basic groups. Table 5.2 shows that the exception classes are divided into a runtime error group and a logic error group. The runtime error group represents errors that are somewhat difficult to prevent. The logic error group represents errors that are "theoretically preventable."

NOTE:
Although the library defines nine exception classes it does not explicitly use them all.

The C++ standard library throws relatively few exception objects, functions borrowed from the library do not throw exceptions, and most of the library classes do not throw exceptions. Table 5.3 shows the classes that throw exceptions and the type of exceptions that they throw. Most of these are of the range and invalid argument variety. The classes are meant to be used primarily as an architectural guideline for the developers who are providing their own classes. Also, the standard C++ exception classes provide a mechanism for class library producers and application framework producers to have a standard set of errors that their objects can throw.

The logic_error Classes

The logic_error family of classes is derived from the exception class. In fact, most of the logic_error family class functionality is inherited from the exception class. The exception class contains the what( ) method, used to report to the user a description for the error being thrown. Each class in the logic_error family contains a constructor used to tailor a message specific to that class. Figure 5.1 shows the class relationship diagram for the logic_error classes, which are node classes; that is, they are really designed to be specialized; they do not provide much functionality as-is. They give the user a string description of which error has occurred.

Because they are classes, they also have a type. Unless the user adds some functionality to these classes, they cannot do anything other than report the error and the type. The nine generic exception classes provide no corrective action or error handling.

Table 5.2 Exception Class Groups

RUNTIME_ERROR	LOGIC_ERROR
length_error	range_error
domain_error	overflow_error
out_of_range_error	underflow_error
invalid_argument	

Table 5.3 Classes That Throw Exceptions

STANDARD CLASSES	EXCEPTION THROWN
Allocator	bad_alloc
basic_string	length_error
	out_of_range
locale	runtime_error
	bad_cast
bitset	out_of_range
	overflow_error

The runtime_error Classes

Figure 5.2 shows the class relationship diagram for the runtime_error family of classes. The runtime_error family of classes is derived from the exception class. Three classes are derived from runtime_error: range_error, overflow_error, and underflow_error. The runtime_error classes report internal computation or arithmetic errors. The functionality of these classes is similar to the logic_error classes. The runtime_error classes get their primary functionality from their exception class ancestor. The what( ) method, assignment operator=( ), and the constructors for the exception class provide the capability of the runtime_error classes. Like the logic_error classes, the runtime_error classes provide an exception framework and architectural blueprint to build upon. They offer very little inherent functionality; the programmer must specialize them through inheritance or by including them in an interface class.

Let's look at how the basic exception classes work with no specialization. Listing 5.1 shows how an exception object and a logic_error object can be thrown.

The basic exception classes have only construction, destruction, assignment, copy, and reporting capabilities. They do not contain the capability to correct a fault that has occurred. In the program in Listing 5.1, the catch blocks call the what( ) method. For the base class exception, the what( ) message may be different depending on the compiler.

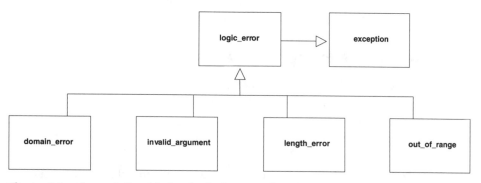

Figure 5.1 Class relationship for the logic_error classes.

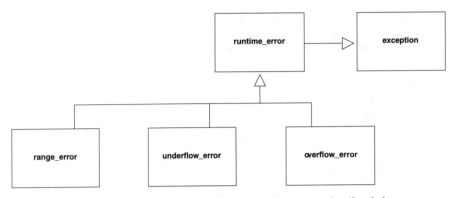

Figure 5.2 Class relationship diagram for the runtime_error family of classes.

For example, some messages currently generated by popular compilers are:

"An unnamed exception has occurred."

"A no named exception has occurred."

"An exception has occurred."

"A generic exception has occurred."

The error message returned by the what( ) method of the logic_error object in Listing 5.1 will be determined by the string passed to the constructor for the logic_error object. Here, the string "Logic Mistake" passed to the constructor will be returned by the what( ) message in the catch block on line 27. The throw( ), catch( ), and what( ) sequence represents the primary way that the exception classes are put to work.

Classifying the Exception Family of Classes

As stated, the exception-handling family of classes are *node* classes. Remember that node classes are easy to use in inheritance hierarchies. Therefore, because the exception classes are node classes, they can be used as base or foundation classes upon which the user can build. And because the exception classes do not do much other than report errors, the consumer of the classes must use inheritance or class containment to give the classes more functionality.

Constructing the Exception Classes

The exception classes are constructed with a string that will describe the error that the exception is intended to represent. For example:

```
logic_error   SubscriptException("Subscript Out Of Bounds");
range_error   CharCheckException("Value Not In CharacterSet");
length_error StringException("String Too Long");
```

We construct logic_error, range_error, and length_error objects with messages that will describe the kind of error that each object is intended to represent. The what( ) method for each object will return the message used to construct the object.

Listing 5.1   Throwing an Exception

```
1  // Listing 5.1 demonstrates how to throw an exception and
2  // print out its description in a catch block.
3
4   #include <exception>
5   void main(void)
6   {
7
8
9       try{
10
11              exception X;
12              throw(X);
13      }
14      catch(const exception &X)
15      {
16              cout << X.what() << endl;
17
18      }
19
20      try
21      {
22              logic_error Logic("Logic Mistake");
23              throw(Logic);
24      }
25      catch(const exception &X)
26      {
27              cout << X.what() << endl;
28      }
29
30
31
32  }
33
```

Destructing an Exception Class

Unless the exception class has been specialized through inheritance or as a part of an interface class, it is not necessary that the user define additional destructor information. However, if the class has been specialized, and the new derived exception class requires memory deallocation, closing of files, or device manipulation in some form, the user must specify a destructor.

Assignment and the Exception Classes

The assignment operator and copy constructor have been defined for the exception family of classes. Therefore, objects of these types can be copied and assigned during the processing of an exception. This means that operations such as:

```
logic_error A;
logic_error B;
 B = A;
 A = B;
```

are legal. The assignment or copy constructors may be used when the exception objects are used as return values or function arguments, or to throw arguments and catch parameters.

Using the Exception Classes

The exception classes can be used as-is; that is, they can be used simply to report an error message describing the error that has occurred. This is done by constructing the object with the string that will describe what has gone wrong. But the real value of the exception classes is the architectural road map that they provide for the designer and developer. The exception classes provide basic error types that the developer can specialize. Most of the exceptions that the designer and developer will encounter can be placed into either the logic_error or runtime_error family of classes.

To demonstrate how to specialize an exception class, let's use the domain_error class as an example. The domain_error class is a descendant of logic_error. We can specialize the domain_error class through inheritance. For instance:

```
class range_exception : public domain_error{
protected:
    string DetailedExplanation;
public:
    range_exception(const string &What_Arg);
    string validDomain(void);
  ...
};
```

Our class range_exception specializes the domain_error class by giving the class more functionality through inheritance. We add a mathematical exception capability that specializes in domain and range errors. Since many mathematics functions have a restriction on which arguments they may be given or on the values they can return, knowing those restrictions is helpful. For example, the sqrt( ) function should only be passed numbers >= 0. Calling the sqrt function with a negative number such as:

```
sqrt(-4)
```

is an error.

Likewise, calling a function such as factorial(500000) returns a number that creates numeric overflow on 32-bit and 64-bit computers. The value returned is *out of range*. To show how exception objects can be helpful in such situations, we'll specialize the domain_error class exception. The range_exception class adds a new method named validDomain( ). The validDomain( ) method reports a valid or safe domain function that causes the exception to be generated. This method is used to enhance the what( ) description of the domain_error object. The what( ) is used to describe what kind of error has occurred. In the case of the domain_error object, the what( ) method will report that some kind of domain error has occurred. The validDomain( ) method is used to report what the valid domain objects or ranges are. With the addition of the validDomain( ) method, we can report to the error handler both what kind of error has occurred and what the valid domain or range choices are.

Managing the Exception Classes

The exception objects are thrown when some software component encounters a software or hardware anomaly. But note, the exception objects themselves do not throw exceptions. This has many implications. If the processing of the exception is complex enough to potentially cause another exception to be generated, then the exception processing should be redesigned and simplified where possible. The exception-handling mechanism is unnecessarily complicated when exceptions can generate exceptions. Therefore, most of the methods in the exception classes contain the empty throw( ) specification. For example, here is a simplified version of the standard C++ exception class:

```
class exception {
public:
    exception() throw();
    exception(const exception&) throw();
    exception& operator=(const exception&) throw();
    virtual ~exception() throw();
    virtual const char* what() const throw();

};
```

Note the throw( ) declarations with empty arguments. The empty argument shows that the method cannot throw an exception. If the method attempts to throw an exception, an error condition is generated. If a method cannot throw an exception, then the corresponding method in any derived type cannot throw an exception.

Specializing the Exception Classes

The exception classes can be extended through inheritance or through interface classes. When using inheritance to specialize the exception classes, keep these points in mind:

- If the method in the base class does not throw exceptions, the corresponding method in the derived class cannot throw exceptions.

- The assignment operator and constructors should be defined for the new derived class. This includes the copy constructor.

- The derived class can override any method in the exception classes declared virtual. Here, the two methods declared virtual are the what( ) method and the base class destructor.

Once the appropriate operators and constructors have been overloaded and the appropriate operators and constructors have been overridden, the exception class can be extended by adding new functionality through defining additional methods. Let's take a closer look at our range_exception class (see Figure 5.3). The declaration for the range_exception class is shown in Listing 5.2.

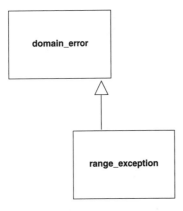

Figure 5.3 Class relationship diagram for range_exception class.

We specialize the domain_error class by providing two new methods for setting and returning domain information:

```
validDomain(string X);
string validDomain(void);
```

The validDomain( ) methods are used to set and return a message describing what the proper domain for an object should be. For example, we can define a factorial function as shown in Listing 5.3.

The addition of the validDomain( ) methods allows the specialization of the domain_error class to return both the type of error that has occurred and a valid domain or safe domain. The factorial( ) function in Listing 5.3 calculates the factorial of

Listing 5.2 Declaring range_exception Class

```
1  //Listing 5.2
2  class range_exception : public domain_error{
3  protected:
4      string DomainExplanation;
5      int LowerLimit;
6      int UpperLimit;
7  public:
8      range_exception(void) : domain_error(DomainExplanation) {}
9      range_exception(const string &X) : domain_error(X) {}
10     range_exception(const range_exception &X);
11     range_exception &operator=(const range_exception &X);
12     void lowerLimit(int X);
13     int lowerLimit(void);
14     void upperLimit(int X);
15     int upperLimit(void);
16     string validDomain(void);
17     void validDomain(string X);
18  };
19
```

Listing 5.3 Defining a Factorial Function

```
1    //Listing 5.3 definition of a factorial function
2
3    int factorial(int X)
4    {
5
6        int M;
7        int N;
8        if(X == 0){
9            return(1);
10       }
11       else{
12
13            M = X - 1;
14            N = factorial(M);
15            if((X * N) > 0){
16                return( X * N);
17            }
18            else{
19                int Factor = numeric_limits<int>::max();
20                int Increment = 2;
21                while(Factor > 0)
22                {
23                    Factor = Factor / Increment;
24                    Increment++;
25
26                }
27                stringstream SafeDomain;
28                SafeDomain << "A safe domain is from 0";
29                SafeDomain << " To " << Increment << ends;
30                range_exception RangeException("Range Error");
31                RangeException.lowerLimit(0);
32                RangeException.upperLimit(Increment);
33                RangeException.validDomain(SafeDomain.str());
34                throw(RangeException);
35
36            }
37        }
38
39        return 0;
40   }
```

positive integers. A factorial of N is written N!, and is calculated by multiplying the factors between 1 and N. For instance, the factorial of 5 is written 5!, and is calculated:

$$5 * 4 * 3 * 2 * 1 = 120$$

If we calculate the factorial for a number just a little larger than 5, say 10!, then we have:

$$10 * 9 * 8 * 7 * 6 * 5 * 4 * 3 * 2 * 1 = 3,628,800$$

Note that 10! is much larger than 5!. If we continue to attempt to calculate the factorial of larger integers, it will not take long to create numeric overflow conditions. For example, 500! is a number larger than the value that most inttypes can represent on 32-bit computers. This means that 500! would be beyond the range of representable integers for the int data type. If we attempt to call our factorial function with a number that would generate an answer that could not be represented with an int data type, then our factorial function throws an exception. This is where our specialization of the domain_error class comes in handy. Ordinarily, the standard exception objects can report only the kind of error that has occurred. Our specialization of the domain_error class allows us to return information to the user that can potentially be used to correct the error condition. The factorial( ) function in Listing 5.3 will throw an object of type range_exception. The range_exception object has a message containing the type of error that has occurred.

Besides reporting what type of error has occurred, our range_exception class returns a message describing a safe domain that can be used in case the user wishes to reexecute the factorial function. The range_exception object can also return an acceptable lower-Limit( ) and upperLimit( ). These two methods can help the user correct the conditions that caused the original exception. However, the user must decide what to do after the exception is caught.

Dealing with Exceptions

Once an exception is thrown and caught, there are two basic courses of action, representing major differences of philosophy in approaches to exception handling. One approach is to catch the exception and attempt to correct the condition or adjust for the condition that caused the exception, then resume execution at the point where the exception was thrown. This approach is called *resumption*. The second approach is to catch the exception and perform a graceful exit of the subsystem or subroutine that caused the exception. The graceful exit is accomplished by closing the appropriate files, destructing the appropriate objects, logging the error if possible, deallocating the appropriate memory, and handling any devices that need to be dealt with. This approach is called *termination*. By default, the C++ exception-handling mechanism follows the termination method, but a resumption approach can be implemented. It is important to note that the termination model does not require that the program be aborted every time an exception occurs. Usually, only a subsystem or subroutine of a complete program gets terminated. Ideally, the program continues to run; after all, the point of the exception-handling mechanism is to give the programmer a chance to build more robust programs. Programs that need to survive software or hardware anomalies require some kind of exception-handling mechanism. In many cases, aborting the complete program is simply not an option.

The Resumption Model

In the resumption model of exception handling, an exception is thrown and caught. The condition or conditions that created the exception are either corrected or adjusted for, and the program resumes from the point where the exception occurred. This sounds straightforward, but there are some complexities. For example, if we have a succession of nested procedure calls, such as:

A calls B

B calls C

C calls D

D calls E

E (exception occurs here)

and an error condition arises in E and an exception is thrown, there is the issue of what to do about the call stack. There are also object destruction issues and suspended return values that need to be resolved. Even if we fix the condition that caused the exception in procedure E, how can we return the program to the state it was in just prior to the exception? We will have to keep stack information, object construction and destruction tables, interrupt tables, and so on. This requires a lot of overhead and cooperation between the callee and the caller.

These issues represent only the surface. It is because of the complexity of implementing the resumption model and the fact that large-scale systems can be developed without it that the termination model was chosen for C++. In *The Design and Evolution of C++* Stroustrup (1994) presents a complete rationale as to why the ANSI committee eventually selected the termination model of exception handling.

Although the resumption model was ultimately rejected as a general exception-handling approach in C++, it can be successfully used in C++ where it makes sense to do so. The architecture of the software system in question will determine whether the resumption model is appropriate. There are several major software architectures in which a resumption model can be used:

Client/server

Event-driven

Blackboard

Multithreaded

Distributed

The Termination Model

Exception handling using the termination model does not attempt to resume execution at the point where the exception occurred. Rather, the function or procedure where the exception occurred is exited, and steps are taken to put the system in as stable a state as possible. The program continues to run, and the user has the option of attempting to retry the failed operation from the beginning. Whereas the resumption model attempts to restart from the point of origin of an exception, the termination model exits the offending subsystem and allows the user to start again where possible.

Summary

Thorough testing, then debugging, of a piece of software should be the primary defense against software defects. Exception handling should be added to the software system or subsystem after the software has undergone rigorous testing. Throwing exceptions should not be used as a generic error-handling technique, because it destroys the flow of control of the program. Again, throwing exceptions should be used only as a last resort. The standard exception-handling classes should be used as architectural road maps for the programmer who wishes to design more complete and useful exception classes. If not specialized, the standard classes can only report errors. More useful exception classes can be built that have corrective functionality, as well as more information.

In general, both the termination and resumption models allow the program to continue to execute. Both models resist simply aborting the program when an error occurs. Exception-handling logic should be kept separate, and should be approached as a self-contained software module. For a more complete discussion of exception handling, see *The Design and Evolution of C++* (Stroustrup, 1994) and *Software Reliability Measurement, Prediction, Application* (Musa, 1986).

CHAPTER 6

Runtime Type Information Classes

*"Why does it work in domains where the
physical phenomena are unknown?"*

—MORRIS KLINE
*MATHEMATICS AND THE
SEARCH FOR KNOWLEDGE*

P olymorphism is the capability to take many forms. A user uses one name or interface that has different implementations. This is why polymorphism is sometimes described as "one interface, multiple implementations." A message is sent to an object as a request to perform a task. Polymorphism lifts the responsibility from the user to determine the correct implementation and places it on the receiver of the message. The resolution of the function call may be outside the source file in a library or other file, for instance. The function is resolved when the call is replaced with the address of the function definition. This resolution can be made at compile time or runtime, and is called *static* or *early binding* and *dynamic* or *late binding,* respectively. Table 6.1 lists the types of polymorphism, the mechanisms in which they work, along with a brief description of each.

Binding is the process by which modules or functions are incorporated to make executable code. Memory addresses are assigned to each module or function call, and external references are patched with correct memory addresses. Early binding occurs at compile time, during which the call is bound to the correct implementation. This means that all information needed to detect which function or module is to be executed is known at compile time. Standard function calls, overloaded function calls, and overloaded operator calls are examples of early binding.

Late binding occurs at runtime, when the call is bound to the correct implementation. This means that all information needed to detect which function or module is to be executed is not known until runtime. Late binding can be activated by using virtual methods and pointers to a base class that can also point to a derived class. If a function is written to accept a pointer to a base class, when the function is called, it can be passed a pointer to the base class or any of the derived classes.

Table 6.1 Types of Polymorphism

POLYMORPHISM TYPES	DESCRIPTION
Static (Early Binding)	*Mechanism: Function and Operator Overloading*
When the specific function to be executed is determined at compile time.	• Function names are the same but the return and argument list does not match.
	• Operator overloading allows an operator to take a specific meaning relative to a user-defined class.
Runtime (Late Binding)	*Mechanism: Overriding*
The specific function to be executed is determined at runtime.	• The use of virtual functions declared in the base class can be redefined in the derived class.
	Mechanism: Pure Virtual Functions
	• The virtual function in the base class has no meaning; the derived class has to define the function or it will also be considered a pure abstract base class.
	Mechanism: Pointers to Derived Type
	• A pointer to a base class can also point to a derived class; all members of the derived class inherited from the base class are accessible, but members specific to the derived class are not accessible.

Runtime Type Information

When pointers can be of a base or derived types, detecting the object type at runtime may be necessary. Knowing the object type may be necessary to determine which operations to perform or which action to take. The standard C++ library has components to support runtime type information (RTTI). These components are used only on class hierarchies that have virtual functions. The typeid operator returns a value that identifies the exact type of object. It returns a reference to the type_info object, which has the operator==( ) and operator!=( ) defined to compare types.

Consider these three classes:

expression_component

operator_type

operand

The expression_component is the base of the operator_type and operand classes; it represents the components of an expression stored in a string, such as:

"5 + 4"

"10 * 7"

"3 / 8 * 7 + 4"

The class operator_type and operand specialize the components of the expression. The operand class encapsulates the traditional mathematical notion of an operand, whereas the operator_type is used to encapsulate the notion of an operator. The expression_component has a virtual method called value( ), which returns the value of the expression component. The method value( ) is specialized by both operator_type and operand classes. The expression "3 / 8 * 7 + 4" is stored in a string:

```
string Expression("3 / 8 * 7 + 4");
```

Each part of the expression is to be stored in a list of expression_components:

```
list<expression_component>::List;
string::iterator StrStart = Expression.begin();
string::iterator StrStop = Expression.end();

while(StrStart != StrStop){
     if(*StrStart is in set of Numbers){
        insert new operand in List
     }
     else{
          if(*StrStart is in set of Operators){
             insert new operator_type in List
          }
     }
     ++StrStart;
}
```

The accumulate algorithm is used to count the number of operands in the expression. The check function object uses the typeid operator to decide if a particular component is an operator or an operand. If it is an operand the object can be counted. The function object will return true if the expression_component is a type operand:

```
class check{
     .
     .
     .
public:
     check(void);
     bool operator() (expression_component X);
};
check::check(void)
{
     ...
}

bool check::operator() (expression_component X)
{
     if(typeid(X) == typeid(operand){
```

```
            return 1;
        }
        else {
                return 0;
        }
    }

    void main(void)
    {
        int sum = 0;
        // insert components into list.
        accumulate(List.begin(), List.end(), sum, check);
        list<expression_component>::iterator Start = List.begin();
        while(Start != List.end()){
                cout << (*Start).value();
        }
    }
```

The number of operands is stored in sum. The if statement:

```
if(typeid(X) == typeid(operand){return 1;}
```

evaluates to the bool value true if X points to an object of type operand. What is actually being compared are the type_info objects returned by the typeid operators. The while loop iterates through the list. Each component's value is sent to the standard output. The statement:

```
cout << (*Start).value():
```

demonstrates the use of dynamic binding. When the Start iterator is dereferenced, an operator_type or operand type object is returned. The correct implementation of the method value( ) is called. Because expression_component, operator_type, and operand all contain a value( ) function, it is not known until runtime which implementation of value( ) is to be executed.

The type_info Class

The type_info class stores a pointer to the type name of an object. It also stores an encoded value used for comparing two types to decide equivalence or ordering. Figure 6.1 is the class relationship diagram for type_info. The type_info class does not inherit, nor does it contain any classes; it is a small class consisting of five public methods:

```
virtual ~type_info();
bool operator==(const type_info&) const;
bool operator!=(const type_info&) const;
```

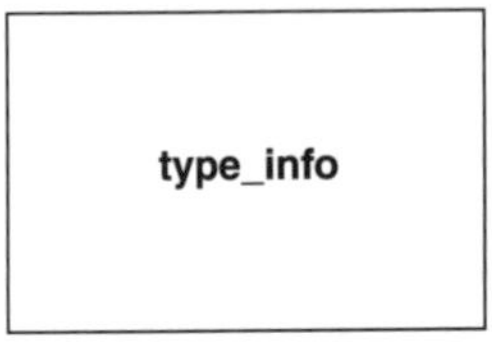

Figure 6.1 Class relationship diagram for the type_info class.

```
bool before(const type_info&) const;
const char* name() const;
```

The equality operator will return a bool value true if the type_info objects describe the same type. The inequality operator will return a bool value true if the type_info objects are not equal. The before( ) method is used to determine the order of these objects, allowing type_info objects to be sorted. Note that the ordering has nothing to do with inheritance order; it is not used to determine if X derived type was derived before Y derived type of the same base type. The before( ) method returns a bool value true if the calling type_info object precedes the type_info object passed as a parameter. The manner in which the type_info objects are sorted is not defined, and may differ from one program to another or even among different executions of the same program. It is safe to assume that the collating sequence is similar or connected to the address operator. The name( ) method will return the name of a type. It returns a const char* to a null-terminated string.

The bad_typeid Class

The typeid operator will accept a pointer when dereferenced evaluates to a type:

```
typeid(*P);
```

If the pointer points to a null value, the typeid operator will throw a bad_typeid exception. The bad_typeid class inherits the exception class. Figure 6.2 shows the class relationship diagram. The bad_typeid class has a default constructor, copy constructor, and a destructor:

```
bad_typeid() throw();
bad_typeid(const bad typeid&) throw();
bad_typeid& operator=(const bad_typeid&) throw();
virtual ~bad_typeid() throw();
```

The default constructor will construct a bad_typeid object. The copy constructor copies a bad_typeid object, and the assignment operator assigns one bad_typeid object to another bad_typeid object. The destructor destroys the object.

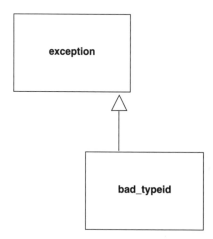

Figure 6.2 Class relationship diagram for the bad_typeid class.

The method:

```
virtual const char* what() const throw();
```

is implementation-defined. The purpose of this method is to return a message, which may be a null-terminated string that can be displayed as a wide character string.

Dynamic Casting and the bad_cast Class

Sometimes, casting an object may be necessary. There are four cast type operators:

const_cast

reinterpret_cast

static_cast

dynamic_cast

Table 6.2 lists these operators along with a brief description of each. The purpose of a dynamic_cast is to *upcast* an object within a class hierarchy. The object to be upcast has to be a direct or indirect descendant of the type that is casting. For example:

```
expression_component* Expression;
operator_type* Operator;
...
Expression = dynamic_cast<expression_component *> Operator;
```

This statement assigns Expression a pointer to expression_component object. The Operator object of type operator_type has been cast to expression_component. The expression_component is the base class for operator_type. If operator_type had not been derived from expression_component, the operation would have returned a null pointer. It is called an upcast because the hierarchy has the base classes closer to the root of the hierarchy, therefore casting to base classes moves upward in the structure.

If the dynamic_cast uses a reference instead of a pointer, as here:

```
dynamic_cast<R& > (p);
```

and the reference is not to a direct or indirect base class of type p, then a bad_cast exception is thrown by dynamic_cast. Table 6.3 lists some results of casting expressions and when an exception is thrown.

The bad_cast class has a default, a copy constructor, and an assignment operator:

```
bad_cast() throw();
bad_cast(const bad_cast&) throw();
bad_cast& operator=(const bad_cast&) throw();
```

The default constructor constructs a bad_cast object. The copy constructor and assignment operator create a copy of a bad_cast object.

The purpose of this bad_cast method:

```
virtual const char* what() const throw();
```

Table 6.2 Cast Operators

CAST OPERATORS	DESCRIPTION
static_cast<T>(a)	Converts *a* to *T*; *T* and *a* must be pointer, reference, arithmetic type or enum type.
dynamic_cast<T>(a)	Performs upcasts within a class hierarchy; *T* must be a pointer, reference, or a pointer to void; *a* must be an expression that resolves to a pointer or a reference.
const_cast<T>(a)	Removes the type's constness; *T* and *a* must be of the same type except for const or volatile modifiers.
reinterpret_cast<T>(a)	Any pointer can be converted into any other pointer; *T* must be a pointer, reference, arithmetic type, pointer to a function, or pointer to a member of a class.

EXAMPLES OF CASTING	<T>	(A)
static_cast<T>(a)	enum type	integral type
	null pointer	null pointer
	*derived class	*base class
	*X	X
	&X	X
	*member A of X	*member B of X
dynamic_cast<T>(a)	*void	pointer
	*B derived of X	*C derived of X
		(result is *unique subclass)
	&B derived of X	&B derived of X
		(result is &unique subclass)
	derived class	polymorphic base class
const_cast<T>(a)	*non-const	*const
	&non-const	&const
	non-const	const
	*non-volatile	*volatile
	&non-volatile	&volatile
	non-volatile	volatile
reinterpret_cast<T>(a)	integral type	pointer
	pointer	integral type
	*object type	*function
	*function	*object type

Table 6.3 Casting Expression Results

EXCEPTION TYPE	EXCEPTION THROWN
Dynamic Cast	
bad_cast	Failed cast to a reference type.
Type Identification	
bad_typeid	Dereference a null pointer.

is to return a message determined by the implementor. Figure 6.3 shows the class relationship of bad_cast.

Summary

Polymorphism makes the receiver of a message responsible for determining the correct implementation of a function to execute. The function is resolved when the function call is replaced with the address of the function definition. This is called *binding,* the process by which modules or functions are incorporated to make executable code. Binding can occur at compile time (static) or at runtime (dynamic or late binding). Dynamic binding occurs when pointers to base types are pointing to derived types and the base type is invoking a method declared virtual.

When it becomes necessary to determine the exact type of object, the standard C++ library supports RTTI, information obtained about an object's type during runtime. The typeid operator returns a type_info object that contains the type name of an object. These type_info objects can be used in comparisons to determine if two objects are of the same type. The method name( ) of the type_info class returns the type name as a null-terminated string. The typeid operator accepts a pointer when dereferenced returns a type. But if it is passed a pointer to a null character, typeid will throw a bad_typeid exception.

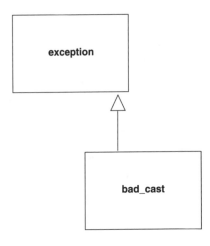

Figure 6.3 Class relationship diagram for the bad_cast class.

Dynamic casting upcasts an object within a class hierarchy. The object that is to be upcast has to be a direct or indirect descendant of the type that is casting:

```
dynamic_cast< P > (c);
```

P has to be a direct or indirect base class of c. P can be a pointer or a reference. If P is a pointer but not a base class of c, then dynamic_cast will return a null pointer. If P is a reference and not a base class of c, then dynamic_cast will throw a bad_cast exception. Both exception classes' bad_typeid and bad_cast have a what( ) method that returns an implementation-defined message as a null-terminated string.

CHAPTER 7

The Standard C++ Containers

"Structural inertia is as least as important as mass inertia . . ."

—CYRIL SMITH
STRUCTURAL HIERARCHY IN
SCIENCE, ART, AND HISTORY

The container class library has seven basic containers: vector, deque, list, set, multiset, map, and multimap. By using adaptors, the seven basic containers are extended to include stack, queue, and priority queue. These 10 containers are the object-oriented equivalents of the most common data structures used in business, industry, and the literature of computer programming.

What Are Containers?

Containers are objects designed to hold or contain groups or collections of objects. In the same fashion that a box can contain a number of pencils or a bag can hold a collection of books, a C++ container can contain an object or collection of objects. Containers act as *generic holders*. Groups or collections of objects may be placed into containers, removed from containers, organized within containers, and accessed. There is no restriction on the types or numbers of objects that can be placed into containers. Containers can contain objects that are all of the same type or that are all related; containers can even be made to hold an assortment of object types, meaning they may contain collections of different kinds of objects or objects that are all of the same type. When a container comprises a group of mixed objects, it is called a *heterogeneous* container; when the container is holding a group of objects that are all the same, it is called a *homogeneous* container.

Containers get their name from their function. Containers are used to *manage* groups of objects. Once we have containers to store objects in and retrieve objects from, we next think about the kinds of operations we can perform on the objects stored or associated with containers, as well as the operations we can perform on the containers.

The container class library divides these ten containers into two broad categories: *sequence* and *associative* (see Table 7.1). These terms refer to how the containers are logically ordered and how they are accessed. On the one hand, the organization of the objects within the containers dictates how the objects can be accessed; on the other hand, the way we would like to access the objects dictates how we must organize the objects within the container. For example, the stack container is known as a last in first out (LIFO) organization. In a LIFO organization, the objects are stored in a sequential fashion, where the last object stored is the first to be removed. The stack structure allows the user to access only one object at a time, and only the object that was last onto the stack.

A stack is a sequential structure. To see the first object pushed onto the stack, we must remove each object one at a time, starting with the last object placed on the stack continuing until we have reached the first. The stack container does not support access or removal from the middle or bottom of the stack; only the object on the top of the stack may be viewed or removed. The stack organization has many applications in computer programming, and has an important access method.

If, however, we want to insert or remove objects at any location in a container, we might want to use a vector or deque container, objects that have a direct access method. Containers with direct access methods allow objects to be inserted or retrieved from any location in the container. Each container in the library has an access method. Table 7.2 shows the access methods and logical view of the standard containers.

Container Class Architecture

The container class library is a flat *template-based* library. This is in contrast to the traditional *object-based* collection and container libraries. There are very few class hierarchies in the container class library. Whereas traditional collection and container class libraries are vertical and driven by inheritance and polymorphism, the container class library is horizontal and driven by genericity and templates.

The container class library containers have fat interfaces (Stroustrup 1991, pg. 452), in contrast to the object-based collection and container classes that have interfaces based

Table 7.1   Sequence and Associative Containers

SEQUENCE CONTAINERS	
vector	list
deque	queue
priority queue	stack
ASSOCIATIVE CONTAINERS	
set	multiset
map	multimap

Table 7.2 Access Methods and Logical View of Standard Containers

CONTAINERS	LOGICAL VIEW	ACCESS METHODS Sequential	Direct	Relational
Stack	push / pop / top / bottom	✓		
Deque	insert, back / add, remove / front, remove	✓	✓	
Vector	insert / remove	✓	✓	
Set	x			✓
Map	A B C D → 1 2 3 4		✓	✓
List	head / tail	✓		

on taxonomy hierarchies. Consequently, it can be used with user-defined objects and built-in types. The container class library emphasizes the genericity constructs in C++, and favors heavy use of templates and pointers. Encapsulation of the container functionality is relaxed in the container class library. Instead of each container class being a self-contained bundle of data and functions, the class library's containers implement only a minimum of the behavior required for the class. Most of the containers' behavior is implemented by the standard algorithms. In this way, the containers and the algorithms form *cooperative patterns*, as opposed to encapsulated objects (see Soukup 1994, pg 48, for a discussion of software building using *pattern* classes). The container class library provides a balance between the goals of object-oriented programming and the goals of genericity.

Objects Stored in Sequences

The logical representation of certain containers is linear or sequential. The objects in these types of containers are understood as being logically stored in contiguous memory. The objects in sequence containers have logical positions within the container relative to start, end, top, bottom, front, or back of the container. Access to the sequence containers can be classified as either sequential or direct (sometimes called random). When a container has sequential access, the programmer must access the first and second objects in order to get to the third object. There is no way to jump to the middle of a container that supports only sequential access. When a container has direct access, the programmer can move directly to any object in the container, without having to process other objects. The container class library vector and deque provide direct access, and the list provides sequential access.

NOTE:

Do not confuse the terms "sequence" and "sequential" here. Sequence refers to the way the objects are logically stored in memory; sequential refers to the way the objects are accessed. Although the vector is a sequence container, it has a direct access method. The list is a good example of a sequence container whose objects are accessed sequentially. The objects in a list container may be accessed either from the front of the list or the rear of the list.

Containers and the Interface View

In Chapter 1, we introduced the idea of the interface view for the C++ standard library, noting that the classes in the library are accessed though a core set of method and operator types. Understanding the core interface view of the container classes is important before we can use them effectively. Three core interface views can be found in the container class library:

- Common methods and operators shared by all containers.
- Common methods and operators shared by the sequence containers.
- Common methods and operators shared by the associative containers.

In addition to the core interface for each container, each container has a set of public methods and operators that make up that container's interface. (Recall that a class interface contains the protocol that the programmer must use to access the class's data and functionality.)

Methods and Operators Common to All Containers

The common methods and operators that all containers share come in two forms:

- Types of methods and operators
- Particular methods and operators

Types of Methods and Operators Shared by All Containers

Each container has one or more public constructors and destructor and accessor methods. Remember that accessor methods allow the user to access the characteristics and attributes of a class. The container classes have access methods that allow the user to access container attributes and characteristics, as well as methods that provide access to the objects stored within the container. Each container has iterator methods.

Particular Operators Shared by All Containers

All standard containers support a core set operators, container accessor methods, and container content accessor methods. Table 7.3 contains the core set of operators that each container defines. These operators each take linear time. The operators perform lexicographical comparisons. The < operator performs a lexicographical comparison. The operators <=, >=, and > are indirectly defined by the < operator and therefore also perform lexicographical comparisons.

Let's see how lexicographical comparisons work. Figure 7.1 shows the results of four lexicographical comparisons. In a < lexicographical comparison of two containers, A and B, the corresponding values from each container are compared. If they are equal, then the comparison moves to the next pair of values. If A < B, then the lexicographical comparison returns true; if A > B, then the lexicographical comparison returns false. If A == B, then the comparison moves onto the next pair of values. Notice the comparisons in Figure 7.1. In Case 1, the comparisons continue until the last pair is reached. Since the last value in B is less than the last value in A, A < B returns false. In Case 2, the comparison stops after the first comparison since the first element in A is < the first element in B. In Case 3, since

Table 7.3 Operators Defined by All Standard Containers

COMMON CONTAINER OPERATORS	DESCRIPTION
a == b	Equality operation on containers of the same type; returns bool true if a.size( ) == b.size( ) and the sequence of elements in container a and the sequence of elements in container b are equal using: X::value_type::operator==( ).
a != b	Inequality operation on containers of the same type; equivalent to !(a == b).
a > b	Returns bool true if b < a.
a >= b	Returns bool true if !(a < b).
a < b	Compares containers lexicographically.
a <= b	Returns bool true if !(a > b).
r = a	Assignment operator for containers; requires that r == a.

NOTE: X is a container class; a and b are values of type X; r is a value of type X&.

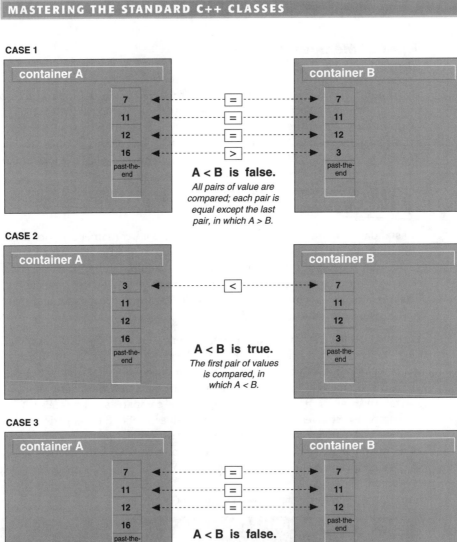

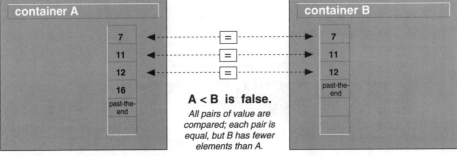

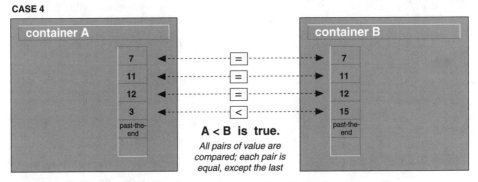

Figure 7.1 How lexicographical comparisons work with container objects.

B is shorter than A, else they are equal, then B < A, so A < B will return false. In Case 4, the comparisons continue until the last two elements are reached; and since the last element in A < last element in B, then A < B returns true. From these four cases, we see it is not always necessary to compare each element. Remember, the <=, >=, == operators will also use lexicographical comparison since they are indirectly defined by the < operator.

Particular Methods Shared by All Containers

In addition to constructors, copy constructors, and destructors, all containers have at least four iterator methods and four accessor methods (see Table 7.4). Notice the two levels of accessors in the table; the four iterator methods are used to access objects within the containers, and the four accessor methods are used to access information about the container.

Common Methods Shared by All Sequence Containers

In addition to the common operators and methods that all containers share, the sequence containers also share a set of insertion and deletion methods, called *modifiers* because they change the state of the containers.

Modifiers Common to Sequence Containers

Every sequence container will have at least three insert modifier methods and three deletion modifier methods. The insert methods are used to place objects in a container, and the deletion objects are used to remove objects from a container.

Table 7.4 Iterator and Accessor Methods Defined by Every Container

ITERATOR METHODS	DESCRIPTION
begin( )	Returns an iterator that points to the first object in the container.
end( )	Returns an iterator that points to the past-the-end value of the container.
rbegin( )	Returns reverse_iterator(end( )).
rend( )	Returns reverse_iterator(begin( )).
ACCESSOR METHODS	**DESCRIPTION**
size( )	Returns the number of elements in the container.
max_size( )	Returns the largest number of objects a container can hold.
swap( )	Swaps two containers of the same type.
empty( )	Returns true if the container is empty or if size( ) = 0.

insert(L,O)

insert(L,N,O)

insert(L,i,j)

erase(L)

erase(L1,L2)

clear(void)

Insertion Modifiers

The three insert( ) methods place copies of the object(s) they receive into the container. The insert(L,O) method inserts a copy of the O object before position L. The insert(L,N,O) method inserts N copies of object O before position L. The insert(L,i,j) method inserts copies of the object in the range in [i,j) before position L. Copy constructors are called for the objects inserted into the container.

When objects are inserted to a container, any objects already in the container may or may not be moved to different locations. The effect an insert modifier has on iterators depends on the sequence container. Whereas the insert( ) method does not invalidate iterators in the list container, it can invalidate iterators in the vector or deque containers; it may cause reallocation within the deque or vector containers. If reallocation occurs, then objects already in the container may be moved. If iterators were pointing to the objects before the reallocation and before the objects were moved, then those iterators may no longer be valid. A good rule of thumb is to be very careful when referencing iterators following insertions or deletions.

Deletion Modifiers

The three deletion modifiers remove objects from the container. The erase(L) method removes the object pointed to by L. The erase(L1,L2) removes objects in the range [L1,L2). The clear( ) method removes all objects in the container. For each deletion modifier, destructors are called for each object removed from the container. The erase( ) methods return either the iterator after the last object removed, or end( ) if there are no more objects beyond the last object removed.

The erase( ) and clear( ) methods also can invalidate iterators. Iterators for deleted objects are always invalidated after the deletion operation. When an iterator has been invalidated, the programmer should not attempt to dereference that iterator, nor use any value

Range Notation

Square brackets—[ ]—and parentheses—( )—have a special meaning when referring to ranges of objects. If we specify a range of objects [A,B], we mean all the objects in the range from A to B, including the object A and the object B. If we specify the range (A,B], then we mean all the object in the range A to B, not including A; however, we do include B. If we specify the range (A,B), we mean all the objects in the range A to B, not including A and not including the object B. If we specify all the objects in the range [A,B), we mean all the objects in the range A to B, including object A but not including object B.

returned as a result of using operation *. The erase( ) and clear( ) modifiers only invalidate the iterators removed for the list container; this is not true for the vector and the deque containers. If objects are removed from either the front or the back of a deque container, only the iterators pointing to those objects become invalid. If objects are removed from the middle of a deque, all iterators should be considered invalid. Likewise, if objects are removed from a vector, all iterators should be considered invalid.

Methods Common to All Associative Containers

Besides the common methods and operators that all containers share, the associative containers define a set of accessors and modifiers. The accessors provide iterator and statistical access for the objects in the associative containers, and the modifiers are used to insert or remove objects from the associative containers.

Iterator Accessors Common to All Associative Containers

There are four iterator accessors:

find(Obj)

lower_bound(Obj)

upper_bound(Obj)

equal_range(Obj)

The find(Obj) method will return an iterator pointing to the Obj object, if that object is in the container; otherwise, it returns the value end( ). The lower_bound( ), upper_bound( ), and equal_range( ) methods behave in the same fashion as their algorithm counterparts (discussed in Chapter 9). The lower_bound(Obj) method will return an iterator pointing to the Obj object, if that object is in the container; otherwise, it will return an iterator pointing to the next largest object in the container. The upper_bound(Obj) method will return an iterator pointing to the next largest object in the container whether Obj is in the container or not. The equal_range(Obj) method will return a pair<iterator,iterator> object that contains two iterators. The first iterator will return the same value that lower_bound(Obj) would return. The second iterator will return the same value that upper_bound(Obj) would return. If the object requested has a larger value than the largest value in the container, then lower_bound( ), upper_bound( ), and equal_range( ) will return end( ).

Insertion Modifiers Common to All Associative Containers

The associative containers have at least three insert( ) methods:

insert(Obj)

insert(L,Obj)

insert(i,j)

These methods work a little differently from the insert modifiers for the sequence containers. The first important difference between the insertion with sequence containers and with associative containers occurs because associative containers are sorted, and maintain their sorted order during the insertion process. Second, the insertion modifiers are different for associative containers because the map and set associative containers do not allow duplicate keys. Attempting to insert an object into a set or map container whose key is already present results in a failure.

The insert(Obj) methods insert the Obj object in the container at a location that leaves the container in sorted order. Although specifying the location where an object is to be inserted in an associative container is not necessary, doing so can save time, especially if the number of objects in the container is large, say 10,000 or more. This is where the container can begin to search for a location. Thus, insert(L,Obj) gives the container a possible starting place, L, where the Obj object might be inserted. The insert(i,j) method inserts all objects in the range [i,j). Recall from the range notation sidebar that [i,j) means all objects starting from i and including i, up to j, but not including j.

Deletion Modifiers Common to All Associative Containers

All associative containers support four object deletion or removal modifiers:

erase(Obj)

erase(L)

erase(L1,L2)

clear( )

The erase(Obj) method will remove all objects whose key is equal to Obj. The erase(L) method will remove the object at position L. The erase(L1,L2) method will erase all objects in the range [L1,L2). The clear( ) method removes all objects within the containers.

Keep in mind that the destructors for these objects will be called when they are removed from the container. Also, iterators associated with any of the deleted objects will be invalid. A good rule of thumb is to refresh any iterators used with a container after object removals have taken place. The same holds true for insertions that may cause containers to be reallocated. The rules for when iterators are valid and not valid often cause confusion. In general, refreshing or resetting the iterators after object removals and object insertions will take care of many problems of invalid iterators.

The count( ) Accessor

In addition to the iterator accessors, all associative containers define a count(Obj) method that returns the number of objects in the container whose key is equal to Obj. The count(Obj) is also a quick way to find out whether an object is in a set or map.

Containers and Automatic Memory Management

All standard container classes are dynamic structures and all the container classes have a default memory management allocator class. The allocator class is a data member of the container class, and this data member type is a parameter to the container. This implies that the user can supply a user-defined allocator. The allocator class is responsible for allocating memory for the objects that will be placed in the container; it presents the memory model to the container. The allocator class has two member functions, allocate( ) and deallocate( ), that request and return memory for the container. Each container's allocator class is responsible for the automatic memory management for that container. In general, each container "owns" the objects it contains, is responsible for calling the copy constructors to make copies of new objects, and will invoke the destructors for those objects when the container goes out of scope.

There are two accessors, size( ) and max_size( ), that can be used to get information about the number of objects in a container and the number of objects that a container can hold. The size( ) method reports how many objects are currently in the container. The max_size( ) method reports the largest number of objects the container can hold; it will return different amounts based on the size of the objects. A vector can hold more char types than double types. If the container is going to hold a user-defined object that has a size of 16,384 bytes, then the maximum number of user-defined objects will be less than an object that has a size of 4 bytes.

Using the Sequence Containers

The standard library defines three basic sequence containers: list, vector, and deque. By using interface classes (adaptors), the library defines three additional sequence classes: queue, priority_queue, and stack. Each of the sequence containers is declared in its own header files. So to use the container, you must include the header files. For instance, to use the vector container, you must include <vector>, and then a vector class can be declared. If a deque is needed, then <deque> must be included, and so on.

Interface Protocol for Sequence Containers

If user-defined classes are going to be used with the sequence containers, in general, the == and < operators will have to be defined for the user-defined class. These operators comprise the primary minimum defined interface that the standard container classes assume will be supplied for each object. Listing 7.1 shows one way a vector container could be declared.

After <vector> is included, objects of type vector can be declared. Because vector is a template class, when an object of type vector is declared, the user must provide a type to the class declaration. In the declarations in this listing, we have declared four vector

Listing 7.1 Declaring a Vector Container

```
// Listing 7.1
// Declaration of vector containers

#include <vector>
void main(void)
{
    vector<int>     MyVector1;
    vector<char>    MyVector2;
    vector<float>   MyVector3;
    vector<char *>  MyVector4;
}
```

containers, each of which stores a different type. We have containers that can store ints, chars, floats, and pointers to char. This emphasizes an important point about template container classes: Because they are parameterized, the code implementing the container and the logic needed to access the objects within the container has to be defined only once. The parameters to the container allow it to hold any kind of object, built-in or user-defined.

Constructing Sequences

The sequence containers provide several ways to construct a container. All sequence containers provide either a constructor that requires no arguments or constructors that have default arguments. These constructors are often called *default constructors.* When the constructor that takes no arguments is used, it is constructed with a size of zero. The sequence containers also provide a constructor that allows the user to specify the number of objects the container is to hold initially, and to what those objects should be initialized. For instance, the program in Listing 7.2 declares an object of type list<double> called Sequence.

The declaration for Sequence specifies that the container should be initially constructed to hold 10 objects of type double. Furthermore, the declaration specifies that all of the doubles should be initialized with the value 1812.23. Table 7.5 shows the output from the program in Listing 7.2. Notice that Sequence contains 10 objects, all whose value is 1812.23.

All sequence containers provide the *copy constructor,* used for certain types of object initialization, and when objects are passed by value to and from functions. The next type of constructor that all the sequences provide constructs the container with a group of objects from another container. This constructor basically copies the elements from the provided container into the new container. For example, Sequence2 in program Listing 7.3 is constructed with the contents of Sequence1.

There are two lists in the program in Listing 7.3. Sequence2 is constructed with the members of Sequence1. Sequence1 is constructed with the default constructor. The output from the program in Listing 7.3 is shown in Table 7.6. This brings us to an important feature of the container objects.

Listing 7.2   Using a Constructor to Initialize a Container

```
// Listing 7.2 demonstrates how a constructor can be used to
// initialize a container with a certain number of objects
// initialized to a specific value.

#include <list.>
#include <iostream>

using namespace std;

void main (void)
{
    list<double>  Sequence(10,1812.23);
    list<double>::const_iterator N = Sequence.begin();
    int Count = Sequence.size();
    while(Count)
    {
        cout <<  "List Element " << Count << ":" << *N << endl;
        Count--;
        N++;
    }
}
```

Sequence Containers
and Dynamic Allocation

The declaration of Sequence1 in the program in Listing 7.3 tells us we don't have to declare in advance how many objects a container will hold. The storage for the objects of a sequence container is *dynamically allocated*, meaning that the space for objects in a container is allocated during the execution of the program, and thus can grow or

Table 7.5   Output from Listing 7.2

List Element 10: 1812.23
List Element 9: 1812.23
List Element 8: 1812.23
List Element 7: 1812.23
List Element 6: 1812.23
List Element 5: 1812.23
List Element 4: 1812.23
List Element 3: 1812.23
List Element 2: 1812.23
List Element 1: 1812.23

Listing 7.3 Constructing One Container from Another

```
1   // Listing 7.3
2   // This program demonstrates how one container can be
3   // used to construct another container
4
5
6   #include <list>
7   #include <iostream>
8   #include <iomanip>
9
10  using namespace std;
11
12  void main (void)
13  {
14      list<double> Sequence1;
15      double Count = 1;
16      while(Count < 6)
17      {
18          Sequence1.push_front(Count / 3);
19          Count++;
20      }
21      list<double> Sequence2(Sequence1);
22      list<double>::const_iterator O = Sequence2.begin();
23      list<double>::const_iterator N = Sequence1.begin();
24      cout.precision(3);
25      cout.setf(ios::fixed | ios::showpoint);
26      Count = Sequence2.size();
27      while(Count)
28      {
29          cout << "Sequence 1 " << Count << ":" << setw(8) << *N
30              << "\t" << "\t";
31          cout << "Sequence 2 " << Count << ":" << setw(8) << *O
32              << endl;
33          N++;
34          O++;
35          Count--;
36      }
37  }
```

shrink during runtime. This is in contrast to static structures like the traditional array in C++. When a traditional array is declared in C++, the size of the array remains fixed for the duration of the program or until the entire array is deallocated. Static structures cannot change their size during runtime. Although a static structure can be dynamically allocated at runtime, it is not a dynamic structure.

We can dynamically allocate a static structure during runtime using the new operator.

```
A = new int[200];
```

Table 7.6 Output from Listing 7.3

Sequence 1 5: 1.66667	Sequence 2 5: 1.66667
Sequence 1 4: 1.33333	Sequence 2 4: 1.33333
Sequence 1 3: 1	Sequence 2 3: 1
Sequence 1 2:0.666667	Sequence 2 2:0.666667
Sequence 1 1:0.333333	Sequence 2 1:0.333333

The array A will consist of space for 200 ints. Although we allocated the space for A during runtime, we cannot change its size. A will consist of space for 200 ints for the duration of the program or until the entire array is destroyed using the delete operator.

Keep in mind that each container has an allocator object. It is the allocator object's responsibility to acquire memory for the objects that will be inserted to a container. Regardless whether the container is constructed with a particular size or no size, when objects are inserted to the container, the container's allocator object will allocate the memory during runtime. Again, dynamic structures are structures whose size can change during the execution of a program. For instance, the program in Listing 7.4 uses a method from an allocator class called Storage and three vector methods to demonstrate the notion of a dynamic container. The three vector methods are max_size( ), size( ), and clear( ). The max_size( ) method of the allocator object is also used. The max_size( ) method of the allocator class reports the maximum number of bytes that can practically be allocated by an allocator object.

Listing 7.4 Demonstrating a Dynamic Structure

```
// Listing  7.4
// This program demonstrates that the sequence container vector
// is a dynamic structure.

#include <vector>
#include <iostream>
#include <memory>

using namespace std;

void main(void)

{
    vector<int> *A;
    allocator<int> Storage;
    A = new vector<int>((Storage.max_size() / 100),10);
    cout << "Size Of A " << A->size() << endl;
    cout << "Cap. of A " << A->max_size() << endl << endl;
    A->clear();
    cout << "Size after clear " << A->size() << endl;
    delete A;
}
```

A container of type vector<int> is declared. As designated by the int parameter, this container will hold integers. The container is called A. Notice the statement:

```
cout << "Size Of A" << A.size() << endl;
```

in Listing 7.4. It sends the number of objects stored in A to the standard output by calling the size( ) member function of A. The size( ) method returns the number of elements stored in the vector. The max_size( ) member function of the vector container returns the largest number of objects that can be stored in the vector. The space for the objects in vector A in this listing is dynamically allocated, therefore, the space for the objects that will be stored in A is allocated at runtime, as opposed to compile time. The allocation of this space will be handled by A's allocator object.

We use the size( ) method to see how many objects were allocated. We use the max_size( ) method to determine the largest number of objects that vector A can store. We use the clear( ) method to remove the objects from A. It is important to note that, although the objects have been removed from vector A, the storage for those objects can be still owned by the vector, depending on the memory management scheme in place. This means that vector A may unintentionally prevent other objects from using this memory. The memory allocated for the objects is not technically free until we issue the

```
delete A;
```

statement. At this point, the memory for the objects held by vector A is released, as is the memory vector A used for data members. So, although we call the clear( ) method, the space the objects occupied might continue to be owned by vector A. However, the number of objects contained in A will be zero.

Destructing Sequences

Every container has a destructor that will invoke the destructors of the objects it contains. The destructor will also use its allocator object to deallocate the memory that the objects used. The basic operation of the destructor is to:

1. Remove all elements from the container, effectively calling the destructors for all contained objects.

2. Deallocate the memory for the container, effectively returning all requested memory back to the operating system or memory pool.

Sequence Insertion Modifiers

All containers must provide some method to add objects to the container. This can be done with constructors, as for vector A in program Listing 7.4, or it can be done with an insertion member function. All sequence containers provide three basic types of insertion member functions. First, are the push_front( ) and push_back( ) member functions, which add an element to the front or back of a container. Next are the insert( ) member functions. Each of the sequence classes has several versions of this function, which can insert an element or group of elements at a specific position or range of positions within a container. Where the push_front( ) and push_back( ) member functions add a single element either to the front or to the back of a container, the insert( ) member functions can insert a single element or a group of elements into any position or positions within the container. The insert( ) member function can also be used to insert *n* copies of an element starting at any specific position in the container that the user specifies. The third way to add objects to a container is through use of the assignment operator. A container that is empty may be populated by assigning it the objects from another container. Using calls to the push_back( ), push_front( ), insert( ), and operator=( ) member functions, along with the constructors that accept arguments, is the standard way to allow the user to add objects to any sequence container.

Sequence Deletion Modifiers

All of the sequences provide methods to remove objects from the containers. Remember, removing objects from a container is different from deallocating the space that those objects take up, as demonstrated in Listing 7.4. If an object has a constructor that allocates space for that object, that constructor is called when the object is created. The container's allocator data member creates space upon construction of the container or when there is not enough memory allocated during an insertion request. When the object is removed from the container, the object's destructor is called, not the destructor for the container. The container returns the memory it has allocated for an object once the container has left scope, or when the container has been deleted using the delete operator. The destructor for the container will remove all remaining objects and use the allocator object to deallocate space that those objects occupied. The destructor for the container will be called when the container leaves scope or when the delete operator is called.

Each sequence container has three basic kinds of removal: a pop( ) member function or functions, a collection of erase( ) member functions, and the container's destructor. There are two kinds of pop( ) member functions: pop_front( ) and pop_back( ). The pop_front( ) member function removes an object from the front of a container and the pop_back( ) member function removes an object from the back of a container. Like the insert( ) member functions, the erase( ) member functions are *position* functions; that is, they can erase either an element or group of elements from a specified position or positions.

Other Sequence Container Accessors

Table 7.7 shows the three basic ways to access objects in a sequence container. These accessors allow access to the objects without changing the objects or changing the container.

The front( ) and back( ) member functions are used to access single objects in a container. The front( ) member function can be used to access the front or first element in a container. The back( ) member function can be used to access the back or last element in a container. The subscript[ ] operator is available only for the vector and deque containers. The subscript operator provides direct access often referred to as random access to an object in a container. For instance, if we have a deque named A that consists of 15 elements, then we can retrieve any element in A by specifying its relative position to the beginning of the container. For instance, A[7] returns the seventh element in A, or A[N]

Table 7.7   Nonmodifying Access to Objects in Containers

NONMODIFYING ACCESS METHODS	DESCRIPTION
front( )	Used to access the front or first element in a container.
back( )	Used to access the back or last element in a container.
subscript[ ] operator	Used for direct or random access of an element in a container.

returns the *Nth* element in A. As with the front( ) and back( ) member functions, the subscript[ ] operator is a method for accessing objects within the container.

Sequence Iterator Accessors

The third method of accessing objects in a container is through the use of iterators, object-oriented generic pointers. The *dereferencing* of an iterator using the * operator returns the object to which the iterator points. Just as a pointer contains an address, or points to where an object is in memory, an iterator contains a position, or points to where an object is within the given container. When a pointer is dereferenced, the object to which the pointer is pointing is returned, as opposed to the address that the pointer contains. When an iterator is dereferenced, the object to which the iterator is pointing is returned, as opposed to the position that the iterator contains.

Whereas a pointer is a built-in type in C++, the iterator is a class defined in the container class library or by the user. This means that iterators can engage in encapsulation, polymorphism, and inheritance. Just as arithmetic can be performed on pointers in C++, arithmetic can be performed on the container class library iterators. These iterators are distinguished by the services they provide. Each has member functions that implement a certain minimum set of services.

There are five kinds of iterators in the container class library (Table 7.8), in contrast to one type of pointer in C++. The iterators form a hierarchy moving from least to most powerful. The least powerful iterators are the input and output iterators, followed by the forward iterator, the bidirectional iterator, and finally, the random-access iterator, the most powerful and flexible. Table 7.9 shows the fundamental services provided by each class of iterator. Moving down in the table, notice that each iterator offers more services and greater flexibility. Also notice that the random-access iterator class offers the full range of *iterator arithmetic* by defining operator++, operator--, operator+, operator--, and all of the relational operators.

The program in Listing 7.5 demonstrates how bidirectional iterators can be used to move forward and backward in a container.

The iterator for the list container is a bidirectional iterator. Along with its capability to be dereferenced and written to, a bidirectional iterator allows forward as well as backward movement in a container by providing definitions for the ++ and -- operators. The program in Listing 7.5 inserts six numbers into MyList, then the program does a forward iteration or forward traversal through the list container, inserting each element of the list into cout. Notice the statement on line 20:

Table 7.8 Basic Iterator Types and Their Descriptions

ITERATOR TYPES	DESCRIPTION
input	Reads objects from an input source and stores the object.
output	Writes objects to an output source.
forward	Writes and reads objects to and from containers or streams.
bidirectional	Writes and reads objects to and from containers or streams; can sequentially iterate through the objects in a container in a forward or backward direction.
random access	Writes and reads objects to and from containers or streams; can sequentially iterate through the objects container in a forward and backward direction; can directly access any object in the container.

```
list<double>::iterator M = MyList.begin();
```

It declares M to be of type iterator, and initializes it with the location of the first element in the container. Since the iterator for the list class is bidirectional, the M object will provide forward and backward iteration through the container. M is an object, and provides at least the services shown in Table 7.9 in the row for bidirectional iterators. The ++ operator causes M to traverse from the beginning of the MyList container to its end.

Next, notice the statement on line 28:

```
M = MyList.end();
```

It assigns one position beyond the last element in the container to M. This is a "beyond the end position," and it should not be dereferenced. It is a housekeeping construct. Once we have this position, we can traverse backward through the MyList container using the −− operator.

In each case, the * operator is used to return the object to which the iterator is pointing to. The statement

```
cout << "MyList : " << *M << endl;
```

Table 7.9 Iterator Objects Services

ITERATOR	READ	WRITE	ACCESS	ITERATION	COMPARISON
input	= *p		* ->	++	== !=
output		*p =	*	++	
forward	= *p	*p =	* ->	++	== !=
bidirectional	= *p	*p =	* ->	++ −−	== !=
random access	= *p	*p =	* ->	++ −− +	== != <
				+= −−=	<= > >=

Listing 7.5   Demonstrating Bidirectional Iterators

```
1    // Listing 7.5
2    // This program demonstrates the usage of
3    // the bidirectional iterator for the list container
4
5
6    #include <list>
7    #include <iostream>
8
9    using namespace std;
10
11   void main(void)
12   {
13       list<double> MyList;
14       int N = 0;
15       while(N < 6)
16       {
17           MyList.push_back(N + 3.14);
18           N++;
19       }
20       list<double>::iterator M = MyList.begin();
21       while(N)
22       {
23           cout << "MyList : " << *M << endl;
24           M++;
25           N--;
26       }
27       N = MyList.size();
28       M = MyList.end();
29       M--;
30       cout << " Reverse Direction-----------" << endl;
31       while(N)
32       {
33           cout << "MyList : " << *M << endl;
34           M--;
35           N--;
36       }
37   }
```

in Listing 7.5 on lines 23 and 33 uses the * operator, which dereferences the M iterator and returns the object to which M is pointing. Therefore, instead of a location being inserted to cout, the object to which M is pointing is inserted to cout.

Although we classify deque and vector as sequential containers, their access methods are not restricted to sequential access. The sequence containers that have only a sequential access method will only allow objects to be accessed at the beginning or end of the container. The third object in a container that has sequential access can only be accessed after the first and second objects have been passed. The vector and deque classes provide both sequential and direct access methods. This means that the programmer can access an object anywhere within a deque or vector container without having to access an object before or after the object that is being requested. The subscript[ ] operator is used to specify a location within the container. Iterator arithmetic can also be used to specify a particular location within a container. After using iterator arithmetic, the programmer can dereference the iterator with the * operator to access the object that is located at the position to which the iterator is pointing.

The program in Listing 7.6 demonstrates how the random access iterators can be used with containers that support direct access.

Listing 7.6 Using Random-Access Iterators

```
// Listing 7.6
// This program demonstrates some of the uses
// of the random-access iterators, the subscript[ ]
// operator, and iterator arithmetic

#include <deque>
#include <iostream>

using namespace std;

void main(void)
{
    deque<double> MyDeque(10,5);
    deque<double>::iterator P = MyDeque.begin();
    P = P + 5;
    *P = 25;
    P = P - 3;
    *P = 15;
    P++;
    *P = 30;
    P += 5;
    *P = 125;
    MyDeque[0] = 0.005;
    MyDeque[9] = 500.05;
    int N = MyDeque.size();
    P = MyDeque.end();
    P--;
    while(N)
    {
        cout << "MyDeque : " << N << " " << *P << endl;
        P--;
        N--;
    }
}
```

Object-Oriented Vectors

A vector that has been designed using the object-oriented constructs and is encapsulated within a class or struct is an object-oriented vector. The C++ language supports a basic array container, but it is not object-oriented. It cannot be specialized with polymorphism, it has no member functions, and it does not support encapsulation. The array container in C++ is a fixed-size container; although it can be dynamically allocated, it is not a dynamic structure. The amount of space allocated for a traditional C++ array does not change throughout the life of that array. This is in contrast to the object-oriented vector, which *is* a dynamic structure. Its size is not fixed; it may grow or shrink during program execution. This is one of the primary advantages of using the object-oriented vector over the traditional C++ array.

Like the traditional C++ array, a vector is a container that provides direct access to the objects it contains. This is in contrast to lists, queues, and stacks, which only provide sequential access, meaning that the objects stored in lists, queues, and stacks can only be accessed in a serial fashion; objects can be processed only at the beginning, end, top, bottom, front, or back. Before an object in the middle of a container can be accessed, all of the objects that precede that object must first be processed. When objects are stored in a vector, they may be directly accessed by an index. The index specifies the relative location of the object in the list. The relative position may be relative to either the beginning or the end of a logical block of memory. For example, an index of 5 would specifically be referring to the fifth object in the vector. If we had a vector called Vect, then the operation Vect[5] would return the fifth object in the vector. There would be no need to first access objects 1 thru 4. The fifth object may be accessed directly, hence the term *direct access.* The vector is an indexed structure.

Like the traditional C++ array, vectors also provide *constant time* access. Constant time refers to the amount of time that it takes to locate an object in the vector container. When a container has constant time access, it should take no longer to access the last item in the container than it takes to access the first item. Although the vector is a sequential structure, like a list, the access methods of the vector allow direct as well as sequential access. Figure 7.2 shows the logical structure of a vector container. The vector container does not impose specific order on the member. However, each of the members is assigned a *position* or *index* within the container. By specifying the object's position or index, direct access can be achieved.

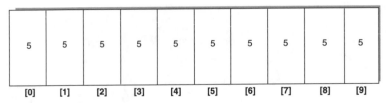

Figure 7.2 Logical structure of a vector container.

Why Vectors Are Useful

The vector can be used to implement queues, stacks, lists, and other more complex structures; in fact, the vector can be used to implement virtually any other container. The only other container that has this distinction is the list. In languages such as C, Pascal, Fortran and COBOL, the array or vector is the only built-in container provided. It is assumed that all other containers can be simulated using the array or vector container. Many important sorting and searching algorithms require that the objects to be sorted and searched be stored in a vector. One of the most used searches in computer science, the *binary search,* is often implemented with objects stored in a vector. The fact that the vector is a dynamic, direct-access structure means that it can be used in any situation where the programmer needs to store a group of objects for later access in an efficient manner. Because the vector has constant time access, the vector's performance as a container is predictable. We can determine the efficiency of this structure easily. Another major reason vectors are so useful is that they are easy to implement. The user can easily insert, remove, and access objects stored in a vector. Vectors do not require advanced knowledge of data structures and algorithms.

The standard class library provides a vector container. This vector can be used to store built-in as well as user-defined data types. If the vector is used to store user-defined data types, it is assumed that the == operator and < operator are defined.

Constructing a Vector

The container class library vector has four constructors. One takes no arguments; this is the default constructor. It builds a vector with size zero.

The vector class also has a constructor that accepts the size of the constructed vector and the value to which the vector is to be initialized:

```
vector(size_type n, const T& value = T());
```

For this constructor, n is the number of elements of type T the vector will be able to hold when it is constructed. Notice, this constructor has a default value of T( ). If this argument is not passed, the constructor uses the default constructor of type T to initialize all of the elements in the vector.

The vector class also has a constructor that accepts another vector as its argument. This means that a vector can be constructed using a copy of another vector. The final constructor for the vector class takes two iterators as arguments. This means that a vector can be constructed with a range of objects from some other collection or container. The program in Listing 7.7 illustrates how a vector can be constructed with a range of objects.

Destructing a Vector

As with all of the standard class library collections and containers, the vector has automatic storage management. The programmer does not have to manually allocate or deallocate memory for the objects a vector will store; the vector automatically allocates memory. When a vector object leaves scope, the vector's object destructor is called. The

Listing 7.7 Constructing a Vector with a Range of Objects

```
// Listing 7.7
// Example of constructing one vector
// with a range of objects from another vector

#include <algorithm>
#include <iostream>
#include <vector>

using namespace std;

void main(void)
{
    vector<char> VectB;
    vector<char>::iterator P;
    VectB.push_back('B');
    VectB.push_back('@');
    VectB.push_back('#');
    VectB.push_back('Z');
    VectB.push_back('%');
    P = VectB.begin();
    P += 2;
    vector<char> VectA(P,VectB.end());
    int N = 0;
    for(N = 0;N < VectA.size();N++)
    {
        cout << VectA[N] << endl;
    }
    vector<char>VectC(VectA);
    ostream_iterator<char> Out(cout," ");
    copy(VectC.begin(),VectC.end(),Out);

}
```

destructor first removes any objects that remain in the container. The destructors are called for each of these objects. After the objects have been removed, the vector uses its allocator class to deallocate any memory that it has allocated for objects.

NOTE:

Removing an object from a container does *not* deallocate the memory that the object occupied. It only causes that object's destructor to be called. Neither does using the erase( ) member function deallocate memory; it only removes the object from the container. Allocated memory is not returned to the free store until the container leaves scope or is deleted.

Accessing Vector Information

The vector container has four member functions that return information about vectors: size( ), max_size( ), capacity( ), and empty( ).

The size( ) and max_size( ) Accessors

The size( ) and max_size( ) member functions of the standard class library collection and container classes are somewhat misnomers. On the surface, you might assume they would report the container's size, measured in kilobytes, megabytes, gigabytes, and so on. But they do not. The size( ) member function reports how many objects are currently in the container, and the max_size( ) member function returns the largest number of objects that can be placed in the container. The max_size( ) member function's calculation is memory-model-dependent. For instance, the max_size( ) member function will return the number of objects that take up no more than 64K in an MS-DOS or 16-bit Windows environment. It will return a much larger number of objects in operating system environments like Unix, NT, or VM, because of their virtual memory management capabilities and flat memory models. Since these operating systems do not have 64K segment limits, all available RAM can be used to store objects. Furthermore, because these OSes are virtual paging operating systems, the operating system can use disk space as an internal memory supplement.

The capacity( ) Accessor

The capacity( ) member function reports the largest number of objects that can be stored without reallocating more memory. In contrast to the max_size( ) member function, which returns largest possible number of objects that can be stored in the container, the capacity( ) member function only reports how many can be stored before more memory has to be reallocated. Because the vector container has automatic memory management, it increases the amount of memory that it needs as necessary. If the container does not have enough memory available when the user inserts objects to the container, the container allocates more memory. How much memory? This is dependent upon the operating system environment, because the OS is ultimately responsible for supplying the program with memory. Figure 7.3 shows the flow of a memory request.

This process is somewhat transparent to the user. If the container does not have enough memory to hold the object being inserted, the container automatically allocates more memory. This request is initially handled by the allocator data member of the container. The allocator's request is translated into a call to functions such as operator new( ), cmalloc( ), or malloc( ), and memory is ultimately returned by operating system-specific functions such as DosAllocMem( ), the OS/2 memory allocation function.

Virtual paging operating systems are pretty much standard issue these days. Systems including VM, Unix, OS/2, VMS, or Windows NT manage memory in blocks called *pages*. The smallest *page size* for these operating systems is 4096 bytes. When a container needs to allocate more memory for an object, it makes a request to the operating system. The operating system returns a block of memory that is evenly divisible by the operating system's page size. For example, if an empty container got a request to store 5003 1 byte objects, the container would make a memory request of the operating system. An operating system with a 4096 byte page would return 8192 bytes. This is why the capacity( ) member function can return a different number from the

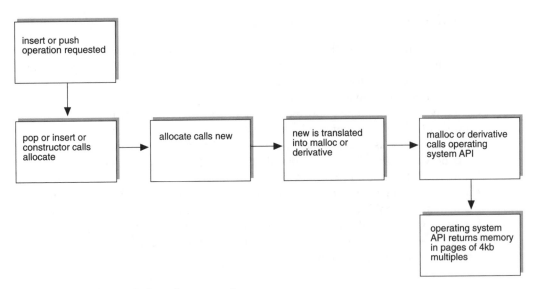

Figure 7.3 Basic translation of a request for memory.

size( ) member function. Although our container would actually have 5003 1 byte objects, the container has the *capacity* to store 8192 1 byte objects. This process is demonstrated in Listing 7.8.

Table 7.10 shows the output of the program is Listing 7.8. Notice the capacity of X in the table immediately after we used the push_back( ) member function to insert the number 1 to the container. The capacity( ) member function returned a value of 1024. This means X can now hold as many as 1024 ints without having to reallocate. You might be wondering, if only one int was placed into the container, where does the 1024 come from? The answer to this question lies in the fact that the operating system is ultimately responsible for supplying the program with memory. Refer back to Figure 7.3, which shows the basic translation of a request for memory. When we added an int to the container, the container's automatic memory facility ultimately requested memory from the operating system. The smallest block of memory the operating system could supply was one page. So, although we only asked for a block the size of an int, we got 4096 bytes. The 1024 that the capacity( ) function reports in Table 7.10 can be calculated by dividing the size of the block of memory returned by the size of an int. For our compiler, an int is 4 bytes; hence, 4096/4 = 1024. For a 16-bit environment like Windows or MS-DOS, the capacity would report 2048 because the size of an int is 2 bytes as opposed to 4 bytes.

After adding the number 1 to container X in Listing 7.8, the capacity( ) was 1024. The addition of objects to the container was done with a for loop:

```
for(int N = 1;N < 10000;N++)      // Loop 1
{
    X.push_back(N);
}
```

Listing 7.8 Using size( ), capacity( ), and max_size( )

```
1    // Listing 7.8
2    // This program demonstrates how the size(), capacity()
3    // and max_size() are used. It also demonstrates how
4    // a container can be constructed from another container
5    // using the constructor or the insert() methods
6
7    #include <iostream>
8    #include <vector>
9    #include <list>
10
11   using namespace std;
12
13   void main(void)
14   {
15
16       vector<int> X;
17       vector<int> Y;
18       X.push_back(1);
19       Y.push_back(1);
20       Y.push_back(3);
21       Y.push_back(5);
22       Y.push_back(7);
23       cout << "X size     " << X.size() << endl;
24       cout << "X capacity " << X.capacity() << endl;
25       cout << "X max size " << X.max_size() << endl;
26       X.insert(X.begin(),Y.begin(),Y.end());
27       cout << "X size     " << X.size() << endl;
28       cout << "X capacity " << X.capacity() << endl;
29       cout << "X max size " << X.max_size() << endl;
30       cout << "Y size     " << Y.size() << endl;
31       cout << "Y capacity " << Y.capacity() << endl;
32       cout << "Y max size " << Y.max_size() << endl;
33       vector<int> Z(Y);
34       Z.insert(Z.end(),13,Y.front());
35       cout << "Z size     " << Z.size() << endl;
36       cout << "Z capacity " << Z.capacity() << endl;
37       cout << "Z max size " << Z.max_size() << endl;
38
39
40
41   }
```

Although the current capacity is only 1024, the container is forced to make room for 10000 more ints. Once the container makes room, the new capacity, as shown in Table 7.10, is 16384 ints. The container has grown in size. This is what we mean by dynamic structure. As long as no more than 16384 int objects are added to the container, the container will not have to be reallocated.

Table 7.10   Output from Listing 7.8

X size 1
X capacity 1024
X max size 1073741823
X size 5
X capacity 1024
X max size 1073741823
Y size 4
Y capacity 1024
Y max size 1073741823
Z size 17
Z capacity 17
Z max size 1073741823

The empty( ) Accessor

The empty( ) member function returns a Boolean true if the vector contains no objects and a Boolean false if the vector contains objects.

Using Modifier Methods to Place Objects into Vectors

Objects can be placed in a vector using:

- Constructors
- push_back( ) method
- insert( ) methods
- [ ] operator
- = operator
- swap( )

The modifier methods may be used to change the contents of a vector container. Objects may be inserted to the vector using vector constructors, one of the insert( ) member functions, the push_back( ) member functions, or using assignment with the [ ] operator as an rvalue or using assignment from one vector to another. Objects can also be placed into a vector using the swap( ) member function. The vector class has three constructors and three forms of the insert( ) member function that can be used to insert objects. The insert( ) member functions allow the programmer to place either a single object at a particular location, a range of objects starting at a particular location, or *n* copies of a single object starting at a given location. This means the program can place objects in the middle or at the end of a container. The push_back( ) member function inserts a single object to the rear of the vector. The [ ] operator and an index position can also be used to insert an object at a particular location within the vector. Because the vector does have automatic memory management, the constructors, the insert( ) member functions, and the push_back( ) member functions will automatically allocate as much memory as is necessary to fulfill the object insertion request. The swap(X) member function takes the elements from X and stores them in the vector; those objects will be placed in the vector called X. These member functions can be used with whatever legal *object type* the vector has been constructed to hold.

The vector container has a member function called reserve( ). When this member function is called, it informs the vector container that a change is planned in the number of objects the vector will be holding. It is important to note that calling the reserve( ) member function does not actually cause any new memory to be allocated; calling the reserve( ) member function is only an alert to the container that more memory may be needed. More memory will not be allocated until the memory that the objects are taking up exceeds capacity( ). After the reserve( ) member function is called, capacity( ) is greater than or equal to the argument of reserve( ), if there is a reallocation. Note that any reallocation of a vector container invalidates all the pointers, iterators, and references that refer to elements in a vector.

Removing Objects from a Vector

There are two ways to remove objects from a vector object: the pop_back( ) and erase( ) modifiers.

The pop_back( ) Modifier

The pop_back( ) member function removes the last object in the vector. If the vector has n elements, pop_back( ) removes the object at the $n - 1$ position. For the vector container, this is the same as end( ) $- 1$.

The erase( ) Modifier

The vector class has two erase( ) member functions: erase(X) erases the element pointed to by X; erase(First,Last) erases all of the elements in the range [First,Last), where First and Last are iterators. Using *interval notation,* this means all of the objects, including the object pointed to by First, up to but not including the object pointed to by Last. Remember that Last is a past-the-end container value. The last iterator should not be dereferenced; its value should be used only to test the end of the container. In the event the last parameter is not actually the end( ) of some container, the values are removed up to but not including the value to which Last points. Recall that using the erase( ) member function to remove objects from the container does not deallocate the space that these objects occupied in that container. It only serves to remove the objects and call destructors for those objects, not the destructor for the container. When the destructor for the container is called, any remaining objects in the container are removed. At that point, the memory that those objects took up is returned.

Accessing Objects from a Vector

The front( ) member function can be used to return the first element in a vector. If we have a vector A, then calling front( ) accesses the A[0] element of the vector. As in the traditional C++ array, the vector's first element is found at index 0. Calling the front( ) member function returns this object. The back( ) member function can be used to return end( ) – 1 element in the vector.

The operator [N] can be used to access the object located at the *Nth* position relative to the beginning of the vector. The operator [N] is one that gives the user direct access to any object that is stored in a vector. Although the user could begin at position 0 and step through each subsequent position in the vector for a sequential or linear access, using the [ ] operator, the user can jump right to the middle of the container.

The vector class also supports random-access iterators. The program in Listing 7.9 uses the front( ), back( ), insert( ), erase( ), push_back( ), size( ), max_size( ), capacity( ), and [ ] operator to demonstrate how vectors are accessed and how some of the vectors member functions work.

Table 7.11 shows the output of this program. Notice that the call to the front( ) and back( ) member functions is equivalent to calls to VectorA[0] and VectorA[VectorA.size( ) – 1], respectively. This demonstrates that the vector container is accessed in the same manner as the traditional C++ array. Another important feature of the vector class is demonstrated on line 19 in Listing 7.9. This is an example of iterator arithmetic, the object-oriented version of pointer arithmetic available in C++. Only random-access iterators support iterator arithmetic. Using iterator arithmetic is another method of gaining direct access to any object within a vector container. Also, many of the generic algorithms require random-access iterators. Since the vector class supports random-access iterators, vector objects can be used with any of these algorithms. For example, by adding 2 to the iterator in line 19, we effectively moved the iterator so that it points to the third object in the vector. The reason that this is the third object is because the zero position refers to the first object.

Another interesting characteristic of the vector object is what happens to allocated memory when all of the objects are erased but the destructor for the container has not been called. Notice that on line 38 we erased all of the objects out of the container VectorA; however, the call to capacity( ) on line 41 still shows that VectorA has a capacity of 512. This is because erase( ) only calls destructors for the objects and removes them from the container. Again, the erase( ) member function does not deallocate memory. Another important point Listing 7.9 demonstrates is how the reserve( ) member function affects capacity( ). Even though reserve( ) has been called, the size( ) of the container is still 0; however, the capacity is now 2000.

The erase( ) member function invalidates all references and iterators after the point of the erase( ) call. So, if there are iterators pointing to objects that come after the objects that were erased, these iterators or references will no longer be valid. There is a similar restriction on iterators after an insertion has occurred. If the insertion to the vector does not cause reallocation, any iterators, pointers, or references are still valid. But if the insertion does cause container reallocation, any iterators, pointers, or references that point to objects should be considered undefined.

Listing 7.9 Accessing Vectors

```
 1  // Listing 7.9
 2  // Example of using vector container's
 3  // information, object insertion, object removal,
 4  // and object iterator member functions
 5
 6
 7
 8    #include <vector>
 9
10    void main(void)
11    {
12        vector<double> VectA;
13        vector<double>::iterator P;
14        VectA.push_back(1.1414);
15        VectA.push_back(3.1415);
16        VectA.push_back(-5.3);
17        VectA.push_back(7);
18        P = VectA.begin();
19        P += 2;
20        cout << "The value at 2 + begin() " << *P << endl;
21        VectA.insert(P,9.99);
22        cout << "The value at 2 + begin() " <<  *P << endl;
23        VectA[2] = 0.33333;
24        cout << "The value at VectA[2] " << VectA[2] << endl;
25        cout << "The value at the 0th position in VectA "
26             << VectA[0] << endl;
27        cout << "The value returned by the front() member function ";
28        cout << VectA.front() << endl;
29        P = VectA.end();
30        P--;
31        cout << "The value at the N - 1 position in VectorA ";
32        cout << VectA[VectA.size() - 1] << endl;
33        cout << "The value at the end() - 1 position " << *P << endl;
34        cout << "The value returned by the back() member function ";
35        cout << VectA.back() << endl;
36        cout << "Vector's size before erase " << VectA.size() << endl;
37        cout << "Vector's max size before erase " << VectA.max_size()
38             << endl;
39        cout << "Vector's capacity before erase " << VectA.capacity()
40             << endl;
41        VectA.erase(VectA.begin(),VectA.end());
42        cout << "Vector's size after erase " << VectA.size() << endl;
43        cout << "Vector's max size after erase " << VectA.max_size()
44             << endl;
45        cout << "Vector's capacity after erase " << VectA.capacity()
46             << endl;
47        VectA.reserve(2000);
48        cout << "Vector's capacity after a call to reserve ";
49        cout << VectA.capacity() << endl;
50        cout << "Vector's size after a call to reserve ";
51        cout << VectA.size() << endl;
52    }
```

Table 7.11   Output Listing 7.9

The value at 2 + begin( ) –5.3
The value at 2 + begin( ) –5.3
The value at VectA[2] 0.33333
The value at the 0th position in VectA 1.1414
The value returned by the front( ) member function 1.1414
The value at the N – 1 position in VectorA 7
The value at the end( ) – 1 position 7
The value returned by the back( ) member function 7
Vector's size before erase 5
Vector's max size before erase 536870911
Vector's capacity before erase 8
Vector's size after erase 0
Vector's max size after erase 536870911
Vector's capacity after erase 8
Vector's capacity after a call to reserve 2000
Vector's size after a call to reserve 0

Relational Operations on Type vector

The == and < operators are defined for the vector container. The == operator returns a Boolean true if the objects in both vectors are equal. To determine the equality of vectors, the == operator that has been defined for the objects contained in the vectors are used. In other words, the == operator for the vector will compare each object from the two vectors. It will use the == operator that the user has defined to determine whether those two objects are equal. The first mismatch will cause the == operator to return a Boolean false. Likewise, the < operator compares each object one by one from the two vectors X and Y, and if each object found in X is less than each object found in Y, the operator returns Boolean true. The first object found in Y that is less than the corresponding object in X will cause the operator to return a Boolean false.

Deques

A deque (pronounced deck) is a queue whose restricted access is somewhat relieved. A queue is said to have restricted access because when a group of objects is stored in a queue, they may only be *dequeued* one at a time from the front of the queue, and may only be *enqueued* one at a time to the rear of the queue. In a deque, objects may be enqueued to either the rear or the front of the queue. Likewise, objects may be dequeued from either the front or the rear of the queue. Unlike the priority queue, the deque has no inherent sort order, so, in addition to being able to remove objects from the front or rear of the queue, the standard deque class allows direct access to objects through the use of the subscript [ ] operator.

Object-Oriented Queues, Priority Queues, and Deques

We are all familiar with the notion of a front-to-back ordering. A line in a restaurant or the line at a bank is a front-to-back ordering. The people in the line are serviced based on where they entered the line, starting with the first person in the line and ending with the last person in the line. Queues encapsulate the notion of when by providing first-come, first-served, and last-in-line, last-served concepts. Because queues deal with objects in this fashion, they are well suited to discrete simulation or event-driven programs. By capturing objects in queues, it is possible to simulate a *sequence of events*. The queue allows the programmer to do processing based on changes over time. Attention can be focused on the objects in the system, and the simulation can be regarded as the task of following the changes that occur as the objects move from activity to activity. The queue structure enables the programmer to capture or simulate the history of activities as they are applied to different entities within a program or system. Any program that needs to process events based on the order in which they happen, or "arrive," can use a queue. The place an object occupies within a queue can be used to symbolically represent time of arrival or history of transaction.

A queue is a front-to-back ordering whose logical structure looks like a line. Figure 7.4 shows the logical view of an object-oriented queue.

NOTE:

We use the phrase *logical view* or *logical representation* throughout this book to contrast with physical representation. The logical view or representation is how the programmer conceptually accesses or manipulates a structure or container. The physical representation is how and where the container or structure is actually stored in internal or external memory. In most cases, the logical representation of a container or structure is different from its physical representation.

In a queue, the items are deleted from the front and inserted to the rear of the queue. The queue is known as a FIFO (first in first out) structure, meaning that the first item inserted will be the first item removed. Thus, the queue can naturally represent aging relationships, because the oldest object is removed first and the youngest object is removed last.

Queues are sequential structures, therefore any method accessing a queue is a sequential access method. Queues are also dynamic structures; they can grow or shrink during program execution. When objects are inserted to a queue, the queue grows; when objects are deleted from the queue, it shrinks. The process of removing an object from a queue is known as dequeuing; the process of adding an object to a queue is called enqueuing. The FIFO notion is encapsulated within a single unit, and is accessible only through member functions. The encapsulation, together with the member function access, gives us an object-oriented queue. We can use inheritance, polymorphism, and encapsulation with queue classes to derive new collection and container classes. The runtime version of the queue class can be passed as parameters, and compared with relational operators. Object-oriented queues can be used as return values from func-

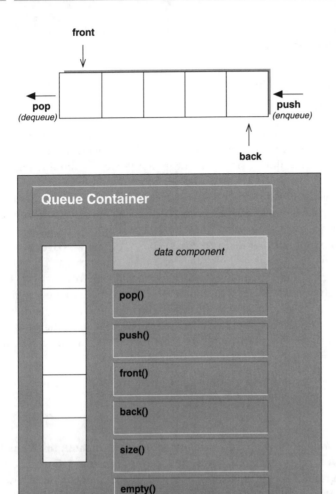

Figure 7.4 Logical view of an object-oriented queue.

tions. We may declare arrays of queues or structs whose fields consist of queues. We can have pointers to queues, linked lists of queues, and so on.

The Standard Deque

The deque is a concrete class, in contrast to the container class library queue and priority queue, which are interface classes. The C++ standard deque deviates somewhat from the traditional notion of a deque, in that the container class library deque provides the programmer with direct access in conjunction with sequential access. The deque class is declared in <deque>. Any user-defined object that will be used with a deque collection must define the == and < operators.

Constructing the Deque

The deque has four constructors:

```
deque(const Allocator& = Allocator());
deque(size_type n, const T& value = T(),
      const Allocator& = Allocator());
deque(const deque<T,Allocator>& x);
deque(InputIterator fi, InputIterator la,
      const Allocator& = Allocator());
```

The first is the default constructor, which will construct a deque where size( ) is zero. The second constructor initializes a deque of size *n*, and initializes all the objects in the deque with T( ) or the value of some other object that is passed to the constructor. The object passed must be of the same type as the objects that the vector holds. The third constructor initializes the deque with the copy of another deque x. The final constructor builds a new deque from a range of elements from another container that supports const_iterators.

Accessing Deque Information

The size( ) member function returns the number of objects in the deque, *not* the deque's size in bytes. The max_size( ) member function returns the largest number of objects of the current type that can be inserted to the deque. The empty( ) member function returns Boolean true if there are no objects in the deque and Boolean false if size( ) > 0.

Using Modifier Methods to Insert Objects into a Deque

Objects can be placed into a deque in a variety of ways:

- Constructors
- push_back( ) method
- push_front( ) method
- insert( ) methods
- [ ] operator
- == operator
- swap( ) method

Each of these may be used to change the contents of a deque container. The push_front(X) member inserts the object X to the front of the deque. The push_back(X) member function inserts the object x to the rear of the deque. The push( ) methods used will depend on the allocator class making room for the objects they are inserting into the deque container.

The Deques' Insert Modifiers

The deque class has three insert( ) member functions that allow the user to insert either a single object or range of objects to the deque. Unlike the push_front(x) and push_back(x) methods, which only allow insertion at either end of the deque, the insert( ) member functions let the programmer insert an object or objects anywhere in the deque. Objects can also be inserted to a deque using a constructor or the assignment operator. When objects are inserted to the deque, previously assigned iterators become invalid.

The Deque Deletion Modifiers

Three methods can be used to remove objects from a deque container:

- pop_back( )
- pop_front( )
- erase( )

The pop_front( ) member function removes the object currently at the front of a deque; pop_back( ) removes the object at the rear of the deque, and any iterators or references to the objects that are removed become invalid. Only iterators that have been "popped" are invalidated; other iterators to locations in the deque remain valid.

The erase(x) member function erases the object pointed to by the iterator x. The erase( ) methods will cause any reference or iterator to objects in the deque to become invalid. The erase(First,Last) member function erases all objects in the range from [First,Last). The destructors for any objects that are popped or erased will be called.

Deque Object Accessors

The deque provides for both sequential and direct access. Objects in the deque can be sequentially accessed by using the front( ) and back( ) member functions in conjunction with the pop_front( ) or pop_back( ) member functions. The front( ) member function returns the object at the beginning of the deque, and the back( ) member function returns the object at the rear of the deque. Iterators can also be used to sequentially traverse a deque; however, because they are random-access iterators, they support iterator arithmetic. For instance, if X is a deque object and P is an iterator supported by the deque class, then:

```
P = X.begin();
P = P + 5;
cout << *P;
```

will move directly to X[5]. Likewise, X[5] can be used to return the same object. Because deques support random-access iterators and the [ ] operator, they can be used for the same types of applications as vectors (see Listing 7.10).

As stated, the deque container supports direct access and has a random-access iterator. The random-access iterator is the most flexible of the iterators, providing read and write dereferencing, forward and backward iteration, all of the relational operations, and iterator arithmetic capability. The statement:

```
deque<double> Dq(10,5);
```

in Listing 7.10 declares Dq to be a deque collection containing doubles. The container is constructed to hold 10 doubles, each of which has a value of 5. The statement:

```
deque<double>::iterator P = Dq.begin();
```

Listing 7.10   Using Random-Access Iterators

```
// Listing 7.10
// This program demonstrates some of the uses
// of the random-access iterators, the subscript[ ]
// operators, with the deque container

#include <deque>
#include <iostream>

using namespace std;

void main(void)
{
    deque<double> Dq(10,5);
    deque<double>::iterator P = Dq.begin();
    P = P + 5;
    *P = 25;
    P = P - 3;
    *P = 15;
    P++;
    *P = 30;
    P += 5;
    *P = 125;
    Dq[0] = 0.005;
    Dq[9] = 500.05;
    int N = Dq.size();
    P = Dq.end();
    P--;
    while(N)
    {
        cout << "Dq : " << N << " " << *P << endl;
        P--;
        N--;
    }

}
```

in the listing declares P to be an iterator. Since deque containers have random-access iterators, the P object will provide the full set of iterator services on Dq. Figure 7.5 shows how the P object is used to iterate through Dq.

Notice in Listing 7.10 that in the iterator, P can be used in arithmetic expressions such as the statement:

```
P = P + 5;
```

This type of a statement uses pointer or iterator arithmetic, because we are performing addition and assignment on the iterator. This statement adds 5 to the current location of P. The 5 is used as a multiplier. In general, this kind of operation uses the numerical constant times the size of the object to determine what value to place in the iterator. In this statement, 5 is the numerical constant and the object has a size of double. So, in

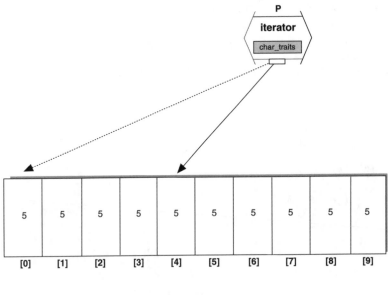

deque<doubles> Dq(10,5);

Figure 7.5 Iteration process through a deque.

simple terms, 5 times the sizeof(double) is added to P. Although this is not exactly what occurs in the container class library, it does describe the general logic of iterator or pointer arithmetic. Another important point to note about the processing in Listing 7.10 is that the first position in Dq is Dq[0] and the last position is Dq[9]. This corresponds to the traditional C++ array where the array index starts at position 0. Also note that the * operator is being used both as a read and write operator. The statement:

```
*P = 25;
```

demonstrates how the * operator can provide write dereferencing, because the number 25 is being assigned to the object to which the iterator P is pointing. Note that P itself contains the location of the object. The location is not being set to 2; the object at the location is set to 25. The object P is used to move to any position within the container that is required, allowing read and write dereferencing.

Table 7.12 shows the output for the program in Listing 7.10, generated by using the P object to iterate backward through the container using the statement:

```
P--;
```

After each insertion to cout, the P iterator is decremented. Notice the statements:

```
P = MyDeque.end();
P--;
```

The first assigns past-the-end position to the P iterator; the next statement ensures that P is referring to a valid position before the while look is entered.

Table 7.12 Output from Listing 7.10

Dq: 10 500.05
Dq: 9 125
Dq: 8 5
Dq: 7 5
Dq: 6 25
Dq: 5 5
Dq: 4 30
Dq: 3 15
Dq: 2 5
Dq: 1 0.005

Container Class Library Adaptors

The standard class library supports seven basic containers: vector, list, deque, set, multiset, map, and multimap. They provide the fundamental capabilities to store, retrieve, and access objects. The containers and collections are augmented by a set of algorithms bundled with the container class library. Missing from the list of basic containers are stack, queue, and priority queue. These are standard data structures and are requirements in many important applications. To meet that necessity, the standard class library provides three template classes called adaptors that can be used in conjunction with the sequence containers to provide the functionality of stacks, queues, and priority queues.

What Are Adaptors?

Adaptors are classes that modify or adjust the interface of other classes to simplify, restrict, make safe, disguise, or change the view of the set of services provided by the modified class. When a class is used for the sole purpose of changing the interface of another class, it is called an adaptor, or interface, class (see Stroustrup 1991, pg. 457). The container class library provides three types of adaptors: container, iterator, and function.

Container Adaptors

Container adaptors are used to extend the seven basic containers to include stack, queue, and priority queue containers, but they require virtually no new code to do so, because they largely reuse code from existing containers. For instance, the stack adaptor can be used to change or map the interface of the vector, list, or deque containers; the queue can be used to change or map the interface of the list and deque containers; the priority queue can be used to change the interface of the vector and deque containers. Table 7.13 shows which adaptors can be used with which containers. There are several ways the container classes can be approached and understood from an object-oriented design (OOD) or OOP perspective:

Table 7.13 Adaptors and Their Containers

CONTAINER ADAPTOR	IMPLEMENTATION
queue	list, deque
priority_queue	vector, deque
stack	vector, list, deque

- Logical views
- Geometrical views
- Access methods
- Mathematical descriptions
- Implementation representations
- Physical representations

The common collection and container classes are listed in Table 7.14.

The adaptor classes present one logical view of a class, while offering a different implementation of the class. When we look at the stack adaptor class that has been instantiated with a vector, we say that the class has the logical look of a stack but the implementation of a vector, or that it is a stack implemented as a vector. Likewise, we could have a stack instantiated by a list, in which case we would say that we have a stack implemented as a list. Figure 7.6 shows how the services of a stack can be mapped onto some of the services of a vector. Be aware: The standard class library adaptor classes don't really provide any new services, they simply change the names, order of execution, or syntax of services already in the container class library. For example, Listing 7.11 shows one definition declaration of the standard stack adaptor.

Notice that the familiar stack push( ) and pop( ) operations are not implemented by new functions. Instead, they are implemented by a call to Container's push_back( ) and pop_back( ) member functions. The stack is a parameterized class, so any class that provides empty( ), size( ), back( ), Push_back( ), and pop_back( ) can be used.

Table 7.14 Collection and Container Classes

CONTAINERS	
list	matrix
vector	file
COLLECTIONS	
queue	stack
set	multiset
map	multimap
graph	tree

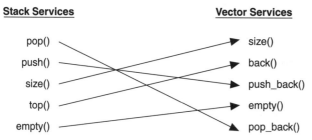

Figure 7.6 Mapping the services of a stack onto services of a vector.

In the stack adaptor in the listing, Container c is protected. This prevents nonderived classes or users from directly accessing the Container's member functions. In this way, the implementor of the stack adaptor can restrict how Container's member functions are used and how they are named. The stack adaptor class demonstrates one of the primary uses for interface classes. By restricting the use of certain member functions and masking the use of others with new names, the implementor of the stack adaptor can give the user new functionality while reusing code.

The declaration in Listing 7.11 illustrates another important point about adaptors, namely that they don't use inheritance. Adaptors are flat classes, just like the seven basic containers provided by the container class library.

Listing 7.11   Declaring the Stack Adaptor Class

```
// Listing 7.11
// This is a declaration of the stack adaptor class

template <class Container>
  class stack {
    friend bool operator==(const stack<Container>& x,
                           const stack<Container>& y);
    friend bool operator<(const stack<Container>& x,
                          const stack<Container>& y);
  public:
    typedef Container::value_type value_type;
    typedef Container::size_type size_type;
  protected:
    Container c;
  public:
    bool empty() const { return c.empty(); }
    size_type size() const { return c.size(); }
    value_type& top() { return c.back(); }
    const value_type& top() const { return c.back(); }
    void push(const value_type& x) { c.push_back(x); }
    void pop() { c.pop_back(); }
};
```

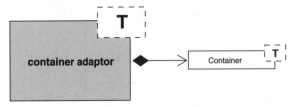

Figure 7.7   Basic class relationship for the container adaptors.

Declaring Container Adaptors

As templates, adaptors must be passed arguments during declaration. The arguments for the container adaptors are chosen from the list of sequence containers. For instance, to declare a stack of characters implemented as a vector, we would use the declaration:

```
stack < vector <char > > MyStack;
```

Once an adaptor container is declared, it can be used in the same manner as a sequence or associative container. For instance, to add objects to or remove objects from Sk, we could call the push( ) and pop( ) member functions:

```
Sk.push('a');
Sk.pop( );
```

To use the adaptor classes, their header files must be included. The stack is declared in <stack>, and priority queue and queue adaptors are declared in <queue>. Adaptors are primarily interfaces to existing sequence containers, therefore adaptor construction and destruction are handled by the constructors and destructors of the particular sequence container that is being mapped. The container adaptors all have a Container type as protected data members. Figure 7.7 shows the basic class relationship diagram for the container adaptors.

Object-Oriented Stacks

Stacks are containers that can hold an arbitrary number of objects; they are dynamic containers. When objects are inserted to a stack, the stack's size grows; when objects are removed from a stack, the stack size shrinks. The stack is a restricted-access container, meaning objects may be removed from a stack only one at a time. The stack is known as a LIFO (last in first out) structure, whereby the first item inserted to a stack is the last item removed, and vice versa. As with vectors, the stack's functionality is encapsulated within a single unit, and we say that the stack is object-oriented. An object-oriented stack can only be accessed by its member functions; thus, the block of memory that the stack uses to store objects can be properly controlled through a selective implementation of member functions. The runtime version of the stack class is an object. This means that stacks can be used in the same way as any other object in the C++ environment. We can use inheritance, polymorphism, and encapsulation with these stack classes to derive new collection and container classes. The runtime version of the stack class can be passed as parameters and compared with relational operators. Object-oriented stacks can be used as return values from functions. We may declare arrays of stacks or structs whose fields consist of stacks. We can have pointer to stacks, linked lists of stacks, and so on.

Figure 7.8 shows a logical view of an object-oriented stack container. The process of inserting objects to a stack is called *pushing* the stack; the process of removing or deleting objects from a stack is referred to as *popping* the stack. Objects are pushed onto the top of the stack and objects are popped from the top of the stack. The logical notion of the stack also includes a top( ) function, used to view what is on the top of a stack without popping it. Although the stack is accessed only from its top, it is still considered a sequence of objects, because a stack does not have a hierarchical structure. It is logically construed as a sequence of objects in a linear space.

Stacks have a wide variety of applications. They are used in everything from graphical user interface processing to mathematical expression and computer language parsing. They can also be used to process aging relationships. The stack implements the notion of *when*. It is used to process the latest element first, then the object that arrived before the latest, until it gets to the earliest element, which is processed last. Stacks permit only sequential access. If a stack contains a collection of objects, there is no way to jump to the middle of a stack to access an object. The stack must be popped for the appropriate number of times before an object in the middle of the stack can be removed.

The basic stack operation includes popping the stack, pushing the stack, looking at the top member of the stack, and checking the stack for underflow conditions. Theoretically, a stack is *upward unbounded.* This means that there is no conceptual limit to how

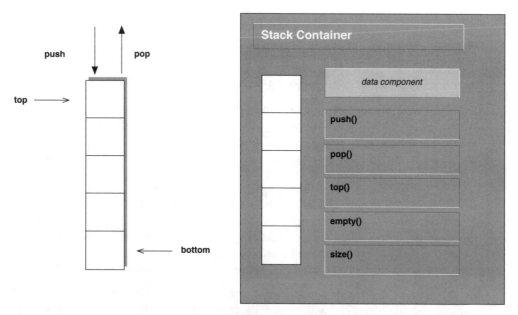

Figure 7.8 Logical view of an object-oriented stack container.

large a stack may grow. But though there is no theoretical limit, there is a physical limit, which is dictated by how much computer memory is available to a stack. When a stack operation exceeds the physical limit of the memory available, it is said to cause a *stack overflow*. On the other hand, stacks do have a lower bound. Once the last item has been popped from a stack, no more items are available. When an operation attempts to pop an item from an empty stack, the operation is said to have caused a *stack underflow*.

In the traditional data structure version of a stack, underflow and overflow are potential problems that may lead to program crashes. Using object-oriented stacks offers the programmer an extra level of protection. Because the memory block that implements the stack is encapsulated within the stack object, and access to that memory block is controlled by member functions, underflow and overflow conditions can be caught before they happen. If a user requests a pop( ) when there are no more objects to be popped, the stack object can decide how to respond. With traditional stack data structures, this response must be explicitly coded everywhere the stack is used and for each type of object the stack is used on.

The Standard Stack

The standard class library stack is implemented by an adaptor. Remember, adaptors are the container class library versions of Stroustrup's interface classes (see Chapter 2 for a discussion of interface classes). Because the stack is implemented as an adaptor, the programmer can change the implementation of the stack without changing the logical view of the stack. The logical view of the stack presents the programmer with the:

empty( )

size( )

top( )

push( )

pop( )

member functions and a LIFO access order.

But to declare a stack object, the user must provide it with an implementation. A container class library stack may be implemented by a vector, list, or deque container. This means that the block of memory where the objects are stored can be implemented as a vector, list, or deque container; furthermore, because vectors, lists, and deques produce different memory performances under different conditions, the user can pick which implementation best suits a given application. The logical view remains the same while the implementation changes. The stack adaptor provides an interface to functions that are available in the implementation containers. Table 7.15 lists the member functions that are used as implementations of the stack member functions based on Container. Also, any user-defined class that supports the back( ), push_back( ), and pop_back( ) functions can be used as an implementation structure for the stack.

As an adaptor, the stack does not have its own constructors or destructors. Instead, it uses the constructors and destructors of the implementation class. The == and < oper-

Table 7.15 Member Functions Used as Implementations of Stack

STACK METHODS	CONTAINER METHODS
push( )	push_back( )
pop( )	pop_back( )
top( )	back( )

ators are assumed to be implemented by any user-defined object placed into the stack. Figure 7.9 shows the class relationship diagram for the stack implemented as vector, list, and deque. Notice the relationship is containment as opposed to inheritance; this is what allows the stack to be an effective interface class. Because a stack is an adaptor, the declaration involves instantiating one template with an instantiated template. For example, to declare a stack of doubles implemented with a vector, the user would declare:

```
stack<vector<double> > MyStack;
```

This declaration creates a stack object called MyStack that consists of doubles. The vector<double> argument is used to instantiate the containment relationship shown in Figure 7.9.

Stack Member Functions

The top( ) member function returns the object at the top of the stack without removing the object. The push(X) member function pushes X onto the stack. The pop( ) member function removes the element at the top of the stack (because it is implemented by the remove member function of the implementor class, the same memory management that applies to the implementor class applies to the stack). The pop( ) member function only causes the object to be removed; it does not deallocate any memory. The size( ) member function returns the number of objects that are on the stack. The empty( ) member function returns Boolean true if there are no objects on the stack and Boolean false if there are objects on the stack. Any stack object can be compared to another stack object for equality using the == operator or for greater than using the > operator, and less than using the < operator.

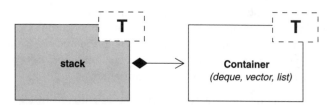

Figure 7.9 The stack adaptor relationship is one of containment, not inheritance.

The Standard Queue

Like the container class library stack, the container class library queue is an interface class. It offers a new logical view of another embedded class. The container class library refers to these interface classes as adaptors. Although the queue class is implemented with either a list container or a deque, it has the logical view of a queue. The queue adaptor is declared in the stack.h header file. Any user-defined object that will be used with the queue must define the < and == operators. Any user-defined class that supports the front( ), push_back( ), and pop_front( ) member functions can be used as an implementation structure for the queue. A queue can be declared as a list or deque using the syntax:

```
queue< list <UserDefinedType> > MyQueue;
queue< deque <UserDefinedType> > MyQueue;
//or
queue<list <BuiltInType> > MyQueue;
queue<deque <BuiltInType> > MyQueue;
```

The logical view of the queue presents the programmer with six operations:

front( )

back( )

push( )

pop( )

empty( )

size( )

The front( ) member function returns a reference to the object that is at the front of the queue; the back( ) member function returns a reference to the object at the rear of the queue. Neither of these functions will cause the object to be removed from the queue. And although the front( ) and back( ) member function return references, the programmer cannot change the value of the objects that are returned because these functions are const member functions. The push(X) member function inserts X at the rear of the queue, and because the queue has automatic storage management, if there is not enough space for X, more space will be allocated. The pop( ) member function removes the object at the front of the queue, in contrast to the front( ) member function, which returns the object. Note also that the pop( ) member function does not deallocate memory; it only removes the object at the front of the queue. The empty( ) member function returns Boolean true if the queue contains zero objects, and Boolean false otherwise. The size( ) member function returns the number of objects in the queue *not* the size of the queue in terms of bytes. Table 7.16 lists those member functions used as implementations of the queue member functions based on container.

Any container class library queue container can be compared with any other container class library queue container using the == or < operators. The comparison between elements in the queue is made using the user-defined == operator for those objects. The < operator does a lexicographical comparison of the objects in the queues; for example,

Table 7.16 Member Functions Used as Implementations of Queue

QUEUE METHODS	CONTAINER METHODS
push( )	push_back( )
pop( )	pop_front( )
front( )	front( )
back( )	back( )

the lexicographical comparison of two container objects, X < Y, causes a traversal of X and Y comparing pairs of objects A and B. If:

A < B, stop the traversal and return true

or if:

B < A, stop the traversal and return false

The traversal will continue until one of these cases is true. If the end of both containers is reached and no stopping condition has occurred, the containers are equal. If one of the containers has fewer objects than the other, the container with the fewest number of objects is said to be less than the container with the most.

Priority Queues

A *priority queue* is an ordered queue. The objects placed into a priority queue are sorted according to some kind of order. This does not change the restriction of only being able to dequeue from the front of the queue and enqueue to the rear of the queue.

There are two types of priority queues: *descending* and *ascending*. In a descending priority queue, the objects are sorted from largest to smallest; the largest object is dequeued from the queue first, followed by the next largest object, and so on. In this way, the queue is said to be descending, because as the values are dequeued they get smaller. The ascending priority queue is just the opposite; the objects are stored from smallest to largest, so as the objects are dequeued, they begin with the smallest and proceed to the largest.

Although the priority queue maintains a sort order, it can still be used for aging relationships or, as the names suggest, priority relationships. If the importance of an object can be associated with its position in the queue, then the queue can be used as a sort of emergency room, where the most critical objects get attention first.

The Container Class Library Priority Queue

Like the container class library queue, the container class library priority_queue is an adaptor or interface class. It, too, is declared in stack.h. But unlike the container class library queue, which can be implemented as a list or deque, the priority_queue can be implemented as a vector or a deque. Any user-defined class that supports random-access iterators and front( ), push_back( ), and pop_back( ) can be used as an implementation structure for the priority_queue.

The priority_queue supports the same set of member functions as the queue, with a couple of exceptions. The priority_queue container cannot be compared with other priority queue containers using the == or < operators. Instead, because it maintains the elements in a sorted order, it requires a comparison function object. The function object will be used to put the objects in the queue in order. The priority_queue has two constructors. One accepts a single function object as an argument. By changing the function objects, the priority_queue can be set up as either a descending or an ascending priority queue. The other constructor accepts a range of elements from another container and a function object. Figure 7.10 shows the class relationship diagram of the priority_queue implemented as a vector and deque. Notice that each implementation contains a function object as a data member.

The Associative Containers

The container class library provides four basic kinds of associative collections:

- Set
- Multiset
- Map
- Multimap

The term associative is used here to denote the logical way objects are stored and held in these collections. Unlike the sequence containers, the associative collections are not thought of as containing objects in a sequential fashion. A sequential traversal from the beginning to the end of the associative collection has no special meaning in terms of position, as it does with the sequential containers. We understand the definition of a set more by the group of operations that are performed on the set than by any other factor: set intersection, set union, set membership, and subsetting. No operations in the definition of a set specify how to access the set or the order that members in the set are to be stored in.

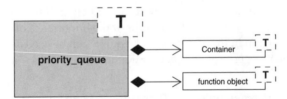

Figure 7.10 The priority_queue implemented as a vector and deque. Each implementation contains a function object as a data member.

Maps and multimaps are mathematical notions that implement the concept of relations. A map associates the elements in one set with the elements in another set. Let's say we have two sets: A = {a,b,c,d,e,} and B = {fish,fred,flea,flower,fox}. A map is a structure that associates pairs of elements, one from each set; for instance, (b,flower), (d,fox), (a,fish), and so on. Figure 7.11 shows a complete mapping between set A and set B. Multisets, sometimes called *bags,* allow more than one copy of a particular element to be stored. Multimaps, sometimes called *dictionaries,* allow more than one copy of a particular element to be stored.

Because sets, multisets, maps, and multimaps have no specified order in their descriptions, the implementor is at liberty to designate an order. The designers of the standard class library let the user of the associative collection determine what the order is. One difference the user will notice immediately between the sequence containers and the associative collections are the extra parameters in their declarations.

Using the Associative Collections

The associative collections are declared in four header files: set.h, multiset.h, map.h, and multimap.h. To declare objects of these collections, the user must include the appropriate header file. Noted: If these containers are to be used with user-defined classes, the == and < operators will have to be defined for the user-defined class. The associative collections make use of these operators in many ways. The primary use is to insert and find elements in the collection. In contrast to the sequence containers, which require only one argument in the declaration of a container, sets and multisets require two, and maps and multimaps require three. The program in Listing 7.12 declares M to be a set of ints.

Notice the declaration:

```
set<int, less<int> > M;
```

The first argument to the set template is int. This argument designates M to be a collection of ints. The next argument, less<int>, is new to our discussion of the container class library components. It determines the sort order of the objects that will be placed into the set container. Table 7.17 shows the output of the program in Listing 7.12.

Notice in Listing 7.12 that the integer values were inserted to M in no specific order. However, Table 7.17 shows the integer values to be in the set from smallest to largest.

Figure 7.11 Complete mapping between set A and set B.

Listing 7.12   Declaring a Set

```
// Listing 7.12
// This program demonstrates the declaration
// of a set container and how no duplicate
// Members are allowed.

#include <set>
#include <iostream>
using namespace std;

void main(void)
{
    set<int, less<int> > M;
    M.insert(1960);
    M.insert(1952);
    M.insert(1771);
    M.insert(1812);
    M.insert(1960);
    M.insert(1996);
    set<int, less<int> >::iterator N= M.begin();
    cout << "Number Of Elements " << M.size() << endl;
    while(N != M.end())
    {
        cout << *N << endl;
        N++;
    }
}
```

This is because the less<int> argument imposes an order from smallest to largest; it is a function object. The function object is another major component of the container class library. The less<T> function object is just one of the 15 provided by the container class library. Table 7.18 lists the container class library function objects and their basic descriptions. All associative collections require a function object in their declarations.

The less function object in the container class library provides a less-than relationship between X and Y. When the less<int> parameter was passed in the declaration of M in List-

Table 7.17   Output from Listing 7.12

NUMBER OF ELEMENTS: 5
1771
1812
1952
1960
1996

Table 7.18 Container Class Library Function Objects

TYPE	FUNCTION OBJECTS	DESCRIPTION
Base	unary_function	Simplifies the typedefs of the argument
	binary_function	and result types.
Arithmetic	plus	Provides arithmetic operations.
Operations	minus	
	times	
	divides	
	modulus	
	negate	
Comparisons	equal_to	Provides comparison operators.
	not_equal_to	
	greater	
	less	
	greater_equal	
	less_equal	
Logical	logical_and	Provides logical operations.
Operations	logical_or	
	logical_not	

ing 7.12, we were requesting that the set be ordered from smallest to largest. As the insert member function adds members to M, the less<int> function object is called to determine where the object should be placed in the set, based on its value being less than some other value in the set. In Table 7.17, the members in M appearing from smallest to largest is a result of the less<int> function object that was passed as the second argument in the declaration of M. We could, of course, have used the standard class library greater-than function object as the sort order, to order the objects in the set from largest to smallest.

The program in Listing 7.12 also demonstrates that only one copy of each member is allowed in the set. Note that we attempted to add the value 1960 twice to M. This request was ignored. Looking at Table 7.17, we can see that the number of elements in M is 5, not 6. This was determined by using a call to the size( ) member function of M. The less<T> function object is also useful in determining whether an object is already in the set. Since object, or key, equality is determined by the function object, if an object is equal to an object already in the set, it is not added.

NOTE:

Object equivalence for the associative collections is not determined by the == operator defined for the class. It is determined by two calls to the function object; for example:

```
MyObject(X,Y) == False, MyObject(Y,X) == FALSE
```

Constructors and Destructors for Standard Associative Collections

Each associative collection has three constructors. Each collection provides a default constructor, which takes one argument. However, the function object used to provide the sort order for the collection is used as the default for this argument, so the user does not have to specify an argument for the default constructor. It will build an empty collection.

The second constructor builds a collection with copies of another collection. For instance, if we declare two sets, A and B:

```
set<int, less<int> A
A.insert(5);
A.insert(6);
set<int,less<int> B(A);
```

then B will contain a copy of the members in set A.

The third type of constructor provided by the association containers is the range constructor. The containers are supplied with two argument iterators that meet the requirements of input iterators. The first argument represents the beginning of the range and the second argument represents the end of a range. The program in Listing 7.13 declares three sets: MySet, MySet2, and MySet3. M is constructed using the first type of constructor; remember, technically, this constructor requires one argument, but since the sort order function object is the default for this, the user does not have to supply an argument. The collection MySet2 is constructed with a copy of MySet with the statement:

```
set <int,less<int > > MySet2(MySet);
```

Table 7.19 shows that MySet2 contains the same elements as MySet; the elements in MySet2 are copies of the elements in MySet. MySet3 has been constructed using a range. The range that MySet3 accepts as an argument comes from the array of ints named A. Traditional pointers in C++ meet the requirements of input iterators, so we are able to specify the starting and ending address of the array as arguments to the constructor of MySet3.

Table 7.20 shows the output of the program in Listing 7.13. Again, note that MySet and MySet2 have the same elements because of the way MySet2 was constructed. The while loop in the program in this listing demonstrates how iterators can be used for loop control. Since Q originally points to the beginning of MySet, we can traverse the set using the ++ operator. Eventually, Q will be equal to MySet.end( ), causing the loop to exit.

Maps and multimaps are constructed the same as the sets and multisets. The program in Listing 7.14 uses arrays, sets, and maps to demonstrate how maps can be constructed and how elements can be inserted and accessed in map collections. One of the container class library pair objects is used to build objects that will be inserted to a map collection. Like the function objects, the pair object is one of the *pattern* objects the container class library uses to complete the functionality of the collections and containers. The definition for the pair object can be found in pair.h.

The program in Listing 7.14 declares three map collections: MapA, MapB, and MapC. MapA is built with the constructor that acts as the default for the association collection. This means MapA is constructed as an empty collection and has a sort order based on the function object passed as part of the collection declaration. Three objects are placed into

Listing 7.13 Declaring a Set Container

```cpp
// Listing 7.13
// This program demonstrates the declaration
// of a set container and the usage of the
// three types of constructors for a set

#include <function.h>
#include <set.h>
#include <iostream.h>

void main(void)
{
    int A[5];
    A[0] = 1960;
    A[1] = 1952;
    A[2] = 1771;
    A[3] = 1812;
    A[4] = 1996;
    set<int, less<int> > MySet;
    MySet.insert(1960);
    MySet.insert(1952);
    MySet.insert(1771);
    MySet.insert(1812);
    MySet.insert(1960);
    MySet.insert(1996);
    set<int, less<int> >::iterator Q = MySet.begin();
    cout << "Number Of Elements " << MySet.size() << endl;
    set <int,less<int > > MySet2(MySet);
    set <int,less<int > >::iterator N = MySet2.begin();
    set<int,less<int> > MySet3(A,A+5);
    set <int, less<int > >::iterator P = MySet3.begin();

    while(Q!= MySet.end())
    {
        cout << "MySet" << *Q << " : MySet2 " << *N;
        cout << " : MySet3 " << *P << endl;
        Q++;
        N++;
        P++;
    }
}
```

MapA: "bird", "bear", and "goblin". Elements placed into map collection are retrieved by specifying the keys they are associated with. This is similar to how elements of an array are retrieved. When accessing elements in an array, the user specifies the index of the element, and the element is returned. For example, by specifying A[5], we are asking for the fifth element from the array called A. Maps provide a similar functionality. Instead of associating each element with an integer value, a map allows any kind of

Table 7.19 Contents of MySet and MySet2

SET < INT, LESS <INT> > MYSET2(MYSET)	
MySet Contents	*MySet2 Contents*
1771	1771
1812	1812
19521	1952
1960	1960
1996	1996

object to be associated. This association is called a relation. In Listing 7.14, we associated "blue" with "bird", "brown" with "bear", and "green" with "goblin". This was done by using the [ ] subscript operator of the map class. When the container receives the request to assign an element, as in:

```
MapA["blue"] = "bird";
```

it checks to see whether an element called "bird" is already associated with "blue". If there is no such pairing, the pair is added to the container; from then on, when we select "blue" as the key, the element "bird" is returned. After the three elements and keys have been placed into MapA, MapB is constructed with a copy of the elements in MapA with the statement:

```
map<string,string,less<string> > MapB(MapA);
```

Table 7.21 shows the output of the program in Listing 7.14. Notice that MapB contains the same elements as MapA. Copying elements from one container to another can be done in a number of ways. One of the simplest is through the use of this constructor. MapB could also receive a copy of the elements in MapA by using the assignment statement:

```
MapB = MapA;
```

The MapC collection has been constructed using a range of input iterators, which, in this example, belong to an array named Group. Group is an array of four pair objects. The pair class has two data members: first and second. Each element in the Group

Table 7.20 Output from Listing 7.13

NUMBER OF ELEMENTS: 5
MySet1771: MySet2 1771: MySet3 1771
MySet1812: MySet2 1812: MySet3 1812
MySet1952: MySet2 1952: MySet3 1952
MySet1960: MySet2 1960: MySet3 1960
MySet1996: MySet2 1996: MySet3 1996

Listing 7.14 Using Map Constructors and Accessing Elements

```cpp
// Listing 7.14
// This program demonstrates the usage of the three
// constructors for the map collection. It also
// demonstrates how map elements can be accessed
// using associations. The last loop demonstrates
// how a set iterator can be used as an association
// element for a map.

#include <string>
#include <map>
#include <set>
#include <iostream>

void main(void)
{
    map<string,string,less<string> > MapA;
    pair<string,string> Group[4];
    Group[0].first = "orange";
    Group[0].second = "clock work";
    Group[1].first = "red";
    Group[1].second = "Herring";
    Group[2].first = "white";
    Group[2].second = "Knight";
    Group[3].first = "silver";
    Group[3].second = "bullet";
    MapA["blue"] = "bird";
    MapA["brown"] = "bear";
    MapA["green"] = "goblin";
    map<string,string,less<string> > MapB(MapA);
    cout << MapB["green"] << endl;
    cout << MapB["blue"]  << endl;
    cout << MapB["brown"] << endl;
    map<string,string,less<string > > MapC(Group,Group+4);
    set<string,less<string> > SetA;
    SetA.insert("white");
    SetA.insert("silver");
    SetA.insert("orange");
    SetA.insert("red");
    set<string,less<string> >::iterator P = SetA.begin();
    while(P != SetA.end())
    {
        cout << *P << " " << MapC[*P] << endl;
        P++;
    }
}
```

Table 7.21 Output from Listing 7.14

goblin
bird
bear
orange clock work
red Herring
silver bullet
white Knight

array is initialized to a pair of strings. The first string will be used for a key; the second will be used for an element. The MapC collection receives the starting and ending address of Group. These two addresses serve as the beginning and ending range for the constructor. The constructor initially builds the collection as empty, then, one by one, it inserts elements from the range, or interval [First,Last), where First represents the starting input iterator and Last represents the ending input iterator.

Table 7.21 shows the elements of MapC. Notice the statement:

```
while(P != SetA.end())
{
    cout << *P << " " << MapC[*P] << endl;
    P++;
}
```

Here, set iterator P is used to traverse SetA. SetA contains elements that are used as associations, or keys, for MapC. When P is dereferenced, it returns a string. This string is used as a key to retrieve an element from MapC. Table 7.21 shows the output of this statement.

All sequence containers provide destructors. The basic operation of the destructor is to:

1. Remove all elements from the container, effectively calling the destructors for all contained objects.

2. Deallocate memory for the container, effectively returning all requested memory back to the operating system or memory pool.

Associative Containers Insertion Modifiers

The set and multiset collections provide three basic ways to add objects, whereas the map and multimap collections provide four basic ways to add objects. Objects can be added to sets and multisets through constructors, the insert( ) member functions, and through assignment. Objects can be added to maps and multimaps through constructors, the insert( ) member functions, assignment, and the [ ] subscript operator. Refer back to Listing 7.13 to recall how the insert member function is used for sets and how the [ ] subscript operator is used for maps. There are four versions of the insert( ) member function, shown in Table 7.22, along with their definitions.

Table 7.22 The insert( ) Member Functions and Their Definitions

INSERT( )	RETURN TYPE	DESCRIPTION
a_uniq.insert(t)	pair<iterator, bool>	■ a_uniq is a value of the associative container class when the associative container class supports unique keys.
		■ *t* is inserted into the container if and only if there is no element in the container with key equal to the key of *t*.
		■ The bool component of the return type indicates whether the insertion takes place.
		■ The iterator component of the return type points to the element with key equal to the key of *t*.
a_eq.insert(t)	iterator	■ a_eq is a value of the associative container class when the associative container supports multiple keys.
		■ *t* is inserted into the container.
		■ iterator returns points to the newly inserted element.
a.insert(p, t)	iterator	■ *a* is a value of the associative container class.
		■ *p* is a valid iterator to *a* where the insert( ) should start to search.
		■ *t* is inserted into the container if and only if there is no element with key equal to the key of *t* in a container with unique keys; always inserts *t* in containers with equal keys.
		■ iterator returns points to the element with key equal to the key of *t*.
a.insert(i, j)	result is not used	■ *a* is a value of the associative container class.
		■ *i* and *j* comprise a range of elements inserted to the container.

Associative Containers
Deletion Modifiers

Objects are removed from the associative collections in two ways: when the collections leave scope and when an erase( ) member function is used. When an associative collection leaves scope, any objects that remain in the collection are removed and the destructors for those objects are called. After the objects have been removed, any space that the collection has allocated for those objects is released and the collection object is deleted. The erase( ) member function can be used to remove an interval of objects, as in [a,b], (a,b), [a,b) or (a,b]. The erase( ) member function can be used to delete all the elements in a collection that have a particular value, or to erase an element at a specific position. Table 7.23 shows the various versions of the erase( ) member function and its uses.

Associative Containers
Iterator Accessors

The associative collections iteration functionality is fundamentally the same as that for the sequence containers. The iterators for associative collections are bidirectional. The insert( ) member function does not affect the validity of the iterators and references to the collection. The erase( ) member function invalidates only the iterators and references to the erased elements.

The Set Container

A set is a collection of objects. Sets are more than just containers. They specify a rich interface and restrictions on the objects that can be a part of the set. Consider a set of

Table 7.23   The erase( ) Member Function and Its Uses

ERASE( )	RETURN TYPE	DESCRIPTION
a.erase(k)	size_type	■ *a* is a value of the associative container class.
		■ *k* is the key in which all elements with a key equal to *k* in the container are erased.
		■ When size_type is returned, it is the number of erased elements.
a.erase(q)	void	■ *a* is a value of the associative container class.
		■ *q* is a pointer to an element that is erased.
a.erase(q1, q2)	void	■ *a* is a value of the associative container class.
		■ *q1* and *q2* comprise a range of elements erased from the container.

red balls, a set of blue blocks, a set of even numbers, and so on. Membership in a set is determined by whether an object meets a condition or set of conditions. For instance, if we have a set of even numbers, any number divisible by 2 with no remainder can be an element of that set. Obviously, this excludes odd numbers, but this point serves to emphasize that not only does set membership specify the conditions for *inclusion,* it also implies *exclusion.* This is an important characteristic of sets, because sometimes it is as important to know if an object is *not* in a set as it is to know if an object *is.*

Another important characteristic of sets is that they allow an object to be included only once in the set. Then, along with the characteristics of set membership, inclusion and exclusion, the set operations provide powerful means for grouping and counting collections of objects. Set intersection, set union, set difference, set complement, and set subsets operations give the user the ability to identify groups of objects based on very complex set membership rules. Because the set membership conditions are virtually infinite, we can identify sets that are highly specific and that contain few or no members. For example, we can specify the set of all U.S. presidents elected under the age of 18. We can specify broad categories of objects, such as the set of blue products sold before the year 1960. Set membership inclusion and exclusion conditions can be very intricate and complex, or simple with very few exclusions.

Sets form the basis for many of the areas in mathematics and computer science; in fact, the entire field of database theory is founded on the notion of the set and set operations. Traditional languages such as Pascal provide elementary set data structures. Usually, the set operations for these types of languages are limited to testing set membership. Typically, no native data type is called set. Using C++ object-oriented constructs or template facilities, we can build set classes. Because C++ has support for object-oriented programming, we can extend the techniques of object orientation to the notion of sets, to design set classes, and specialize those classes with inheritance and virtual member functions. Further, we can instantiate the set classes to get set objects. Once we have set objects, we can store them in vectors, queues, stacks, lists, or even other set objects. We can use multiple inheritance to create hybrid sets. And because sets can take advantage of object orientation, we can store all kinds of diverse objects in sets, including bitmaps, sound files, built-in types, images, function objects, and more.

Once we have objects stored in our object-oriented sets we can use the set operations to build new sets, with new membership conditions. The set is one of the most versatile and expressive structures available to the C++ programmer. A set can be a collection of people, places, things, or ideas. For example, we may specify the set of all men over the age of 35 who are married and own pink cars, or the set of all of fish that grow to a length of 100 feet, or the set of all C++ compilers that require less than 1 meg to execute.

We call the people, places, things, or ideas in a given set its members, or elements. If x represents something or someone that is a member or element of a set we call A, we use the notation:

$$x \in A$$

to mean that x is a member or an element of A. If x is not an element of A, we use the notation:

$$x \notin A$$

This means x does not satisfy the membership rules for inclusion into set A.

When we want to explicitly list elements of a set, we use curly brackets—{ }—notation. For example, if we have a set named B that consists of all the odd whole numbers between 0 and 6, we write:

$$B = \{1,3,5\}$$

This notation works fine for sets that have only a few elements. But if we wanted to use set notation to denote a large set—for instance, the set of all telephone numbers in Los Angeles—then this type of notation is not appropriate since it is not practical to explicitly list every phone number in Los Angeles. So we use another form of notation. To talk about large, compound, or complex sets, we use *set-builder notation,* a form of set shorthand. For instance, if the set A is to contain all telephone numbers in Los Angeles, we would write:

$$A = \{x : x \text{ is a Los Angeles telephone number}\}$$

We read this as, "A is the set of all values of x such that x is a Los Angeles telephone number." By using set-builder notation, we are able to circumvent the enumeration of all of the members of a particular set. In general set-builder notation takes the form:

$$M = \{x : P(x)\}$$

where P(x) is a predicate describing the membership rules or conditions for the set M. Note that the colon is used to represent the phrase "such that." Any element meeting the conditions or rules stated in P(x) are members of the set M.

Set Relationships

The set that contains all of the elements or members under consideration is called the *universal set.* Two sets, A and B, are equal if every member in set A is in set B, and every member in set B is in set A. Set A is a subset of set B if every member in set A is also a member of set B. We denote this relationship with the $\subset$ sign, such as:

$$A \subset B$$

This statement expresses that A is a subset of B. For example, if set M is the set of all people who use computers, and set N is the set of all teenagers who use computers, we could denote the sets and their relationship as follows:

$$M = \{x : x \text{ is a person that uses computers}\}$$

$$N = \{x : x \text{ is a teenager who uses computers}\}$$

$$N \subset M$$

Figure 7.12 shows how the subset relationship between N and M is depicted using a Venn diagram. Venn diagrams are used to illustrate relationships between sets. When

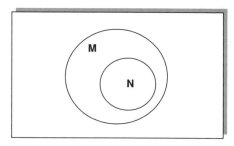

N ⊂ M

Figure 7.12   Venn diagram of a subset relationship between N and M.

we have two sets, such as N and M, where $N \subset M$ but $N \neq M$, then we say that N is a proper subset of M. However, if $N = M$, then we can say that N is a subset of M, or M is a subset of N. In this case, we write:

$$N \subseteq M$$

to denote that although N is not a *proper* subset of M, it is a subset of M.

If we have a set A, then A′ is the set of all elements that are not members of set A. The set A′ is called the *complement* of A. If:

$$A = \{x : x \text{ is a Los Angeles phone number}\}$$

then

$$A' = \{x : x \text{ is not a Los Angeles phone number}\}$$

Figure 7.13 shows the Venn diagram of the relationships between A and its complement A′. The empty set is the one that has no elements; it is denoted by $\varnothing$ or { }.

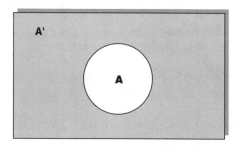

A'

Figure 7.13   Venn diagram of the relationship between A and its complement A′.

Common Set Object Types

There are several common types of set objects:

- Empty sets
- Singleton sets
- Power sets
- Universal sets
- Cartesian products
- Infinite sets
- Partition sets
- Multisets

As just stated, the *empty set* contains no members. It is also sometimes called the *null* set, and is denoted by { }. A set with exactly one element is called a *singleton set*.

For any set A, the *power set* of A, denoted by P(A), is the set of all subsets of A, and is written:

$$P(A) = \{X \mid X \subseteq A\}$$

The power set is a *set of sets*. If we have a set M, then P(M) is the power set. The power set of M is all of the possible subsets of M. For instance, if M = {a,b,c}, then the P(M) is:

$$P(M) = \{\{\ \},\{a\},\{b\},\{c\},\{a,b\},\{a,c\},\{b,c\},\{a,b,d\}\}$$

Notice that each element in the P set is also a set. And since the empty set is an element of every set, it is also an element of the power set. If P is a power set of M, and the *cardinality* of M is N, then the cardinality of P is:

$$|P| = 2^N$$

In other words, the number of elements in a power set P of set M is equal to 2^N, where N is the number of elements in set M. We can use the container class library set container to implement a power set. But note that because the cardinality of a power set is 2^N, memory resources can be quickly exhausted. Depending on the real size of the objects that are placed into a power set, power set operations can be extremely expensive. Let's say set M = {x | x is a common modem baud rate < 9600}, then:

$$M = \{300,1200,2400\}$$

The power set of M is:

$$P(M) = \{\varnothing,\{300\},\{1200\},\{2400\},\{300,1200\},\{300,2400\},\{1200,2400\},M\}$$

Note that $\varnothing$ set is a part of every set, including the power set.

The *universal set* is the set of all members or elements under consideration. It is only a subset of itself. When we use the container class library set container to declare a set, the instantiation of that set represents the universal set.

The *Cartesian product* is a set that has pairs of elements that come from two sets. Let A and B be sets. The Cartesian product of A and B, denoted by:

$$A \times B$$

is the set of all ordered pairs (x,y) where x is an element of A, and y is an element of B. If:

$$A = \{1,2\}$$
$$B = \{a,b,c\}$$

and if C is the Cartesian product of A and B, denoted by:

$$C = A \times B$$

then:

$$C = \{(1,a),(2,a),(1,b),(2,b),(1,c),(2,c)\}$$

An *infinite set* is a set without bounds. For instance, the set of all even numbers, or the set of all fractions between the 1 and 2, are infinite sets. Infinite sets can be denoted by:

$$A = \{2,4,6,8 \ldots\}$$
$$B = \{1 \tfrac{1}{2}, 1,\tfrac{1}{4},1\ 1\ \tfrac{1}{16}, 1\ \tfrac{1}{32} \ldots\}$$

Or they can be stated using set-builder notation; for instance:

$$M = \{x : x \text{ is a negative number}\}$$

Let M and N be two sets. If M and N have no members in common, then M and N are said to be *disjoint sets*. A separation of a nonempty set A into mutually disjoint non-empty subsets is called a *partition* of set A. For example, if:

$$M = \{300,1200,2400,9600,14400,28800\}$$

then one partition of M is:

$$M1 = \{300,2400\},$$
$$M2 = \{14400,1200\},$$
$$M3 = \{28800,9600\}$$

since $M = M1 + M2 + M3$. Another partition is:

$$M1 = \{300\}, M2 = \{14400,1200,2400,9600,28800\}$$

since $M = M1 + M2$. Note that the partition uses every member of the universal set.

A *multiset* is a set that can contain duplicates of members. Where a set is an unordered collection of unique elements, a multiset is an unordered collection of not necessarily unique elements.

What Is an Object-Oriented Set?

An object-oriented set is a class that models our notion of a set. The class encapsulates the attributes and characteristics of the set, and its member functions provide the traditional set operations. Once we have a set class, we can use polymorphism and inheritance to generate specializations of the set class, and it can be instantiated to create set objects. An object-oriented set will take advantage of the object-oriented constructs; it should allow the inclusion of built-in or user-defined types. Although an object oriented set could be normally treated as a collection of data structures and algorithms, it is treated as a self-contained single object within a program. We are able to declare a vector of set objects or pass set objects as parameters, and store set objects into other set objects.

Logical Representation versus Implementation of Set

The logical representation of the set gives the programmer the familiar set operations and the set notion. Set intersection, union, complement, and subsets are part of the logical representation of the set, as is the fact that it is an unordered collection of unique elements. The logical representation represents how the programmer or user of the structure accesses it. In the case of a set, the logical representation is totally different from the actual implementation. A set may be implemented by many high-level collections or containers, as well as by low-level data structures. A set could be implemented by a list, a vector, a tree, a graph, and so on. This is true of any container or collection.

Once we have a block of internal or external memory that can hold objects, we can begin to build a container or collection around that block of memory. The block of memory serves as the generic holder for the objects, and by providing member functions to access that block of memory in certain ways, the programmer has logical representations of various collections and containers. Figure 7.14 illustrates the layers of abstraction between internal or external memory and an object-oriented set class. Once

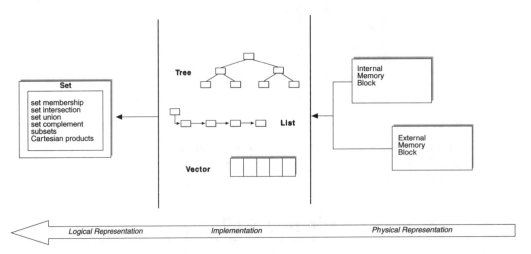

Figure 7.14 Layers of abstraction between internal or external memory and an object-oriented set class.

we have some data structure that provides a block of memory to store objects in, we can encapsulate the data structure within a class and provide set operations against that data structure.

The implementation of the collection and container class dictate the efficiency and flexibility of any class. If the set class is implemented with a fixed structure, then the set's allocation is efficient; however, the fixed size poses an undesirable restriction in some cases. If the set is implemented by a list, we have a dynamic structure that can grow or shrink during program execution, accessing the elements in the set will have a linear performance. If we want to test for set inclusion, conceivably, we could have to access every element in the list. The intersection operation would also suffer, because we might have to access N * M elements, where N is the number of objects in each set and M is the number of sets to be intersected. We could improve on the efficiency of the set's operations by implementing the set with a tree structure. Although the complexity of the set's implementation increases, the performance of the set's member functions dramatically improves. The trade-offs must be evaluated when deciding how to implement a collection or container class. Obviously, the best-case scenario is to provide a number of implementations and then use the implementation appropriate for the job at hand.

Whatever the implementation, the logical representation of a set should offer at least the core functionality of a set. Table 7.24 lists the core attributes and services a set class should provide. We use the set class from the container class library. Currently, it is implemented by a tree. This gives very efficient implementations for the set's member functions.

The Standard Set Container

The standard set is an ordered collection, in contrast to the formal notion of a set, which is an unordered collection. When a collection or container is unordered, the interface to that collection or container does not depend on the members being in a specific order. When a collection or container is ordered, the services and member functions for that container depend on and take advantage of the fact that the container is ordered. Because the traditional set notion is that of an unordered collection, without a particular manner by which to access the elements in the set, set iteration is undefined. Therefore, the container class library implementors have imposed an artificial order on the set class for efficiency purposes. Many operations are more efficient when they are performed on ordered data. For instance, if we wanted to make sure that an object about to be inserted into a list was unique, in an unordered list, we would have to examine every member of the list. In an ordered list, we could move to the position in the list where the object would be inserted and examine only surrounding objects. In the set container, object insertion, removal, and certain object access take advantage of the fact that the set has been put into a specific order. Note, however, that the user must specify a function object that designates the sort order for the set. (See Chapter 9 for a discussion on function objects and how they are used with the standard class library.)

Table 7.24 Core Attributes and Services of a Set Class

METHODS	DESCRIPTION
swap( )	Swaps elements with the given set.
clear( )	Erases all the values in the set container; same as erase( ).
key_comp( )	Returns the comparison object used in constructing the set container.
value_comp( )	Returns an object of the value_compare type.
find( )	Returns an iterator that points to the element equal to the given value.
count( )	Returns the number of elements in the set container.
lower_bound( )	Returns an iterator to the first element with a key not less than given value.
upper_bound( )	Returns an iterator to the first element with a key greater than given value.
equal_range( )	Returns a pair whose first member is lower_bound( ) and whose second member is upper_bound( ).
TYPEDEF ATTRIBUTES	**DESCRIPTION**
Key key_type	Same as value type.
Key value_type	Value type.
Compare key_compare	Binary predicate; same as value_compare.
Compare value_compare	Binary predicate; used to compare the stored values; has a default value of less<value_type>.

The set class is declared in <set>. As a template class, the user must supply the template with certain arguments in order to declare a set class. The user also must supply the type of object that will be stored in the set, along with a function object that specifies the sort order for the set's objects. Any class to be used with the set is required to have the == and the < operators defined for that class. To summarize, the user or "client" of a set container is responsible for supplying four things:

- A type for the set to store
- A function object for set's sort order
- A definition for the < operator
- A definition for the == operator

Client Responsibilities for Built-in Types

Because the < and == operators are already defined for all of the built-in data types in C++, the user or client of the set container can provide any of the built-in types without worrying about this requirement. Furthermore, the container class library provides two function objects that can be used with any of the built-in data types: less and greater. These function objects are templates, and therefore take arguments; for example:

```
less<double>

greater<int>
```

The declaration for the greater and the less function templates look like this:

```
template <class T>
struct greater : binary_function<T, T, bool> {
    bool operator() (const T& x, const T& y) const { return x > y; }
};

template <class T>
struct less : binary_function<T, T, bool> {
    bool operator() (const T& x, const T& y) const { return x < y; }
};
```

Notice the operator( ) defined in both classes. The operator( ) for the greater function object template returns the result of the > operator applied to its two argument x and y. The operator( ) for the less function object returns the result of the < operator applied to its two arguments x and y. To use the greater and less function objects with user-defined classes, the user must define the > operator for use with the greater function object and the < operator for use with the less function object.

If a set container is declared with the less function object, the members in the set would be sorted from the smallest to the largest element. Conversely, if a set container is declared with the greater function object, the set would be sorted from the largest to the smallest element. To declare a set A of doubles that will be sorted from the largest to the smallest, the code would look like this:

```
#include <set>
set < double, greater<double> > A;
```

After the user has supplied the set template with the type the set is to hold, the only other action the user must take is to decide whether the set should be sorted in ascending order (using the less function object) or in descending order (using the greater function object). In this code, the doubles would be in descending order.

Client Responsibilities for User-Defined Objects

When using user-defined objects with the set container, the user must define the < and the == operators. The user must also provide the set container declaration with a function object that will be used to designate the sort order for the set. For instance:

```
class user_defined{
...
public:
    bool operator() (user_defined &Obj)
    bool operator<(user_defined &Obj) ;
    bool operator==(user_defined &Obj);
    ...
};
```

Here, class user_defined has the correct operators defined. Although it is only necessary to define the == and the < operators for the user-defined class, the user should define any other operators that make sense for the class. The user should also supply copy constructors if the compiler-supplied copy constructor will not be adequate. If the user does supply a copy constructor, it is important to remember to also supply a destructor that deletes any temporary objects. Once a class with the appropriate operators has been supplied, along with a function object, the user can declare a set object. The set object initially is empty or can be constructed with objects.

Set Construction

The standard set class has three constructors:

```
explicit set(const Compare& comp = Compare(),
             const Allocator& = Allocator());
template <class InputIterator> set(InputIterator first,
                                   InputIterator last,
                                   const Compare& comp = Compare(),
                                   const Allocator& = Allocator());
set(const set<Key,Compare,Allocator>& x);
```

The first constructor takes a function object as a parameter and constructs an empty set. The function object will be used to determine the sort order for the set. It is interesting to note here that the instantiation of the set template already requires a function object, as in:

```
set < user_defined, less<user_defined> > X;
```

If the instantiation of the template requires a function object, why is there a constructor that accepts a function object as a parameter? First, for convenience. A second reason depends on the type of instantiator that the user's C++ compiler or linker uses. The typedef declaration is often used to simplify numerous, complex, ugly, or long declarations. For instance, we could use a typedef to simplify our set instantiation:

```
typedef  set <user_defined, less<user_defined> >  Set;
```

Because this is a typedef, the Set declaration does not occupy any space. It only acts as a shortcut for specifying set <user_defined, less<user_defined>>. Everywhere we declare an object of type Set, the compiler knows to use set <user_defined, less<user_defined>>. So, we can declare a list of set<user_defined, less<user_defined>> objects by using only the shortcut Set. For example:

```
Set SetA(greater<user_defined>);
Set SetB;
Set SetC;
```

These sets all hold user_defined objects. SetB and SetC hold user_defined objects and are sorted in ascending order based on the less<user_defined> function object that was provided in the typedef of Set. Notice, however, that SetA provides its own function object; it does not rely on the function object supplied in the typedef. SetA will be sorted in descending order based on the greater<user_defined> function object. This is one of the primary uses of a constructor that accepts a function object. It allows sets declared from a typedef to supply different sort orders. Depending on the compiler's or linker's template instantiator, the user could save code generation and prevent code bloat with typedef. For a thorough discussion of template instantiators, see *Designing and Coding Reusable C++*, by Martin D. Carrol and Margaret A Ellis (1995).

The second constructor takes three arguments. The third argument defaults to the function object used to instantiate the template. The first and second arguments are input iterators for the types of objects that will be stored in the set; they represent a range [i,j) of elements to be copied into the set, where i is the first element that will be stored and j is a past-the-end element for the range. For example:

```
#include   <set>
...
set<int,less<int> > A;
A.insert(3);
A.insert(5);
A.insert(7);
A.insert(9);
A.insert(11);
set <int, greater<int> > B(A.begin(),A.end(),less<int>);

...
```

B is constructed with the elements from the A set in the range A.begin( ) and A.end( ).

The third constructor accepts another set container as an argument. When this constructor is used, the set being constructed will receive a copy of the another set.

Set Destruction

When a set container leaves scope or when the delete function is called, all the space that was allocated by the set is returned. Before the space is returned, any members in the set are erased. The destructors for the members are called.

Set Container Information Accessors

Four member functions provide information about the set container:

size( )

max_size( )

empty( )

count( )

The size( ) member function returns the number of objects currently in the set. The max_size( ) member function returns the maximum number of objects that can be stored in the set container. The empty( ) member function returns Boolean true if the set is empty, and false otherwise. The count(X) member function returns the number of objects in the set equal to X. This member function can be used to test for set *inclusion*. If the count function returns a 1, we know the element is in the set; if it returns a 0, we know the element is not in the set.

Set Container Insertion Modifier Methods

There are three ways that objects can be added to a set container, using constructors, the = assignment operator, and insert( ) methods.

There are two set constructors that accept elements. One accepts a range of objects to be inserted into the set; the other accepts a set of objects to be inserted.

```
set<float,less<float> > A;
set<float,less<float> > B(A.begin(),A.end());
set<float,less<float> > C(B);
```

Assignment is defined for the set container. Therefore, we can assign all of the elements of a set A to an empty set B, as follows:

$$B = A$$

This statement will assign copies of all of the elements in A to B. The assignment statement uses the *shallow copy*. If the objects stored in the set do not have data members that are pointers, then the shallow copy poses no problem; however, if the objects stored in the set do have data members that are pointers, the shallow copy will only copy the pointers. This means A and B would have objects pointing to the same block of memory for the elements that had pointers. It follows, then, that any elements changed in B would also be changed in A, for those members that had elements that were pointers.

The insert( ) Modifiers

The set class has three insert( ) member functions. The single-object insert( ) member function is used only if that object is not already a member of the set. The second insert( ) member function inserts a range of objects into the set, assumed to be taken from some container that supports iterators. The third type of insert( ) member function inserts a single object into a particular position. This insert( ) member function takes two arguments: first, the object to be inserted; second, a "hint" to where the collection should place the object (the actual location will be determined by the objects that are already in the set container, along with the sort order in effect). In general, the time complexity for the range insert( ) member function is linear; for the other two types of insert( ) member functions, it is logarithmic.

The program in Listing 7.15 demonstrates the usage of set constructors, assignment statements, and the insert( ) member function.

The erase( ) Modifiers

The standard set container class has three erase( ) member functions: an erase(X) member function that removes the object located at position X; an erase(X) member function that removes object X from the set; an erase(i,j) member function that removes all of the elements from the *i*th location through the *j*th location. As far as deallocation of memory, they work in the manner previously described.

Listing 7.15   Using the Set Constructors and insert( ) Member Functions

```
1    // Listing 7.15
2    // This program demonstrates how to insert
3    // elements into set containers using constructors
4    // and insert methods
5
6
7
8    #include <vector>
9    #include <list>
10   #include <deque>
11   #include <set>
12   #include <iterator>
13   #include <iostream>
14   #include <algorithm>
15
16   using namespace std;
17
18   void main(void)
19   {
20       ostream_iterator<double> Out(cout,"\n");
21       vector<int> Vect(10,1);
22       list<float> List(10,2);
23       deque<double> Deque(10,3);
24       set<double,less<double> > X;
25       X.insert(Vect.begin(),Vect.end());
26       set<double,less<double> > Y(X);
27       Y.insert(List.begin(),List.end());
28       set<double,less<double> > Z(Deque.begin(),Deque.end());
29       Z.insert(Y.begin(),Y.end());
30       cout << "Z's size " << Z.size() << endl;
31       cout << "Z's max size " << Z.max_size() << endl;
32       cout << "Z's contents " << endl;
33       copy(Z.begin(),Z.end(),Out);
34   }
```

Set Container Accessors

Remember, traditionally the set does not specify a particular manner by which the elements or members of a set are accessed, in contrast to other collections and containers like stacks, queues, or priority queues. For instance, the last element placed into a stack must be the first element removed. Therefore, while iterating through a stack using pop( ) functions, the user is moving from the most recent member inserted to the member that has been in the stack the longest. Likewise, with a queue, the first object placed into the queue must be the first element out. In other words, a queue is a first come, first served structure. With structures like stacks, queues, and priority queues, iteration is defined, whereas with the set container no such specification is made for how to move from one element to the next. Therefore, we must invent the notion of iteration for a set.

The standard class library set is well ordered. Its objects have a sort order based on the function object passed in the constructor or in the instantiation of the template of the set. The set container supports bidirectional and reverse iterators. The bidirectional iterators allow us to move one object at a time forward or backward in the container. The reverse iterators switch the front with the back and the back with the front. Using the reverse iterator, we can also move one object at a time through the container. We can start at the beginning of a set container and traverse to the end, or we can start at the end and traverse to the beginning.

The iterators are like traditional C++ pointers in that they can be dereferenced. We can compare the iterators for equality or inequality using the == and != operators, respectively. We can assign iterators to other iterators. We can also save the values for iterators through iterator assignment. This allows us to jump into the middle of a set. This cannot be done with all collections and containers. For instance, by definition, we could not get to the middle of a stack until we have popped all of the objects that precede the middle. The iterators for the set class support the capability to move to the middle of the container through assignment.

NOTE:

Keep in mind that iterators are just C++ classes that have the necessary member functions and operators defined. Think of iterators as object-oriented pointers. We can assign one of the set's smart pointers to point to the first object in the container or to the last object in the container, then we can increment or decrement the pointer accordingly. Once we are at the location in the container that we want, we can dereference the smart pointer to get the object to which it is pointing.

Every set container knows the value of four iterators:

iterator::begin

iterator::end

reverse_iterator::rbegin

reverse_iterator::rend

These iterators, or smart pointers, point to the first object in the container and to one past the last object in the container. The values of these pointers are returned by four member functions:

begin( )

end( )

rbegin( )

rend( )

The programmer can declare objects of an "appropriate iterator type"; for instance:

```
set<T, Compare>::iterator P;
// or
set::<T,Compare>::reverse_iterator P;
```

Once an object of the appropriate iterator type has been defined, the user can initialize that iterator with a call to one of the set's iterator member functions, such as:

```
P = MySet.begin();
```

After the iterator has been initialized with a valid object location in the set, the iteration through the set container can begin. It is important to note that iterator P in this case must first be initialized with a valid position within the collection before it can be dereferenced. This can be done in a couple of ways: by assignment of one iterator to another, or by calling one of the set's iterator functions. Dereferencing an unintialized iterator will not return an element from the set. The begin( ) member function returns the iterator that points to the first object in the set. The end( ) member function returns a value that can be used to test the end of the set. The value the end( ) member function returns should not be dereferenced, as the primary purpose of this value is to test whether the iteration is at the end of the set. The rbegin( ) member function turns the set container upside down and starts to iterate from the bottom up. The rend( ) member function is used to test whether a reverse_iterator has reached the end of the set container. In the case of the reverse_iterator, the end of the collection is actually the beginning of the collection. Like the value the end( ) member function returns, the value the rend( ) member function returns also should not be derefenced.

Using the objects of bidirectional iterator type, we can visit every object in a set container in a sequential fashion. The set iteration does not support random or direct access. If direct or random access is required, a container such as the vector, deque, or map can be used. The set only enables sequential access. But because the set is ordered, the set algorithms intersection, union, difference, and includes are sufficient.

An object can also be visited using the find(X) member function, which returns an iterator pointing to X if it is in the set. If X is not in the set, the find( ) member function returns the value stored at end( ). This iterator can be used to retrieve the object from the set. The member functions lower_bound( ), upper_bound( ), and equal_range( ) can also be used to visit specific objects in a set container. The lower_bound(X) member function returns an iterator to the first object in the set container that is not less than X; if X is in the set, it will return an iterator that is pointing to X. By using the iterator, you can go directly to the object. The upper_bound(X) member function returns the first object in the set container that is greater than X; if X is not in the set, then lower_bound( ) and upper_bound( ) return end( ). The equal_range( ) member function returns the pair, lower_bound( ), and upper_bound( ).

Set Container Operators

The set container supports the relational operators ==, !=, <, >>, <=>, and >=. This means that given two sets, A and B, we can do comparisons such as A == B, A <= B, B != A, and so on. These comparisons will return Boolean true or false. The logical operators and arithmetic operators are not defined for the set container, but nothing prevents the user from doing so.

Set Operations

Some of the most powerful features of the set structure are the operations available on sets. These operations include:

- Set intersection
- Set union
- Set difference
- Set membership
- Subset membership

The set container supports each of these operations. Testing set membership can be done by using the count( ) member function of the set container. The other set operations are implemented as standard class library *generic* algorithms; they are not a part of the set class. In this sense, the standard set object is not self-contained, because it depends on procedures and functions that are not members of the class to complete its functionality. The generic set operations work with the set container because the set container has iterators that are compatible with the arguments that the set algorithms expect. Put in equation format, generic set algorithms + the set collection class = complete set functionality. Although this departs from the object-oriented implementation of the set class, it is a valid implementation of parameterized set functionality. Fortunately, C++ provides the programmer with object-oriented constructs as well as generic programming constructs, so we can choose the most flexible methods for implementing structures.

The set operations enable the programmer to deal with collections of objects based on how they are related to other collections of objects, or how a collection is related to a condition or set of conditions. Any set of objects have *identifying characteristics* that are based on set membership. The identifying characteristics give information about the objects in the set. For instance, we can conclude many things from the set of integers. We know that each integer is contained only once in the set. We know that there are no real or complex numbers in the set. We know that alphabets are not allowed in the set. We can be sure that the number 1 is in the set. We know that the set is infinite, and so on. We can, therefore, classify sets based on their membership rules or conditions. Subsequently, we can classify groups of objects by placing them into sets. This is important because it allows the programmer to organize and manipulate groups of objects based on category and classification.

NOTE:

The categories and classifications the set structure supports are based on the membership rules or conditions. The membership rules designate which objects are included in a set and which objects are not allowed. These membership rules or conditions are totally under the control of the programmer. By specifying the requirements an object must meet, the programmer has full control over each set's membership.

In any application, object-oriented or otherwise, there will be many groups of items that need to be classified, categorized, organized, compared, and counted, based on some set of rules or conditions. This is where the set container comes in. Two of the primary functions of a set are:

- Object classification based on rules or conditions
- Counting objects based on rules or conditions

The rules are specified by the programmer in the form of if-then-else sequences, looping conditions, template parameter specifications, object hierarchies, and "pattern matching." The program in Listing 7.16 demonstrates how the set operations are used with the set container.

This program determines if a set of keywords is contained in a text document. The program makes sure that it contains one set of keywords, but does not contain another set of keywords. The program uses set_difference to filter unwanted words and set_intersection to include wanted words. Finally, it uses the includes( ) algorithm to determine whether the document meets all of the search criteria. The program takes three text files: the first containing a list of words that are being searched for; the second containing a list of words that should not be in the text file; and the third containing the text document to be searched.

The Standard Multiset Container

The standard multiset container, sometimes called a *bag,* is an ordered collection. When a collection or container is ordered, the services and member functions for that container depend on and take advantage of that characteristic. And, remember, the traditional notion of the set is of an unordered collection; it does not specify a particular manner by which to access the elements in the set, so the multiset iteration is undefined. As for sets, the standard class library designers have imposed an artificial order on the multiset class for efficiency purposes. To repeat, many operations are more efficient if they are performed on ordered data. In the multiset container, object insertion, removal and certain object access take advantage of a specific order.

The multiset has the same functionality as the traditional set, but in addition, it allows the user to add duplicate objects into the set. The user of a multiset collection must specify a function object that designates the sort order of the set.

Listing 7.16   Using Set Operations with Set Containers

```
1    // Listing 7.16
2    // This program demonstrates the use of insert methods,
3    // the set_difference(), set_intersection(), and includes()
4    // set algorithms
5
6
7    #include <fstream>
8    #include <iostream>
9    #include <set>
10   #include <algorithm>
11   #include <string>
12
13   using namespace std;
14
15   int main(int argc, char *argv[ ])
16   {
17
18       if(argc == 4){
19           string Word;
20           ifstream Fin1(argv[1]);
21           ifstream Fin2(argv[2]);
22           ifstream Fin3(argv[3]);
23           ostream_iterator<string> Out(cout," ");
24           set<string,less<string> > Good;
25           set<string,less<string> > Bad;
26           set<string,less<string> > Document;
27           set<string,less<string> > X,Z;
28           while(!Fin1.eof())
29           {
30               Fin1 >> Word;
31               if(!Fin1.eof() && Fin1.good()){
32                   Good.insert(string(Word));
33               }
34           }
35           Fin1.close();
36           while(!Fin2.eof())
37           {
38               Fin2 >> Word;
39             if(!Fin2.eof() && Fin2.good()){
40                 Bad.insert(string(Word));
41             }
42         }
43           Fin2.close();
44           while(!Fin3.eof())
45           {
46               Fin3 >> Word;
47               if(!Fin3.eof() && Fin3.good()){
48                   Document.insert(string(Word));
```

Listing 7.16 *(Continued)*

```
49                    }
50            }
51        Fin3.close();
52        set_difference(Document.begin(),Document.end(),Bad.begin(),
53                       Bad.end(),inserter(X,X.begin()));
54        set_intersection(Good.begin(),Good.end(),X.begin(),X.end(),
55                         inserter(Z,Z.begin()));
56        if(includes(Z.begin(),Z.end(),Good.begin(),Good.end())){
57            cout << "Match Found" << endl;
58        }
59        else{
60                cout << " no match " << endl;
61        }
62        copy(Good.begin(),Good.end(),Out);
63        copy(Document.begin(),Document.end(),Out);
64        return(0);
65    }
66    else{
67            cerr << "Program requires 3 text files" << endl;
68            return(1);
69    }
70
71  }
```

The multiset class is declared in <multiset>. It is a template class, therefore the user must supply certain arguments to declare a multiset class. The user also must supply the type of object that will be stored in the multiset and a function object that specifies the sort order for the objects that will be placed into the set. Any class that is to be used with the multiset is required to have the = = and the < operators defined.

Multiset Insertion Modifiers

There are three ways that objects can be added to a multiset container, using constructors, assignment, and insert( ) methods.

Two multiset constructors accept elements. One accepts a range of objects to be inserted into the multiset; the other accepts a multiset of objects to be inserted. Assignment is defined for the multiset collection; therefore, we can assign all of the elements of a SetA multiset to an empty SetB multiset, as follows:

$$SetB = SetA$$

This statement will assign copies of all of the elements in SetA to SetB. The assignment statement uses the shallow copy, as described with a set.

Multiset insert( ) Modifiers

The multiset class has three insert( ) member functions:

```
iterator insert(const value_type& x);
iterator insert(iterator position, const value_type& x);
template <class InputIterator> void insert(InputIterator first,
                                           InputIterator last);
```

The single-object insert( ) member function inserts only one object into the container. Unlike the set class, when this member function is used, the multiset class will allow object duplication, meaning that even if the object is already a member of the multiset, it will be inserted. An insert( ) member function inserts a range of objects into the multiset. The range is assumed to be taken from some container that supports input iterators. The third type of insert( ) member function inserts a single object into a particular position. It performs as described for the set container. The time complexity for these insert( ) methods is linear and logarithmic.

Multiset erase( ) Modifiers

The standard multiset container class has three erase( ) member functions: an erase(X) member function that removes the object located at position X; an erase(X) member function that removes every occurrence of the object X from the set (in the set class, this function removes only one object; in the multiset class, this function removes every object that is equal to X and returns the number of elements or members that were erased); and an erase(i,j) member function that removes all of the elements from the *i*th location through the *j*th location. The first erase( ) member function has a time that is an *amortized constant.* The second and third erase( ) member functions have a size that is logarithmic, relative to the number of objects being removed from the multiset.

Multiset Accessors

Like the set, the multiset does not specify a particular manner by which the elements or members are accessed. Also like the set, the multiset is well ordered. Its objects have a sort ordered based on the function object that was passed in the constructor or in the instantiation of the template of the multiset. The multiset container supports bidirectional and reverse iterators.

Every multiset collection has four iterators:

iterator::begin

iterator::end

reverse_iterator::rbegin

reverse_iterator::rend

The values that these pointers hold are returned by four member functions:

begin( )

end( )

rbegin( )

rend( )

The programmer can declare objects of an "appropriate iterator" type; for instance:

```
multiset<T, Compare>::iterator P;
// or
multiset::<T,Compare>::reverse_iterator P;
```

Once an object of the appropriate iterator type has been defined, the user can initialize that iterator with a call to one of the multiset's iterator member functions, such as:

```
P = MySet.begin();
```

After the iterator has been initialized with a valid object location in the multiset, the iteration through the multiset collection can begin.

Using the objects of bidirectional iterator type, we can visit every object in a multiset collection in a sequential fashion. Like the set container, multiset iteration does not support random or direct access, only sequential access. But because the multiset is ordered, the set algorithms intersection, union, difference, and includes are sufficient.

An object can also be visited by using the find(X) member function, which returns an iterator pointing to X if it is in the multiset. Because a multiset may include an object more than once, the find(X) function only returns the iterator to one of those objects. If X is not in the multiset, find( ) returns the value stored at end( ). If at least one X is in the multiset, the iterator that find( ) returns can be used to retrieve the object from the multiset. The member functions lower_bound( ), upper_bound( ), and equal_range( ) can also be used to visit specific objects in a multiset collection.

NOTE:
Any member function or algorithm that returns at least a bidirectional iterator can be used to get an iterator that can visit objects in a multiset container.

The multiset count( ) member function behaves differently from the count(X) member function for the set. The count(X) member function for the set returns a 1 if X is in the set and a 0 if X is not in the set, whereas the count(X) member function for the multiset returns the number of elements in the set equal to X.

Multiset Operators

The multiset collection supports the relational operators ==, !=, <, >>, <=, >=. This means that given two multisets, A and B, we can do comparisons such as A == B, A <= B, B != A, and so on. These comparisons will return Boolean true or Boolean false. The logical operators and arithmetic operators are not defined for the multiset container, but nothing prevents the user from doing so.

Relations, Maps, and Multimaps

We have shown how containers can be used to store, retrieve, organize, manipulate, and search groups of objects. These are some of the primary uses for collections and containers. This section explains how containers can be used to relate or associate groups of objects. The relation describes a connection or association between objects. Concepts, persons, places, things, or ideas can be related with other concepts, persons, places, and ideas. Describing how objects are related can be done in many different ways; it is *context-dependent*. For example, a phone number can be related to a person. If no more is said other than that the phone number is related to the person, we do not know exactly how the phone number is related. We only know that there is some connection. What is the connection? How are they related? The phone number could belong to that person. The phone number may belong to the person's employer. The phone number could be the last phone number the person dialed. And so on.

A relation also defines a connection or association between items in a set or sets. For example, given two sets, a set of phone numbers and a set of geographical locations, we can specify a relation. The relation can be restricted to the geographic locations associated with specific area codes. Given the set of area codes {212,215,301,707}, we relate cities in the United States. The phone numbers and geographic locations can be expressed in this way:

Area Codes = {212,215,301,707}

Locations = {x : x is a city in the United States}

The relation of phone numbers to geographic location can be expressed in this way:

Relation = Area Codes X Locations

This statement reads: "Relation is a subset of the Cartesian product of Area Codes and Locations." This relation describes a *belonging* relation, which in these examples associates phone numbers with certain area codes to certain geographic locations. This example also illustrates an important point about relations: they are normally associations between groups of objects or sets.

A set of phone numbers with certain area codes could likewise be related to a set of residential or commercial locations. A phone number belongs to a residential or commercial location. There might be cases in which one location has multiple phone numbers because it has separate telephone lines, in which case, several phone numbers would be related to one location. Therefore, there may be a one-to-one correspondence between a phone number and a location, or there may be a many-to-one correspondence between phone numbers and locations. Inasmuch as the phone numbers are related to locations, can locations be related to the phone numbers in the same way? Would it also be true to say that for every location there is a phone number? What about locations without phones? Figure 7.15 illustrates possible relations between phone numbers with a 707 area code and addresses in Los Angeles, California. Determining to what extent phone numbers and locations are related helps in the description of the relation of phone numbers to locations. All relations have certain properties.

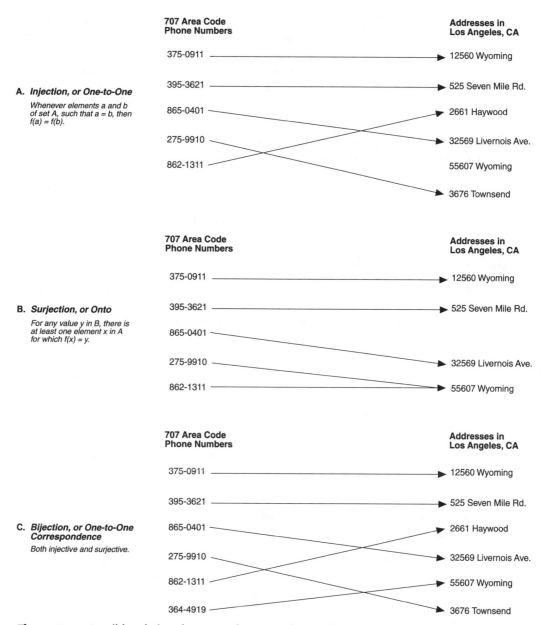

Figure 7.15   Possible relations between phone numbers with a 707 area code and addresses in Los Angeles, California.

A Map Container

A map container is a special type of set. The map collection, also called a *dictionary* or an *associative array,* is used to create a collection of related pairs. The map collection associates the elements of one set to the elements of another set. It is an indexed structure similar to a vector. But where a vector uses integers as the index values, a map collection can use any type as the index value. The map collection consists of related ordered pairs. The first element of the pair serves as the *key,* and the other element the *value.* The value can be accessed by using the key as the index value within a subscript operator. The key and the value can be of the same type or any mix of types. Map containers are associative structures where the key is one dimension and the value is another. It can be considered multidimensional. Figure 7.16 shows the geometrical view of a map collection.

Map collections are also nonlinear structures. The objects that it contains cannot be thought of as a sequence of objects. Map collections utilize both direct- and relational-access methods. They use direct access because an object can be retrieved from any position within the collection without the need to process other objects first. They use relational-access methods for the storage, retrieval, and access of one object (value) dependent upon its relationship with another object (key).

Standard Map Container

The standard map container is an associative *set* container that allows unique keys of a given type to be associated with a value of the same or another type. By definition, it is an unordered collection but the implementor has the liberty to designate an order by supplying the function object.

The map collection is declared in <map>. It is a template class, so the user must supply the template with certain arguments in order to declare a map class. The user also must supply the type of object that will serve as the key for the map, the type of object that will serve as the value the key is associated with, and the function object that specifies the sort order. The sort order is imposed on the key, as opposed to the value. Elements of the map collection are stored in pairs. Each map contains at most one pair (key + value) for each key value. A key cannot be associated with more than one value. Figure 7.17 illustrates the type of mapping used in the map container.

Client Responsibilities for Built-in and User-Defined Types

Because the sort order is imposed on the key, the < and the == operators should be defined for the key type. If the key type is a built-in data type, the < and the == opera-

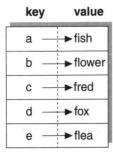

Figure 7.16 Geometrical view of a map collection.

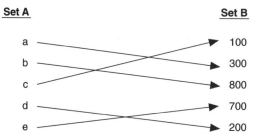

Figure 7.17 Mapping used in the map container.

tors are already defined. Therefore, the user, or client, does not have to be concerned with the operator requirements. The standard class library provides the less (<) and greater (>) function objects that can be used with any of the built-in data types. These function objects are also templates and must be passed the data type.

If the map collection is declared using the less function object, the key values of the map would be sorted from smallest to largest; if the map collection is declared using the greater function object, the key values of the map would be sorted from largest to smallest. For example, to declare a map collection using the built-in data type int for the key values and string for the values sorted in descending order, the code would look like this:

```
#include<map>
#include<string>

...
map<int,string,greater<int> > MapA;
```

The greater function object is used for descending order of the key values; it is passed the same type as the key type: greater<int>. If the key type were a double or a string, the template would be passed a double or a string, respectively: greater<double> or greater<string>.

When user-defined objects are the key type, the user or client must define the < and == operators. The user or client must also provide the map collection declaration with a function object that will designate the sort order on the key values. For example, to declare a map collection with the key values of the user-defined type clock_time and values of type string in ascending order, the code would look like this:

```
#include<map>
#include <string>
#include "clktime.h"
...
map<clock_time, string, less<clock_time> > MapB;
```

The function object uses the standard class library's built-in less function object. This is permissible because class clock_time has defined the < operator.

NOTE:
■■■■■ The client responsibilities for built-in and user-defined types also apply to the multimap collection.

Map Construction

The standard map container has three constructors:

```
explicit map (const Compare& comp = Compare(),
              const Allocator& = Allocator());
map(const map<Key,T,Compare,Allocator>& x);
template <class InputIterator> map(InputIterator first,
                                   InputIterator last,
                                   const Compare& comp = Compare(),
                                   const Allocator& = Allocator());
```

The first is the default constructor; it constructs an empty map. The comp function
object is passed as a parameter. The comp is a comparison function object used to order
the key elements of the map collection. As mentioned earlier, to instantiate a map collection, the function object is passed to the template before the constructor is called. It
may be convenient to use the typedef declaration when instantiating a map collection,
in particular when the declaration of an object is complex or long. The typedef declaration is a shortcut when there are numerous instantiations.

A typedef could be used in the instantiation of a map collection as follows:

```
typedef map<user_defined, string, less<user_defined> > Map;
```

Here, typedef is a shortcut for specifying the map map<user_defined, string,
less<user_defined>>. Then, every time an object is declared using the Map identifier,
the compiler knows to use map<user_defined, string, less<user_defined> >. This is
convenient when a list of Map type objects is declared; for example:

```
Map MapA;
Map MapB;
Map MapC(greater<user_defined>);
```

These maps all contain user_defined objects. MapA and MapB contain user_defined
objects in which the keys are sorted in ascending order based on the function object
less<user_defined>, according to the typedef Map. MapC uses the same typedef but
supplies the greater function object; therefore, MapC keys will be sorted in descending
order. This is one convenience provided by this constructor.

The second constructor accepts another map collection as the argument, the map copy
constructor. When this constructor is used, the map being constructed will be initialized with copies of the elements of the map in its argument.

The third constructor builds an empty map and initializes it with copies of the elements in the range [first,last). This constructor accepts three arguments. The first and
second arguments InputIterator first and InputIterator last are input iterators for
objects that will be stored in the map. The range [first, last) supplies the range of objects
that will be copied to the map collection. In Listing 7.17, a map collection is constructed
using the string object as the key, and string as the values.

Listing 7.17   Initializing a Map Collection with a Constructor

```
1    // Listing 7.17
2    // This program demonstrates how a map collection can
3    // be initialized using the constructor that initializes
4    // an empty map with the elements of a range supplied by
5    // a vector of pairs. This map collection uses the user
6    // standard string class as the key and a string
7    // as the value.
8
9
10   #include<string>
11   #include<map>
12   #include<iostream>
13   #include <vector>
14
15   using namespace std;
16
17
18
19   pair<string,string> Object1("122.22.33.45","www.example1.map");
20   pair<string,string> Object2("122.33.44.55","www.example2.map");
21   pair<string,string> Object3("122.33.55.66","www.example3.map");
22   vector<pair<string,string> > Group;
23   pair<string,string> Temp;
24
25
26   void main(void)
27   {
28       Group.push_back(Object1);
29       Group.push_back(Object2);
30       Group.push_back(Object3);
31       map<string,string,less<string> > MapA;
32       MapA.insert(Group.begin(),Group.end());
33       map<string,string,less<string> >::iterator P = MapA.begin();
34       while(P != MapA.end())
35       {
36           Temp = *P;
37           cout << "The key for MapA is " << Temp.first << endl;
38           cout << "The value for MapA is " << Temp.second << endl;
39           P++;
40       }
41
42   }
```

The program in Listing 7.17 creates a map collection and initializes the map with a range of elements. First the constructor creates an empty map, then it inserts the elements in the range or interval [First,Last) into the map collection. The range is the starting and ending address of a vector of pairs called Group. The map collection, called MapA, uses the standard string class as the key type and string class as the value. Then the keys and the values of the map collection are displayed.

Map Destruction

The map destructor:

```
~map()
```

is called when a map collection leaves scope or when the delete function is called. All the space allocated to the map is returned. Before the space is returned, any members that were in the map collection are erased. The destructors for the members are called individually.

Map Accessor Method Information

Four member functions supply information about the map collection and its objects. They are:

empty( )

size( )

max_size( )

count( )

The empty( ) member function returns a Boolean type, true if the map is empty and false otherwise. The size( ) member function returns the number of elements in the map collection. The max_size( ) member function returns the maximum possible size of the map collection. The count( ) member function accepts an argument X of key_type, which represents the type of the keys of the map collection. The count( ) member function will return the number of elements that have a key equal to X. The map collection has unique keys only, so if the key has been inserted into the map collection, the count( ) member function will return a 1; otherwise, it will return a 0.

Map Insertion Modifiers

There are three ways to add objects into the map container, using constructors, assignment, and insert( ) methods. Two of the three constructors can initialize an empty map collection. One constructor:

```
map(const map<Key, T, Compare>& x);
```

adds objects from one map collection to a newly constructed map collection. The other constructor:

```
template <class InputIterator> map(InputIterator first,
                                    InputIterator last,
                                    const Compare& comp = Compare(),
                                    const Allocator& = Allocator());
```

adds objects in the range [first,last) to a newly constructed map collection.

The assignment operation, which is defined for the map collection, is another way to copy elements from one map to another map:

$$MapA = MapB$$

After this operation is performed, the elements of MapB are copied to MapA.

Map insert( ) Modifier Methods

There are three insert( ) member functions. One accepts an iterator and an argument X of value_type. The value X is inserted into the map collection if it not already there. The iterator argument tells where the insert( ) member function should begin its search. An iterator that points to the element with the key equal to the key of X is returned. An insert( ) member function inserts the X value into the map if it is not already present. It returns a pair object composed of an iterator and a bool component. The iterator points to the element that has a key equal to the key of X. The bool component indicates whether the insertion of the X value has taken place. Another insert( ) member function accepts two arguments, input iterators that point to objects of the same type stored in the map collection. These pointers represent a range of elements. The elements in the range [first,last) are inserted into the map collection. This insert( ) member function has no return value.

The erase( ) Modifiers

The map container has three erase( ) member functions that remove objects from a map collection. One accepts an iterator that points to the element that is to be removed from the map collection. A second accepts a value of the key type. It removes all the pairs that have a key equal the value of its argument. This erase( ) member function returns the number of elements that were erased. Since the map collection has only unique keys, this value will always be 1 if the key is present in the collection; otherwise, it will return a 0. The third erase( ) member function erases elements in a range. It accepts two iterators that are assumed to point to elements in the map collection. The iterators point to the first and last elements of the range [First,Last). All the elements in that range are removed from the map collection. This erase( ) member function has no return value.

Map Object Accessors

The map container supplies a number of ways to perform object visitation: with iterators, the subscript operator, and numerous member functions. The map container supports bidirectional and reverse iterators; bidirectional iterators allow us to visit one object at a time forward or backward, and the reverse iterators allow us to go front to the back, back to front.

The map collection has four member functions that return iterators:

begin( )

end( )

rbegin( )

rend( )

The begin( ) and end( ) member functions return an iterator of bidirectional type. The rbegin( ) and rend( ) member functions return reverse_iterator of reverse type. The begin( ) member function returns a bidirectional iterator that can be used to begin the traversal through all the locations of the map collection. The end( ) member function returns a bidirectional iterator that is used in a comparison to end the traversal through the map collection. The rbegin( ) member function returns the reverse iterator that can be used to begin the traversal to all locations in the map collection in the reverse order. The rend( ) member function returns a reverse iterator that can be used in a comparison for ending a reverse-the-direction traversal through all the locations on the map collection.

One way to traverse through the elements of a map collection is to use the map iterator or reverse_iterator objects. An iterator object is declared, as here:

```
map<user_defined, string, less<user_defined> >:: iterator P;
map<user_defined, string, less<user_defined> >:: reverse_iterator R;
```

The first is a bidirectional iterator and the second is a reverse iterator. They are used with a map collection that has user_defined types for the keys and string types for the values. Once the appropriate type of iterator is declared, the user can initialize them with iterators that point to elements in the map collection with a call to the appropriate member functions mentioned earlier. The incrementation or decrementation of pointers can be used with the iterators to sequentially traverse through the map collection. When the iterator is dereferenced, the value is not a single element but a pair.

The subscript operator can be used to visit elements in the map collection, using a key value. The operator will return the object associated with that key. Unlike the subscript operators for vectors, if the map does not contain the key and its associated element, it will insert the pair into the map. The program in Listing 7.18 demonstrates the usage of iterators and the subscript operator for object visitation of a map collection. The program also demonstrates how the insert( ) member function can be used to initialize a map.

In Listing 7.18, MapA is initialized by using the insert( ) member function. The insert( ) member function is passed an interval [First,Last). The interval is the beginning and ending address of a vector of pairs called Group. Table 7.25 shows the output for the program in Listing 7.18.

Listing 7.18 Initializing a Map Collection with the insert( ) Method

```
1   // Listing 7.18
2   // This program demonstrates how a map collection can
3   // be initialized using the insert method and subscript
4   // operator.
5
6
7   #include<string>
8   #include<map>
9   #include<iostream>
10  #include <vector>
11
12  using namespace std;
13
14
15
16  pair<string,string> Object1("122.22.33.45","www.example1.map");
17  pair<string,string> Object2("122.33.44.55","www.example2.map");
18  pair<string,string> Object3("122.33.55.66","www.example3.map");
19  vector<pair<string,string> > Group;
20  pair<string,string> Temp;
21
22
23  void main(void)
24  {
25      Group.push_back(Object1);
26      Group.push_back(Object2);
27      Group.push_back(Object3);
28      map<string,string,less<string> > MapA;
29      MapA.insert(Group.begin(),Group.end());
30      MapA["122.77.66.77"] = "www.example4.map";
31      map<string,string,less<string> >::iterator P = MapA.begin();
32      while(P != MapA.end())
33      {
34        Temp = *P;
35        cout << "The key   for MapA is " << Temp.first << endl;
36        cout << "The value for MapA is " << Temp.second << endl;
37        P++;
38      }
39
40  }
```

Table 7.25   Output from Listing 7.18

The key   for MapA is 122.22.33.45
The value for MapA is www.example1.map
The key   for MapA is 122.33.44.55
The value for MapA is www.example2.map
The key   for MapA is 122.33.55.66
The value for MapA is www.example3.map
The key   for MapA is 122.77.66.77
The value for MapA is www.example4.map

Other Map Object Accessors

Objects in a map collection can also be accessed using the find( ) member functions to locate an element that is equal to the key supplied by its argument. It accepts an argument x of the key type of the map collection. If the element is present, the find( ) member function will return an iterator pointing to that element. Otherwise, an iterator pointing to the end of the map collection is returned.

The member functions:

lower_bound( )

upper_bound( )

equal_range( )

all accept an argument X of the key type. They can be used to retrieve a specific element from the map collection. The lower_bound( ) member function searches the map collection for the first element whose key is not less than x key. It searches for the first element whose key satisfies this statement:

$$y >= x$$

If the element is present in the map collection, the member function will return an iterator pointing to that element.

The upper_bound( ) member function searches for the first element whose key is greater than x key. It searches for the first element whose key satisfies this statement:

$$y > x$$

If the element is present in the map collection, the member function will return an iterator pointing to that element. If the element is not present in the collection, the lower_bound( ) and upper_bound( ) member functions will return the iterator that points to the end of the collection. The equal_range( ) member function will return the lower_bound( ) and upper_bound( ) pair. Table 7.26 lists the description and the performance of these member functions.

Table 7.26 The lower_bound( ), upper_bound( ), and equal_range Member Functions

FUNCTIONS	PERFORMANCE	DESCRIPTION
upper_bound( )	O(logn)	Searches a sorted input range for a given value; returns an iterator pointing to the next highest value available. If the object is not in the container, an iterator pointing to the next highest value in the container is returned. If that value is not available, the past-the-end iterator is returned.
lower_bound( )	O(logn)	Searches a sorted input range for a given value; returns an iterator pointing to the value for which the container is being searched. If the object is not in the container, an iterator pointing to the next highest value in the container is returned.
equal_range( )	O(logn)	Searches a sorted input range for a given value; returns a pair of iterators: one iterator containing the value lower_bound( ) and the other containing the value upper_bound( ).

Map Collection Operators and Operations

The map collection supports these relational operators: ==, !=, <, > >, <=, >>=. If given two maps, MapA and MapB, relational comparisons such as:

$$MapA > MapB$$

$$MapB == MapA$$

can be performed. These comparisons will return a bool value true if the statement is true and a bool false if the statement is not true.

The map collection can be viewed as a set of pairs, making it appropriate to use set operations on the map collection. As mentioned earlier, the set operations of includes( ), set_union( ), set_intersection( ), set_difference, and set_symmetric_difference( ) are all generic algorithms that can be used on any sorted structure. The map collection is sorted based on the function objects passed to the template during instantiation or during construction of the map collection. (The set operations are discussed in Chapter 9.)

Multimap Collection Class

The multimap collection is a special type of multiset used to create a collection of related pairs. Unlike the map, which includes unique pairs of related items, the multimap may include duplicate pairs. The multimap collection associates the elements of one set to the elements of another set. Multimap collections are structured in the same way as map collections, the only difference being that the multimap collection allows

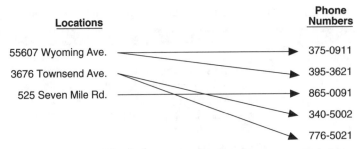

Figure 7.18 Mapping used in a multimap collection. A single location with more than one phone can be mapped to different phone numbers.

key duplication; in other words, the same key can be associated with different values. Figure 7.18 illustrates the type of mapping used in a multimap collection, again using the phone number example with locations as keys and phone numbers as values. In the multimap, a single location with more than one phone can be mapped to different phone numbers.

Standard Multimap Container

The standard multimap container is an associative collection that allows duplicate keys of a given type to be associated with different values of another type. The multimap collection is declared in <multimap>. It is declared and instantiated in the same way as the map collection. The user supplies the type of object that will serve as the key, the type of object that will serve as the values, and the function object. Each multimap contains as many pairs as desired (key + value) for each key value. The multimap collection does not define the subscript operator, which is logical considering there may be more than one value associated with a key.

Multimap Construction

The standard class library multimap container has three constructors:

```
explicit multimap(const Compare& comp = Compare(),
                const Allocator& = Allocator());
multimap(const multimap<Key,T,Compare,Allocator>& x);
template <class InputIterator> multimap(InputIterator first,
                                InputIterator last,
                                const Compare& comp = Compare(),
                                const Allocator& = Allocator());
```

The first is the default; it constructs an empty multimap. The comp function object is passed as a parameter and used to order the key elements of the multimap container. This constructor can also be used with a typedef declaration. The second constructor accepts another multimap container as the argument; it is the multimap copy constructor. When this constructor is used, the multimap is initialized with copies of the elements of the multimap in its argument. The third constructor builds an empty multimap and initializes it with copies of the elements in the range [first,last). The third argument comp is the function object. Even though the multimap may have duplicate keys, no sort is performed on pairs of values with the same keys.

Multimap Destruction

The multimap destructor:

```
multimap();
```

is called when a multimap container leaves scope or when the delete function is called.

Multimap Container Accessor Information

The multimap container has the same member functions as the map container for supplying information about the multimap container and its objects:

empty( )

size( )

max_size( )

count( )

The empty( ), size( ), and max_size( ) member function perform the same for multimap collections as they do for map collections. As for the count( ) member function, it will return the number of all pairs with keys equal to X. Since the multimap container may have duplicate keys, each pair is counted separately. If the pair duplications also have the same values, they will also be counted as individual pairs.

Multimap Container Modifiers

There are three ways to add objects to the multimap container, using constructors, assignment, and insert( ) methods. The assignment operation is defined for the multimap container as:

$$MultimapA = MultimapB$$

After this operation is performed, the elements of MultimapB are copied to MultimapA.

The insert( ) Modifiers

Three insert( ) member functions are defined for the multimap container. They perform differently from their map container counterparts. It is important to note that all the insert( ) member functions for multimaps will always insert the pair element into the container. Two of the insert( ) member functions for map collections will insert the element only under the condition that the key is not already present in the container. It searches the container for an occurrence of the key, and if the key is present, the pair is not inserted. Because the multimap container allows for duplicate keys, the element will always be inserted when using the insert( ) member functions. The member function considers only the keys, not the values; therefore, pairs with duplicate keys and identical values as pairs already present in the container will be inserted as well. When the insert( ) member function is passed a pair element, it does not execute the insert( ) member function that returns a pair object as with the map container; instead, the iterator that points to the newly inserted pair element is returned.

The erase( ) Modifiers

A multimap container has three erase( ) member functions that remove objects from a multimap container. They accept the same arguments and have the same return types as the map container versions. When the erase( ) member function is passed a key, all pairs with that key will be erased, and the number of element pairs erased is returned.

Other Multimap Container Accessors

Object visitation for the multimap container can be performed with iterators and a number of member functions. The multimap container supports bidirectional and reverse iterators. Therefore, the begin( ), end( ), rbegin( ), and rend( ) member functions can be used with the multimap. Objects in a multimap container can also be accessed using the find( ) member functions. Since there may be more than one element with a key equal to X, the find( ) member function will return an iterator pointing to one of those elements.

The lower_bound( ) and upper_bound( ) member functions are very useful when processing elements with equal keys. They can be used to retrieve a specific element from the multimap container. The lower_bound( ) member function searches the multimap container for the first element whose key is not less than X key; for duplicate keys, this will be the first occurrence. The iterator that is returned can be used to traverse through the remaining elements. The upper_bound( ) member function can be used to end the traversal. It searches for the first element whose key is greater than X key. This is illustrated in Figure 7.19.

Multimap Container Operators and Operations

The multimap container supports these relational operators: = =, !=, <, >, <=, >=. Multimap collections are multisets, so it would be appropriate to use set operations on multimap collections. The set algorithms, along with any of the generic algorithms that require input, output, and forward iterators, can be used with the multimap container.

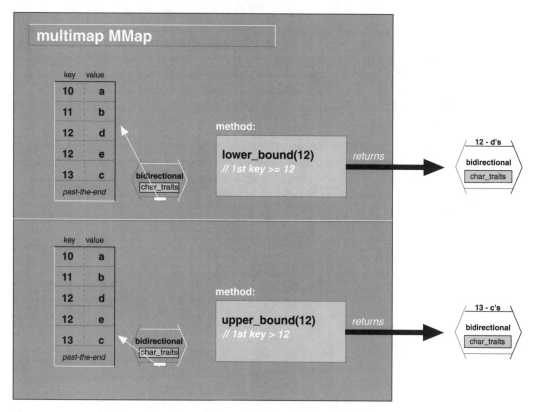

Figure 7.19 Using the range bound algorithms to search a multimap when there are duplicate keys.

Summary

The container classes are object-oriented versions of the classic data structures:

lists	stacks
queues	vectors
deques	priority queues
sets	multisets
maps	(bags) multimaps

These containers come ready to use. The programmer only has to add a few operators to any user-defined objects that will be used with the containers. These operators are: <, =, ==, ( ), and the copy constructor.

Once these operators have been defined, any container class can be used with any user-defined type. The containers work with all built-in data types with no additional coding. The container classes are template classes instantiated with some data type that will determine the containers' content.

Each container has its own memory management in the form of an allocator object. The allocator object is responsible for allocating and deallocating memory for objects in the containers and for calling the destructors of the objects in the containers. The containers are based on parameterized programming, so, in general, they do not have complicated class hierarchies.

The container adapters are user-interface classes designed to provide a new interface for existing containers. The stack, queue, and priority_queue classes are adaptor classes. The set, map, multiset, and multimap are powerful abstractions that can be used in a wide variety of applications, including object-oriented database programming.

CHAPTER 8

Iterators

"By associating each of these properties with a dimension, we create an N-dimensional space. Objects are located at positions (or possibly not located) according to the values of the properties of the objects."

—ALAN WEXELBLAT
"GIVING MEANING TO PLACE"

A n iterator is an object-oriented generalized pointer, used to point to elements in a container or stream. The iterator can be a data member of a container or be implemented as a "friend" member function or as a separate but cooperating class of the container or stream class for which it was designed. The standard C++ library uses both techniques. An iterator provides a method for performing sequential or direct access to any object in a given container or stream, where it acts as a kind of cursor or position locator in a container or stream of objects. Once the iterator has reached the sought object, the iterator can be used to access the object. In the same way that a C++ pointer is dereferenced to access the data to which the pointer is pointing, the iterator is dereferenced to enable the user to access the object. But where pointers refer to the location of an object within computer memory, iterators refer to the location of an object within a container or stream, as illustrated in Figure 8.1. In summary, iterators make it possible to move around in a container or stream and to access and manipulate particular objects.

Some containers provide various methods and operators for sequential access to objects. For example, the deque class uses the subscript operator for sequentially accessing objects in the deque. A function can be written, as follows, to print the contents of a deque:

```
void deque_content(Deque D)
{
    int Count = 0;
    while (Count < D.size()){
        cout << D[Count++] << endl;
    }
}
```

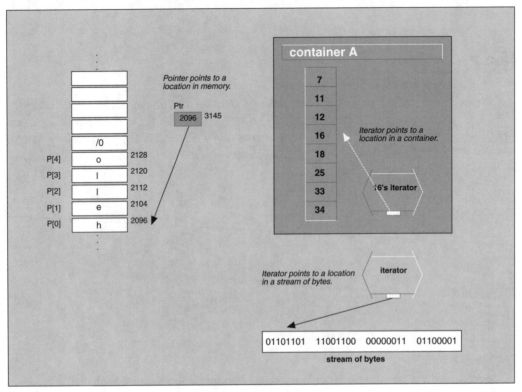

Figure 8.1 Iterators point to locations in a container or stream.

This function sends the content of the deque to the standard output with the use of the subscript operator. Count serves as the index incremented at each iteration through the while loop. But note, if we wanted to generalize this function to print the content of any container, we could not use subscript operators because they are not defined for all containers. One advantage of using iterators is that they supply a method that can be used to traverse the contents of any type of container in a uniform manner. Without iterators there would be no way to sequentially access objects in containers like set and stack. With iterators, the new content function can print the objects of any container. Here:

```
void content (iterator first, iterator last)
{
    while(first != last){
        cout << *first++ << endl;
    }
}
```

points first to the beginning of the container and points last to one element past the last element, or the past-the-end value in the container, as discussed in earlier chapters. Each object in the container is sent to the standard output. The beginning iterator is incremented until it reaches the past-the-end value.

Container and sequence classes can provide member functions, such as current( ), that return either a pointer or reference to the current object. The iterator, like a pointer, can be moved sequentially to point to new objects in the container by calling member functions like next( ) or previous( ). The current( ), next( ), and previous( ) type member functions let the user visit or access every object in the container or sequence. Furthermore, iterators can be used with operators, using the ++, − −, +=, or *= notation to navigate through a group of objects. When iterators are implemented as methods, they are usually part of the class that they will be accessing. However, iterators can also be implemented as separate classes. The standard C++ class library defines five categories of iterators, each of which has a certain minimum set of services that serve as a blueprint for the design of any future iterator classes. A class implementing these services (also known as requirements) is considered an iterator of that type. Therefore, a container could be considered an iterator, too, if it meets the necessary set of requirements. The standard C++ class library also has predefined several iterator classes. The five iterator categories and the predefined classes will be discussed later in this chapter.

Iterator Processing: Sequential and Direct Access

Iterator processing can be divided into two fundamental types: *sequential* and *direct access*. Sequential processing describes iterators that move through a container one object at a time. Sequential iterators can move forward and/or backward using the ++, − −, next( ), or previous( ) notations.

The user cannot jump to the middle of the container with a sequential iterator; to get to the third object in the container, the user must iterate through the first and second objects. For example, the third object in a set is sent to the standard output:

```
...

myIterator = MySet.begin();

for(int Count = 0; Count <= 2; Count++)
{
    if(count == 2){
        cout << "this is third "<< *myIterator;
    }
    myIterator++;
}
```

Here, myIterator is a sequential iterator that points to objects in the MySet set. It is initialized with an iterator that points to the first object in the set; myIterator is incremented using the operator++( ) at each iteration of the for loop. It iterates through the first and second objects in the set. Then, at the third iteration of the for loop, where count == 2, the third object is sent to the standard output. In the content function, the first iterator is also an example of a sequential iterator.

Iterators also can move sequentially in the reverse direction using operator − − ( ) or previous( ). Reverse or backward iteration might look something like this:

```
myIterator--;
  // or
mySet.previous();
```

These iterators, whether forward or backward, would return either the location, a pointer, or a reference to the object to which they were referring.

In contrast, direct-access iterators do not need to process the top half of the container before accessing an object in the middle of the container. The operator[ ]( ) is an example of a direct access iterator that works for vectors, deques, and arrays and is used for sequential iteration. When using the subscript operator and specifying an index value, the user can directly access any object in the container. For instance, to access the fifth object in a deque container, the user could specify:

```
myDeque[4];
```

This would return either a pointer or reference to the fifth object in the deque container.

Direct access can be implemented via the +=, −=, −, +, *= notations. For example:

```
myDeque += 4;
```

This statement will move the myDeque iterator four objects away from its current position. This is called *iterator* or *pointer arithmetic* or *relative addressing*. Figure 8.2 illustrates the difference between sequential and direct iterator processing of a deque.

Using Standard C++ Library Iterators

Iterators are used to sequentially access objects in a stream, or sequentially or directly access objects in the standard C++ containers:

Vector

Deque

List

Set and multiset

Map and multimap

Iterators are also used to define a range of objects to be processed by a method, function, or the standard algorithm. A function or standard algorithm sometimes works on a range of objects in a container. Each object or a specific object in the range may be processed. The range is defined by two iterators that form an *iterator range*. The first iterator points to the first object in the range of objects and the second iterator points to the end of the range. But when the end of the range does not extend to the end of the container, or the second iterator points to an object, the second iterator can point to a position one past the last object in the container if the range extends to the end of the container. Again, this is called the past-the-end value. If the second iterator is not pointing to this position, it can be dereferenced; if it is, though this is a valid iterator, it cannot be dereferenced. The operator++( ) is applied to the first iterator until the first iterator is equal to the second iterator. Let's consider our earlier example:

```
void content(iterator first, iterator last)
{
```

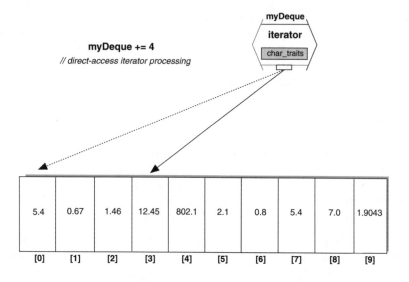

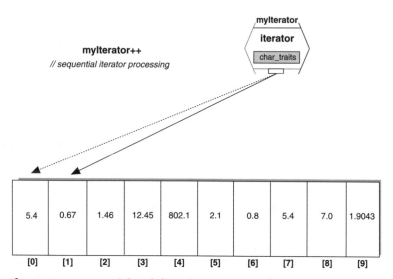

Figure 8.2 Sequential and direct iterator processing of the elements in a deque.

```
    while(first != last){
        cout << *first++ << endl;
    }
}
```

where first and last define an iterator range. The objects in this range are sent the standard output. This range is written as:

```
[first,last)
```

and can be understood as a *half-open interval* in which x (a value in the container) >= first, and x < last. All of the objects in the container are sent the standard output. When first is pointing to the past-the-end value, it cannot be derefenced. The range [first, last) describes the entire contents of a container by constructing an iterator that points to the beginning of the container and a special iterator that points to the past-the-end value of the container.

Ranges can also describe a subsequence of objects within the container by using two iterators in which the first iterator points to the first object or some other object in the container and the last iterator points to past-the-end value or to some other object in the container. Such ranges are illustrated in Figure 8.3. To define a range that is a subsequence of objects, the iterators must be direct-access iterators; only these can use pointer arithmetic, or relative addressing. An empty range occurs when first == last. Empty ranges are valid but they do not include any iterators.

Iterators can also be used to work with input and output streams as defined in the C++ iostreams library. They are called *stream iterators*. The stream iterators also work in pairs to provide a way to write and read objects to and from permanent storage. In other words, a stream iterator can be associated with an istream or ostream. Iterators associated with an istream can read objects from an input stream and then place the objects in a container and so on or process them. Iterators associated with an ostream can write objects to an output stream associated with a file, thereby giving the object a type of persistence. The stream iterators use the insertion (<<) and extraction operators (>>). If user-defined objects are used, these operators must be defined for that object. Figure 8.4 illustrates the stream iterator concept.

Iterator Classification

Iterators are passed to algorithms so that work can be performed on containers. Instead of the algorithm directly accessing the container and the contents of the containers, the algorithm *manipulates* the container's iterators. To specify which standard algorithm and containers are compatible, iterators are classified. Because the containers are templates, iterators can enable the algorithms to be generic. The sequence of actions, or *algorithm,* is reusable because it is independent of the object type and the container that holds the object.

But though the algorithms are generic, they still must perform certain operations on the container. The container must provide the required access methods. For example, searching for a particular object in a container requires the inequality and dereference operations, and sequential access to all the objects in the container. Replacing an object with another object in the container requires equality, dereference, assignment, and sequential access to all the objects in a container. The find and replace algorithms are compatible with any container. These operations may be global functions or operations, defined by the container or assisted by iterator functions.

Performing a sort requires direct access to any object in the container, but all containers do not provide or support the direct access of objects. The sort algorithm is efficient when direct access of objects is possible. Lists, sets, or maps do not support this operation, but this does not mean that objects in these containers cannot be sorted. In the

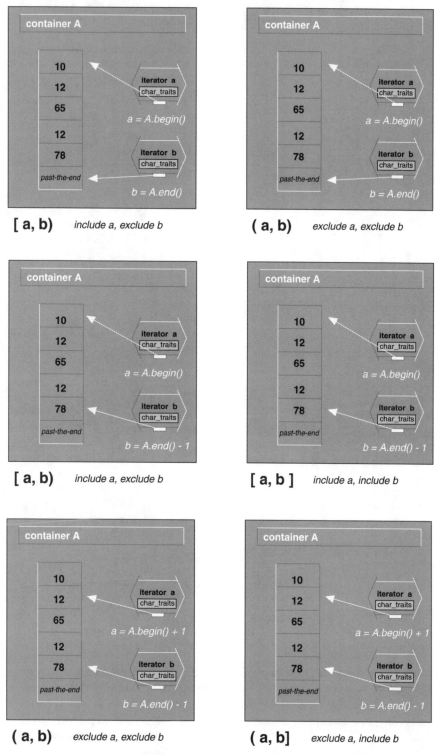

Figure 8.3 Possible ranges that can be represented with iterators. (Note: *a* and *b* are random-access iterators.)

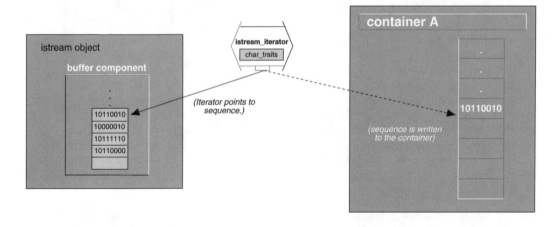

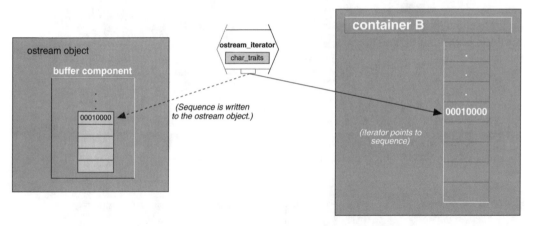

Figure 8.4 The stream iterator concept.

object-oriented model, each container class would define a method that sorts the objects in the most efficient way for that container. When using the standard algorithms or designing a generic algorithm, be aware that they may not be compatible to work efficiently with all containers. The purpose of iterators is to give the algorithm the appropriate container-access operations.

The iterator is the "middle man" between the algorithm and the container. Iterators are classified by the container access operations for a family of data representations or group of containers. The algorithms, by requiring only certain types of iterators, define the container access operations needed for the algorithm to perform work. The algorithm does its work on the container by means of the iterators that give it access to the elements in the container. This is illustrated in Figure 8.5.

An iterator is any type that performs like an iterator. Any type can be considered an iterator if it has the basic capabilities to:

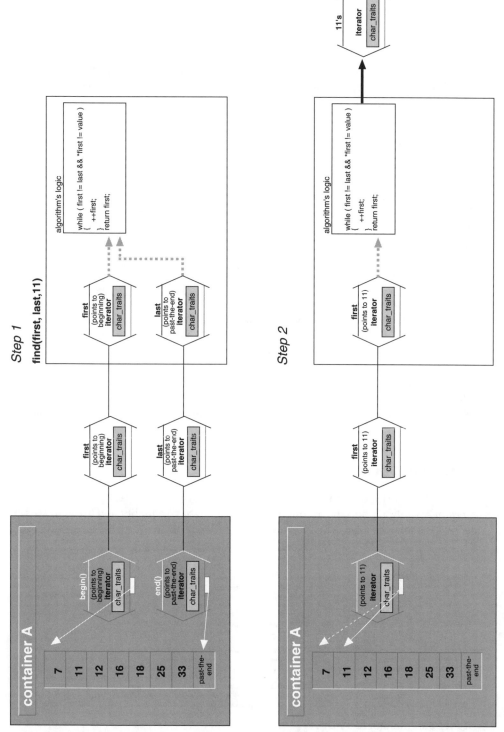

Figure 8.5 Using an iterator to access the elements in a container.

- Point to an element and dereference using the –> or * operators.

- Point to the next element in the container using the ++ operator.

- Test for equality between iterators to determine that the end of the container has been reached.

These basic operations must be defined in order for a type to be considered an iterator. (There is one exception that will be discussed momentarily.) Most containers provide their own iterators because they have methods and operators that perform these operations.

As mentioned earlier, the standard C++ library defines five categories of iterators:

- Input
- Output
- Forward
- Bidirectional
- Random-access

Each category has a set of requirements that describe the operations an iterator of that category can perform. Any class that meets those requirements would be considered an iterator of that category. Starting from the input and output iterators, each category of iterator increases its capability by adding to that of the previous category, until the iterator emulates a full-blown pointer. In other words, all iterators do not possess the same capabilities. The forward iterator has all of the capabilities of the input and output iterators, plus some additional ones. The bidirectional iterator has all the capabilities of the input, output, and forward iterators, plus some additional ones. The random-access iterators have the capabilities of *all* the iterator categories, plus others; they are the most powerful of all the iterators, and emulate a fully object-oriented pointer. Figure 8.6 shows the hierarchy of iterators.

Input and Output Iterators

The least powerful of the iterators are input and output. They perform only the basic iterator operations; and the output iterator does not have equality and inequality operations defined (see Table 8.1). The input iterator reads objects from an input source and

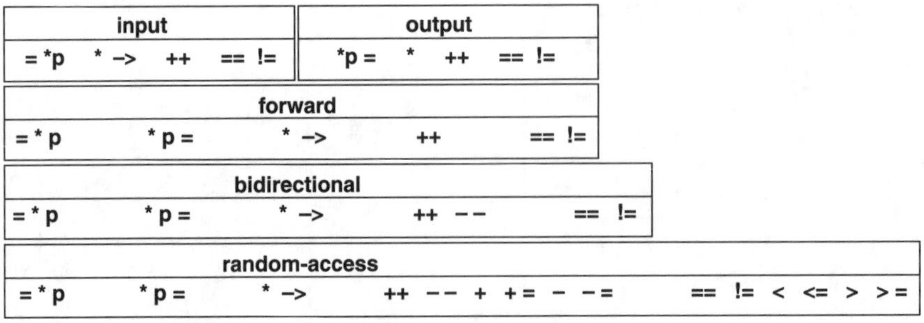

input					output				
= *p	* –>	++	== !=		*p =	*	++	== !=	

forward						
= * p	* p =	* –>	++		== !=	

bidirectional						
= * p	* p =	* –>	++ ––		== !=	

random-access								
= * p	* p =	* –>	++ –– + += – –=		== != < <= > >=			

Figure 8.6 Iterator hierarchy.

Table 8.1 Input and Output Iterators Operations and Requirements

INPUT ITERATOR REQUIREMENTS	DESCRIPTION
X(a)	Copy constructor.
X u(a)	u is a copy of a.
X u = a	u is a copy of a.
a == b	== must be the equivalence relation; the return type must be convertible to bool.
a != b	The same as !(a == b); the return type must be convertible to bool.
*a	a must be dereferenceable; the return type must be convertible to T. If a == b, and (a,b) is in the domain of ==, then *a == *b.
a->m	Same as (*a).m.
++r	r must be dereferenceable; the return type must be convertible to const X&. If r is dereferenceable, or is the past-the-end value of a container, then &r == &++r.
r++	The result must be the same as X temp = r; ++r; return temp; the return type must be convertible to const X&.
*++r	The return type must be convertible to T.
*r++	The return type must be convertible to T.

OUTPUT ITERATOR REQUIREMENTS	DESCRIPTION
X(a)	*a = t is the same as *X(a) = t.
X u(a)	u is a copy of a.
X u = a	u is a copy of a.
*a = t	t is assigned to the position to which a points.
++r	r must be dereferenceable on the left side of the assignment operator; the return type must be convertible to const X&. If r is dereferenceable, or is the past-the-end value of a container, then &r == &++r.
r++	The result must be the same as X temp = r; ++r; return temp; the return type must be convertible to const X&.
*++r	The return type must be convertible to T.
*r++	The return type must be convertible to T.

X is the iterator type; a and b are of type X; r is a value of X&; T is the type to which the iterator points; t is a value of type T; m is a method of type T.

stores the object; examples of input sources are containers or istreams. The dereferencing of an input iterator must allow the object to be read and assigned, but it does not have to allow the object to be altered. Dereferencing appears on the right side of the assignment operation, not on the left side:

```
... = *p;   // reading a value
*p = ...;   // writing a value
```

Input iterators are sequential iterators. If an input iterator points to the first object in the input source, the iterator can be incremented until it points to the past-the-end value. Therefore, all of the objects from the input source must be accessible by means of the *post-* and *prefix* incrementation. The prefix operation returns a reference to itself; the postfix operation returns a copy of itself before incrementation. Algorithms using input iterators should not attempt to traverse an input source, copy the value of the iterator, then use it to traverse an input source a second time. Input iterators should be used only for *a single pass* through the input source.

Input iterators must also define equality and inequality operations. If two iterators are equal, it does not guarantee that subsequent iterators are also equal. In other words:

```
if a == b, does not mean ++a == ++b
```

But if the iterators are equal, it does imply that the objects the iterators are pointing to are equal. In other words:

```
if a == b, does mean *a == *b
```

For this iterator or any other iterator that defines an equality, there must be a difference_type that holds the distance between two elements.

These are the requirements of the input iterators:

- Read, dereference, and assign (on right sides of assignment).
- Increment.
- Test for equality or inequality.

Output iterators, too, are sequential iterators, but they write objects to a container or ostream. The dereferencing of an output iterator must allow objects to be altered and written, but this does not guarantee that objects can be read. In this case, dereferencing appears on the left side of an assignment operation, and assignment occurs only once. Post- and prefix incrementation must be allowed. Also like input iterators, output iterators should be used for a single pass. Figure 8.7 illustrates the use of input and output iterators on containers and streams. These are the requirements of the output iterators:

- Write, dereference, and assign (on the left side of the assignment).
- Increment.

The content function can be altered to show the use of input and output iterators, as in this code:

```
void new_content(InputIterator first, InputIterator last,
              OutputIterator out)
{
    while (first != last){
```

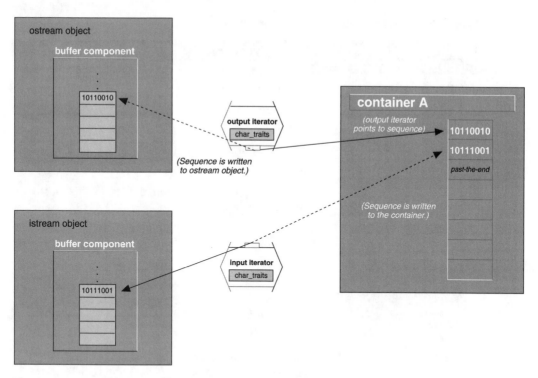

Figure 8.7   Use of input and output iterators on containers and streams.

```
                            *out++ = *first++;
              }
          }
```

Here, first and last are both input iterators. Objects pointed to by first are sequentially assigned to the out output iterator. The out iterator can be another container or associated with a file or standard output. If out is associated with standard output, then this function will produce the same results as the original content function.

Forward Iterators

Forward iterators must perform all of the operations of input and output iterators. They can, therefore, write and read objects to and from containers or streams, and dereferencing can appear on either side of the assignment operator. They, too, are sequential iterators; therefore both postfix and prefix incrementation must be defined (see Table 8.2). Figure 8.8 illustrates how the forward iterator can be used.

Unlike the input and output iterators, subsequent iterations of equal iterators are also equal.

These statements:

```
  if a == b, then ++a == ++b
  if a == b, then *a == *b
```

Table 8.2 Forward Iterator Operations and Requirements

FORWARD ITERATOR REQUIREMENTS	DESCRIPTION
Xu	The result may be singular.
X ( )	May be a singular value.
X (a)	Copy constructor.
X u (a)	u is a copy of a.
X u = a	u is a copy of a.
a == b	== is the equivalence relation; the return type must be convertible to bool.
a != b	Same as !(a == b); the return type must be convertible to bool.
r = a	Same as r == a; the return type is X&.
*a	a must be dereferenceable; the return type must be convertible to T. If a == b, then *a == *b. If X is mutable, then *a = t is valid.
a->m	Same as (*a).m.
++r	r must be dereferenceable; the return type must be convertible to const X&. If r is dereferenceable, or is the past-the-end value of a container, then &r == &++r. If r == s and r is dereferenceable, then ++r == ++s.
r++	The result must be the same as X temp = r; ++r; return temp; the return type must be convertible to const X&.
*++r	The return type must be convertible to T.
*r++	The return type must be convertible to T.

X is the iterator type; a and b are of type X; r and s are values of X&; T is the type to which the iterator points; t is a value of type T; m is a method of type T.

are guaranteed. Forward iterators allow multiple passes through the input or output sources, but only in the forward direction. These are the requirements for the forward iterators:

- Read, dereference, and assign (on right side of assignment).
- Write, dereference, and assign (on left side of assignment).
- Increment.
- Test for equality or inequality.

The new_content function can be altered to demonstrate how forward iterators can be used:

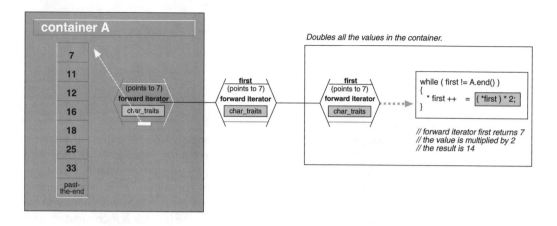

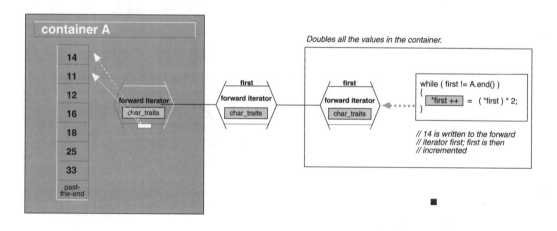

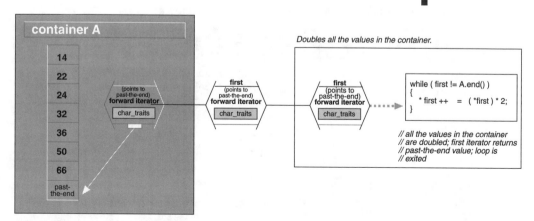

Figure 8.8 Using the forward iterator on a container.

```
void change_content(ForwardIterator first,
                     ForwardIterator last,
                     Function Func)
{
    while(first != last){
         *first++ = Func(*first);
    }
}
```

The new function change_content accepts two forward iterators. The first parameter is a forward iterator that points to the beginning of a container; the second is a forward iterator that points to the end of the same container; the third parameter is a function. The forward iterator first reads each object from the container. The Func function is applied to the object, altering it in some way. Next the new object is written back to the container at the same location where it was read. Then the iterator is incremented. This demonstrates how the forward iterator can be used for reading, modifying, and writing objects.

Bidirectional Iterators

Bidirectional iterators can perform all of the operations of the forward iterators with the additional capability to move in either direction sequentially (see Table 8.3). Figure 8.9 illustrates how a bidirectional iterator can be used. The term bidirectional means "two directions." Consequently, the bidirectional iterator must perform postfix and prefix decrementation. These iterators can make multiple passes in either direction. These are the requirements for the bidirectional iterators:

- Read, dereference, and assign (on right side of assignment).
- Write, dereference, and assign (on left side of assignment).
- Increment and decrement.
- Test for equality or inequality.

Table 8.3 Bidirectional Iterator Operations and Requirements

BIDIRECTIONAL ITERATOR REQUIREMENTS	DESCRIPTION
- -r	- -r must be dereferenceable, and &r == &- -r; the return type must be convertible to const X&. If there exists an s such that r == ++s, then - -r == s. These properties must also hold: - -(++r) == r, if - -r == - -s, then r == s.
r- -	The result must be the same as X temp = r;- -r; return temp; the return type must be convertible to const X&.
*- -r	The return type must be convertible to T.

X is the iterator type; r and s are of type X&; T is the type to which the iterator points.

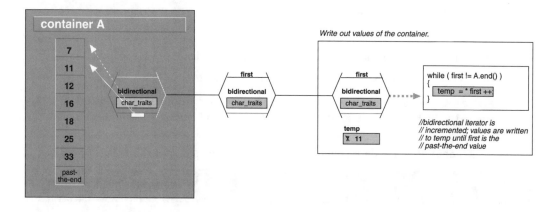

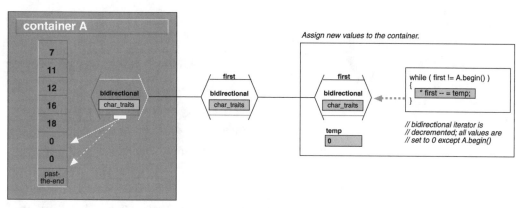

Figure 8.9   Using a bidirectional iterator on a container.

Random-Access Iterators

The most powerful iterators, which fully model a pointer, are the random-access iterators: They define postfix and prefix increments and decrements; they are sequential
and direct-access iterators; they can read objects from an input source and write objects
to an output source; they can perform all of the operations of the bidirectional iterators
with the additional capability to jump directly to any element in the container. But
note: In order for the random-access iterator to jump to and access any element in the
container, the subscript operator must be defined. This iterator must also be able to do
relative addressing using pointer arithmetic. Operators such as +, −, +=, and −= all must
be defined for this category of iterator, along with relational operations for ordering
the elements. The >, <, >=, and <= operators are defined for this iterator type.

These are the requirements for random access iterators:

- Read, dereference, and assign (on right side of assignment).
- Write, dereference, and assign (on left side of assignment).
- Increment and decrement.

- Test for equality or inequality.
- Perform subscript operation.
- Perform relative addressing with pointer arithmetic (+, −, +=, −= operators).
- Carry out relational operations for ordering elements (>, <, >=, <=).

Table 8.4 lists the operations and requirements of the random-access iterators, and Figure 8.10 illustrates how a random-access iterator can be used.

Table 8.4   Random-Access Iterator Operations and Requirements

RANDOM-ACCESS ITERATOR REQUIREMENTS	DESCRIPTION

r += n	The result must be equivalent to this computation:
	<pre>{ Distance m = n;
	  if(m >= 0){
	      while(m--)++r;
	  }
	  else{
	        while(m++)--r;
	  }
	  return r;
	}</pre>The return type must be X&.

a + n	The result must be equivalent to this computation: {X temp = a; return temp += n;}; the return type must be X.
n + a	Same as a + n.
r −= n	The result must be equivalent to this computation: r += -n; the return type must be X&.
a − n	The result must be equivalent to this computation: {X temp = a; return temp -= n;}; the return type must be X.
b − a	A value n of type Distance exists such that: (a + n) == b; Distance n is returned.
a[n]	The result must be equivalent to this computation: *(a + n); the return type must be convertible type T.
a < b	< must be a total ordering relation; the return type must be convertible to bool.
a > b	> must be a total ordering relation opposite to <; the return type must be convertible to bool.
a >= b	The result must be equivalent to this computation: !(a < b); the return type must be convertible to bool.
a <= b	The result must be equivalent to this computation: !(a > b); the return type must be convertible to bool.

X is the iterator type; a, b and r are of type X; T is the type to which the iterator points; t is a value of type T; m and n are scalar values.

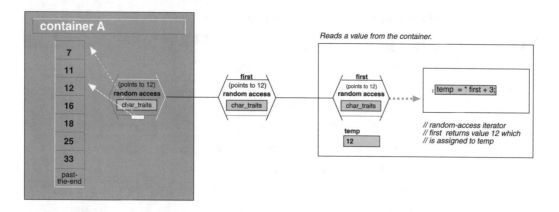

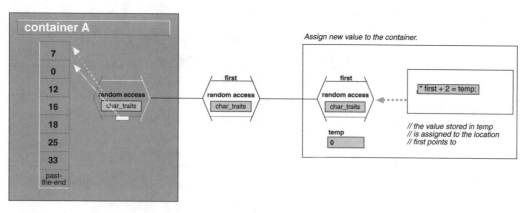

Figure 8.10 Using a random-access iterator on a container.

Iterators and the Container Classes

Each container class has an iterator type, and this is what determines the kind of traversing that can be performed on the container (see Table 8.5). Usually, the iterator is compatible with the behavior and operations of the container, and is sometimes the only method for moving sequentially through the container. All the containers have the following type definitions (X is the container class):

X::iterator

X::const_iterator

X::reverse_iterator

X::const_reverse_iterator

The iterator points to an object within the container, and const_iterator is a constant iterator that points to a constant object within the container. How these iterators are

Table 8.5 Standard Containers and Supported Iterator Types

CONTAINER	ITERATOR TYPE	ITERATOR
vector	random-access	vector<T>::iterator
	const random-access	vector<T>::const_iterator
	reverse iterator	vector<iterator>::reverse_iterator
	const reverse iterator	vector<const_iterator>::const_reverse_iterator
deque	random-access	deque<T>::iterator
	const random-access	deque<T>::const_iterator
	reverse iterator	deque<iterator>::reverse_iterator
	const reverse iterator	deque<const_iterator>::const_reverse_iterator
list	bidirectional	list<T>::iterator
	const bidirectional	list<T>::const_iterator
	reverse iterator	list<iterator>::reverse_iterator
	const reverse iterator	list<const_iterator>::const_reverse_iterator
set	bidirectional	set<T>::iterator
	const bidirectional	set<T>::const_iterator
	reverse iterator	set<iterator>::reverse_iterator
	const reverse iterator	set<const_reverse>::const_reverse_iterator
multiset	bidirectional	multiset<T>::iterator
	const bidirectional	multiset<T>::const_iterator
	reverse iterator	multiset<iterator>::reverse_iterator
	const reverse iterator	multiset<const_reverse>::const_reverse_iterator
map	bidirectional	map<Key,T>::iterator
	const bidirectional	map<Key,T>::const_bidirectional
	reverse iterator	map<iterator>::reverse_iterator
	const reverse iterator	map<const_iterator>::const_reverse_iterator
multimap	bidirectional	multimap<Key,T>::iterator
	const bidirectional	multimap<Key,T>::const_bidirectional
	reverse iterator	multimap<iterator>::reverse_iterator
	const reverse iterator	multimap<const_iterator>::const_reverse_iterator
data types		
string	random-access	string::iterator
	const random access	string::const_iterator
	reverse iterator	string<iterator>::reverse_iterator
	const reverse iterator	string<const_iterator>::const_reverse_iterator

implemented depends on the compiler. The reverse_iterator and const_reverse_iterator are both constructed from the predefined reverse_iterator class. The reverse_iterator class defines a traversal of the container in the reverse direction.

Each container also defines the following member functions (where *a* is a particular instance of the container type):

a.begin( )

a.end( )

a.rbegin( )

a.rend( )

The begin( ) member function returns an iterator that points to the first object in the container; end( ) returns the past-the-end value of the container. The rbegin( ) function returns an iterator that points to the last object within the container, and rend( ) returns the object before the first element in the container. In all cases, if the container object is a constant, the iterator returned will also be a constant. The begin( ) function can be used for a forward traversal to all the objects in the container, and rbegin( ) can be used for a reverse traversal through the container. The end( ) and rend( ) functions can be used for comparison for ending the traversal through the container; they should not be dereferenced because they point to values outside the container. Table 8.6 summarizes the common iterator type definitions and member functions.

Traversal is not done automatically by these member functions; the iterators have to be incremented. For example, let's look again at our content function that sends all the objects in a container to the standard output:

```
...

void content(BidirectionalIterator first, BidirectionalIterator last)
{
    while(first != last){
```

Table 8.6 Iterator Type Definitions and Member Functions

CONTAINER'S ITERATOR METHODS	RETURN TYPE	DESCRIPTION
begin( ) begin( ) const	iterator const_iterator	Returns the iterator that points to the first element in the container.
end( ) end( ) const	iterator const_iterator	Returns the iterator that points to the past-the-end element in the container.
rbegin( ) rbegin( ) const	reverse iterator const reverse iterator	Returns reverse_iterator(end( )).
rend( ) rend( ) const	reverse iterator const reverse iterator	Returns reverse_iterator(begin( )).

```
            cout << *first++ << end1;
        }
    }

    ...

    void main(void)
    {
        ...
        // declare start and stop as iterators for container a
        // initialize start with an iterator which points to
        // the first object in the container
        // initialize stop with an iterator which points to the
        // past-the-end value
        start = a.begin();
        stop = a.end();
        // declare rstart and rstop as reverse iterators for container a
        // initialize rstart with an iterator which points to the last
        // object in he container or one past it
        // initialize rstop with an iterator which points to the first
        // object in the container or one before it
        rstart = a.rbegin();
        rstop = a.rend();
        content(start, stop); // forward iteration through a container
        content(rstart,rstop); // backward iteration through a container
        ...
    }
```

Here, start and stop are iterators of container a. They are initialized with iterators that point to the first object and the past-the-end value of container a. These iterators are then passed to the content function that accepts bidirectional iterators. Next, first is dereferenced then incremented. The object is sent to the standard output until first has the same value as last. For reverse traversal, rstart and rstop are declared as reverse iterators for container a, then initialized with the iterators returned by rbegin( ) and rend( ):

```
    ...
    rstart = a.rbegin();
    rstop = a.rend();
    ...
```

This would cause a traversal in the reverse order. Figure 8.11 shows how the iterators are used for forward and backward traversal through a container.

Constant and Mutable Iterators

In addition to having forward, bidirectional, or random-access capabilities, an iterator can also be *constant* or *mutable*. A constant value is a value that cannot be modified, denoted by the keyword const. Iterators can be constant or mutable (modifiable) depending on whether the begin( ) or rbegin( ) member functions return a constant iterator. If the iterator returned is mutable, the object the iterator points to can be over-written; if the return value is a constant, the object cannot be changed—that is, it can be

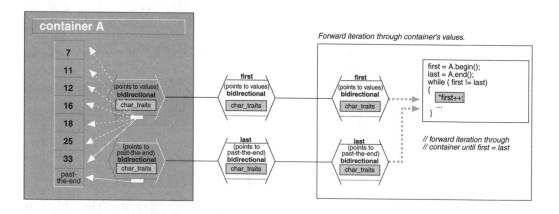

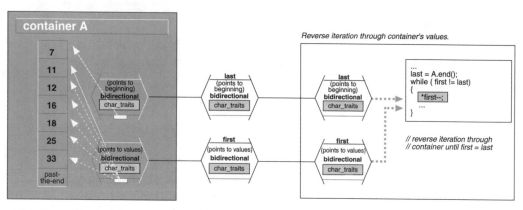

Figure 8.11 Using an iterator to traverse a container forward or backward.

read but not written to. The following are the return types for the begin( ), rbegin( ), end( ), and rend( ) methods:

```
iterator begin();

const_iterator begin() const;

reverse_iterator rbegin();

const_reverse_iterator rbegin();

iterator end()

const_iterator end() const;

reverse_iterator rend();

const_reverse_iterator rend();
```

If the container object is mutable, or nonconstant, a constant or mutable iterator can be used. But if the container object is constant, only constant iterators can be used. For example, deque iterators can be declared as mutable and constant:

```
deque<int>:: iterator X;
deque<int>::const_iterator Y;
```

X is a mutable iterator and Y is a constant iterator. Y can be used on a mutable or a constant container object, but X can only be used on a mutable container object. Therefore, the Y iterator can be initialized with a constant or mutable deque iterator. When the deque iterator is mutable, a conversion is performed:

```
const deque<int> cdec;
deque<int> const_iterator Y = cdec.begin();
    // or
deque<int> mdec;
deque<int> const_iterator Y = mdec.begin(); // conversion performed
```

To initialize a mutable iterator with a constant iterator pointing to the objects of a constant container would be incorrect:

```
X = cdec.begin();    // incorrect
```

There is no conversion from a constant to a mutable iterator. These assignments and conversions of iterators are also true for the reverse iterators:

```
const deque<int> cdec;
deque<int> const_iterator Y = cdec.rbegin();
    // or
deque<int> mdec;
deque<int> const_iterator Y = mdec.rbegin(); // conversion performed
X = mdec.rbegin(); // initialized with a reference to a mutable
                   // iterator.
```

When X is dereferenced, assignments can be performed, but when Y is dereferenced, no assignments can be performed. All the containers' begin( ) and rbegin( ) functions can return a mutable or constant iterator, except set and multiset, which return only constant iterators.

When the iterator is dereferenced, if the result of the operator*( ) is a reference, modifying the object pointed to by the iterator is possible. If the result is a reference to a constant, no assignments can take place. As noted, certain classes of iterators can be used to read elements from a container or stream, whereas other classes of iterators are used to write elements to containers or streams. Table 8.7 lists the predefined iterator classes and the return type of the dereference operators.

Iterator Adaptors

Recall that we defined adaptors as classes that modify or adjust the interface of other classes to simplify, restrict, make safe, disguise, or change the view of the set of services that the modified class is providing. When a class is used for the sole purpose of changing the interface of another class, it is called an adaptor or interface class (Stroustrup 1991, pg. 457). Extending on that, then, iterator adaptors are iterator classes that have adapted or changed the interface of another iterator class or a component of an iterator

Table 8.7 Predefined Iterator Classes and the Return Type of the Dereference Operator

PREDEFINED ITERATOR TYPES	DEREFERENCE OPERATORS	RETURN TYPE
reverse_iterator	operator*( ) const	Reference
	operator->( ) const	Pointer
back_insert_iterator	operator*( )	back_insert_iterator<Container>&
front_insert_iterator	operator*( )	front_insert_iterator<Container>&
insert_iterator	operator*( )	insert_iterator<Container>&
istream_iterator	operator*( ) const	const T&
	operator->( ) const	const T*
ostream_iterator	operator*( )	ostream_iterator<T,charT,traits>&
istreambuf_iterator	operator*( ) const	charT
ostreambuf_iterator	operator*( )	ostreambuf_iterator<charT,traits>&

class. This creates a new iterator class that supplies new methods that use extant methods of the original class.

The standard defines two iterator adaptors: *reverse* and *insert*. As its name implies, the reverse iterator can traverse through the container in the opposite direction. It is an adaptation of the bidirectional and random-access iterators. Algorithms can use reverse iterator adaptors, functioning as they do with regular iterators except that they will be given access to the elements in the container in reverse order. Table 8.8 lists the reverse_iterator methods that adapt the behavior of the bidirectional and random access iterators.

Insert iterators are an adaptation of the output iterators that supply the write functionality. When output iterators are used to write a value to a container using the assign-

Table 8.8 The reverse_iterator Methods

BIDIRECTIONAL ITERATOR METHODS ADAPTED BY REVERSE_ITERATOR		
operator++( )	operator++(int)	
operator– –( )	operator– –(int)	
RANDOM-ACCESS ITERATOR METHODS ADAPTED BY REVERSE_ITERATOR		
operator+( )	operator+=( )	operator[ ]( )
operator–( )	operator–=( )	operator
global operators		
operator<( )	operator<=( )	operator–( )
operator>( )	operator>=( )	operator+( )

Remember, all bidirectional methods are also implemented by random-access iterators.

ment operator, the value the iterator is pointing to is overwritten. Not surprisingly, the insert iterators insert values into the container.

There are three insert iterator classes:

front_insert_iterator

back_insert_iterator

insert_iterator

The front_insert_iterator inserts objects at the beginning of a container and the back_insert_iterator inserts objects at the back or end of a container. The insert_iterator inserts objects at the location immediately preceding where the iterator is pointing. The front_insert_iterator, back_insert_iterator, and insert_iterator all require a reference to the container in which objects are to be placed. In addition to the reference to the container, the insert_iterator requires an iterator that points to a location in the container. Because the values are not overwritten, the insert iterators increase the size of the container.

This adaptor's primary function is to modify an iterator's behavior by modifying the container's interface. The inserters use container methods to do the insertion. The front_insert_iterator uses a container's push_front( ) method; the back_insert_iterator uses a container's push_back( ) method; the insert_iterator uses a container's insert( ) method (see Table 8.9). These adaptors can be used with any container that supplies the appropriate methods.

Table 8.9 Container Methods Used by Insert Iterators

CONTAINER METHODS USED BY INSERT ITERATORS	CONTAINERS	REQUIREMENTS
front_insert_iterator		
push_front( )	list, deque	■ Container::value_type is a type
		■ Container has a method:
		push_front(Container::value_type&)
back_insert_iterator		
push_back( )	vector, list, deque	■ Container::value_type is a type
		■ Container has a method:
		push_back(Container::value_type&)
insert_iterator		
insert( )	map, multimap	■ Container::value_type is a type
	set, multiset,	■ Container has a method:
	vector	insert(Container::iterator,
		Container::value_type&)

Predefined Iterator Classes

The input, output, forward, bidirectional, and random-access iterators describe categories of iterator types. A class that meets the requirements of a specific iterator category is considered an iterator of that type. The standard C++ class library has predefined iterators classes of the input, output, bidirectional, and random-access iterator types. These predefined iterator classes can be classified as:

- Stream iterators
- Stream buffer iterators
- Reverse iterators
- Insert iterators

The stream and stream buffer iterators are input and output iterator types; the reverse iterators are bidirectional and random-access iterators; the insert iterators are output iterators. Two predefined classes are the basis for every other predefined iterator class: iterator traits and iterator.

Iterator Traits and Iterator Classes

The iterator_traits class is a template class that describes a set of declarations used by any iterator object, which can be dereferenced. The dereferencing will return the object to which the iterator is pointing. Given the iterators, the number of elements in a container or stream can be determined. These operations can be done only by referring to the object type and the type of distance between two iterators. Algorithms must be able to determine if they are being passed the correct iterator type; then based on the iterator type, the algorithm can select the most efficient implementation.

The iterator_traits class declares these type definitions:

```
template<class Iterator> struct iterator_traits {
    typedef Iterator::difference_type difference_type;
    typedef Iterator::value_type value_type;
    typedef Iterator::pointer pointer;
    typedef Iterator::reference reference;
    typedef Iterator::iterator_category iterator_category;
};
```

The difference_type is the type used to represent the difference between two iterators. It is of type ptrdiff_t, which is the result type of pointer subtraction. It is defined in the header <cstddef>, which also defines size_t that is returned by sizeof( ). The value_type is a type used to represent the class of object to which the iterator is pointing. Just as pointers are of some type—character, integer, and so on—the iterator points to a built-in or user-defined type, called the *value type* of the iterator.

The iterator_category is the type used to represent the iterator category. As stated earlier, there are five iterator categories: input, output, forward, bidirectional, and random-access. Different algorithms require different types of iterators as arguments. Each iterator category has a corresponding iterator *category tag* class:

input_iterator_tag

output_iterator_tag

forward_iterator_tag

bidirectional_iterator_tag

random_access_iterator_tag

These category tag classes are used at compile time to enable a template function to select the most efficient algorithm implementation.

An iterator_traits object is defined for every iterator. If a new iterator class is to be defined, an iterator_traits class is implicitly defined for that new class. The iterator_traits class uses the default types of the iterator base class:

```
template<class Category, class T, class Distance = ptrdiff_t,
        class Pointer = T*, class Reference = T&>
struct iterator {
    typedef T value_type;
    typedef Distance difference_type;
    typedef Pointer pointer;
    typedef Reference reference;
    typedef Category iterator_category;
}
```

If these types are not sufficient for the new class, new values can be assigned to Distance, Pointer, and Reference classes.

Stream and Stream Buffer Iterators

The stream and stream buffer iterators make it possible for algorithms to work with the iostream. They are also the connection between the iostream classes and the standard containers. Stream and stream buffer iterators can be used to read data from a stream and write it to a container, or read data from a container and write it to a stream.

The C++ standard has two stream iterators and two stream buffer iterators:

ostream_iterator

ostreambuf_iterator

istream_iterator

istreambuf_iterator

As you might expect, the ostream_iterator and ostreambuf_iterator work with the ostream family of classes, and the istream_iterator and istreambuf_iterator work with the istream family. The ostream_iterator and ostreambuf_iterator are output iterator types, and the istream_iterator and istreambuf_iterator are input iterator types. Figure 8.12 shows the class relationships for these four iterators.

These iterators classes inherit the base class iterator. Any algorithm that accepts input iterators can be used with the istream family of classes, and any algorithm that accepts output iterators can be used with the ostream family of classes. Stream iterators read or write

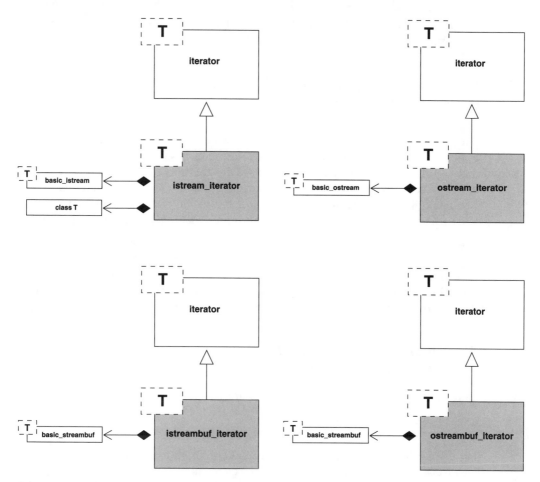

Figure 8.12 Class relationship of stream and stream buffer iterators.

successive elements of a type using the insertion and extraction operators << and >>. Stream buffers do insertion and extraction at a lower level, character by character. If user-defined types or special characters are used, these operators must be defined for them.

Stream and Stream Buffer Iterator Construction

The stream iterators can be constructed with input or output streams. When types are read from an input stream, and the end of the stream is reached, the iterator becomes equal to an *end-of-stream* iterator value. These values are constructed when the istream_iterator default constructor is used. An end-of-stream iterator value can be constructed and used as the ending condition when iterating through an input stream. When types are to be written to the output stream, the stream iterator uses a delimiter to separate one value from another. It is written to the stream after every value is written. The ostream_iterator has a constructor that accepts the output stream and the delimiting character:

```
ostream_iterator(ostream_type& s, const charT* delimiter);
```

If the delimiter is not specified, the delimiting character will be the null character. Each stream iterator has a copy constructor.

The istreambuf_iterator also uses the end-of-stream iterator value. This iterator is constructed when the default constructor or istreambuf_iterator(0) is used. The stream buffers can be constructed with a basic_streambuf, basic_istream, or basic_ostream that supplies the stream buffer to be used by the iterator. The basic_istream and basic_ostream objects' rdbuf( ) method returns a pointer to their stream buffer. For the istreambuf_iterator, if rdbuf( ) returns a null pointer, an end-of-stream iterator is constructed. For the ostreambuf_iterator, it is required that this pointer not be null.

The istreambuf_iterator also supplies a constructor that accepts a reference to an implementation-defined object. This object also supplies the stream buffer. The purpose of this object is to keep the character pointed to by the previous value of the iterator. This object type is returned by the post-increment operator. The stream buffer iterators do not have copy constructors, and no constructors can throw an exception.

Stream and Stream Buffer Iterator Assignment and Access

Only the ostream_iterator defines the assignment operators:

```
ostream_iterator& operator=(const T& value);
ostreambuf_iterator& operator=(charT c);
```

For the ostream_iterator, the element currently pointed to by the iterator is replaced by a const reference value of type T. For the ostreambuf_iterator, only a single character of type charT can replace the current character pointed to by the iterator. The basic_streambufs sputc( ) method writes the character to the write position, then increments the pointer of the output buffer. If the sputc( ) method fails to write the character to the buffer because the end of file was reached, a call to failed( ) will return true.

Elements in a stream pointed to by a stream or stream buffer iterator can be accessed by dereferencing the iterator. The operator*( ) is used for dereferencing both the stream and stream buffer iterators. The operator->( ) can be used the dereference the istream_iterator. The istream_iterator and istreambuf_iterator are used to read values from a stream. When dereferencing the istreambuf_iterator, a character of type charT is read from the stream:

```
charT operator*() const; // defined for the istreambuf_iterator
```

The basic_streambuf's sgetc( ) method reads the character from the stream.

When dereferencing the istream_iterator, a value of type T is read from the stream. To ensure that the value returned will be used only for reading, and will not be altered, it is a reference to a const:

```
const T& operator*() const; // both defined for the istream_iterator
const T* operator->() const;
```

An istream_iterator can be associated with a file. Values can be read from the file by dereferencing the istream_iterator, then placed in a container. The istreambuf_iterator can be associated with the file's buffer from which the characters are read. Figure 8.13 shows how istream_iterator and istreambuf_iterator access sequences with which they are associated. When dereferencing the ostream_iterator and ostreambuf_iterator, values of type T and charT can be written to the output stream of the ostream_iterator and ostreambuf_iterator, respectively. If the ostream_iterator was constructed with a delimiter string, it will be written to the stream each time a value of type T is written.

Stream and Stream Buffer Iterator Incrementation

The prefix and postfix incrementation operators are defined for all of the stream and stream buffer iterator classes. For most of the stream and stream buffer iterators, the operator++( ) and operator++(int) return a pointer to the iterator. For the istream_iterator, the operator++(int) makes a temporary copy of the iterator before a new value is read; the copy is returned. For the istreambuf_iterator, a copy of the iterator is made

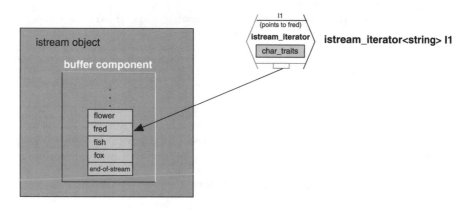

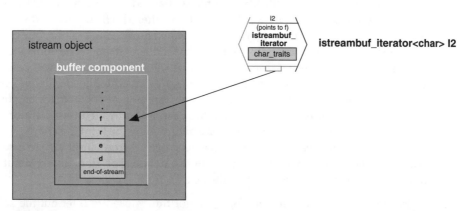

Figure 8.13 Using istream_iterator and istreambuf_iterator to access elements in a stream.

before the basic_streambuf's sbumpc( ) method is called. The sbumpc( ) method reads a character, then increments the pointer to point to the next character in the buffer.

Stream and Stream Buffer Equality and Inequality

The istream_iterator and istreambuf_iterator can be tested for equality and inequality. The standard C++ class library defines operator==( ) and operator!=( ) as global operators:

```
template <class T, class charT, class traits, class Distance>
 bool operator==(const istream_iterator<T,charT,traits,Distance>& x,
                 const istream_iterator<T,charT,traits,Distance>& y);

template <class T, class charT, class traits, class Distance>
 bool operator!=(const istream_iterator<T,charT,traits,Distance>& x,
                 const istream_iterator<T,charT,traits,Distance>& y);
```

The streams x and y are compared for equality and inequality:

```
template <class charT, class traits>
 bool operator==(const istreambuf_iterator<charT,traits>& a,
                 const istreambuf_iterator<charT,traits>& b);

template <class charT, class traits>
 bool operator!=(const istreambuf_iterator<charT,traits>& a,
                 const istreambuf_iterator<charT,traits>& b);
```

The istreambuf_iterator has an equal( ) method that returns true if both iterators are at the end of stream or neither is at the end of stream. If two iterators are not at the end of stream, they are considered equal, regardless of the stream buffers the iterators are using. The a.equal( ) method is called by the operator==( ) and operator!=( ) methods.

Using the istream and ostream Iterators

Listing 8.1 uses the istream_iterator and the ostream_iterator.

This program filters out keys from a text file. The in8-1.txt text file is attached to the ifstream Infile object. The out8-1.txt text file is attached to the ofstream Outfile object. The in8-1.txt file contains the text file that is to be filtered. The filtered text will be sent to out8-1.txt. The istream_iterator In object and the ostream_iterator Out object are associated with an input and output stream that contains strings. The input and output streams in this program are Infile and Outfile. A deque of strings will contain the strings of the input file. The contents of the file are copied to the Dec deque object by means of the copy algorithm, which accepts the iterator that points to the beginning of the input stream, an end-of-stream iterator Last, and a front_insert_iterator for the deque container. The front_insert_iterator is returned by the front_inserter( ). The copy algorithm uses front_insert_iterator objects returned by front_inserter( ) to insert each element of the input stream at the front of the deque. The front_insert_iterator and front_inserter( ) are both discussed in the next section.

Notice at line 65 that the remove_copy_if algorithm is used to filter out the keys and write the filtered text to the output file. The remove_copy_if algorithm removes ele-

Listing 8.1 Using istream and ostream Iterators

```
1  // Listing 8.1
2  // This program uses the istream and ostream iterators.
3
4    #include <iterator>
5    #include <string>
6    #include <fstream>
7    #include <deque>
8    #include <list>
9    #include <algorithm>
10   #include <iostream>
11
12   using namespace std;
13
14   class discard{
15       list<string> Keys;
16       static float Num;
17   public:
18       discard(void);
19       int operator()(string X);
20       float number(void);
21   };
22
23   float discard::Num = 0;
24
25   discard::discard(void)
26   {
27
28       ifstream Keyfile("key8-1.txt");
29       istream_iterator<string> Inkey(Keyfile);
30       istream_iterator<string> eof;
31       copy(Inkey,eof,back_inserter(Keys));
32       Keyfile.close();
33
34   }
35
36   int discard::operator()(string X)
37   {
38
39       int Temp = 0;
40       Temp = count(Keys.begin(),Keys.end(),X);
41       discard::Num = discard::Num + Temp;
42       return Temp;
43
44   }
45
46   float discard::number(void)
47   {
48
```

Continues

Listing 8.1 Using istream and ostream Iterators (*Continued*)

```
49          return(discard::Num);
50
51    }
52
53
54    void main(void)
55    {
56
57          float Percent = 0;
58          discard Discard;
59          ifstream Infile("in8-1.txt");
60          ofstream Outfile("out8-1.txt");
61          istream_iterator<string> In(Infile),Last;
62          ostream_iterator<string> Out(Outfile," ");
63          deque<string> Dec;
64          copy(In,Last,front_inserter(Dec));
65          remove_copy_if(Dec.begin(), Dec.end(),Out, Discard);
66          cout.precision(2);
67          Percent = (Discard.number() / Dec.size()) * 10;
68          cout << Percent << "%";
69          Infile.close();
70          Outfile.close();
71
72    }
73
```

ments that cause the predicate function Discard to return true. The remove_copy_if algorithm accepts input iterators that point to the beginning and end of the deque, the output iterator, and the predicate. The iterators supply the range of objects the algorithm will process. Discard returns the number of times a key appears in a list. In the Discard function object, the text file is associated with an istream_iterator InKey object. In line #31, the istream_iterator is used to write the contents of the key8-1.txt file to a Keys list by means of the copy algorithm. These are the strings that are to be filtered from the in8-1.txt file. (Table 8.10 shows the content of both files.) In line #40, discard returns the number of times a string appears in a list. In line #41, a count is incremented if the string was found in the list of keys. If the string was not found in the list, the string is written to the ostream_iterator Out by the remove_copy_if algorithm. The number of keys found in the text file is stored in static Discard::Num. This value is returned by the number( ) member function. Percent in line #67 is the percentage of keys contained in the text file. This value is sent to the standard output. (Chapter 9 discusses in more detail algorithms and function objects.)

Insertion Iterators

Insertion iterators are adaptations of the output iterators that supply the write functionality. When insert iterators are used, the values are inserted to a location in the container;

Table 8.10 Contents of Files in Listing 8.1

CONTENTS OF KEY8-1.TXT TEXT FILE
man time enough
CONTENTS OF IN8-1.TXT TEXT FILE
The man has too much time on his hands.
CONTENTS OF OUT8-1.TXT TEXT FILE
hands. his on much too has The

they do not overwrite an already existing value. The insert adaptor puts the container into *insert mode* rather than *overwrite mode*. The front_insert_iterator insert objects at the beginning of a container and the back_insert_iterator insert objects at the back or end of a container. The insert_iterator inserts objects at the location immediately preceding where the iterator is pointing. The front_insert_iterator, back_insert_iterator, and insert_iterator all require a reference to the container where the objects are to be inserted. The insert_iterator also requires an iterator that points to a location in the container.

The inserters use the container's methods to do the insertion: The front_insert_iterator uses a container's push_front( ) method; the back_insert_iterator uses a container's push_back( ) method; the insert_iterator uses a container's insert( ) method. Any container that supplies the appropriate method can be used by these inserters, as listed in Table 8.9. Figure 8.14 shows the class relationship diagram for three iterators. They inherit the base class iterator and contain a reference to the container.

Insert Iterator Construction

The front_insert_iterator and back_insert_iterator are constructed with explicit constructors that accept references to the container where the objects will be inserted:

```
explicit front_insert_iterator(Container& x);
explicit back_insert_iterator(Container& x);
```

The insert_iterator constructor requires the container reference and the iterator for the container. The element will be inserted just prior to this location:

```
insert_iterator(Container& x, typename Container::iterator i);
```

The front_insert_iterator and back_insert_iterator do not require an iterator for the container because elements are automatically inserted at the front or back of the container.

Insert Iterator Assignment and Access

Each of the insert iterators defines the assignment operator:

```
front_insert_iterator<Container>&
operator=(const typename Container::value_type& value);

back_insert_iterator<Container>&
operator=(const typename Container::value_type& value);
```

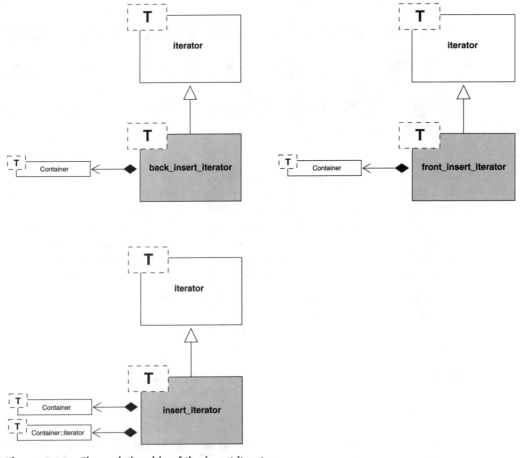

Figure 8.14 Class relationship of the insert iterators.

```
insert_iterator<Container>&
operator=(const typename Container::value_type& value);
```

A const reference to the element to be inserted is passed to the operator's method. The copy of the element is passed to the container's push_front( ), push_back( ), and insert( ) methods, which actually do the insertions. The insert( ) method returns the iterator that points to the copy of the element. This iterator is incremented, and a pointer to the inserter object is returned. Though a container may have several versions of the insert method, the method used by the insert_iterator must meet the requirements listed in Table 8.9. (Table 8.9 also lists the requirements for the push_back( ) and push_front( ) methods.)

Elements in the container can be accessed by dereferencing the insert_iterator:

```
front_insert_iterator<Container>& operator*();
back_insert_iterator<Container>& operator*();
insert_iterator<Container>& operator*();
```

A reference to the front_insert_iterator, back_insert_iterator, and insert_iterator is returned.

Inserter Functions

The class library provides three template functions that can be used to insert objects to a container:

```
template <class Container> back_insert_iterator<Container>
back_inserter(Container& x);

template <class Container> front_insert_iterator<Container>
front_inserter(Container& x);

template <class Container, class Iterator> insert_iterator<Container>
inserter(Container& x, Iterator i);
```

These inserter functions are global. The front_inserter( ) function accepts a reference to a container and returns a front_insert_iterator object. The back_inserter( ) function accepts a reference to a container and returns a back_insert_iterator object. The inserter( ) function accepts a reference to a container and the container's iterator. It returns an insert_iterator object. Listing 8.2 demonstrates how the insert_inserter can be used.

In this program, the contents of a set are inserted to a list, and the contents of another set overwrite the elements in the list. SetA and SetB are sets of integers. SetA contains the integers 1, 3, 5, and 7; SetB contains the integers 2, 4, 6, and 8. A list of integers, ListTest, is constructed, and the integers 12, 34, 89, and 71 are placed in the list using the push_back( ) method.

Each container has two iterators initialized, with the iterator pointing to the beginning and the past-the-end value of the container. The assignment of these iterators precedes the insertion of elements into the container. For example, in:

```
27          set<int,less<int> > SetA(A,A + 4);
            ...
29          set<int,less<int> >::iterator StartA = SetA.begin();
30          set<int,less<int> >::iterator StopA = SetA.end();
```

the iterators StartA and StopA are constructed and initialized with values after the set is constructed and initialized with values. This is an important point: If the iterators are initialized or assigned values before the container has values, once the container's elements have been inserted to the container, the iterators may no longer be valid; the container has been relocated in memory. There are ways to prevent this reallocation, using methods such as size( ), resize( ), max_size( ), and reserve( ). This was discussed further in Chapter 7. In the for loop:

```
44              *(inserter(ListTest,Start)) = *StartA++;
45              *Start++ = *StartB++;
```

you can see how the iterators are used to insert and overwrite values in the container. StartA points to the values that are to be inserted to the list. The value is assigned to the

Listing 8.2 Using the inserter( ) Function

```cpp
1  // Listing 8.2
2  // This program demonstrates the use of inserter() and the
3  // iterators of a list container.
4
5  #include <iterator>
6  #include <iostream>
7  #include <deque>
8  #include <set>
9  #include <algorithm>
10  #include <list>
11
12  using namespace std;
13
14  void main(void)
15  {
16
17      int A[4];
18      A[0] = 1;
19      A[1] = 3;
20      A[2] = 5;
21      A[3] = 7;
22      int B[4];
23      B[0] = 2;
24      B[1] = 4;
25      B[2] = 6;
26      B[3] = 8;
27      set<int,less<int> > SetA(A,A + 4);
28      set<int,less<int> > SetB(B,B + 4);
29      set<int,less<int> >::iterator StartA = SetA.begin();
30      set<int,less<int> >::iterator StopA = SetA.end();
31      set<int,less<int> >::iterator StartB = SetB.begin();
32      set<int,less<int> >::iterator StopB = SetB.end();
33      list<int> ListTest;
34      list<int>::iterator Start;
35      list<int>::iterator Stop;
36      ListTest.push_back(12);
37      ListTest.push_back(34);
38      ListTest.push_back(89);
39      ListTest.push_back(71);
40      Start = ListTest.begin();
41      for(int Count = 0; Count <= 3; Count++)
42      {
43
44          *(inserter(ListTest,Start)) = *StartA++;
45          *Start++ = *StartB++;
46
47      }
48      Start = ListTest.begin();
```

Listing 8.2 *(Continued)*

```
49          Stop = ListTest.end();
50          while(Start != Stop)
51          {
52
53              cout << *Start++ << endl;
54
55          }
56
57      }
58
59
60
```

location preceding the location pointed to by Start, the iterator for the list. The inserter( ) returns the insert_iterator that puts the container in insertion mode during the assignment. StartB points to the values that will overwrite the current value in the list. The assignment at line 41 overwrites the values pointed to by the Start iterator. Figure 8.15 demonstrates what occurs at each iteration of the for loop.

The inserter( ) increases the size of the container, so the iterators are reassigned the beginning and ending iterators of the list container:

```
48          Start = ListTest.begin();
49          Stop = ListTest.end();
```

Then the contents of the list container are sent to the standard output.

Reverse Iterators

Reverse iterators are adaptations of bidirectional and random-access iterators. They transform the bidirectional and random-access iterators to do a traversal in the reverse direction, meaning they move through the container in the opposite direction. The interface is the same as that for the bidirectional or random-access iterator, except that the container traversal is done in reverse.

There are two types of reverse iterators:

reverse_iterator

const_reverse_iterator

The reverse_iterator is mutable; const_reverse_iterator is constant. The reverse iterators are a part of every container.

To use the reverse iterator for a list, for example, an object P could be declared of type:

```
list<double>::reverse_iterator P;
```

P could be initialized with an iterator that points to the end of the container MyList:

```
list<double> MyList;
P = MyList.rbegin();
```

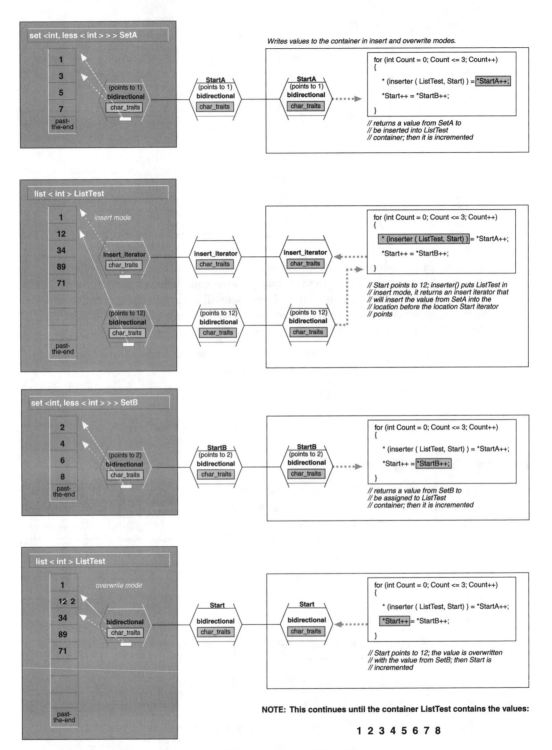

Figure 8.15 Activity at each iteration of the for loop in Listing 8.2.

Any traversing through the list—for example, P++ —would actually be moving in the reverse direction. The rbegin( ) and rend( ) methods can return both constant and mutable reverse iterator types. The rbegin( ) method points to the same element as the end( ) method: the rend( ) method points to the element prior to the element pointed to by the begin( ) method. The end( ) method actually points to the past-the-end value of the container, so an adjustment is made when the reverse iterator returned by rbegin( ) is dereferenced. The dereference operator will return current − 1 to compensate. Therefore, if the iterator is dereferenced, it will not attempt to dereference the iterator pointing to the past-the-end location of the container; it will return the element preceding that location. This is illustrated in Figure 8.16.

Whether the reverse iterator is random-access or bidirectional will depend on which type of iterator the container supports. If the container supports bidirectional iterators, the reverse iterator will be an adaptation of the bidirectional iterator. If the container

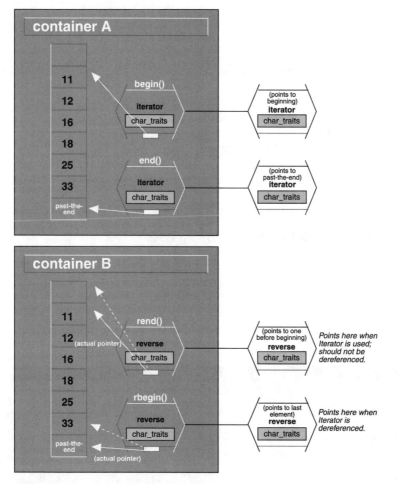

Figure 8.16 The return from the rbegin( ) and rend( ) methods in contrast to the return by the begin( ) and end( ) methods of a container.

supports random-access iterators, the reverse iterator will be an adaptation of the random-access iterator (Table 8.4). The rbegin( ) and rend( ) methods will return either a reverse bidirectional or a reverse random access iterator. If the reverse iterator is a random-access iterator, then all of the iterator arithmetic and subscript operations can be done. Table 8.11 summarize the operations available for each type of iterator.

Algorithms can use reverse iterators, and will function as they do with regular iterators except in reverse. For example, a sort algorithm would sort the elements of the container in reverse order. The find algorithm would find the last occurrence of an element instead of the first occurrence. Figure 8.17 demonstrates how the find algorithm locates the last occurrence of an element in a container. With the reverse iterators, incrementation decrements the iterator, and decrementation increments the iterator.

Reverse Iterator Construction

The reverse iterator can be constructed with an explicit constructor:

```
explicit reverse_iterator(Iterator x);
```

It accepts a bidirectional or random-access iterator that points to the container. This iterator points to the current position in the container; it also has a default constructor:

```
reverse_iterator();
```

A reverse_iterator object is constructed that is not associated with any container. The iterator passed to the reverse_iterator associates the reverse_iterator with a container. If there is no iterator passed to the object, there is no container associated with the reverse_iterator. The reverse_iterator is said to have a *singular value*. This value can be overwritten with a nonsingular value, which can be the past-the-end value of a dereferenced iterator.

Reverse Iterator Assignment and Access

Elements in the container can be accessed using the dereferencing operators:

```
Reference operator*() const;
Pointer   operator->() const;
```

Table 8.11 Summary of Iterator Operations

ITERATOR	READ	WRITE	ACCESS	ITERATION	COMPARISON
Input	= *p		* ->	++	== !=
Output		*p =	*	++	
Forward	= *p	*p =	* ->	++	== !=
Bidirectional	= *p	*p =	* ->	++ --	== !=
Random-Access	= *p	*p =	* ->	++ -- +	== != <
				+= - -=	<= > >=

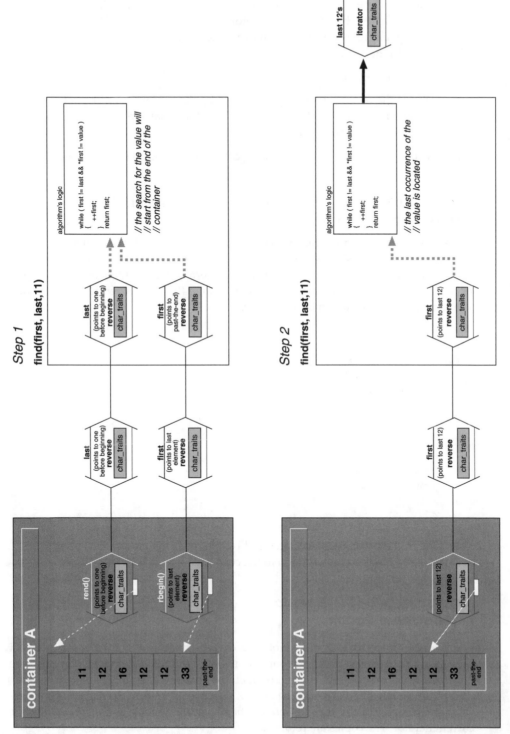

Figure 8.17 Using the find( ) algorithm to locate the last occurrence of an element in a container by passing it reverse iterators.

The operators return a reference and a pointer to the element. The current iterator is copied, then the copy is decremented and returned. Remember, with the reverse iterator, the iterator had to be decremented before the value is returned to compensate for the rbegin( ) pointing to the past-the-end value of the container. There is a method that returns the current iterator:

```
Iterator base() const;
```

which returns the reverse iterator type defined by the container, bidirectional, or random-access iterator. No adjustments are made to the iterator returned; it is explicitly the current iterator for the container.

If the reverse_iterator is a random-access iterator, the subscript operator can be used:

```
Reference operator[](Distance n) const;
```

where n is a Distance type. The method will return the element that is n distance + 1 from the end of the container.

Since reverse iterators are bidirectional and random-access adaptors, they can appear on either side of the assignment operator. The reverse_iterator can be used to alter the contents of a container. For example, a reverse_iterator for a container of integers can be used to read an element in the container, change the value, then reassign the new value to the same location in the container:

```
...
deque<int> dec;
dec.push_back(12);
dec.push_back(10);
dec.push_back(90);
deque<int>::reverse_iterator start = dec.rbegin();
deque<int>::reverse_iterator stop = dec.rend();

while(start != stop)
{
    *start = (*start) / 2;
    cout << *start++ << endl;
}

...
```

The value in the dec container is accessed by the reverse_iterator start, divided by 2, then reassigned to the same location in the container. The output is: 45, 5, 6.

Reverse Iterator Incrementation and Decrementation

The prefix and postfix incrementation and decrementation operators are defined for the reverse iterator class. The prefix operator++( ) decrements the current iterator, then returns a reference to itself; the prefix operator– –( ) increments the current iterator, then returns a reference to itself. The postfix incrementation and decrementation operators make copies of the current iterators before decrementing and incrementing the current iterator. The copies are returned.

Reverse Iterator Equality and Inequality

The standard C++ library uses global operators to define the equality and inequality operations:

```
template <class Iterator>
  bool operator==(const reverse_iterator<Iterator>& x,
                  const reverse_iterator<Iterator>& y);

template <class Iterator>
  bool operator!=(const reverse_iterator<Iterator>& x,
                  const reverse_iterator<Iterator>& y);
```

The current iterator of reverse_iterator x is compared with the current iterator of reverse_iterator y for equality and inequality. A bool value is returned.

Reverse Iterators and Iterator Arithmetic

The reverse_iterator class defines the +, −, +=, and −= operators, along with the global operators operator+( ) and operator−( ). Iterator arithmetic can only be performed on random-access iterators, therefore random-access reverse_iterator objects are manipulated and returned. The operator+( ) subtracts n of type difference_type to the current iterator and returns the resulting reverse_iterator object. The operator+=( ) assigns the new iterator to the current iterator, then returns the reverse_iterator. The global operator+( ) subtracts n of type difference_type from a reverse_iterator object:

```
template <class Iterator>
  reverse_iterator<Iterator> operator+(
    typename reverse_iterator<Iterator>::difference_type n,
    const reverse_iterator<Iterator>& x);
```

This operator subtracts n from x.current and returns the resulting iterator.

The operator−( ) adds n of type difference_type to the current iterator and returns the resulting iterator. The operator−=( ) assigns the new iterator to the current iterator and returns the reverse_iterator. The global operator−( ) subtracts a reverse_iterator from another reverse_iterator object:

```
template <class Iterator>
  typename reverse_iterator<Iterator>::difference_type
    operator-(const reverse_iterator<Iterator>& x,
              const reverse_iterator<Iterator>& y);
```

This operator subtracts x.current from y.current and returns the difference as a value of type difference_type.

Reverse Iterator Relational Operators

All of the relational operators—<, <=, >, and >=—are global and used only to compare random access reverse_iterator objects. They act in the normal manner; the reverse direction does not affect the way the iterators are compared. Each operator returns a bool value.

The Global Methods: advance( ) and distance( )

The advance( ) and distance( ) methods are used to increment or decrement an iterator and determine the distance between two iterators. They are global functions:

```
template <class InputIterator, class Distance>
    void advance(InputIterator& I, Distance n);

template <class InputIterator>
    iterator_traits<InputIterator>::difference_type
    distance(InputIterator first, InputIterator last);
```

The advance( ) function accepts a reference to an input iterator and the distance to be incremented or decremented from the iterator. The iterator can be any iterator type, except output. The function will decrement the iterator if passed a negative value for n, and if the iterator is bidirectional or random-access. If the iterator is random access, the function performs the same operation as operator+( ) or operator–( ). For all other iterators, successive operator++( ) and operator– –( ) are used. The advance( ) function serves as a relative addressing mechanism for iterators that do not perform it. The new iterator value is assigned to the original iterator. For example, if a set contained the integers 5, 6, 7, 9, 8, and 90, and two iterators Start and Stop were initialized:

```
Start = myset.begin();
Stop = myset.end();
```

the advance( ) function could be used to increment and decrement the iterators:

```
advance(Start, 2);
advance(Stop, -3);
```

Start is now pointing to 7 and Stop is pointing to 8.

The distance( ) function returns the number of increments or decrements needed to move from the first iterator to the last iterator. It can be used with any iterator except output. It requires that last be reachable from first; in other words, the iterators must be of the same container or stream. The distance( ) function can be used to determine the number of elements in a container by counting the distance between the iterator pointing to the beginning of the container and the iterator pointing to the past-the-end value of the container:

```
distance(myset.begin(), myset.end());
```

The value returned in this case is 6.

The distance( ) method can also be used to determine the number of elements in an input stream:

```
ifstream Infile;
Infile.open("in.txt");
istream_iterator<int> In(Infile);
istream_iterator<int> Last;

...
```

```
cout << distance(In, Last);

. . .
```

The number of elements in the file is sent to standard output. The value returned is a difference_type.

Summary

An iterator is an object-oriented, polymorphic, generalized pointer. It is used to point to elements in a container or stream. Iterators provide a method for accessing any object in a container or stream sequentially or directly. They can be dereferenced in the same way that a pointer in C++ is dereferenced, to access the data to which the pointer is pointing. But where pointers refer to the location of an object in computer memory, iterators refer to the location of an object within a container or stream.

An iterator range is defined by two iterators. The first points to the first object in the range of objects and the second points to the end of the range. When passed this range, a function or standard algorithm works on the objects in the container. The second iterator can point to a past-the-end value that is one beyond the last object in the container. The operator++( ) is applied to the first iterator until the first iterator is equal to the second iterator.

There are five types of iterators: input, output, forward, bidirectional, and random-access. Each has a set of requirements, and a type that meets a set of requirements can be considered an iterator of that type. Random-access iterators encapsulate the notion of a pointer. These iterator types are all scaled-down versions of a pointer, and each incorporates the requirements of the preceding iterator.

Each container supports an iterator type, supporting either bidirectional or random-access iterators. The begin( ) and end( ) methods will return the iterator supported by the container. Each container also support a reverse version of the bidirectional or random-access iterator. It is returned by the rbegin( ) or rend( ) methods.

The standard C++ library has several predefined iterator classes:

reverse_iterator (bidirectional and random-access)

back_insert_iterator (output)

front_insert_iterator (output)

insert_iterator (output)

istream_iterator (input)

ostream_iterator (output)

ostreambuf_iterator (output)

istreambuf_iterator (input)

The reverse and insert iterators are iterator adaptors, iterator classes that have adapted or changed the interface of another iterator class or a component of an iterator class. The reverse iterator changes the bidirectional and random-access iterators by traversing the container in the reverse order. The insert iterators change the behavior of the output iterator by inserting objects to a container instead of overwriting the value. The insert adaptors use methods supplied by the container itself by calling push_back( ), push_front( ), and insert( ). The inserter functions return insert iterators: front_inserter( ) returns a front_insert_iterator; back_inserter( ) returns a back_inserter_iterator; inserter( ) returns an insert_iterator.

The advance( ) function is used to increment and decrement the iterators. If passed two iterators, the distance( ) function will return the distance or difference between the two iterators.

CHAPTER 9

Algorithms

"In order to make a start in so complex a subject, one must ruthlessly strip away detail and arrive at a few broad, very approximate 'constants of operation.' By studying the variations of these constants, one can then perhaps begin to see how to improve the operation."

—PHILLIP M. MORSE
HOW TO HUNT A SUBMARINE

The C++ standard library contains 70 algorithms designed to work in conjunction with the container classes and iterators, both those that are part of the C++ standard library or those that are user-defined. Likewise, the algorithms can work with library or with user-defined iterators. The standard C++ algorithms cover a lot of territory. There are algorithms that do searching, sorting, erasing, counting, comparison, transformations, permutations, and container management. One of the most important features of these algorithms is that they are generalized, and so can be used with wide varieties of objects and with built-in data types.

What Are Algorithms?

Algorithms are sequences of instructions that represent well-defined problem solutions that are suitable for implementation in a computer programming language. Specifically, an algorithm is a procedure or process that uses a set of well-defined steps to solve a problem. And because algorithms are independent of specific computer language, no computer language is required to specify an algorithm; algorithms can be represented in plain English. For instance, an algorithm for printing a list of files stored on a computer could be stated as follows:

Step 1. Change to the directory containing the files to print.

Step 2. Pick the next file alphabetically that has not already been printed.

Step 3. If a file was chosen in step 2, then print it; otherwise stop.

Step 4. Do step 2.

Algorithms can also be represented mathematically: For instance:

$$SUM(X) = \sum_{I=1}^{n} (X - 1) + 1$$

But frequently, algorithms are represented in *pseudocode*, as a mix of English (or another natural language) and a small sampling of computer language keywords, that usually includes looping commands, decision commands, assignment commands, and some generic input/output commands. The advantage of using pseudocode is that the programmer can specify the logic for a routine or computer program without having to worry about syntax, rules, or other language-specific features and requirements. There is no right or wrong way to use pseudocode; it is simply used to capture the list of steps and the logic that a solution must follow. Pseudocode is also a design tool and a method of informal communication of solutions or approaches to a problem.

An algorithm expressed in pseudocode could be written as follows:

```
Start
Set N = 10
Set X = 6
Set I = 1
Set SUM = 0
While I <= N
    SUM = (X - 1) + 1
    I = I + 1
End While
Stop
```

The commands in this sample do not belong to a particular computer language, though they do have a familiar ring. They are similar to commands from a computer language, and are used as a shortcut for some real computer programming language.

NOTE:

Most algorithms start out written in pseudocode and are later implemented in a computer language.

The Importance of Algorithms

Algorithms are important because they enable the programmer to develop one general solution that can be used for many different problems. To show what we mean by "general solution," let's take the problem of adding to large numbers.

4343431231225343431231221 + 344432121123455454.23

We could write a program to add and print the results of the addition. Look at Listing 9.1.

Though this program works just fine—a computer running this program would add these two numbers much faster than a person could—the problem is that it works only for these two numbers. To add another set of numbers, we would have to write another

Listing 9.1 A Simple Addition

```
// Listing 9.1

void main(void)
{
    cout << 4343431231225343431231221 + 344432121123455454.23;
}
```

program. In fact, if we wrote all our programs in this fashion, for each set of numbers that we wanted to add, we would have to write a separate program.

Clearly, what we need to do is generalize our program. Most computer languages support the notion of *variables*, features that allow the programmer to generalize a program. For example, we could generalize our two-number addition program by including variables, as shown in Listing 9.2.

This program can now add *any* two large integers that the user enters. This is a much more general solution than our first program, but it is not general enough: It can add only whole numbers, and only two at a time. What if we wanted to add fractions? What if we wanted to add 1,000 numbers?

To make this program more general, we need some way to vary how many numbers the user can type in and how many numbers the add statement can work with. We might change the program to look like Listing 9.3.

This program is more general than our second program. We can use it under many more conditions, but it still is not general enough. Again, we can only use this program to add a list of whole numbers; we still cannot add fractions or numbers with decimals, so if we wanted to add numbers representing dollars and cents (e.g., checkbook entries), we could not use this program. To do so, we need to make it more general.

Algorithms provide general *and* reusable solutions. The C++ standard algorithms provide extremely general and reusable solutions. To show how the C++ algorithms rep-

Listing 9.2 Addition Using Variables

```
// Listing 9.2

void main (void)
{
    long X;
    long Y;
    cout << "input first Number";
    cin >> X;
    cout << "input second Number";
    cin >> Y;
    cout << X + Y;
}
```

Listing 9.3 Further Generalizing the Addition Program

```
//Listing 9.3

void main(void)
{
    long X;
    long Count;
    long N;
    long Total = 0;
    cout << "How many Numbers?";
    cin >> Count;
    for (N = 1; N <= Count;N++)
    {
        cin >> X;
        Total = Total + X;
    }
    cout << Total;
}
```

Listing 9.4 Using the accumulate Algorithm

```
1   // List 9.4
2   // Demonstrates use of accumulate with vector of doubles
3
4   #include <numeric>
5   #include <vector>
6   #include <iostream>
7
8
9   using namespace std;
10
11  void main(void)
12  {
13
14      vector<double> Doubles;
15      int Count;
16      int N;
17      double X;
18      cout << "How Many Numbers ";
19      cin >> Count;
20      for(N = 1;N <= Count;N++)
21      {
22          cin >> X;
23          Doubles.push_back(X);
24      }
25      cout << accumulate(Doubles.begin(),Doubles.end(),0.0);
26  }
```

resent very general *ready-to-use* solutions, let's solve our adding problem with the C++ accumulate algorithm shown in Listing 9.3.

Line 25 in Listing 9.4 contains the accumulate algorithm, which will add all the numbers in whatever container the user gives it. It has no restriction on the number of values it can add. Notice one of the differences between this program and the program in Listing 9.3. The latter contains instructions that accumulate the sum. This code is not necessary in this listing. The accumulate algorithm comes built-in with its own accumulator. The programs in Listings 9.1, 9.2, and 9.3 also suffer from the fact that they can only add integers, whereas the accumulate algorithm will add any kind of values in the container the user passes to it. For instance, the program in Listing 9.5 uses the accumulate algorithm to add a list of integers.

Notice that we did not have to use a different accumulate algorithm; it represents a truly general solution to the problem of adding a group of numbers. It can get the objects it adds from lists, vectors, deques, sets, and so on. This means that it can be used to add numbers from virtually any kind of container that supports the proper iterators.

In fact, the accumulate algorithm is so general that it can add any kind of object for which the addition and assignment operator have been properly defined. For example,

Listing 9.5 Adding a List of Integers

```
1    // List 9.5
2    // Demonstrates use of accumulate with list of integers
3
4    #include <numeric>
5    #include <list>
6    #include <iostream>
7
8
9    using namespace std;
10
11   void main(void)
12   {
13
14       list<int> Integers;
15       int Count;
16       int N;
17       int X;
18       cout << "How Many Numbers ";
19       cin >> Count;
20       for(N = 1;N <= Count;N++)
21       {
22           cin >> X;
23           Integers.push_back(X);
24       }
25       cout << accumulate(Integers.begin(),Integers.end(),0);
26
27   }
```

if we wanted to add apple objects, triangle objects, or car objects, as long as operator+( ) and operator=( ) are appropriately defined for those objects, the accumulate algorithm can do the job. To demonstrate this, we will use accumulate to add several clock_time objects. The clock_time class represents hours and minutes. Listing 9.6 shows the declaration of the clock_time class.

This class can be used to do clock arithmetic. For example, operations such as:

$$90 \text{ minutes} + 90 \text{ minutes} = 3 \text{ hours}$$

$$1 \text{ hour} - 45 \text{ minutes} = 15 \text{ minutes}$$

can be done using objects of type clock_time. Next let's see what the C++ standard accumulate algorithm does with a list of clock_time objects. The program in Listing 9.7 has three clock times.

The times are:

3 hours and 10 minutes

5 minutes

95 minutes

So far, we have used the accumulate algorithm to add a list of integers and a vector of doubles. The accumulate algorithm can work with both lists and vectors; it can accu-

Listing 9.6   Declaring the clock_time Class

```
1    // Listing 9.6
2    // Declaration of the clock_time class
3
4    #include <iostream>
5
6    class clock_time{
7    protected:
8        int Minutes;
9        int Hours;
10   public:
11       clock_time(void);
12       clock_time(int Hrs,int Min);
13       clock_time(const clock_time &Time);
14       clock_time &operator=(clock_time &Time);
15       friend ostream &operator<<(ostream &Out,clock_time &Time);
16       clock_time &operator+(clock_time &Time);
17       clock_time &operator-(clock_time &Time);
18       int operator>(clock_time &Time);
19       void minutes(int M);
20       void hours(int H);
21       int minutes(void);
22       int hours(void);
23   };
```

mulate both doubles and integers. The program in Listing 9.7 uses the same accumulate algorithm to add a vector of clock times; it reports:

4 hours and 50 minutes

Without changing the accumulate algorithm, we were able to add a collection of user-defined objects, with the only requirement that the objects define the addition operator+( ) and the assignment operator=( ). All of the algorithms in the standard C++ library are just as general as accumulate, providing generalized ready-made solutions that can be put to work immediately.

Algorithm Generalization

The generalization in the standard C++ algorithms is accomplished using iterators and templates. The iterator acts as "middle man" between the algorithm and the container. The algorithm requests an object from the iterator, and the iterator knows where the object is within the container. The iterator locates the object and gives the algorithm access to it. The algorithm is unaware of the specifics of where the objects are stored within the container; usually, the algorithm is also unaware of the kind of container in which the objects are stored. The algorithm simply requires the next object, whatever that object may be and wherever that object may be stored. Think of

Listing 9.7 Using accumulate to Add Clock Times

```
1   // Listing 9.7
2   // This program uses the accumulate algorithm to add clock times.
3
4   #include <iostream>
5   #include <numeric>
6   #include <vector>
7   #include <clktime.h>
8   using namespace std;
9
10
11  void main(void)
12  {
13      clock_time X(3,10);
14      clock_time Y(0,05);
15      clock_time Z(0,95);
16      clock_time ZeroTime;
17      vector<clock_time> Clocks;
18      Clocks.push_back(X);
19      Clocks.push_back(Y);
20      Clocks.push_back(Z);
21      cout << accumulate(Clocks.begin(),Clocks.end(),ZeroTime);
22  }
23
```

the algorithm as a surgeon performing an operation: The iterator is the surgeon's assistant. When the surgeon calls for a scalpel, the assistant supplies it; when the surgeon calls for scissors, the assistant supplies them. The surgeon is focusing on the operation to be performed, not where the objects for the operation are or in what kind of container they are stored.

Iterators are used to generalize the kinds of objects the containers can contain. Because the algorithms are concerned only with iterators, the algorithms do not need to know the kind of container it is working on. And because the container is parameterized using the C++ template construct, the container can contain virtually any kind of object. Consequently, then, a standard algorithm can manipulate almost any kind of container, and a container can potentially contain any kind of object. This kind of generalizing lets the programmer use code and solutions repeatedly without any extra effort. Furthermore, the standard algorithms and containers are tested, so the programmer can build more stable programs in less time.

The diagram in Figure 9.1 shows the relationships between the standard C++ algorithms and parameterized containers. The containers in the figure can be used to hold data or objects of all kinds. The containers (object-oriented versions of data structures) are used to organize the objects in some fashion. The iterators as shown in Figure 9.1 are used to locate particular objects within the organization. Iterators can be used to locate objects at the beginning of a container, the end of a container, or somewhere else within the container's organization. The algorithms simply request the next required object; it is the iterator's job to locate that object wherever it may be and return it to the algorithm. The algorithms make requests of the iterators, and the iterators in turn make requests of the containers.

The C++ Standard Algorithms

Now that we know what makes the algorithms generalized solutions, let's look at the types of general solutions provided by the standard C++ library. As noted at the beginning of the chapter, the standard C++ library contains 70 algorithms (listed in Table 9.1). The algorithms are divided into eight categories, based on the kind of work each does:

- Search
- Sort
- Numeric
- Comparison
- Set
- Container management
- Statistical
- Heap

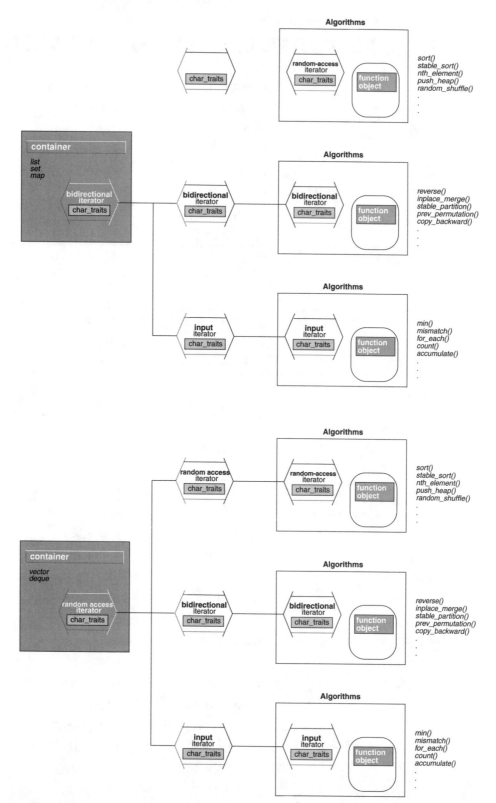

Figure 9.1 The relationships between the standard C++ algorithms and parameterized containers.

Table 9.1 C++ Standard Algorithms

ALGORITHM TYPE	ALGORITHMS	
sort	sort( )	stable_sort( )
	partial_sort( )	partial_sort_copy( )
	merge( )	inplace_merge( )
search	find( )	find_if( )
	find_end( )	find_first_of( )
	adjacent_find( )	search( )
	search_n( )	binary_search( )
	nth_element( )	lower_bound( )
	upper_bound( )	equal_range( )
set operations	set_union( )	set_difference( )
	set_intersection( )	set_symmetric_difference( )
	includes( )	
numeric operations	next_permutation( )	prev_permutation( )
	accumulate( )	partial_sum( )
	inner_product( )	adjacent_difference( )
heap operations	push_heap( )	pop_heap( )
	make_heap( )	sort_heap( )
statistical information	min( )	max( )
	min_element( )	max_element( )
	count( )	count_if( )
comparison operations	equal( )	lexicographical_compare( )
container management	copy( )	copy_backward( )
	replace( )	replace_if( )
	replace_copy( )	replace_copy_if( )
	reverse( )	reverse_copy( )
	mismatch( )	swap( )
	swap_ranges( )	iter_swap( )
	transform( )	fill( )
	fill_n( )	remove( )
	remove_if( )	remove_copy
	remove_copy_if( )	unique( )
	unique_copy( )	rotate( )
	rotate_copy( )	random_shuffle( )
	partition( )	stable_partition( )
	generate( )	generate_n( )
	for_each( )	

Each algorithm has one primary task—for example, search algorithms locate particular objects; sort algorithms sort collections of objects; comparison algorithms compare two or more objects; and so on. To use the algorithms, the user must follow the algorithm's argument requirements and include the appropriate header files. The C++ standard requires that the declarations for the algorithms be included in the <algorithm> header file and the <numeric> header file. The <algorithm> header file contains all of the algorithms except:

accumulate( )

inner_product( )

partial_sum( )

adjacent_difference( )

NOTE:

These algorithms will be found in <numeric>. If your compiler is nonstandard, the algorithms may be found in algo.h, algobase.h or function.h.

Algorithm Arguments

The algorithms may require up to four different kinds of arguments from this list:

- Iterators
- Function objects
- Predicates
- User objects

The arguments are the first thing to tackle when using the algorithms. After satisfying the argument requirements, the next thing to consider is the behavior and performance of the algorithms.

Iterator Arguments

Each algorithm works with objects stored in some kind of container (data structure). The objects may be built-in data types, such as float, int, or char, built-in objects such as string and complex, or user-defined objects. The algorithms access the objects in a container through the iterators, which perform locator services for the algorithm (see Table 9.2). Algorithms require different types of iterators based on the type of work that it does and the kind of container it uses. Logically, therefore, algorithms are classified according to the type of work they do and the kind of container they access. Similarly, containers are classified according to the access methods they support. Table 9.3 lists the algorithm classifications, and Figure 9.2 shows the access mechanisms the containers support.

Table 9.2 Algorithm Iterators

ALGORITHM	ITERATORS	ALGORITHM	ITERATORS
Sort			
sort( )	Random-Access	stable_sort( )	Random-Access
partial_sort( )	Random-Access	partial_sort_copy( )	Random-Access
merge( )	Input, Output	inplace_merge( )	Bidirectional
Search			
find( )	Input	find_if( )	Input
find_end( )	Forward	find_first_of	Forward
adjacent_first( )	Input	search( )	Forward
search_n( )	Forward	binary_search( )	Forward
nth_element( )	Random-Access	lower_bound( )	Forward
upper_bound( )	Forward	equal_range( )	Forward
Set Operations			
set_union( )	Input, Output	set_difference( )	Input, Output
set_intersection( )	Input, Output	set_symmetric_difference( )	Input, Output
includes( )	Input		
Numeric Operations			
next_permutation( )	Bidirectional	prev_permutation( )	Bidirectional
accumulate( )	Input	partial_sum( )	Input, Output
inner_product( )	Input	adjacent_difference( )	Input, Output
Heap Operations			
push_heap( )	Random-Access	pop_heap( )	Random-Access
make_heap( )	Random-Access	sort_heap( )	Random-Access
Statistical			
min( )	None	max( )	None
min_element( )	Input	max_element( )	Input
count( )	Input	count_if( )	Input
Comparison			
equal( )	Input	lexicographical_compare( )	Input
Container Management			
copy( )	Input, Output	copy_backward( )	Bidirectional
replace( )	Forward	replace_if( )	Forward

Table 9.2 *(Continued)*

ALGORITHM	ITERATORS	ALGORITHM	ITERATORS
replace_copy( )	Input, Output	replace_copy_if( )	Output
reverse( )	Bidirectional	reverse_copy( )	Bidirectional, Output
mismatch( )	Input	swap( )	None
swap_ranges( )	Forward	iter_swap( )	Forward
transform( )	Input, Output	fill( )	Forward
fill_n( )	Output	remove( )	Forward
remove_if( )	Forward	remove_copy	Input, Output
remove_copy_if( )	Input, Output	unique( )	Forward
unique_copy( )	Input, Output	rotate( )	Forward
rotate_copy( )	Output, Forward	random_shuffle( )	Random-Access
partition( )	Bidirectional	stable_partition( )	Bidirectional
generate( )	Forward	generate_n( )	Output
for_each( )	Input		

Table 9.3 Algorithm Classifications

ALGORITHM CLASSIFICATION	DESCRIPTION
Divide and Conquer	A problem is broken down into several subproblems that are similar in nature to the original problem but smaller in size. The subproblems are solved recursively. The solutions are combined to create a solution to the original problem.
Greedy	Optimal choices are made at each step with the hope that these choices will produce a global solution that is optimal.
P, NP, and NP Complete	A classification of decision problems. The *class P* problems include decision problems that have a reasonably efficient algorithm. The *class NP* problems include decision problems for which a given solution for a given input can be checked to see if it is a solution that satisfies all the requirements of the problem. If a reasonably efficient algorithm exists for an *NP complete* problem, then there would be a reasonably efficient algorithm for each problem in the NP class of problems. NP complete problems are the hardest problems in the NP of problems.
Dynamic Programming	The results or solutions of small subproblems are stored; the program then looks them up when it needs them to solve the larger problems.

Containers	Access Methods		
	Sequential	Direct	Relational
Stack	√		
Deque	√	√	
Vector	√	√	
Set			√
Map		√	√
List	√		

Figure 9.2 Access mechanisms supported by containers.

For example, let's say we have an algorithm that "looks through" some kind of container for a particular object or objects. The primary function of this algorithm is to find objects, so we classify it as a search algorithm.

NOTE:

Certain algorithms also require specific types of containers before they can operate properly. For instance, a binary search algorithm requires that its container be sorted. Depending on the implementation of a binary search algorithm, it may also require direct access to the elements of its container. If an algorithm requires direct access to a container, the algorithm would require a random-access iterator, as opposed to one of the simpler iterators, such as the input, output, or forward iterator.

Passing Iterators to Algorithms

The two most commonly used methods of passing iterators to algorithms are:

- Passing begin( ), rbegin( ), end( ), rend( ) iterators that belong to some container.
- Passing declared iterators initialized with begin( ), rbegin( ), end( ), rend( ) iterators that belong to some container.

To see how begin( ), and end( ) iterators are passed to algorithms, let's look at the accumulate program in Listing 9.4; it contains the code:

```
...
vector<double> Doubles;
int Count;
int N;
double X;
cout << "How Many Numbers ";
cin >> Count;
for(N = 1;N <= Count;N++)
{
    cin >> X;
    Doubles.push_back(X);
}
cout << accumulate(Doubles.begin(),Doubles.end(),0.0);
...
```

It declares a container called Doubles. We want the accumulate algorithm to add all of the numbers in the container, so we pass the algorithm an iterator pointing to the first object in the Doubles container, and an iterator pointing to beyond the last object in the Doubles container.

```
accumulate(Doubles.begin(),Doubles.end(),0.0);
```

The accumulate algorithm then uses these iterators; specifically, it uses the Doubles.begin( ) iterator to get the first object to be added. Then the accumulate algorithm uses the operator++( ) to increment the iterator to get the next object to be added. The process of incrementing the iterator to get to the next object in the container is called *iteration*. The accumulate algorithm will keep iterating through the container until it reaches an iterator that is equal to Doubles.end( ). At that point, the algorithm terminates and returns the sum of the objects that have been added. One of the most common implementations of the accumulate algorithm is shown in Listing 9.8.

When we invoke the accumulate( ) algorithm:

```
accumulate(Doubles.begin(),Doubles.end(),0.0);
```

the InputIterator first is assigned the value of Doubles.begin( ), and the InputIterator last is assigned the value of Doubles.end( ). Once these iterator assignments are made, the algorithm can iterate through the container. The begin( ), end( ), rbegin( ), and rend( ) iterators are defined and maintained by the container to which they belong. The rbegin( ) and rend( ) iterators can be used in the same fashion as begin( ) and end( ).

```
accumulate(Doubles.rbegin(),Doubles.rend(),0.0);
```

Listing 9.8   Common Implementation of Accumulate Algorithm

```
//Listing 9.8
// A common implementation of the accumulate algorithms

template <class InputIterator, class T>
T accumulate(InputIterator first, InputIterator last, T init)
{
    while (first != last)
        init = init + *first++;
    return init;
}
```

Passing the begin( ), end( ), rbegin( ), and rend( ) iterators to the algorithm is the first, commonly used, method of giving the algorithm access to a container. The second method requires a declaration of a container iterator. Take, for instance, the statements in Listing 9.9.

Two iterators are declared:

```
Location1
Location2
```

Both are initialized with valid container positions. We then perform some iterator arithmetic:

```
Location1 = Location1 += (Doubles.size() / 2);
Location2 = Location2--;
```

This causes the iterators to point to new objects within the container. Then we invoke the accumulate( ) algorithm with the new iterators:

```
accumulate(Location1,Location2,0.0)
```

The first time we used the accumulate algorithm with the Doubles container, it added all the objects in the container. When we changed the iterators, as we did with Loca-

Listing 9.9   Using Container Iterators for Accumulate

```
// Listing 9.9
// Demonstration of using container iterators for algorithms

vector<double> Doubles(NumOfObjects,Object);
vector<double>::iterator Location1;
vector<double>::iterator Location2;
Location1 = Doubles.begin();
Location2 = Doubles.end();
Location1 = Location1 += (Doubles.size() / 2);
Location2 = Location2--;
accumulate(Location1,Location2,0.0);
```

tion1 and Location2, the accumulate algorithm could add only the objects found between the objects located at Location1 and Location2.

We also passed iterators that pointed to containers holding user-defined objects. Notice that Listing 9.7, line 19, contains a call to the accumulate( ) algorithm:

```
cout << accumulate(Clocks.begin(),Clocks.end(),ZeroTime);
```

Two iterators were passed to the accumulate( ) algorithm:

```
Clocks.begin();
Clocks.end();
```

The accumulate algorithm will use these two iterators to add all the objects in the Clocks container. The accumulate algorithm is typical of how iterator arguments are used with the standard C++ library algorithms.

Function Objects and Predicates

Besides iterator arguments, many standard C++ algorithms accept function objects or predicates as arguments. These can increase the functionality of the generalized solution that the algorithm offers. Function objects and predicates can make algorithms that are already very general even more general.

Function Objects

A *function object* is a class that overloads the ( ) operator. Function objects can be used in the same places as pointers to functions. The difference is that a function object can take advantage of the benefits of object-oriented programming—encapsulation, polymorphism, and inheritance.

Let's define a function class to see how function objects work. The declaration:

```
class root{
public:
    double operator() (double X, double Y) { return(sqrt(X+Y)); }
};
```

declares a function object. The operator( ) has been defined for the root object, a typical function object. This operator accepts any two numbers, adds them, and returns their square root. Though this function object has no data members and only one operator, we can define function objects to contain data members and other member functions. The following percent function object contains a data member P.

```
class percent{
    double P;
public:
    percent(double X) { P = X;}
    double operator() (double X, double Y) { return (P * ( X + Y));}
};
```

The percent function object is used to return a percentage of two numbers that have been added.

Now let's see how the percent and root function objects can be used with one of the standard C++ algorithms. Most C++ standard algorithms have two forms: the first does not take a function object, and the second form expects either a function object or predicate. The declarations for the accumulate algorithm are examples of the two forms that the standard C++ algorithms can take.

```
// Form 1 (no function object)
template <class InputIterator, class T>
T accumulate(InputIterator first, InputIterator last, T init)
{
    while (first != last)
        init = init + *first++;
    return init;

}
//Form 2 (contains a function object)
template <class InputIterator, class T, class BinaryOperation>
T accumulate(InputIterator first, InputIterator last, T init,
            BinaryOperation binary_op)
{
    while (first != last)
        init = binary_op(init, *first++);
    return init;

}
```

Passing Function Objects to Algorithms

Again, the first form does not expect a function object and the second form does. The program in Listing 9.10 demonstrates how functions objects are used with algorithms.

The two calls to the accumulate algorithm on lines 34 and 35 contain function objects. The first has a percent object and will return a sum of values in container C that has been multiplied by 0.10. The Percent object is initialized with 0.10. As the accumulate object adds values from the container C, the sums will be multiplied by 0.10. We could have chosen any multiplier for the constructor of the Percent object. The accumulate algorithm that contains the root function object will return a sum of the container C values, with the sqrt operation applied.

Figure 9.3 shows how the arguments to an algorithm are resolved with iterator parameters, objects, and function objects. The important connection to note is between accumulate's binary_op( ) and the function object's operator( ) definition.

```
init = binary_op(init, *first++);

double operator() (double X,double Y);
```

Here, wherever the algorithm calls the binary_op( ) function, it is really referring to the operator( ) function defined by the function object passed to the algorithm. So, when binary_op( ) is called for the accumulate algorithm that has a Percent function object in Listing 9.10, the behavior of binary_op( ) is actually:

```
double   binary_op(double X,double Y)
{
    return (P * (X + Y));
}
```

Listing 9.10 Using Function Objects with Algorithms

```
1    // Listing 9.10
2    // Demonstrates how to use function objects
3
4    #include <iostream>
5    #include <vector>
6    #include <numeric>
7    #include <cmath>
8    #include <iterator>
9
10   using namespace std;
11
12   class percent{
13       double P;
14   public:
15       percent(double X) { P = X;}
16       double operator()(double X, double Y){ return (P * ( X + Y));}
17
18   };
19
20   class root{
21   public:
22       double operator()(double X, double Y) { return(sqrt(X+Y)); }
23   };
24
25
26   void main(void)
27   {
28
29       vector<double> C;
30       percent Percent(0.10);
31       root Root;
32       for(int N = 0;N < 5;N++){
33           C.push_back(N);
34       }
35       cout << accumulate(C.begin(),C.end(),0.0,Percent) << endl;
36       cout << accumulate(C.begin(),C.end(),0.0,Root) << endl;
37
38   }
39
```

Let's trace through the execution of the accumulate function in this case (see Table 9.4).

A function object can be as simple or as complicated as needed, to give any algorithm added functionality. We have seen how the accumulate algorithm and function objects can be used to do simple summations. Next, the program in Listing 9.11 demonstrates the use of a function object, the accumulate algorithm, and an istream_iterator to count the number of occurrences of a specified word in a text file.

Algorithm

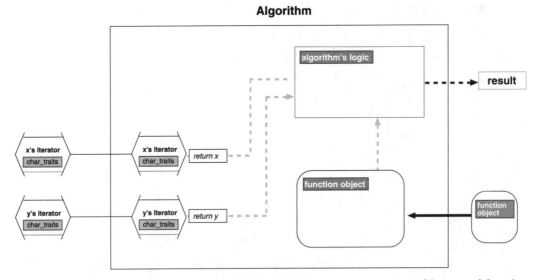

Figure 9.3 Resolving arguments to an algorithm with iterator parameters, objects, and function objects.

The function object same_word is used to compare the words passed to the function object, with the word used to construct the function object. On line 35 the function object Same was constructed with the string contained in argv[2]. The program in Listing 9.11 is invoked as:

```
list9-11.exe mytextfile searchword
```

where list9–11 refers to the program in Listing 9.11 and mytextfile refers to the text file that is to be searched; searchword refers to the word that is to be counted. The text file is searched with the help of the In istream_iterator. The In iterator returns strings that are compared using the function operator of same_word.

Built-in Function Objects

The standard C++ Library comes with a collection of ready-to-use function objects. These function objects provide important helper functions for the standard algorithms. Understanding these function objects is necessary to make effective use of the standard

Table 9.4 A Trace of the Accumulate Algorithm's use of the Percent's Function Object

P =0.100	,X = 0.000	,Y = 0 0.10* (0.00 + 0.00) = 0.00
P =0.100	,X = 0.000	,Y = 1 0.10* (0.00 + 1.00) = 0.10
P =0.100	,X = 0.100	,Y = 2 0.10* (0.10 + 2.00) = 0.21
P =0.100	,X = 0.210	,Y = 3 0.10* (0.21 + 3.00) = 0.32
P =0.100	,X = 0.321	,Y = 4 0.10* (0.32 + 4.00) = 0.43

Listing 9.11 Using Function Objects

```
1    // Listing 9.11
2    // Demonstrates How to Use Function Objects
3
4    #include <iostream>
5    #include <numeric>
6    #include <cmath>
7    #include <iterator>
8    #include <string>
9    #include <fstream>
10
11   using namespace std;
12
13   class same_word{
14   string SearchWord;
15   public:
16       same_word(string X) { SearchWord = X;}
17       double operator() (int X, string Y);
18   };
19
20
21   double same_word::operator() (int X,string Y)
22   {
23       if(Y == SearchWord){
24           return (X + 1);
25       }
26       return(X);
27   }
28
29
30
31   void main(int argc, char *argv[])
32   {
33
34       if(argc == 3){
35           same_word Same(argv[2]);
36           ifstream Fin(argv[1]);
37           istream_iterator<string> In(Fin),eos;
38           cout << accumulate(In,eos,0,Same) << endl;
39       }
40       else{
41
42               cerr << "Usage: list9-11 Filename Word" << endl;
43       }
44
45   }
46
```

C++ algorithms, as some of the most powerful features of the standard algorithms rely on the use of function objects.

These function objects are found in the <function> header file, and are divided into these six categories:

- Arithmetic operations
- Negators
- Comparison
- Binders
- Logical operations
- Adaptors

In addition to the regular function object, there is a special-purpose function object called a *predicate,* a function object that returns a value representing true or false. The helper objects in these categories are either regular function objects or predicates. Figure 9.4 shows how the algorithms use function objects and iterators to perform work.

Arithmetic Operations

The arithmetic operations provide function object definitions for the most commonly used operators (see Table 9.5). The arithmetic operations are easy to use. For example, we can use the multiplies function object in a familiar accumulate algorithm.

```
accumulate(C.begin(),C.end(),1,multiplies<double>>);
```

Listing 9.12 demonstrates how the arithmetic function objects can be used with the algorithms, and Table 9.6 traces the multiplies<double> function object.

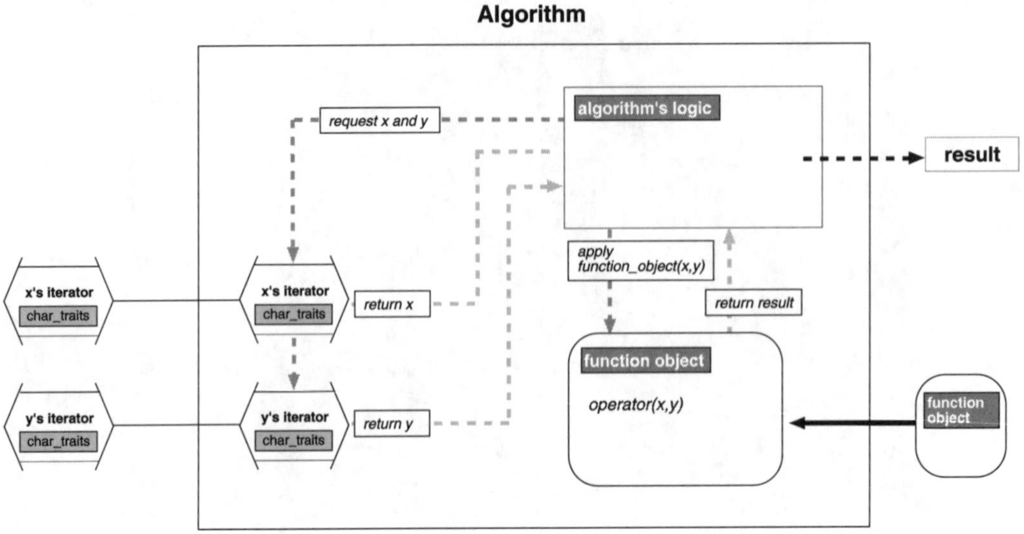

Figure 9.4   How algorithms use function objects and iterators to perform work.

Table 9.5 Arithmetic Function Objects and Their Operations

ARITHMETIC FUNCTION OBJECT	OPERATION	DESCRIPTION
plus	Binary	addition: $x + y$
minus	Binary	subtraction: $x - y$
multiplies	Binary	multiplication: $x * y$
divides	Binary	division: x / y
modulus	Binary	modulus: $x \% y$
negate	Unary	negation: $-x$

Comparison Operations

The comparison operations provide function definitions for the most commonly used comparison operators. They are used with the algorithms in the same manner as the arithmetic operations (see Table 9.7). The comparison function objects are predicates. They return type bool, representing either true or false.

The most convenient places to see how the comparison operations work is with the set, multiset, map, and multimap containers. These containers require a comparison operation that defines their sort order. For example, the program in Listing 9.13 demonstrates how the less and greater predicates can be used with a set container and a copy algorithm.

Listing 9.12 Using Arithmetic Function Objects with Algorithms

```
1  // Listing 9.12
2  // Demonstrates how a built-in function object is used with
3  // an algorithm
4
5  #include <iostream>
6  #include <list>
7
8  using namespace std;
9
10  void main(void)
11  {
12
13      list<double> C;
14      C.push_back(3);
15      C.push_back(4);
16      C.push_back(5);
17      cout << accumulate(C.begin(),C.end(),0,multiplies<double>())
18          <<endl;
19
20
21  }
```

Table 9.6 A Trace of the multiplies<double> Function Object

1 * 3 = 3
3 * 4 = 12
12 * 5 = 60
Result is 60

Logical Operations

The logical operations provide function objects for the basic logical operators. Table 9.8 lists these logical operators and their definitions.

Negators and Binders

Negators and binders transform the original function object in some way. The negators reverse the logic of the original predicate. For example, if a predicate returns true if object X < object Y, by negating that predicate, it will return true if object X > object Y. When a predicate is negated, the condition(s) that causes the predicate to return true will cause it to return false and the condition(s) that causes it to return false will cause it to return true. Figure 9.5 shows how negators work on function objects.

Binders are also objects used to transform the argument requirements of a function object or predicate. They can be used to reduce the argument requirements of a function object from two down to one. They can also be used to pick either the left or the right argument during the reduction process. Figure 9.6 shows the flow of the bind1st and bind2nd binders; bind1st binds the first argument, causing a two-argument function object to generate a one-argument function object; bind2nd binds the second argument. Table 9.9 lists the binders, what they bind, and an example of their use.

Search Algorithms

One of the most important functions performed in computer programming is searching for a specific object, a piece of information, or data in a collection of other objects or information. We use computers to search for names, social security numbers, dates, account numbers, addresses, documents, license numbers, identification numbers, e-mail aliases, and so on. We search among networks, relational databases, object-oriented databases, files, and data structures of all types. There are literally dozens of

Table 9.7 Comparison Function Objects and Their Operations

COMPARISON FUNCTION OBJECT	OPERATION	DESCRIPTION
equal_to	Binary	equality: x == y
not_equal_to	Binary	inequality: x != y
greater	Binary	greater than: x > y
less	Binary	less than: x < y
greater_equal	Binary	greater than or equal to: x >= y
less_equal	Binary	less than or equal to: x <= y

Listing 9.13   Using Predicates with Algorithms

```
1    // Listing 9.13
2    // Demonstrates how built-in predicates are used with algorithms
3
4    #include <iostream>
5    #include <iterator>
6    #include <algorithm>
7    #include <set>
8
9
10   void main(void)
11   {
12
13       set<int,less<int> > X;
14       set<int,greater<int> > Y;
15       X.insert(3);
16       X.insert(1);
17       X.insert(2);
18       Y.insert(5);
19       Y.insert(7);
20       Y.insert(6);
21       ostream_iterator<int> Out(cout,"\n ");
22       copy(X.begin(),X.end(),Out);
23       copy(Y.begin(),Y.end(),Out);
24
25   }
```

commonly used search algorithms available to help us find the objects we want (see Table 9.10). Finding and developing good search algorithms continues to be an active area of research among computer scientists.

A search has three basic goals:

1. To find and report the location of an object within some type of collection or container.

2. To find and return the object or its value from some type of collection or container.

3. To report whether an object or piece of information is in some type of container.

To accomplish these goals efficiently, we need a good search algorithm. It might seem that we should be able to write one good search algorithm capable of effectively locat-

Table 9.8   Logical Operators

LOGICAL FUNCTION OBJECT	OPERATION	DESCRIPTION
logical_and	Binary	and: x && y
logical_or	Binary	or: x ∥ y
logical_not	Unary	not: !x

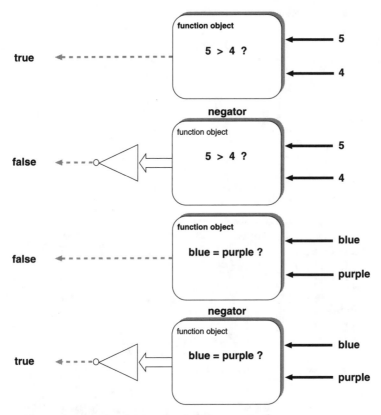

Figure 9.5 Negators work on function objects that accept built-in and user-defined values.

ing any kind of object or information we needed. But any search algorithm depends on how information is organized in the computer or computer storage, and there are many approaches to storing and organizing information. Consequently, we must design algorithms that deal efficiently with each of these approaches.

We call the organization of information within a computer a *data structure*. Some examples of data structures are lists, stacks, queues, arrays, matrices, sets, and maps. Each has its own access methods (see Figure 9.7). For example, a stack allows the user to access only what is on the top of the stack. The last object placed on a stack is the first object removed from it, an access method called LIFO (last in first out), as we've discussed throughout this book. The reverse of LIFO is FIFO (first in first out). The queue data structure uses FIFO access; we place objects at the rear of the queue and remove objects from the front of a queue. The first object in is the first object removed, and the last object in is the last object removed. A search algorithm can only access the data structure based on its access method. Certain search algorithms work better with one data structure than another, meaning it will find the information more quickly and with less effort. The goal, then, is to match the right search algorithm with the right data structure, or in C++ terms, the right algorithm with the right container.

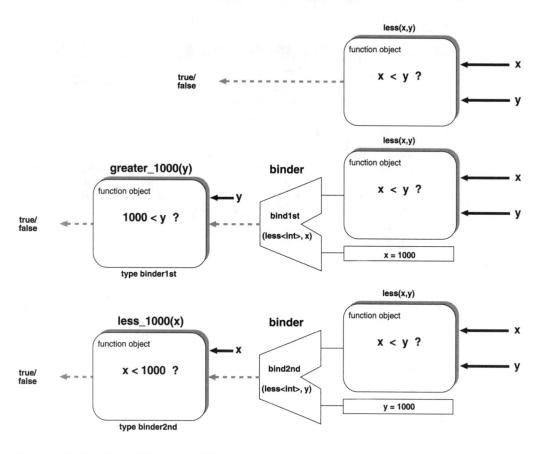

Figure 9.6 The flow of bind1st and bind2nd.

The standard C++ library includes 13 search algorithms, each of which is most properly suited to a certain situation. We determine how well a search algorithm performs by looking at how much work it must do to accomplish the goals of the search. Specifically, we measure the amount of work the algorithm does based on how many comparison or identification instructions will be executed before the search item is found and how much extra space the algorithm will need to do its job. In short, we look at the number of *primary* steps (instructions) an algorithm must perform.

We use the O notation to describe the amount of work an algorithm must perform. It gives us a number of steps (instructions) based on the amount of data the algorithm must work on. For instance, if a search algorithm has to look through 1,000 names in a list to find a particular name, the O notation would give us the number of steps the algorithm has performed based on 1,000. By comparing the O notation numbers for the different algorithms under consideration, we can easily see which algorithm is best for the job. (O notation is described more fully later in this chapter.)

Although the standard C++ library does not contain all of the commonly used search algorithms, it does contain a number of the most effective ones. A very important search algorithm is binary_search( ). Beating the binary_search( ) is hard when consid-

Table 9.9 Binders and Their Use

BINDERS	DESCRIPTION	EXAMPLE
bind1st	Takes two arguments, a function object and a value, and binds them into a single construction where the value is the first argument. Returned is a unary function object, *binder1st,* to be used as a single argument in a function.	bind1st(less<int>( ), 000); Returns a unary function object that performs: 1000 < y?
bind2nd	Takes two arguments, a value and a function object, and binds them into a single construction where the value is the second argument. Returned is a unary function object, *binder2nd,* to be used as a single argument in a function.	bind2nd(less<int>( ), 1000); Returns a unary function object that performs: x < 1000?

ering the worse case. For our discussion on searches, the worst-case scenario occurs when the object we are looking for is not in the container we are searching. When we have the worst-case scenario binary_search( ) performs well. When we have the average case scenario binary_search( ) performs well. For our discussion on searches, the average case occurs when the object we are searching for is anywhere in the container. Furthermore, the probability of the object appearing at any one place in the container is equal to it appearing any where else in the container. There are very few search algorithms that can out perform binary_search( ) in the average case.

Table 9.10 Common Search Algorithms

SEARCHED ALGORITHMS	CONTAINERS SEARCHED
find( )	All containers
find_if( )	All containers
find_end( )	All containers
find_first_of( )	All containers
adjacent_find( )	All containers
search( )	All containers
search_n( )	All containers
binary_search( )	All containers
nth_element( )	deque, vector
lower_bound( )	All containers
upper_bound( )	All containers
equal_range( )	All containers

Containers	Logical View	Access Methods		
		Sequential	Direct	Relational
Stack	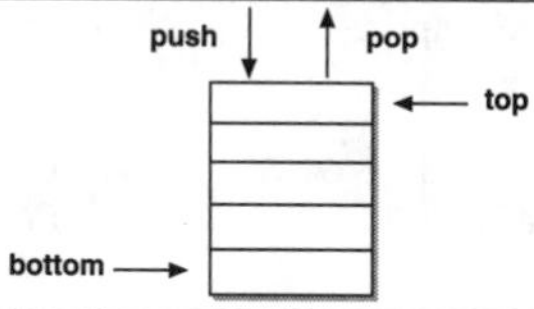	✓		
Deque	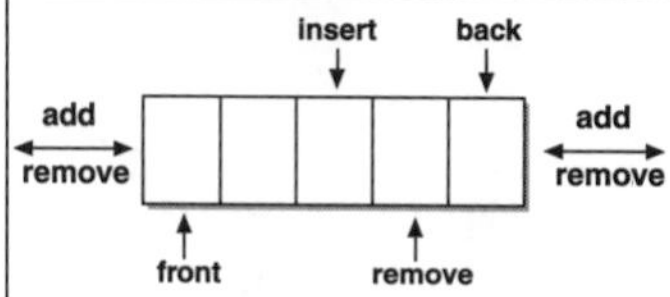	✓	✓	
Vector	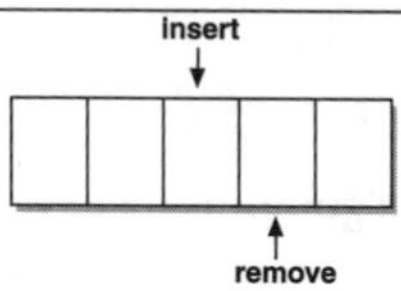	✓	✓	
Set	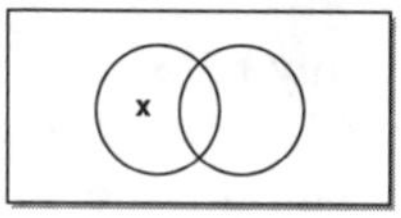			✓
Map	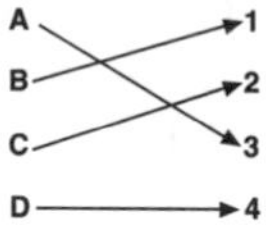		✓	✓
List	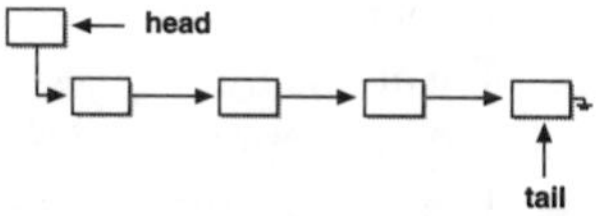	✓		

Figure 9.7 Common data structures, their logical view, and access methods.

Figure 9.8 compares the number of steps some commonly used algorithms would take to find an object in a list of 5,000 objects. Note that the interpolation search does better than binary_search( ) on the average. However, binary_search( ) does better than an interpolation search in the worst-case scenario. For many situations, the binary_search( ) algorithm is the best choice, especially if we want to know absolutely the longest time that a search will take. It is one of the most efficient algorithms searching a sorted collection of objects.

Note in Figure 9.8 that the standard C++ library binary_search( ) algorithm performs on par with the best algorithms. (The number of steps [instructions] represents how these algorithms will do in the worst case. Most do better in the average case.) The

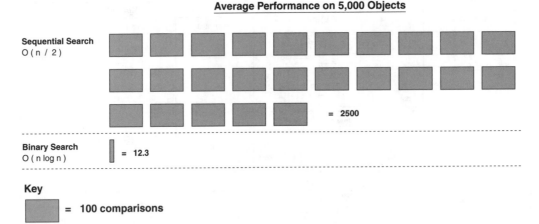

Average Performance on 5,000 Objects

Sequential Search
O (n / 2)

= 2500

Binary Search
O (n log n)

= 12.3

Key

= 100 comparisons

Figure 9.8 Comparing steps some commonly used algorithms take to find an object in a list of 5,000 objects.

worst case tells us that an algorithm will only require a certain number of steps no matter how complicated the data is arranged; the average case indicates the number of steps an algorithm will take when the data is not organized according to worst-case scenario. The O notation is useful in determining the maximum number of primary steps a given algorithm will perform under any situation. The top partition in Figure 9.8 represents how a sequential search performs on a typical data set in the average case. The bottom partition shows the performance of the binary search in the average case.

These two basic kinds of searches are supported by the standard library. The first type is a sequential search, which will look at each object in the container one by one until the item being searched for is found or until there are no more objects to check. The sequential searches found in the standard C++ library are represented by the find( ) and find_if ( ) family of algorithms (see Table 9.11). The second type of search uses the *bisection* method. This method requires that the container being searched be in a sort order. Sequential searches are not concerned with order; the container may be sorted or unsorted. Sequential searches will visit every object in the container if necessary. In contrast, the bisection searches work by checking successively smaller halves of a container until the object is located or until it runs out of halves to check. The binary_search( ) algorithm uses a bisection method.

Sequential Searches

Let's look more closely at how the sequential and bisection methods work. Figure 9.9 shows an array of words to be searched. Let's say our search word is "Voyages." Our sequential search must inspect every word in the container until it finds "Voyages," or until it reaches the end of the container. Remember, sequential searches cannot jump around in the container they are searching; they must look at each element one at a time from beginning to the end, or from end to beginning.

Table 9.11 The find( ) and find_if( ) Family of Algorithms

ALGORITHM	PERFORMANCE	SEARCH OBJECTIVE
find( )	n	Searches the range defined by first and last for an element. Returns the iterator.
find_if( )	n	Searches the range defined by first and last for an element in which the predicate function returns true for that element. Returns the iterator.
find_end( )	n	Searches the first range for a subsequence defined by the second range. Returns the last iterator in the range where the subsequence has been located.
find_first_of( )	n	Searches the first range for a subsequence defined by the second range. Returns the first iterator where the match starts in the first range.
adjacent_find( )	n	Searches the range defined by first and last for a pair of adjacent elements that are equal. Returns the first iterator of the pair.

Bisection Searches

As stated, most of the searches that use a bisection method require that the containers they are searching be in some type of sort order. Thus, even if the containers hold something other than numbers or characters, they must be sorted. For instance, if a container holds fruit objects, we must define the operators <, >, and == on the fruit objects so the

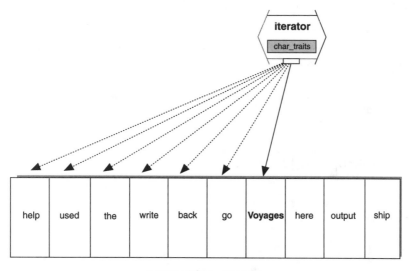

Figure 9.9 An array of words to be searched for "Voyages," using a sequential search.

algorithms will know whether apple is < orange, banana >= grape, peach < pear, and so on. The bisection searches work by searching successively smaller halves of a sorted container. For example, if we were searching for the letter k in the vector shown in Figure 9.10, the search would proceed by bisecting the container as shown. We first check to see if the letter k is in the top half or the bottom half. The figure shows what happens in a sequential and binary search. We find that k is not in the first half, so we consider only the bottom half of the vector from that point. We divide the bottom half of the vector into halves, then check to see whether k is < the letter that is at the dividing point of our two new halves. We find that k is not in the top half, so we *bisect* the vector again. We continue with this process until either we have located k or we cannot bisect the vector any further. Again, the binary_search( ) algorithm uses this type of search method. Figure 9.11 shows a flowchart of a typical implementation of the binary search algorithm. There, the objects are stored in the vector k[ ]. The standard C++ library contains four search algorithms that use different variations of the bisection method; these are listed in Table 9.12.

The search algorithms in the standard C++ library return either iterators or bool values representing true or false. Consider the sequential search find( ). The find( ) algorithm can be used to search any kind of container; it does not matter whether the container is sorted.

```
Loc = find(C.begin(),C.end(),15);
if(Loc != C.end()){
    cout << *Loc
}

    . . .
```

In this example, the find( ) algorithm looks for the value 15 in container C. If the search is not successful, the find( ) algorithm will return the value C.end( ). If the search is successful, the find( ) algorithm will return an iterator pointing to the position in the container where 15 is located. We can then access that value by dereferencing the iterator:

```
*Loc
```

returns the value located at the iterator position Loc. Notice that the find( ) algorithm accomplishes two of the three sorting objectives:

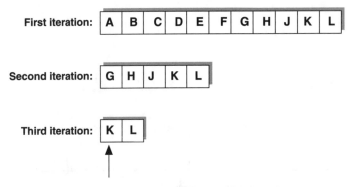

Figure 9.10 A bisection search cuts a vector in halves until the search item is located. In this case, the search item is the character k.

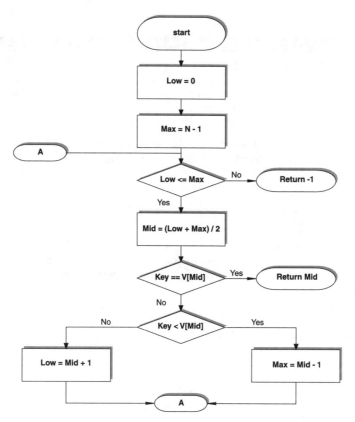

Figure 9.11 A flowchart of a typical implementation of the binary search algorithm.

- To find and report the location of an object within some type of collection or container.

- To find and return the object or its value from some type of collection or container.

The find( ) family of algorithms returns an iterator. The iterator is a pointer to the location of the object in the container. The iterator can also be used to gain direct access to the object value at that location.

Next, we will look at how the binary_search( ) algorithm is used to accomplish the third objective of a search: To report whether an object or piece of information is present within some type of container.

Using Searches with User-Defined Objects

Search algorithms can also be used to find user-defined objects. It is important to make sure that the != operator, == operator, and < operator are defined for any user-defined objects that will be used with the searches. It is a good policy to define all of the com-

Table 9.12 Bisection Algorithms

BISECTION SEARCHES	DESCRIPTION
upper_bound( )	Searches a sorted input range for a given value; returns an iterator pointing to the next highest value available. If the object is not in the container, an iterator pointing to the next highest value in the container is returned. If that value is not available, then the past-the-end iterator is returned.
lower_bound( )	Searches a sorted input range for a given value; returns an iterator pointing to the value for which the container is being searched. If the object is not in the container, an iterator pointing to the next highest value in the container is returned.
binary_search( )	Searches a sorted input range for a given value; calls lower_bound( ) to find the value.
equal_range( )	Searches a sorted input range for a given value; returns a pair of iterators: one iterator containing the value lower_bound( ) and the other containing the value upper_bound( ).

parison operators for user-defined objects that might be compared to each other. The program in Listing 9.14 uses the find( ) algorithm to locate and return a user-defined Clock object.

The find( ) algorithm in this listing locates and prints a value of 40 hours and 31 minutes. We can use our user-defined clock_time object because we defined the operator !=( ) for the clock_time class. The clock_time declaration contains operator!=( ) and operator==( ).

```
class clock_time{
protected:
    int Minutes;
    int Hours;
public:
    clock_time(void);
    clock_time(int Hrs,int Min);
    clock_time(const clock_time &Time);
    clock_time &operator=(clock_time &Time);
    friend ostream &operator<<(ostream &Out,clock_time &Time);
    clock_time &operator+(clock_time &Time);
    clock_time &operator-(clock_time &Time);
    int operator>(clock_time &Time);
    int operator<(clock_time &Time);
    int operator==(clock_time &Time);
    int operator!=(clock_time &Time);
    void minutes(int M);
    void hours(int H);
    int minutes(void);
    int hours(void);
};
```

Listing 9.14   Using the find( ) Algorithm on a User-Defined Object

```
1    // Listing 9.14
2    // Demonstrates find with a user-defined object Clock.
3
4    #include <iostream>
5    #include <vector>
6    #include <clktime.h>
7    #include <algorithm>
8
9    using namespace std;
10
11
12
13   void main(void)
14   {
15
16       vector<clock_time> List;
17       clock_time Clock(40,31);
18       List.push_back(clock_time(13,50));
19       List.push_back(clock_time(21,20));
20       List.push_back(clock_time(40,31));
21       List.push_back(clock_time(15,10));
22       cout << *(find(List.begin(),List.end(),Clock));
23
24   }
25
```

Let's see why our comparison operator definitions were necessary. A common implementation for the standard find( ) algorithm is shown in Listing 9.15.

Notice how the comparison operator!=( ) is used to see if we have found a match that contains the != operator:

```
*first != value;
```

Listing 9.15   Common find( ) Implementation

```
// Listing 9.15
// A common implementation of the find( ) algorithm

template <class InputIterator, class T>
  InputIterator find (InputIterator first, InputIterator last,
                      const T& value) {
      while (first != last && *first != value) ++first;
      return first;
}
```

If the object that we are attempting to pass to the find( ) algorithm has not defined the operator!=( ), the program will not compile. However, we have defined the operator!=( ) for the clock_time class, so when the

```
*first != value;
```

comparison is made, the operator!=( ) will refer to our definition in the clock_time class. In the same manner that the sequential find( ) algorithms require us to define the != operator, the binary_search( ) algorithms require us to define the < operator for any user-defined class that will be used with one of the binary_search( ) algorithms.

Keep in mind that any container used with one of the binary search type algorithms will have to be sorted. Since our clock_time object has the operator<( ) defined, we can use it with a sort and, therefore, use it with any of the bisection algorithms. The program in Listing 9.16 calls the sort( ) algorithm to sort the Clock container.

Listing 9.16 Using binary_search

```
1    // Listing 9.16
2    // Demonstrates binary_search() with a user-defined object Clock.
3
4    #include <iostream>
5    #include <vector>
6    #include <algorithm>
7    #include <clktime.h>
8
9
10   using namespace std;
11
12
13
14   void main(void)
15   {
16       vector<clock_time> List;
17       clock_time Clock(21,21);
18       List.push_back(clock_time(13,50));
19       List.push_back(clock_time(40,31));
20       List.push_back(clock_time(21,20));
21       List.push_back(clock_time(15,10));
22       sort(List.begin(),List.end());
23       if(binary_search(List.begin(),List.end(),Clock)){
24           cout << "Found It";
25       }
26       else{
27               cout << "No Hit";
28       }
29   }
30
```

After the sort( ) algorithm does its work, the binary_search( ) algorithm can determine whether a clock time of 21 hours and 21 minutes is stored in the clock container. (The sorting process is necessary with the binary_search( ), upper_bound( ), lower_bound( ), and equal_range( ) algorithms.) The binary_search( ) algorithm returns a bool representing true or false. If the value that the binary_search( ) was looking for is found, the algorithm will return true, otherwise it will return false.

The binary_search( ) algorithm is one of the easiest bisection searches to use in the standard library. The upper_bound( ), lower_bound( ), and equal_range( ) algorithms are a little trickier. The lower_bound( ) algorithm returns an iterator pointing to the first object equal to or greater than the object for which the container is being searched. To use the lower_bound( ) algorithm to search for the number 16 in two containers, A and B, we would code the call as:

```
lower_bound(A.begin(),A.end(),16);
lower_bound(B.begin(),B.end(),16);
```

Container A has the value 16; container B does not. Figure 9.12 illustrates which iterators the searches will return in both cases. The lower_bound( ) algorithm is designed to return an iterator pointing to the object of the search, if it is present. If the object is not in the container, the lower_bound( ) algorithm will return the next largest object in the container. Figure 9.12 also shows that the lower_bound( ) algorithm returns 17 when container B is searched because 16 is not in container B.

The upper_bound( ) algorithm behaves similarly. The upper_bound( ) algorithm will return an iterator pointing to the next largest value available. The upper_bound( ) algorithm is invoked in the same fashion as lower_bound( ).

```
upper_bound(A.begin(),A.end(),16);
upper_bound(B.begin(),B.end(),16);
```

Figure 9.13 shows what happens when the upper_bound( ) algorithm is used on container A and container B. Again, the value 16 is in container A, but not in container B. The upper_bound( ) returns the next largest object whether the value is in the container or not, hence their name. The lower_bound( ) algorithm will find an object that has a sort order no lower than the object for which the container is being searched. The upper_bound( ) algorithm will also return an object that has a sort order that is no lower than the object for which the container is being searched. Listing 9.17 demonstrates the use of the lower_bound( ), upper_bound( ), and equal_range( ) algorithms.

The equal_range( ) algorithm is a combination of lower_bound( ) and upper_bound( ). If the object we are looking for is in the container, the equal_range( ) algorithm will return a *pair* of iterators that point to the object *and* the object with the next smallest value. If the object we are looking for is not in the container, the algorithm will return a pair of iterators, one containing the value:

```
lower_bound(X);
```

the other containing the value:

```
upper_bound(X);
```

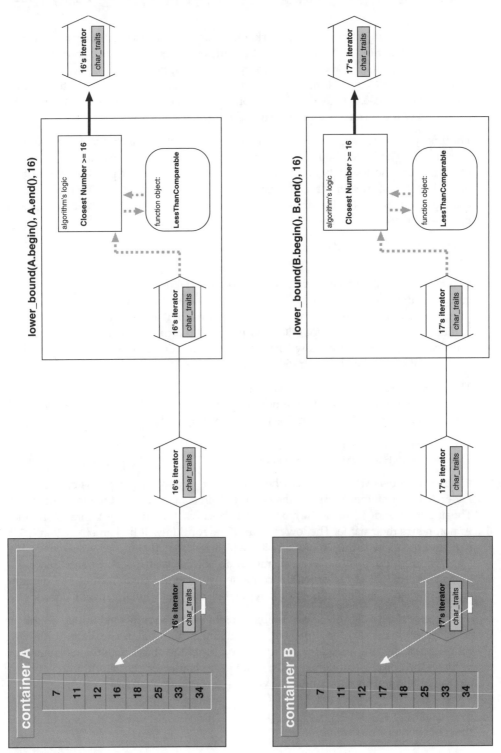

Figure 9.12 The lower_bound( ) algorithm returns 17 when container B is searched because 16 is not in the container.

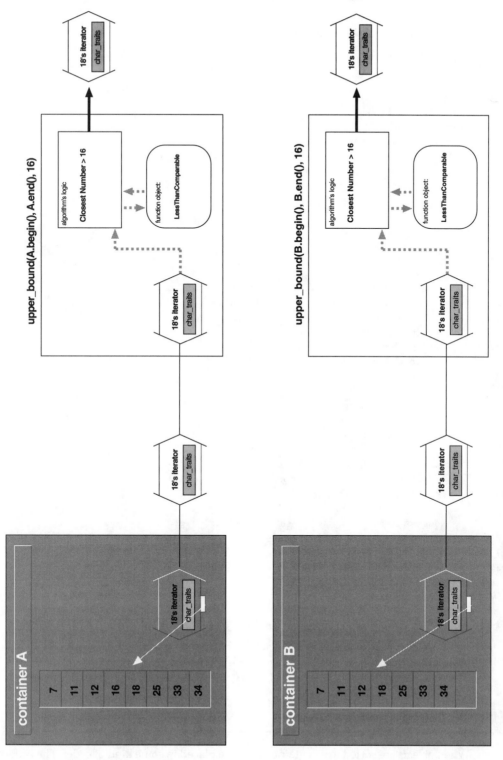

Figure 9.13 Using the upper_bound() algorithm to call on container A and container B.

Listing 9.17 Searching with User-Defined Objects

```
1  // Listing 9.17 demonstrates the use of lower_bound(), upper_bound()
2  // and equal_range()
3
4  #include <iostream>
5  #include <list>
6  #include <algorithm>
7  #include <iterator>
8
9  using namespace std;
10
11  void main(void)
12  {
13      list<char> List;
14      list<char>::iterator I1;
15      list<char>::iterator I2;
16      pair<list<char>::iterator,list<char>::iterator> I3;
17      ostream_iterator<char> Out(cout,"\n");
18      List.push_back('x');
19      List.push_back('z');
20      List.push_back('e');
21      List.push_back('k');
22      List.push_back('r');
23      List.push_back('h');
24      List.push_back('g');
25      List.sort();
26      copy(List.begin(),List.end(),Out);
27      I1 = lower_bound(List.begin(),List.end(),'f');
28      I2 = upper_bound(List.begin(),List.end(),'f');
29      I3 = equal_range(List.begin(),List.end(),'f');
30      cout << *I1 << endl;
31      cout << *I2 << endl;
32      cout << *I3.first << " " << *I3.second << endl;
33      cin.get();
34
35
36  }
```

Figure 9.14 shows what happens when equal_range( ) is called to search container A and container B. It returns an object of type pair< >. Remember, the bisection searches, including binary_search( ), upper_bound( ), lower_bound( ) and equal_range( ), require containers to be sorted.

Sort Algorithms

When objects are sorted in a container, they are placed in some kind of order. The order of characters and numbers in a computer character set is called its *collating sequence,* to

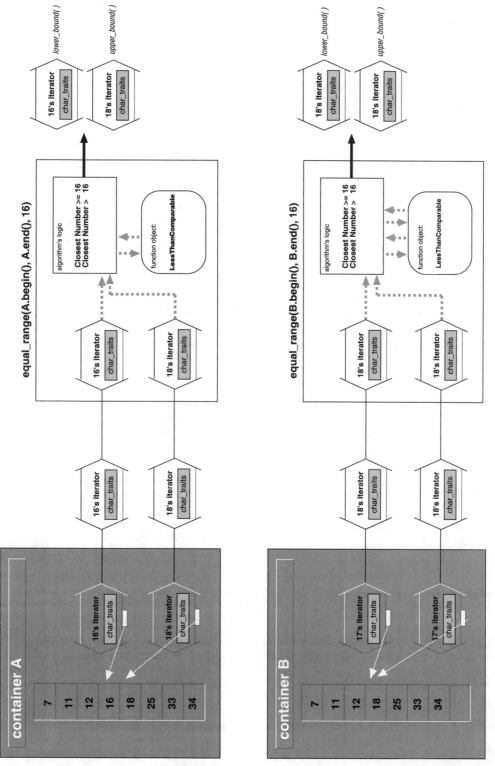

Figure 9.14 Using equal_range( ) to search container A and container B.

determine which character comes before another. If a container holds numbers, a sort based on the collating sequence rearranges them in the container either in ascending— 1, 2, 55, 77 . . .—or in descending order— . . . 77, 55, 2, 1. Likewise if the objects are characters, a sort based on collating sequence arranges them in either ascending or descending alphabetical order.

However, we are working with C++ and object-oriented programming, so we often deal with more than simply numbers and characters. We are often dealing with strings and user-defined objects. How do we sort a container of colors, shapes, or weather condition objects? If C++ is capable of modeling virtually any kind of object, it follows that we may need to sort any kind of object. The standard algorithms use either the comparison operators or predicates when performing sorts. Ordinarily, the standard algorithms use operator<( ) to compare two objects. This means that any objects that need to be sorted should have operator<( ) defined in its class declaration. It is a good idea to define all of these comparison operators for any class that may be used in a comparison: <, >, <=, >=, !=, ==.

The standard library provides eight basic sort algorithms (see Table 9.13). As with the search algorithms, the standard C++ library includes the best of the commonly used sort algorithms. Figure 9.15 shows a chart comparison of the commonly used algorithms based on sorting a container with 5,000 objects. Note that these algorithms sort have performance on par with some of the best sorting algorithms available.

Each standard sort algorithm has two forms, one that relies on a comparison operator (usually operator <) and another that relies on a user-supplied predicate. Using these two forms, we can design very flexible sorts. Let's take the job of sorting a container that holds rectangles. The operator<( ) may be defined as follows:

```
bool rectangle::operator<(const rectangle &X)
{
    if ((Length * Width) < (X.Length * X.Width)){
        return(true);
    }
    return(false);
}
```

Table 9.13 Standard Sort Algorithms

SORT ALGORITHMS	SORT TYPE	AVERAGE PERF.	WORST PERF.
sort( )	quick sort	$O(nlogn)$	$O(n^2)$
stable_sort( )	merge sort	$O(nlogn)$	$O(nlogn * nlogn)$
partial_sort( )	heap sort	$O(nlogn)$	$O(nlogn)$
partial_sort_copy( )	heap sort	$O(nlogn)$	$O(nlogn)$
nth_element( )	partition	$O(n)$	$O(n^2)$
merge( )	merge sort	$O(n)$	$O(n)$
inplace_merge( )	merge sort	$O(n)$	$O(nlogn)$
make_heap( ) + sort_heap( )	heap sort	$n + O(nlogn)$	$3n + O(nlogn)$

Figure 9.15 Comparing the commonly used algorithms based on sorting a container with 5,000 objects.

If we sort a container of rectangles based on this definition, the rectangles will be sorted based on area size (Area = Length * Width). The rectangles with the smallest area will be first in the container. The rectangle with the next largest area would be next and so on.

We could sort our container of rectangles by calling:

```
sort(Rect.begin(),Rect.end());
```

But because each sort algorithm has two forms, we may sort our container in another fashion. Let's assume we need to sort a container that has not only rectangles but other types of polygons, such as pentagons, hexagons, or triangles. We can use the predicate form of the algorithm to pass a built-in or user-defined predicate that will determine when one object is less than or greater than another. For example, we could define a predicate smallerThan(X,Y) as such:

```
bool smallerThan(X,Y)
{
    if X has less sides than Y then
        return true
    }
    return false
}
```

Recall that a predicate is simply a function object that returns true or false.

```
sort(Shapes.begin(),Shapes.end(),smallerThan);
```

This sort would organize the container Shapes so that the object with the least number of sides would be first. The object with the next larger number of sides would be second, and so on.

Using the second form of the algorithm, we could then pass other predicates that might sort the container of shapes based on some different comparison criteria. For example, if the shapes we were sorting were solids, we might sort them based on which objects had the most volume, to learn whether a cube can hold more than a cone.

The predicate argument to the sort algorithms allows for very flexible sorting sequences. The sorting algorithms supplied with the standard library can sort any standard container that has proper iterators defined. Table 9.14 lists the sort algorithms and the iterator types they require.

Sort Characteristics

A sort is either *internal* or *external*. An internal sort works on collections of objects in internal computer memory (RAM). External sorts work with collections of objects stored on disk. When an internal sort is performed, the result is a container stored in internal memory in sorted order. When an external sort is performed, the result is a file on disk or some other type of secondary storage in sorted order. But the definition of internal or external becomes blurred when we are dealing with *virtual memory*. Virtual memory treats disk space as internal memory. For our purposes, we will categorize virtual memory as sorting with internal sorts.

Of the eight standard sort algorithms, only merge can be used as an external sort. The merge( ) algorithm can be used in conjunction with an ostream_iterator to perform external sorts. The other seven algorithms are internal sorts.

Space Requirements

Another important characteristic of a sort algorithm is how much space beyond the number of elements to be sorted is needed. If an algorithm needs more space than that needed to hold the elements to be sorted, it is called an *inplace* algorithm. This means if 100 elements are to be sorted, only the space necessary to hold the 100 elements, plus a small amount for overhead is needed. A fast inplace sorting algorithm is highly desirable when selecting sort algorithms.

Many algorithms, however, require space proportional to the number of elements to be sorted. That is, if an algorithm is sorting a million elements, extra space for a million keys might be needed, or enough space to hold an entire copy of the million elements to be sorted might be needed. The sort( ) algorithm from the standard library is one that

Table 9.14 Sort Algorithms and Their Iterator Types

SORT ALGORITHM	ITERATORS	ALGORITHM	ITERATORS
sort( )	Random-Access	stable_sort( )	Random-Access
partial_sort( )	Random-Access	partial_sort_copy( )	Random-Access
nth_element( )	Random-Access	merge( )	Input, Output
inplace_merge( )	Bidirectional	make_heap( )	Random-Access
		sort_heap( )	Random-Access

requires space proportional to the number of elements to be sorted. The standard library's heap_sort( ) algorithm, on the other hand, is basically an inplace algorithm. Space requirements are not critical for sorts of, say, 500 objects or fewer. But as the number of objects to be sorted moves into the thousands, hundreds of thousands, or even millions, the amount of space a sort algorithm requires becomes an important algorithm selection criterion. Table 9.15 lists the eight standard sort algorithms, with their time and space requirements.

Sort Stability

If a sort algorithm maintains the sort objects in their original positions where possible, it is considered stable. "A sorting method is called stable if it preserves the relative order of equal keys in the file. If an alphabetized class list is sorted by grade, then a stable method will produce a list in which students with the same grade are still in alphabetical order" (Sedgewick 1983). A sort that is not stable usually destroys the original order of a list. To demonstrate, let's take a list of four names to be sorted. We want the sort to arrange the names only according to last name. If we have the names:

Kepler, J

Wakefield, A

Johnson, C

Johnson, B

A stable sort would produce:

Johnson, C

Johnson, B

Kepler, J

Wakefield, A

Table 9.15 Standard Sort Algorithms, with Time and Space Requirements

SORT ALGORITHM	PERFORMANCE	SPACE REQUIREMENTS
sort( )	O(nlogn)	logn
stable_sort( )	O(nlogn)	n
partial_sort( )	O(nlogn)	constant
partial_sort_copy( )	O(nlogn)	constant
nth_element( )	O(n)	constant
merge( )	O(n)	constant
inplace_merge( )	O(n)	n
make_heap( ) + sort_heap( )	n + O(nlogn)	constant

A nonstable sort might produce:

Johnson, B

Johnson, C

Kepler, J

Wakefield, A

Note that although the stable sort and the unstable sort both produced correctly sorted lists, the unstable sort switched the two Johnsons. A stable sort would maintain the relative position where possible. The standard C++ library includes a sort algorithm that ensures that objects are left in their relative position, stable_sort( ). To use stable_sort( ) on our container of names, we could have invoked it as follows:

```
stable_sort(Names.begin(),Names.end());
```

The result of this sort would be a sort order with the Johnsons in the appropriate slots.

Standard Class Library Sort Classifications

The sort algorithms in the standard library are derivatives of three basic types of sorts:

- Quick sort
- Merge sort
- Heap sort

Table 9.16 shows the breakdown of these algorithms. Both quick and merge sort are called *divide-and-conquer* algorithms, which typically work by dividing the problem into small pieces, solving for the small pieces, then putting those solved pieces together to generate a complete solution. The quick and the merge sorts use the divide-and-conquer approach to divide the collection of objects to be sorted into small sections. Once each small section is sorted, they are combined to produce a completed set of sorted objects. The quick and merge sorts are typically implemented using recursion. The heap sort uses the tree data structure to perform its work. The make_heap creates a tree out of the container that needs to be sorted, and sort_heap places the values in the proper nodes.

Table 9.16 Breakdown of the Standard Sorting Algorithms

QUICK SORT	PARTITION
sort( )	nth_element( )
MERGE SORT	**HEAP SORT**
stable_sort( )	make_heap( ) + sort_heap( )
merge( )	partial_sort( )
inplace_merge( )	partial_sort_copy( )

Selecting which sort algorithms to use can be tricky. Some are faster than others on the average; many do poorly under certain circumstances. For instance, the sort( ) algorithm is, on average, faster than the sort_heap( ) algorithm. However, some data arrangements make sort( ) much slower than sort_heap( ). If you need an absolute guarantee the sort will always take a certain amount of time, regardless how the data is organized, then a make_heap( ) followed by sort_heap( ) is the way to go. On the other hand, if you are more concerned with performance on the average, then sort( ) is about twice as fast as sort_heap( ).

And remember these algorithms can take up additional space. The generic merge( ) algorithm needs an additional container equal to the size of the two containers to be merged. Although it may have a better "face value" performance than the other sorts, it requires a considerable amount of extra space. It also requires that the two containers that it is merging already be sorted.

We must also consider whether an algorithm is stable. The standard library does provide a stable_sort( ). If speed is the primary concern, but stability and inplace sorting are issues, then sort( ) based on quick sort is a good choice. If you need to be sure that the algorithm never takes more than a specific number of primary steps to sort, regardless of the organization of the objects to be sorted, then make_heap( ) followed by a sort_heap( ) is the way to go. If, on the other hand, you need a fast method to put a sorted collection on a disk or other external medium, then the merge( ) algorithm is a good choice.

Using the Sort Algorithms

The sort algorithms are easy to use. They are mutable, which means they will modify the containers they are sorting. To use the sort algorithms, simply pass them the appropriate iterators for the container that needs to be sorted. The program in Listing 9.18 demonstrates a typical use of the sort algorithms.

This program uses the make_heap( ) and sort_heap( ) algorithms to perform a heap sort. The program reads all the file names in the directory passed from the command line. It then performs a heap sort on that list of file names and uses the standard copy algorithm to display the sorted list to the console.

The Set Algorithms

The C++ standard library includes a powerful set of algorithms designed to *identify* collections of objects based on some property or set of features. These algorithms are designed to include certain objects in a collection while excluding other objects based on a defined set of characteristics. They are called the set algorithms. They allow the programmer to choose groupings of objects based on a specified set of attributes, capabilities, or values. They also enable the programmer to include one set of objects while excluding another.

Whereas the search algorithms allow the programmer to find an object with a particular value, and the sort algorithms organize objects in collating sequence, the set algorithms give the programmer the capability to group, organize, and find collections of

Listing 9.18 Using the Sort Algorithms

```
1    // Listing 9.18
2    // This program demonstrates the use of heap sort
3
4    #include <iostream>
5    #include <dirent.h> // requires POSIX compatibility
6    #include <algorithm>
7    #include <iterator>
8    #include <deque>
9    #include <string>
10
11   using namespace std;
12
13
14   void main(int Argc, char *Argv[])
15   {
16       deque<string> List;
17       DIR *Directory;
18       struct dirent *Entry;
19       if(Argc == 2){
20           ostream_iterator<string> out(cout,"\n");
21           Directory = opendir(Argv[1]);
22           if(!Directory == NULL){
23               Entry = readdir(Directory);
24               while(Entry != NULL)
25               {
26                   List.push_back(Entry->d_name);
27                   Entry = readdir(Directory);
28               }
29               closedir(Directory);
30               make_heap(List.begin(),List.end());
31               sort_heap(List.begin(),List.end());
32               copy(List.begin(),List.end(),out);
33           }
34           else{
35               cerr << "Bad directory.." << endl;
36           }
37       }
38       else{
39           cerr << "Usage: list9-13 DirectoryName" << endl;
40       }
41   }
```

objects based on the objects' characteristics. The set algorithms can be used for all kinds of identification processing, from database applications to artificial intelligence programming. The set algorithms are based on several operations from set theory. See the sidebar discussion on set operations for a quick review of how the set operations are defined.

Set Operations

There are three basic set operations: set intersection, set union, and set difference. Let's say we have two sets, A and B; the intersection of sets A and B is written as:

$$A \cap B$$

If set M is the intersection of sets A and set B, then set M contains all of those elements common to both A and B. Set M is denoted as:

$$M = A \cap B$$

Let's say that set A is the set of all people who use the Internet and set B is the set of all people who use computers; the intersection A and B is the set of all people who use their computers and use the Internet. Figure 9.16 shows a Venn diagram that depicts the intersection of sets A and B. Further, if set C is the set of all people who use modems, then the intersection of A, B, and C is the set of all people who use computers, modems, and the Internet. Figure 9.17 shows this intersection, where:

$$A = \{x : x \text{ is a person who uses the Internet}\}$$

$$B = \{x : x \text{ is a person who uses a computer}\}$$

$$C = \{x : x \text{ is a person who uses a modem}\}$$

then the complement of A, B, and C is the set of all people who do not use computers, modems, or the Internet.

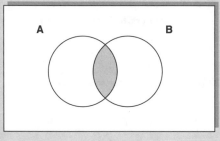

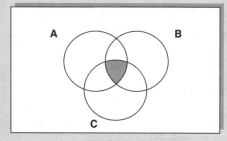

A ∩ B

A ∩ B ∩ C

Figure 9.16 The intersection of sets A and B.

Figure 9.17 The intersection of A, B, and C.

If we have two sets B and C:

$$B = \{x : x \text{ is a person who uses a computer}\}$$

$$C = \{x : x \text{ is a person who uses a modem}\}$$

then the "union" of B and C is denoted as:

$$B \cup C$$

If set M = B ∪ C, then M contains all of the members in set B and all of the members in set C. So, in this case, M is the set of all people who use computers and modems. Figure 9.18 shows the union of set B and C.

Continues

Set Operations (*Continued*)

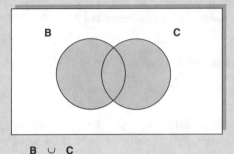

B ∪ C

Figure 9.18 The union of sets B and C.

Now let's say set U is the universal set, and:

U = { x : x is a person who uses a computer}

We have two other sets, M and N, and:

M = { x : x is a person who uses spreadsheets}

N = { x : x is a person who uses databases}

then the set difference M/N denotes the set of all people who use their computers and spreadsheets but *do not* use databases. Note that the set difference between M and N could have also been expressed:

M ∩ N′

Figure 9.19 shows a Venn diagram of the difference between set M and set N. Set difference operations usually imply the existence of some universal set.

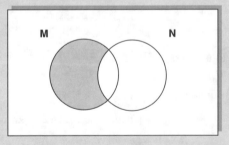

M \ N

Figure 9.19 The difference between set M and set N.

Noting that the operations on sets are important, intersection, union, and difference can be combined in all sorts of ways. If we have five sets:

A = {x : x is a person who uses the Internet}

B = {x : x is a person who uses a computer}

C = {x : x is a person who uses a modem}

M = { x : x is a person who uses spreadsheets}

N = { x : x is a person who uses databases}

Then we may have expressions like:

$$P = ((M \cap N') \cap B) \cup (C \cap A)$$

where P is the set of all people who use computers and modems. We can evaluate the expression in the innermost parentheses first:

$$(M \cap N')$$

This represents the set of all people who use computers.

We then can intersect this set with B. This again leaves us with only the set of people who use computers. Next, we evaluate the expression:

$$(C \cap A)$$

This gives us the set of people who use modems. Finally, we "union" these two sets to get a set containing all the people who use modems and computers.

Set Operations

The standard class library includes five basic set algorithms:

includes( )

set_intersection( )

set_union( )

set_difference( )

set_symmetric_difference( )

Except for the includes( ) algorithm, they require five iterators that represent two sets of input iterators and one output iterator. The two sets of input iterators will represent the two containers that the set algorithms will work on. The output iterator will represent the destination of the result of the set operations. Each set algorithm takes two containers and performs the appropriate operation upon them, storing the resulting set at the location that begins at the output iterator. The includes( ) algorithm does not have an output iterator because its only job is to report true or false. The other algorithms return a set that will be the result of the operation performed.

The includes( ) algorithm is used to determine whether one set is a member, or subset, of another. It can also be used to determine whether one sequence is contained within another sequence. The set_intersection( ), set_union( ), set_difference( ), and set_symmetric_difference( ) are used to perform the set operations discussed in the set operation sidebar. The program in Listing 9.19 demonstrates how the set algorithms are called and used.

Listing 9.19 Using Set Algorithms

```
1  //Listing 9.19
2  //This program demonstrates set union,intersection and set difference
3
4  #include <iostream>
5  #include <dirent.h> // Requires POSIX compatibility
6  #include <algorithm>
7  #include <iterator>
8  #include <set>
9  #include <string>
10 #include <io.h>>
11
12 using namespace std;
13
14 typedef set<string,less<string> > Set;
15
16 void main(int Argc, char *Argv[])
17 {
18     Set A,B,C,D,E,F,G;
19     DIR *Directory;
20     struct dirent *Entry;
21     if(Argc == 2){
22         ostream_iterator<string> out(cout,"\n");
23         Directory = opendir(Argv[1]);
24         if(!Directory == NULL){
25             Entry = readdir(Directory);
26             while(Entry != NULL){
27                     G.insert(string(Entry->d_name));
28                     if(Entry->d_name[0] == 'A'){
29                         A.insert(Entry->d_name);
30                     }
31                     if(Entry->d_name[0] == 'C'){
32                         B.insert(string(Entry->d_name));
33                     }
34                     if(access(Entry->d_name,2) == 0){
35                         C.insert(string(Entry->d_name));
36                     }
37                     Entry = readdir(Directory);
38             }
39             closedir(Directory);
40             set_union(A.begin(),A.end(),B.begin(),B.end(),
41                     inserter(D,D.begin()));
42             set_intersection(A.begin(),A.end(),C.begin(),C.end(),
43                         inserter(E,E.begin()));
44             set_difference(G.begin(),G.end(),D.begin(),D.end(),
45                         inserter(F,F.begin()));
46             copy(D.begin(),D.end(),out);
47             copy(E.begin(),E.end(),out);
48             copy(F.begin(),F.end(),out);
```

Listing 9.19 *(Continued)*

```
49
50                    }
51          }
52   }
```

This program demonstrates how the set algorithms can be used to pinpoint a specific collection of objects. The program reads the names of all of the files in the directory entered on the command line. Set A will contain all of the file names that begin with the letter A. Set B will contain all of the file names that begin with the letter C. Set C will contain all of the file names of the files that have write permission set. Set D is a union of set A and set B. Set E contains an intersection of set A and set C. Set F contains all of the file names that don't begin with either A or C. Figure 9.20 shows the Venn diagrams representing the set operations performed in the program in Listing 9.19.

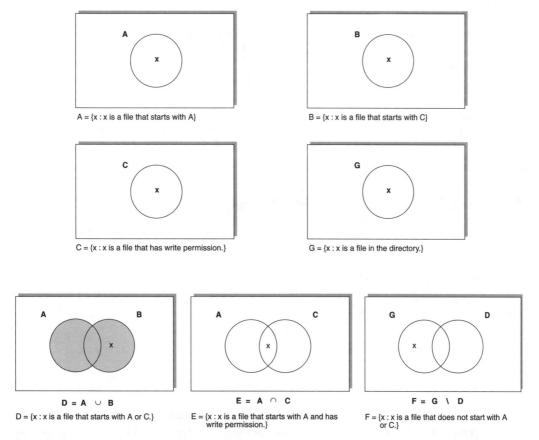

A = {x : x is a file that starts with A}

B = {x : x is a file that starts with C}

C = {x : x is a file that has write permission.}

G = {x : x is a file in the directory.}

D = A ∪ B
D = {x : x is a file that starts with A or C.}

E = A ∩ C
E = {x : x is a file that starts with A and has write permission.}

F = G \ D
F = {x : x is a file that does not start with A or C.}

Figure 9.20 Venn diagrams representing the set operations performed in Listing 9.19.

Container Management Algorithms

Another important set of algorithms in the standard library are the container management algorithms. These algorithms are used to: initialize containers with user-supplied values, copy container contents from one container to another, swap contents between containers, count objects within containers, remove objects from containers, reorder objects within a container, and apply function objects to each object within a container (see Table 9.17). The container management algorithms are basically utility operations for the containers. The program in Listing 9.20 demonstrates how some of these algorithms are called and used.

The standard C++ library also contains several algorithms that are handy for generating numerical results, counts, and comparisons (see Table 9.17). They are numeric in nature.

Algorithm Design Considerations

We have seen that the standard C++ algorithms take iterators, function objects, and predicates as arguments. These arguments are important because they give the algorithms their flexibility and generality. It follows, then, that to design algorithms that are compatible with the style of algorithms in the standard C++ library, you must supply algorithms that accept iterators, function objects, and predicates. But these elements constitute only the interface to the algorithm. If you want to design your own algorithms, you must keep in mind a few important characteristics of algorithms. To begin, let's lay some ground rules for what constitutes an algorithm, because there can be subtle but important differences between algorithms, procedures, functions, and methods.

Five Requirements of All Algorithms

For a set of steps or list of instructions to be considered an algorithm, it must be:

- Finite
- Unambiguous and detailed
- Effective
- Accurate
- Measurable

Be Finite

The set of steps or list of instructions must specify actions that have a definite stopping point. If the steps are not finite, the solution will never be reached or the task

Table 9.17 Container Management Algorithms

ALGORITHM	PERFORMANCE	DESCRIPTION
copy( )	n	Copies the elements in an input range to an object that obeys iterator syntax.
copy_backward( )	n	Copies the elements in an input range from last to first to an object that obeys iterator syntax.
fill( )	n	Sets each value in an input range to a given value.
fill_n( )	n	Sets n consecutive elements to a value.
for_each( )	n	Applies a function to each element in an input range.
generate( )	n	Sets each element in an input range to the return value of a function object that takes no arguments.
generate_n( )	n	Sets the first n elements, starting at the position given by the iterator, to the return value of a function object that takes no arguments.
iter_swap( )	constant	Exchanges two values stored at locations specified by the given iterators.
mismatch( )	n	Searches through two ranges checking each pair of elements for equality; returns a pair of iterators whose elements are not equal.
partition( )	n	Places all the elements that cause a predicate function object to return true in front of all the elements that don't.
random_shuffle( )	n	Randomly rearranges the elements in an input range.
remove( )	n	Removes all occurrences of a given value from an input range and returns a past-the-end iterator for the resulting new range.
remove_copy( )	n	Copies all the elements from an input range to another range; all elements equal to the given value are omitted.
remove_copy_if( )	n	Copies all the elements from an input range to another range; all elements for which the predicate function object returns true are omitted.
remove_if( )	n	Removes all occurrences of a value in an input range for which the predicate function object returns true; returns a past-the-end iterator for the resulting new range.

Continues

Table 9.17 Container Management Algorithms (*Continued*)

ALGORITHM	PERFORMANCE	DESCRIPTION
replace( )	n	Replaces all occurrences of a value in an input range with another value.
replace_copy( )	n	Copies one range to another range; each occurrence of the given value is replaced with another value.
replace_copy_if( )	n	Copies one range to another range; each occurrence of a value for which the predicate function returns true is replaced with another value.
replace_if( )	n	Replaces all occurrences of a value in an input range with another value, if the predicate function object returns true.
reverse( )	n	Reverses the elements in an input range.
reverse_copy( )	n	Copies an input range in reverse order to a second range.
rotate( )	n	Treats an input range as a circular order in which the elements are rotated to the left.
rotate_copy( )	n	Copies an input range to another range in rotated order.
stable_partition( )	n	Places all the elements that cause a predicate function object to return true in front of all the elements that don't; the relative order of each group is preserved.
swap( )	constant	Exchanges two values stored at locations specified by the given references.
swap_ranges( )	n	Exchanges corresponding values in two ranges.
tranform( )	n	Applies a function object to each element in an input range or each of a pair of elements in a pair of input ranges; the return value to the corresponding location is copied to another range.
unique( )	n	Reduces each sequence of two or more equivalent elements in an input range to a single element.
unique_copy( )	n	Reduces each sequence of two or more equivalent elements in an input range to a single element; the new sequence is copied to another range.

Listing 9.20 Using Container Management Algorithms

```
1   // Listing 9.20
2   // This program demonstrates how some of the container
3   // management algorithms are called and used.
4
5   #include <iostream>
6   #include <string>
7   #include <algorithm>
8   #include <deque>
9   #include <vector>
10  #include <set>
11  #include <iterator>
12
13
14
15  using namespace std;
16
17  string change(string &X)
18  {
19      string Y(" From The C++ Standard Library");
20      X.append(Y);
21      return(X);
22  }
23
24
25
26  void main(void)
27  {
28
29      string Sc("String Container");
30      string Sc1("String Data Type");
31      deque<string>::iterator DI;
32      vector<string>::iterator VI;
33      deque<string> Deque(10,"Containers");
34      vector<string> Vector(10,"Function Objects");
35      set<string,less<string> > S;
36      replace(Deque.begin(),Deque.end(),"Containers","Algorithms");
37      ostream_iterator<string,char> Out(cout,"\n");
38      ostream_iterator<char,char> Out2(cout," ");
39      swap_ranges(Sc.begin(),Sc.end(),Sc1.begin());
40      DI = Deque.begin();
41      VI = Vector.begin();
42      DI = DI + 5;
43      VI = VI + 5;
44      sort(Deque.begin(),Deque.end());
45      set_union(Deque.begin(),Deque.end(),Vector.begin(),
46                Vector.end(), inserter(S,S.begin()));
47      reverse(Sc.begin(),Sc.end());                        Continues
```

Listing 9.20 Using Container Management Algorithms (*Continued*)

```
48        random_shuffle(Sc.begin(),Sc.end());
49        random_shuffle(Sc1.begin(),Sc1.end());
50        swap_ranges(Sc.begin(),Sc.end(),Sc1.begin());
51        make_heap(Vector.begin(),Vector.end());
52        sort_heap(Vector.begin(),Vector.end());
53        copy(Deque.begin(),Deque.end(),Out);
54        copy(Vector.begin(),Vector.end(),Out);
55        copy(S.begin(),S.end(),Out);
56        cin.get();
57        for_each(VI,Vector.end(),change);
58        for_each(Deque.begin(),Deque.end(),change);
59        copy(Deque.begin(),Deque.end(),Out);
60        copy(Vector.begin(),Vector.end(),Out);
61        fill(DI,Deque.end(),"These Are The Voyages");
62        copy(Deque.begin(),Deque.end(),Out);
63        copy(Sc.begin(),Sc.end(),Out2);
64        copy(Sc1.begin(),Sc1.end(),Out2);
65    }
```

will never be accomplished. The main purpose of an algorithm is to specify the solution to a problem or sequence of steps for a task; hence, a list of instructions that does not specify a final step, or *stopping case,* is not an algorithm. For instance, the sequence of steps:

```
N = 1
While N < ∞ Do
    N = N + 1
EndDo
```

is not an algorithm because N will never reach ∞, therefore this process will never stop.

Be Unambiguous

Every action specified at any step of an algorithm must be precisely defined. This means every action must be clear and not subject to different interpretations. For example, the following procedure is only a potential algorithm.

Step 1. Get a list of 10 numbers.

Step 2. Sort the list of numbers.

Step 3. Print all very large numbers.

Step 4. Stop.

These instructions fail in step 2 and step 3. In step 2, the sort order of the numbers is not specified. We don't know whether to sort the numbers into descending or ascending order. Step 2 is not detailed enough. In Step 3, how do we determine which are the "very large" numbers? Step 3 is ambiguous.

Be Effective

Every algorithm must consist of effective steps, meaning that each step that an algorithm specifies must be executable. If a list of instructions specifies a step that cannot be done, then we do not have an algorithm. This requirement is closely related to the finite stipulation. A step that cannot be completed because it cannot be done would not allow the algorithm to halt.

Be Accurate

The algorithm must produce the appropriate results based on the conditions and input given, and it must produce the same results every time the same conditions or input are given. A sequence of steps that does not solve the problem it is designed to solve, or only sometimes solves the problem, is not an algorithm. The study of algorithm accuracy occupies much of the computer scientist's time, and entire books have been dedicated to this topic.

Be Measurable

If there is no way to measure the steps in an algorithm, we cannot know whether it is finite or correct. The consequences of each action in an algorithm must be observable or verifiable in some fashion. A sequence of steps must meet at least these five criteria to be considered an algorithm. If we know that we are dealing with bonafide algorithms, then we can predict the behaviors of containers that depend on them. Predictability impacts the design, testing, and usefulness of a container class. If we can predict the behavior of an algorithm or member function, we can measure its performance. If we can measure the performance of the algorithms and member functions for a container, we can determine which containers best meet our needs.

Relationships between Algorithms and Class Methods

Class member functions, sometimes called *methods,* are either functions or procedures. All algorithms can be considered either procedures or functions, but not all procedures and functions are algorithms. Table 9.18 shows the five relationships that normally exist between class member functions and algorithms. Here's how they work:

- Multiple member functions implement a single algorithm.
- A single member function consists of multiple algorithms.
- A single member function is implemented by a single algorithm.
- A single member function is only part of an algorithm.
- Member functions are not related to algorithms.

A class member function may be as simple as one statement that returns a single value, or it may be very complex, consisting of an algorithm or collection of algorithms that work to contribute to part of the behavior of the class. Algorithms play major roles in

Table 9.18 Relationships between Class Member Functions Algorithms

	Single Algorithm	Multiple Algorithms
Single Member Function	1	2
Multiple Member Function	3	4

1. Single member function, single algorithm.
2. Single member function, multiple algorithms.
3. Multiple member functions, single algorithms.
4. Multiple member functions, multiple algorithms.
5. Member function, no algorithm.

the behavior of collection and container classes because the normal use of collections and containers involve iteration, storages, removal, sorting, and searching mechanisms, each of which may consist of one or more algorithms.

A Classic Algorithm

Let's consider the notion of *a factorial*. A factorial of size n is represented as n!. The quantity n factorial is computed as follows:

$$n! = n(n-1)(n-2) \ldots (2)(1)$$

This is a mathematical representation of the algorithm for n!. But we could also represent this algorithm in plain English:

Step 1. Initialize the variable for which the factorial will be computed.

Step 2. Multiply the variable successively by all the positive integers less than the variable.

Or we could represent this algorithm by a flowchart (Figure 9.21), so that we could see the logic that computes the factorial.

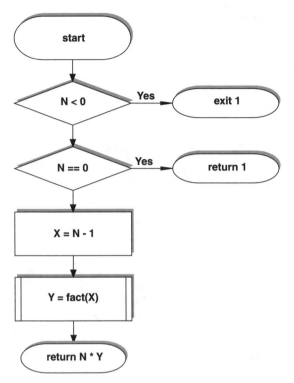

Figure 9.21 The steps used to calculate the factorial.

After we confirm that the algorithm works, the final step is to convert the algorithm into a form suitable for execution by a computer. In our case, we will convert all the algorithms we design into the C++ language. This must be done carefully, because it is easy to change a working "correct" algorithm into a computer program, procedure, or function that does not work. While converting each step in the algorithm we must retain its meaning and relationship to the rest of the algorithm. The program in Listing 9.21 shows a C++ program that represents the mathematical notion of a factorial. The program was converted from the flowchart shown in Figure 9.21.

The factorial function in this listing is an example of a recursive algorithm, an algorithm that calls itself to solve a problem or execute a task (Sedgewick 1983). The use of recursion in this example illustrates the stopping case, one of the important requirements for all algorithms. If a recursive procedure or function is to terminate—not call itself forever—there must be a stopping case. In the factorial function in Listing 9.21, the stopping case is when N is equal to 0. Given that this function is passed an integer and the program is not interrupted in the middle of processing, N will necessarily reach 0 because of the X-- in line 12. Because we take the |N| prior to it being passed to the function, the proper result is guaranteed.

The X-- statement is one of the keys to the algorithm. It ensures that we will be multiplying the original value by all the integers that are less than the original value. This

Listing 9.21   Calculating a Factorial with an Algorithm

```
 1 // Listing 9.21
 2 // This program is the algorithm shown in the flowchart Figure 9.22
 3
 4   include <iostream>
 5
 6   int factorial(int N)
 7   {
 8       int X = N;
 9       if(N == 0){
10           return(1);
11       }
12       X--;
13       return(N * factorial(X));
14   }
15
16   void main(int Argc, char *Argv[])
17   {
18       if(Argc == 2){
19           cout << factorial(abs(atoi(Argv[1])));
20       }
21       else{
22               cout << "Syntax: fact Num";
23       }
24   }
```

brings us to a fundamental characteristic of all algorithms. Namely, algorithms build paths from some *input state* to some *output state*. Given some input or output state, the algorithm moves from the initial state, performing transformations until those transformations meet the conditions of the stopping case. In the factorial program in Listing 9.21, the transformation was the decrementing of the variable X in the statement X--. This transformation ultimately caused the factorial to call itself with a value of 0, causing the recursion to cease. We see that the factorial function meets the five basic requirements of all algorithms: It is finite—the stopping case is N == 0; it is unambiguous, and it is effective because we have implemented it in the C++ language; it has passed the compiler, therefore the level of detail is sufficient and all operations are capable of being executed; the program is correct (note, however, that algorithm proving is beyond the scope of this book—refer to Sedgewick, 1983, and other mathematical texts that address the topic of proofs or proof by induction); finally, the factorial algorithm is measurable because it returns values we can examine. Thus, we can conclude that we have a C++ representation for the factorial algorithm. The factorial function is useful and can easily be made a member function for a container object. In this case, the member function would have a one-to-one relationship with the algorithm; in other words, the algorithm would directly implement the member function. Refer back to Table 9.16 for the relationships between member functions and algorithms.

Table 9.19 Basic Components of All Algorithms

INPUT STATE	TRANSFORMATION	OUTPUT STATE
1. input values	1. operators	1. output values
2. conditions	2. calculations	2. conditions
3. assertions	3. formulas	
4. rules	4. transitions	

Algorithm Components

Table 9.19 shows the three basic components of all algorithms. The input state can be the original condition of a variable or set of variables; it serves as the "precondition" for the algorithm execution. The preconditions for the algorithm are the facts about the algorithm's operands and operators that are assumed to be true before the algorithm begins execution. Every algorithm must perform some kind of operation or transfor-

:: O Notation

Algorithm Analysis and O Notation

Usually more than one algorithm can solve a particular problem or execute a particular task. Therefore, techniques have been developed that help us to measure algorithm performance. These measurements provide us with criteria that enable us to make intelligent choices about which algorithm best addresses the problem at hand. (An in-depth analysis of algorithms is beyond the scope of this book. See Sedgewick 1983, for more on this topic.)

Comparing Algorithms

The same algorithm implemented in C++ but compiled by different compilers may perform differently depending on the optimization capabilities of the compilers. GNU C++ has one set of optimization capabilities; Microsoft Visual C++ has another. A binary search implemented in C++ compiled by GNU C++ may have fewer machine code steps than the same binary search compiled by IBM's Visual Age C++. The computer an algorithm executes on will also have an impact on how well that algorithm performs. Which sort is faster: an insertion sort running on a Cray supercomputer or a heap sort running on a Sun Workstation? Which search is faster: an interpolation sort compiled by Visual C++ or a binary search compiled by Inprise's C++ Builder?

Even if we compare algorithms compiled by the same compiler and executed on the same computer, we still only know how the algorithms compare for that specific compiler and computer. When the compiler and computer changes, the performance of the algorithm will change. In addition to speed differences between compilers and computers, algorithms also differ as to how they handle data. Some algorithms are data-dependent; others are

Continues

:: O Notation (*Continued*)

not. Comparing data-dependent algorithms with algorithms that are not data-dependent is like comparing apples and oranges. What we need is a general method for comparing algorithms, one that is independent of computer, compiler, and data organization.

Comparing the Basic Operation
Every class of algorithm has a few basic algorithms that represent the basic operation of the algorithm. For instance, the basic operation of a search algorithm is the comparison operation. The search does its job by comparing the items in a container with an item that a user is searching for. Thus, the basic operation to concentrate on for the search algorithms is the comparison. The basic operations of a sort algorithm include comparison and rearrangement. It is the job of a sort algorithm to determine where to place a given object among other objects. It does this through comparison and assignment. The basic operation of a numeric algorithm may be multiplication or division. The algorithms are divided into categories based on their basic operations. When comparing algorithms, we compare those that use similar basic operations. We count the number of basic operations each algorithm will perform on its data; the algorithm that performs the fewest number of basic operations is given the highest rating. Clearly, this is an oversimplification of how algorithm analysis is done, but the basic idea is here.

We ask: How many basic operations does the algorithm perform relative to the size of the input? Or, given an input state, what is the ratio or proportion of algorithm performance to an input size increase or input size decrease? We use a notation that describes the relative, or proportionate, running time of an algorithm as it is compared with the size of the input. For instance, if N is the number of data values that an algorithm processes, and we say the algorithm has a performance of N^2, then we mean that the algorithm will perform its basic operations N * N times (N^2). If N doubles, the algorithm will take four times as long to execute. If we say the algorithm has a performance of N^3, then the algorithm will perform its basic operation no more than N * N * N times. If the algorithm has an N^3 performance, when N doubles, the algorithm will take eight times as long to execute. We say that the algorithm is on the order of N, or is on the order of N^2, or that the algorithm is $O(N^2)$ (O is short for "on the order of"). In more theoretical surroundings, the O stands for big Omega. In either case, using this type of notation is just a means of talking about algorithms being measured, relative to the number of basic operations they perform based on the size of the data set to be processed by the algorithm. All the measurements of the algorithm's performance are proportionate to the size of the input the algorithm processes. Formally, this type of measurement states how the algorithm is asymptomatically bounded by a value N (Tenebaum et al., 1992). Note that using big O notation we make no mention of how fast the computer is, how many processors the computer has, or which compiler is used. These questions are beyond the control of someone performing algorithm analysis in a computer-independent manner. Now, if the particular processor is known and is available, then the algorithms may be compared directly, and the actual results can be used to determine which is best. This type of comparison falls under the category of *benchmarking*. Table 9.20 contains some of the common measurements for algorithm performance. Algorithms that have constant running times approach the best performance that can be achieved.

Table 9.20 Common Measurements for Algorithm Performance

ALGORITHM PERFORMANCE	DESCRIPTION
1	Most instructions for most programs are executed once, or at most, only a few times. If this is true, most program instructions have a constant running time.
log n	When the running time of a program is logarithmic, the program goes slightly slower as N grows. This type of running time happens often when programs have to solve a big problem by converting it into smaller problems. The size of the problem is cut by some constant fraction. The running time can be considered to be less than a "large" constant. The base of the logarithm changes the constant.
n	When the running time of a program is linear, generally, a small amount of processing is done on each input element.
n log n	This running time arises in algorithms that solve a problem by breaking it up into smaller subproblems and solving each subproblem independently. The subproblems are combined for one solution.
n^2	When the running time of an algorithm is quadratic, it is practical for use only on relatively small problems. Typically, quadratic running times arise in algorithms that process all pairs of data items (perhaps a double nested loop).
n^3	An algorithm that processes triples of data items (perhaps a triple nested loop) has a cubic running time, and is practical for use only on small problems.
2^n	Very few algorithms with an exponential running time are likely to be appropriate for practical use. These types of algorithms arise as "brute-force" solutions to problems.

mation. If the algorithm doesn't perform a transformation or operation, then the algorithm cannot move toward its stopping case. Again, if it does not eventually reach a stopping case, then it is not an algorithm. The transformations can include assignment, exchange, comparison, calculation, counting, evaluation, iteration, recursion, reading, or writing. Once the transformations reach the stopping case, the algorithm has an output state. The output state will include any conditions that are true or values that are available at the time the stopping case has been reached. The output state must be measurable or verifiable in some manner. Therefore, the basic pattern of all algorithms is Input—>Processing—> Output.

One of the first places to start when analyzing algorithms is to evaluate their input state and problem space. Ask questions such as: How much input does the algorithm handle? How large is the search domain for the algorithm? How many simultaneous inputs does the algorithm take? How large or how small are the values? Once we have a basic understanding of the input state and algorithm preconditions, we can ask how the algorithm processes its input conditions or variables, including: How many times does it access each input value? How many steps does the algorithm have? How many times are the steps in an algorithm executed? How far does the algorithm search the problem space for a solution? How many times does it iterate over a set of values? As the number of values that an algorithm can process gets larger, how does the algorithm behavior change? After questions of this type have been answered, we can start to compare algorithms to see which is preferable to another. One of the primary ways of describing algorithm performance is by O notation.

Summary

The C++ algorithms give the programmer standard implementations for very common operations and tasks. The algorithms are used for searching, sorting, counting, storing, removing, and organizing of data. One or more of these tasks are found in virtually every program that is written. A program can be developed faster and more reliably by using the C++ algorithms. The algorithms have been tested and standardized. This makes the algorithms robust and portable to different platforms. The algorithms are designed to be used with either the built in container classes or user defined container classes. The algorithms provide an effective means to process information that is stored in C++ vectors, lists, stacks, queues, priority queues, maps, and sets. The performance of the algorithms in most cases is optimal. The programmer or software developer can avoid reinventing the wheel by using the standard C++ algorithms wherever they can be used within a program.

CHAPTER 10

Memory Management

"As it turns out, it is actually impossible to find any objective and universally acceptable definition of 'all of space taken at this instant.' "

—RUDY RUCKER
THE FOURTH DIMENSION

The standard C++ library has two classes that help the programmer with memory management: allocator and auto_ptr. Both classes are designed to encapsulate certain types of memory access. They are used to hide the grungy details of memory models, pointer sizes, reference sizes, and resource allocation and deallocation, and to present an object-oriented interface to dynamic memory or runtime memory allocation and destruction.

The computer architecture and the memory management capabilities of the operating system determine how and where we can store objects. The memory acquisition process is specific to the various memory models; for example, systems that support shared memory can differ from systems that support distributed memory, and systems that support distributed shared memory differ from systems that support only single-processor virtual memory schemes. Likewise, garbage collection schemes work differently from nongarbage collection schemes. Certain memory systems are highly segmented with data segments, stack segments, and free store all managed a little differently. In contrast, flat memory models have a simple code segment and data segment.

These differences prompt a number of questions: Should an object be allocated in a stack segment or data segment? Should an object be created on the near heap or far heap? Should the entire memory resources of an object be assigned to a single node, or should the memory resource requirements be distributed among several nodes? What happens if we attempt to allocate a locked object in shared memory? Do we throw an exception, continue to attempt to acquire the memory, or swap the page, semaphore, and mutex out to disk? Should objects be allocated from a precommitted pool of memory, or should we use the new operator to allocate objects one block at a time?

In addition to the software issues inherent in different memory models, we have to determine how to reconcile the difference in pointer sizes between, say, a Cray T3D and an Intel 386 (there are programs that run on both!). There is C++ code that needs to run on an Ultra SPARC and PowerPC. Will the max_size( ) for a container of doubles on an Ultra SPARC be the same as the max_size( ) for a container of doubles on a PowerPC? The differences among 16-, 32-, and 64-bit architectures can wreak havoc on the programmer who has to create objects that will work on all three.

The allocator class is designed to help make some differences between hardware architectures and memory models transparent to the process of object creation and destruction. Figure 10.1 illustrates how an allocator object is used as a "middle man" between a C++ object and a memory model in current use. The allocator class provides a hardware-independent and operating system-independent interface for the iostreams, the string class, the container classes, and any user-defined class, class library, or application framework.

Dynamic Memory Allocation in C++

Dynamic memory allocation is accomplished in C++ using either the new and delete operators or the calloc( ), malloc( ), realloc( ), and free functions. The calloc( ), malloc( ), and realloc( ) functions are used to allocate memory from the *free store*, also called the *heap*. Memory organization for C++ programs depends both on the compiler and the operating system environment. Usually, the memory a C++ program accesses is divided into four logical areas:

- Code segment(s)

- Stack segment

- Data segment(s)

- Free store (heap)

Once a C++ program is compiled, it may have one or more code segments, a stack segment, one or more data segments, and a free store. On some systems, the stack and the data segment share a single set of addresses; on other systems, the stack and the data segments are separate; on still others, the data segment and the heap share a segment with the beginning of the data segment at one end of a block of memory and the heap beginning at the other end. The organization and number of segments are largely compiler-dependent, and how these segments interact with the memory management on a particular system is largely operating system-dependent. Figure 10.2 shows a set of typical memory maps for C++ programs. Although the organization of segments and use of segments will vary from one system to another, memory allocation for C++ objects is divided into two basic types:

- Memory allocated at compile type (statically allocated)

- Memory allocated at runtime through calls to memory allocation functions

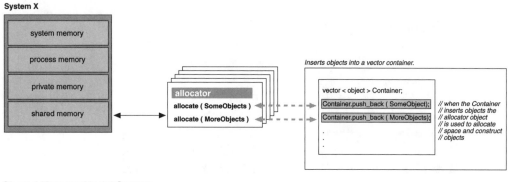

Shared Memory Model System

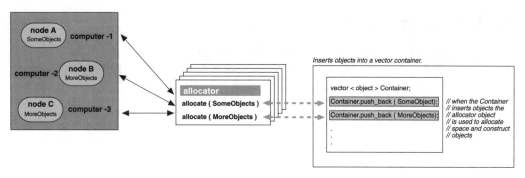

Distributed Memory Model System

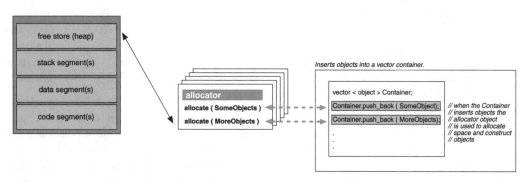

Classic Segmented Memory Model System

Figure 10.1 Allocator objects acting as interfaces to memory models.

Segmented Memory

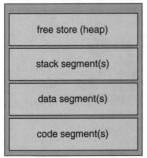

Flat Memory

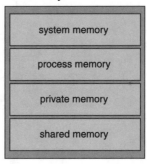

Figure 10.2 Typical segmented memory map and a flat memory map.

Static Memory Allocation in C++

Where and how storage space is allocated for an object in C++ is determined by where and how the object is declared. Take, for instance, the following piece of code:

```
list <int> X;
char Bitmap[1000];

void func(void)
{
     int Y;
     float Z;
}
```

Space for the objects Y and Z declared inside func( ) will be allocated on the call stack (stack segment) whenever func( ) is executed. After func( ) has executed, the space for objects Y and Z will be deallocated. Space for the Bitmap object will be allocated in a data segment during compile time. This space is considered *statically allocated* because the amount of space will not increase or decrease during the execution of the program. The size of Bitmap is determined before the program is loaded into memory; it is placed in a data segment during compile time, and the space remains constant throughout the execution of the program.

The list<int> X container object is allocated a little differently from the Bitmap object. Although both objects are declared outside the function, the list<int> X object is more complex than Bitmap. Since X is a container, it has a set of attributes and will contain a set of objects. Here, the attributes for X will be allocated in the data segment; they consist of a number typedefs, private variables, pointer definitions, and so on. Space for these attributes will be placed in one or more data segments; however, the objects that X will contain will not be inserted into X until runtime. These objects will be dynamically allocated by the allocator object that belongs to X. So, from this, we see that X is part statically allocated and part dynamically allocated. In general, objects declared outside any function will be statically allocated in one or more data segments. Objects that are not declared static and are declared inside a function are generally dynamically allocated.

Dynamic Memory Allocation of Objects

If we want to allocate space for 1,000 ints in C++, there are four standard ways to accomplish this, as shown the next code fragment:

```
...
int main(void)
{
    int * Array;
    allocator<int> Storage;
    Array = calloc (1000, sizeof( int ));       // Method 1
    Array = malloc(1000,sizeof(int));           // Method 2
    Array = new int[1000];                      // Method 3
    Storage.allocate(1000)                      // Method 4
    ...
}
```

Each of these methods will dynamically allocate a block of memory large enough to hold 1,000 ints. Generally, this memory will be allocated in free store, heap, but this is largely system-dependent; there are no specific requirements determining where objects are to be allocated. All we know about the objects is that the space for them will not be statically allocated or allocated during compile time.

It is important to note that the calloc( ) and malloc( ) functions differ in that the calloc( ) function initializes its memory blocks to zero, and the malloc( ) function does not do the initialization. Also notice that these two functions require more information than the new operator or the Storage allocator object; they are considered lower-level allocation functions. The new operator is an improvement over the calloc( ) and malloc( ) functions. For one thing, the new operator removed the sizeof requirement. The new operator determines the size of the object to allocate based on the type of object presented. The programmer can play "tricks" with the malloc( ) and calloc( ) functions to make it possible to declare objects of one type and allocate objects of another. But a word of caution: These tricks are not for the uninitiated. The new operator generally removes the need for some of the trickery of allocating dynamic memory. However, it is important to note that most implementations of the new operator are simply disguised calls to the lower-level calloc( ) and malloc( ) functions. We still have to specify a type when doing allocation, but in many circumstances, this is still troublesome and we can do better.

The allocator Class

The container and stream buffer classes would be more complicated to use if the type of every object inserted was required. The allocator class offers a higher level of abstraction than the new operator. It hides the type of object being allocated as well as the underlying memory model. Memory allocation by an allocator object is normally done through calls to the new operator, which as just explained, normally calls a calloc( ) or malloc( ) type function. The calloc( ) or malloc( ) type function will then make a call to an operating system-specific memory allocation routine. Figure 10.3 shows the generic sequence of an allocator object allocating spaces for N objects. The container classes use allocator objects to allocate memory. The buffer classes use allocator objects to allocate storage for I/O. Table 10.1 lists all of the classes that require the allocator object. The allocator object acts as a middle man between C++ objects and different memory models that a C++ program might encounter. Let's look a little closer at how the allocator class works.

The allocator Class

The allocator class encapsulates information about the memory model being used by the program. It encapsulates information about:

- Pointers and const pointers
- References and const references
- Size of objects
- Difference between pointers
- Allocation and deallocation functions

The information contained in the allocator class is used by any function that performs an operation concerning the memory model. Therefore, a function that inserts, extracts, advances, or has pointers that point to objects in a container needs information from the allocator to determine the size of the object, pointer, or reference. The allocator class is a template parameter, and is passed to the constructor of a container. This allocator object is assigned to the allocator contained in the container. Each container also has type definitions that can be used to access the types of the allocator object and the return types and arguments for its own methods. These typedefs are as follows:

```
typedef typename Allocator::reference          reference;
typedef typename Allocator::const_reference    const_reference;
typedef typename Allocator::size_type          size_type;
typedef typename Allocator::difference_type    difference_type;
typedef typename Allocator                     allocator_type;
typedef typename Allocator::pointer            pointer;
typedef typename Allocator::const_pointer      const_pointer;
```

All of the allocator parameters for the containers default to the standard allocator class. This means that there is already an allocator class, the standard allocator class, that can be used for the containers. This is the interface to the standard allocator class:

```
template <class T> class allocator {
 public:
    typedef size_t size_type;
    typedef ptrdiff_t difference_type;
    typedef T* pointer;
    typedef const T* const_pointer;
    typedef T& reference;
    typedef const T& const_reference;
```

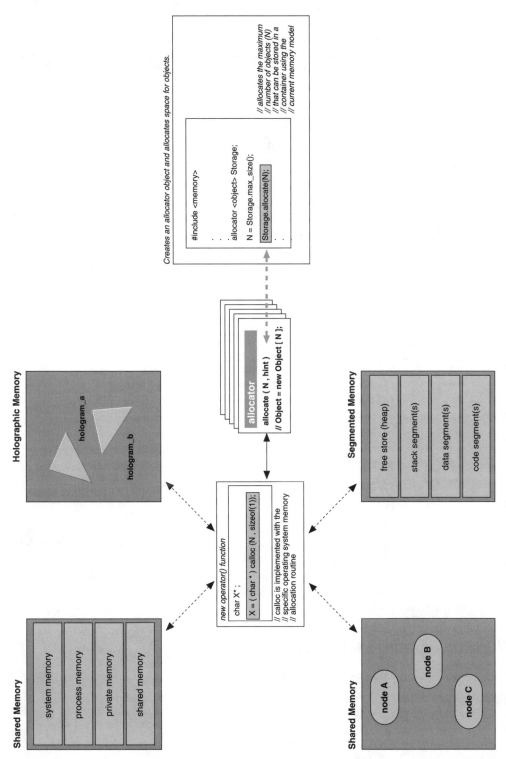

Figure 10.3 A generic memory allocation call sequence for allocator objects.

Table 10.1   Classes That Require the Allocator Object

CLASSES THAT REQUIRE ALLOCATOR OBJECT	
Containers	
deque	multiset
vector	map
list	multimap
set	
Input/Output	
basic_stringbuf	basic_ostringstream
basic_istringstream	basic_stringstream
String	
basic_string	

```
    typedef T value_type;
    template <class U> struct rebind { typedef allocator<U> other; };
    allocator() throw();
    allocator(const allocator&) throw();
    template <class U> allocator(const allocator<U>&) throw();
    ~allocator() throw();
    pointer address(reference x) const;
    const_pointer address(const_reference x) const;
    pointer allocate(
    size_type n, typename allocator<void>::const_pointer hint = 0);
    void deallocate(pointer p, size_type n);
    size_type max_size() const throw();
    void construct(pointer p, const T& val);
    void destroy(pointer p);
};
```

This default allocator class meets the requirements of the allocator class, listed in Table 10.2. Like an iterator, an allocator is a description of a class. Therefore, any class that meets the requirements of the allocator is an allocator type. In addition to those requirements listed in Table 10.1, all instances of an allocator type should be interchangeable and always equal to each other.

allocator Typedef Members

The allocator class has the following type definitions:

```
typedef size_t size_type;
typedef ptrdiff_t difference_type;
typedef T* pointer;
typedef const T* const_pointer;
typedef T& reference;
```

Table 10.2 Requirements of the Allocator Class

ALLOCATOR REQUIREMENTS	DESCRIPTION
X::pointer	Pointer to T.
X::const_pointer	Pointer to const T.
X::reference	&T.
X::const_reference	T const&.
X::value_type	type T.
X::size_type	An unsigned integral type that represents the size of the largest object that can be allocated using the current memory model.
X::difference_type	A signed integral type that represents the difference between two pointers using the current memory model.
X( )	Creates a default instance.
X a(b)	Creates an allocator object a: Y(a) becomes equal to b.
typename X::rebind<U>::other	For all U types, including T, Y::rebind<T>::other is X type; returns a Y type.
a.address(r)	Returns X::pointer, a pointer to r.
a.address(s)	Returns X::const_pointer, a const_pointer to s.
a.allocate(n) a.allocate(n,u)	Memory is allocated for n objects of T type; the objects are not constructed; returns X::pointer, which points to the memory allocated.
a.deallocate(p,n)	Deallocates the memory for all n objects of type T in the area pointed to by p; all objects must be destroyed prior to this call.
a.max_size( )	The largest value that can be passed to X::allocate( ); returns X::size_type.
x.construct(p,t)	Constructs an object of type T in memory at p; effect: new((void*)p) T(t).
x.destroy(p)	Destroys object in memory at p; effect: ((T*p)->~T( ).
a1 == a2	Returns true if and only if the storage allocated from a1 and a2 can be deallocated via the other; returns a bool.
a1 != a2	Same as !(a1 == a2); returns a bool.

T, U is any type; t is a value of type const T&; b is value of type U; X is an allocator class for type T; Y is an allocator class for type U; p is a value of type X::pointer returned by allocate( ); r is a value of type X::reference; s is a value of type X::const_reference; u is a value of type Y::const_pointer returned by Y::allocate( ); n is a value of type X::size_type.

```
typedef const T& const_reference;
typedef T value_type;
```

The typedef size_type is of type size_t that is an unsigned integer type. It describes an object that represents the length of any sequence the allocator can allocate. It can hold the size of the largest object in the memory model, and is seen as the return type for many container methods, such as size( ), max_size( ), resize( ), length( ), and reserve( ). It is also used by functions or methods that perform object counts or accept an object count as an argument. For example, containers that define the subscript operator and the at( ) method accept a type of size_type used as an index to the container:

```
// deque, vector and string
reference operator[] (size_type n);
const_reference operator[] (size_type n) const;
reference at(size_type n);
const_reference at(size_type n) const;
```

It is also used in the constructors and in the return type for the find( ) family of methods for the basic_string class.

The typedef difference_type is of type ptrdiff_t, an integer. This integer is the result of subtracting two pointers. T type is the object type in which the pointer is pointing. In a container, T is the object type the container holds.

allocator Class Member Functions

These are the member functions of the allocator class:

```
pointer allocate(size_type n,
typename allocator<void>::const_pointer hint = 0);
pointer address(reference x) const;
const_pointer address(const_reference x) const;
void deallocate(pointer p, size_type n);
size_type max_size() const throw();
void construct(pointer p, const T& val);
void destroy(pointer p);
```

Allocation of Objects Using the allocator Class

The method:

```
pointer allocate(size_type n,
                 typename allocator<void>::const_pointer hint = 0);
```

allocates memory for n objects of size_type. The memory is allocated, but the objects are not constructed. The standard allocator uses new(size_t) to create the memory block. The "hint" argument is implementation-dependent; it is used to help to the allocator object in systems where locality is an important factor when allocating memory. Where should the space be allocated? If the objects are to be used by another object, maybe the space should be allocated near that object. The self-reference pointer for the object, this, may be used for hint. Pointers to similar objects or an object recently allocated by the same allocator object may be used for hint. Again this is implementation-dependent. The allocate( ) method returns a pointer to this allocated space. This pointer is used by other methods, including construct( ), destroy( ), and deallocate( ).

Deallocation of Objects Using the allocator Class

The method:

```
void deallocate(pointer p, size_type n);
```

deallocates all of the storage of n objects of type size_type pointed to by the pointer p. The standard allocator uses the delete( ) method to free the space for use. The actual objects should be destroyed before the deallocate( ) function is called.

The construct( ) Method

Allocating memory is a separate process from constructing objects. Figure 10.4 contrasts allocation and construction of an object. Before objects are constructed, memory has already been set aside for that object. In other words, memory allocation creates a space for the object to occupy in memory, and constructing the objects actually places the objects in that memory space. For example, when initializing a container with objects, inserting or placing the objects in a container, the allocator object is used. It will allocate the space for the objects, then call the construct( ) method:

```
void construct(pointer p, const T& val);
```

It is passed the pointer returned by allocate( ), then it constructs the T object by invoking its constructor.

Destruction Using the allocator Class

Deallocating memory is a separate process from destroying objects. Figure 10.5 contrasts destruction and deallocation of an object. The method:

```
void destroy(pointer p);
```

uses the pointer returned by the allocate( ) method. This method will explicitly invoke T's destructor to destroy the object at p. The object is destroyed, but the space that it occupied has not been deallocated. The memory cannot be used by the system until the deallocate( ) method is called. When objects are to be destroyed—for example, when a container's destructor is called—each object in the container is destroyed, then the deallocate( ) method returns the memory to the system. Objects are also destroyed and new objects are constructed when the assignment or the pop_front( ) operation is performed. The existing object is replaced by a new object. Actually, the existing object is destroyed and the new object is constructed.

How are the container and its objects destroyed? This is a very interesting question and depends on where the container was declared. If the container was declared within a

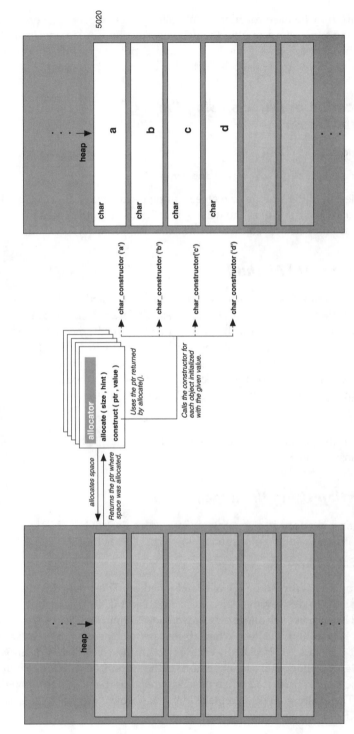

Figure 10.4 Contrasting allocation and construction of an object.

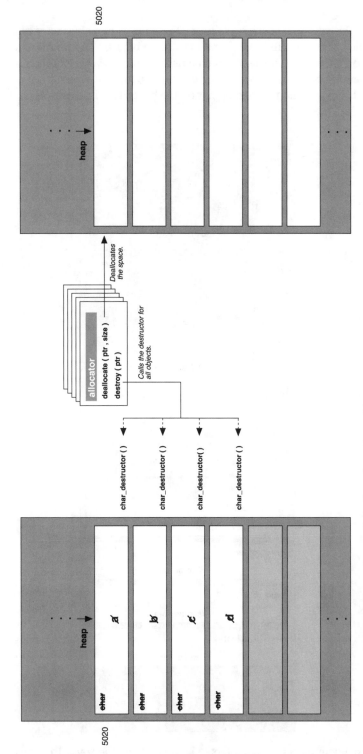

Figure 10.5 Contrasting destruction and deallocation of an object.

function, the container object is placed on the stack. When objects are placed in the container, the container will have pointers to those objects. The pointers to those objects are also on the stack, but the objects themselves are elsewhere in memory. Remember, when memory has been allocated for the objects, the new operator is used. Therefore, the objects are in dynamic memory, or on the heap. This is illustrated in Figure 10.6.

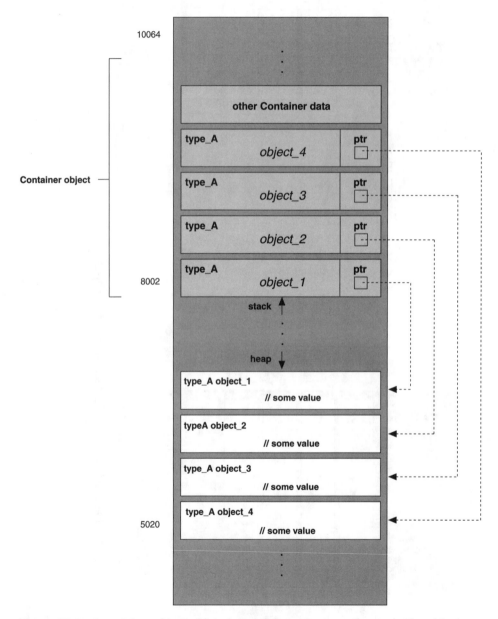

Figure 10.6 A container object with pointers to its contents on the stack. The objects are in dynamic memory.

If new operator was not used to create the container, when the function goes out of scope, the destructor for the container is called automatically. At that point, the objects on the heap are destroyed and the memory is deallocated. The container object is popped from the stack and the stack is destroyed. If the new operator was used to create the container, and the delete operator was not invoked prior to the function going out of scope, the container's destructor is not called. The pointers to the objects in dynamic memory are no longer available, the objects are no longer accessible, and the space occupied by those objects cannot be deallocated. If the container has been declared outside the main( ) function, then the container object is static and placed in the data segment. Table 10.3 summarizes where the container and objects are stored, based on where the container was declared, and what can occur during the destruction of the container.

allocator Class Accessors

There are two accessors for the allocator class:

```
address(reference X) const;
max_size() const;
```

The purpose of the address( ) method is to return the pointer to the X object. When passed a reference to an object, address( ) will return a pointer to that object. The pointer can then be dereferenced, returning the actual object. For example:

```
const_pointer address(const_reference x) const;
```

will return a const pointer of object x.

The other accessor:

```
size_type max_size() const throw();
```

returns the maximum number of objects that can be stored in an object using the current memory model. For example:

Table 10.3 Container and Object Storage

CONTAINER DECLARED	CONTAINER LOCATION	OBJECTS LOCATION	DESTRUCTION OF CONTAINER
inside function	stack	heap	■ Function goes out of scope.
			■ Removes container object from stack.
			■ Destroys objects.
			■ Calls delete to deallocate memory.
outside function	data segment	heap	■ Program terminates.
			■ Removes container from data segment.
			■ Destroys objects.
			■ Calls delete to deallocate memory.

```
void main(void)
{
    allocator<char> Storage;
    cout << Storage.max_size() << endl;
```

creates an allocator object that will create storage for the built-in data type char. Storage.max_size( ) will return the number of characters that can be stored using the current memory model. This will be a theoretical number and will depend on the actual space that is available.

The auto_ptr Class

The auto_ptr class is a pointerlike object. Like a regular pointer, it points to an object in memory; it can be dereferenced and incremented. Unlike a regular pointer, when the auto_ptr object goes out of scope, the destructor uses the delete operator to deallocate the memory occupied by the object to which it points. As mentioned earlier, when a container is declared inside a function and initialized with objects using the new operator, and the function goes out of scope before the delete operator has been called, the pointers to the objects are removed from the stack, but the objects are still in dynamic memory. If the pointer is assigned to an auto_ptr object, when the pointer is removed from the stack, the destructor of auto_ptr will delete the object and free the dynamic memory.

Construction of an auto_ptr Object

An auto_ptr object has three constructors:

```
explicit auto_ptr(X* p = 0) throw();
auto_ptr(const auto_ptr<T>& a) throw();
template<class Y> auto_ptr(const auto_ptr<Y>& a) throw();
```

The first is passed a pointer to an object. The self-reference pointer of the auto_ptr object, this, will hold the pointer p; it owns the object pointed to by p. This is an explicit constructor.

The second constructor is the copy constructor. The newly constructed auto_ptr will hold the same pointer that *a* holds. The constructor calls a.release( ), which returns the pointer *a* holds; *this will own the object returned by *get( ) if and only if *a* owns *a.

An auto_ptr object can be initialized with a pointer or another auto_ptr object. For example:

```
...
double *RegPtr1 = new double;
double *RegPtr2 = new double;
auto_ptr<double> APtr(RegPtr1);
auto_ptr<double> Auto1(RegPtr2);
auto_ptr<double> Auto2(APtr);
...
```

In this example, Auto1 is initialized with a regular pointer to a double, and Auto2 is initialized with another auto_ptr object, APtr. The Auto1 auto_ptr holds the RegPtr2 pointer, and Auto2 and APtr both hold the RegPtr1 pointer. The ownership of the object pointed to by RegPtr1 is transferred from APtr to Auto2. This example is illustrated in Figure 10.7.

The third constructor is a template function. It creates an auto_ptr object in the same way as the second constructor. It requires that Y* be implicitly converted to X*. X is the template parameter for auto_ptr. It is the object for which auto_ptr manages dynamic memory.

Destruction of an auto_ptr Object

The destructor:

```
~auto_ptr();
```

requires that *this owns the pointer returned by get( ). If this is true, then the delete operator can delete the object and deallocate the memory.

The auto_ptr Class Accessors

These are the auto_ptr accessors:

```
X* get() const throw();
X* release() const throw();
X& operator*() const throw();
X* operator->() const throw();
```

The get( ) method returns the pointer *this holds. It is a pointer to an object of type X. The release( ) method returns the pointer *this holds by calling the get( ) method. The purpose of this method is to transfer the ownership of the object to which the pointer returned by get( ) points. The release( ) method is called by the constructor and the assignment operator. The first dereference operator will return *get( ). The object to which the pointer is pointing is returned. It requires that get( ) != 0. The second dereference operator returns get( ).

The auto_ptr Assignment Operator

The assignment operator:

```
auto_ptr& operator=(const auto_ptr& a) throw();
template<class Y> auto_ptr& operator=(const auto_ptr<Y>& a) throw();
```

assigns one auto_ptr to another. The assignment operator calls a.release( ) if and only if *this and *a* are not the same object. If they are the same object, then nothing takes place, and *this will now hold the returned pointer. And *this will own the object only if *a* owned the object; *this is returned. The assignment template function works in the same way. It requires that Y* be implicitly converted to X*.

Implicit type conversions are not performed. An auto_ptr object cannot be assigned to a regular pointer, and a regular pointer cannot be assigned to an auto_ptr object:

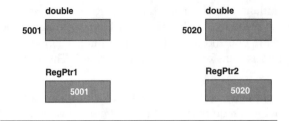

---

auto_ptr < double > APtr (RegPtr1)

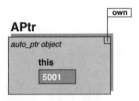

auto_ptr < double > Auto1 (RegPtr2)

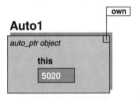

auto_ptr < double > Auto2 (APtr)

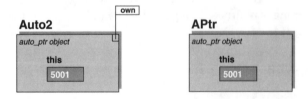

NOTE: The "own" flag on the auto_ptr object means the auto_ptr
      object has ownership of the object to which it points.

Figure 10.7 The initialization of the Auto1 auto_ptr
object with a regular pointer, the initialization of Auto2
with another AutoPtr auto_ptr object, and the transfer-
ence of ownership of the object pointed to by RegPtr1
from APtr to Auto2.

```
...
double *RegPtr = new double;
auto_ptr<double> APtr;
APtr = RegPtr;        // not allowed; implicit type conversion
RegPtr = APtr;        // not allowed; implicit type conversion
```

An auto_ptr object can be assigned to another auto_ptr object:

```
auto_ptr<double> Auto1(RegPtr);
APtr = Auto1;         // allowed; explicit type conversion
```

Both auto_ptr objects hold the same RegPtr pointer. Ownership of the object has been transferred from Auto1 to APtr.

Something about Ownership

When an auto_ptr object is initially constructed, the auto_ptr object owns the object for which it holds the pointer. The auto_ptr that has ownership is responsible for deleting it. Copying one auto_ptr object to another during construction or assignment transfers the object's ownership to the destination auto_ptr. For example:

```
void func1(string& Str)
{
    string *Str2 = new string("the truth is out there");
    auto_ptr<string>Ptr2(Str);    // Ptr2 now has ownership of
                                  // the object Str
    auto_ptr<string>Ptr3(Ptr2);   // Ptr3 now has ownership of
                                  // the object Str;
                                  // Ptr2 no longer has ownership
    auto_ptr<string>Ptr4(Str2);   // Ptr4 has ownership of object Str2
    Ptr2 = Ptr4;                  // Ptr2 has ownership of object Str2
    ...
}
```

Figure 10.8 illustrates the transfer of ownership.

Using auto_ptr

The purpose of auto_ptr is to give the auto_ptr ownership of an object for which it is responsible for the deletion of that object. For example:

```
...
void func2(void)
{
    string *StrPtr = new string("hello out there");
    ...
    return;
}
```

In this example, every time this function is called, the new operator allocates more memory from the heap. The memory is never returned because the delete operator is not called. The result is a memory leak; that is, memory that has been allocated but can no longer be used. It can no longer be used because the pointer to the memory allo-

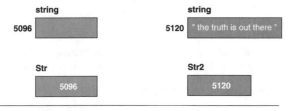

auto_ptr < string > Ptr2 (Str)

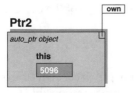

auto_ptr < double > Ptr3 (Ptr2)

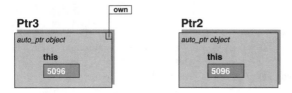

auto_ptr < double > Ptr4 (Str2)

Ptr2 = Ptr4

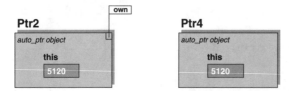

Figure 10.8 Transfer of ownership as described in func1( ).

cated is, in this case, lost every time the function goes out of scope. There is no way to use it or delete it once that happens. If the memory leak grows too large, the program may halt, if it requires more dynamic memory that cannot be allocated. The problem can be solved by adding the delete operator to destroy StrPtr1 before the function goes out of scope; but the delete operator may never be called if the function throws an exception:

```
void func2(void)
{
    string *StrPtr = new string("hello out there");
    . . .

    if(error()){
        throw exception();
    }
    delete StrPtr;
    return;
}
```

If an error occurs, an exception is thrown and the delete operator is never performed.

With auto_ptr, the memory is deallocated:

```
void func2(void)
{
    string *StrPtr = new string("hello out there");
    auto_ptr<string> StrAptr(StrPtr);
    . . .

    if(error()){
        throw exception();
    }
    return;
}
```

When the function goes out of scope, the destructor for auto_ptr StrAptr is called and the memory for StrPtr is deallocated. Listing 10.1 demonstrates initializing the auto_ptr objects with pointers, the use of get( ), and the dereference and assignment operator. Table 10.4 shows the output to Listing 10.1.

Summary

The memory acquisition process is different among various memory models; therefore, the standard C++ library has supplied two classes to help the programmer with memory management: allocator and auto_ptr. The allocator and auto_ptr classes present an object-oriented interface to runtime memory allocation and destruction and dynamic memory management. The classes are used to hide the details of memory models, pointer sizes, reference sizes, and resource allocation and deallocation. The Allocator class is designed to help make the differences in pointer sizes (16, 32, and 64) on different computers—Cray T3D, Ultra SPARC, PowerPC—transparent to the process of

Listing 10.1 Demonstration of the auto_ptr Objects Initialized with Pointers, and the Use of get( ), Dereference and Assignment Operator

```
1    // Listing 10.1
2    #include <memory>
3    #include <iostream>
4    #include <string>
5
6    using namespace std;
7
8    void main(void)
9    {
10       string *Str1 = new string("hello");
11       string *Str2 = new string("out there");
12       auto_ptr<string> AutoPtr1(Str1);
13       auto_ptr<string> AutoPtr2(Str2);
14
15       cout << "auto ptr 1 has object " << *AutoPtr1 << endl;
16       cout << "auto ptr 1 pointer is " << AutoPtr1.get() << endl;
17       cout << "auto ptr 2 has object " << *AutoPtr2 << endl;
18       cout << "auto ptr 2 pointer is " << AutoPtr2.get() << endl;
19       AutoPtr1 = AutoPtr2;
20       cout << "after assignment" << endl;
21       cout << "auto ptr 1 has object " << *AutoPtr1 << endl;
22       cout << "auto ptr 1 pointer is " << AutoPtr1.get() << endl;
23       cout << "auto ptr 2 has object " << *AutoPtr2 << endl;
24       cout << "auto ptr 2 pointer is " << AutoPtr2.get() << endl;
25
26   }
27
```

Table 10.4   Output from Listing 10.1

auto ptr 1 has object hello
auto ptr 1 pointer is 007B0AD0
auto ptr 2 has object out there
auto ptr 2 pointer is 007B0B60
after assignment
auto ptr 1 has object out there
auto ptr 1 pointer is 007B0B60
auto ptr 2 has object out there
auto ptr 2 pointer is 007B0B60

object creation and destruction. The auto_ptr class provides memory management for objects created using the new operator.

The allocator class is a set of requirements, and any type meeting these requirements would be considered an Allocator. It is used by functions that insert, extract, and advance pointers that point to objects in a container; it also provides necessary information about the size of the object, pointer, or reference. There is a standard allocator class. This class supplies services that allocate, deallocate, construct, and destroy an object or objects. Allocation and construction, deallocation and destruction are separate processes. Memory is allocated or set aside for an object or objects; then the objects can be constructed or placed in the memory already set aside. Objects are destroyed or removed from memory, after which the memory can be deallocated or returned to the available memory pool.

The auto_ptr class manages dynamic memory for an object or objects. If an object is created in dynamic memory from inside a function, and if the delete operator has not been called when the function goes out of scope, the memory is not deallocated. If the function is called many times within a program, a memory leak will occur, which if it grows too large can halt the program. The auto_ptr object class is assigned a pointer to an object. When the function goes out of scope, the auto_ptr destructor will destroy the object and deallocate the memory. This will prevent a memory leak. But note, the auto_ptr class can only delete objects that it owns. Ownership of an object can be transferred between auto_ptr objects during construction or assignment. These methods call the release( ) method, which transfers ownership of an object. The auto_ptr objects can be initialized with regular pointers or other auto_ptr objects. There are no implicit type conversions; therefore, an auto_ptr object cannot be assigned to a regular pointer, and a regular pointer cannot be assigned to an auto_ptr object.

CHAPTER 11

Numerics

"If androids were encased in fur, given attractive voices, and made to look like teddy bears, we might be more accepting of them than we otherwise would be . . ."

—N. FRUDE
THE INTIMATE MACHINE:
CLOSE ENCOUNTERS WITH THE NEW COMPUTERS

The standard class library defines several numeric classes that are important to software engineers, developers, computer scientists, engineers, scientists, and mathematicians. Software developers interested in maximum portability or machine-independent programming will find the numeric_limits class indispensable. Those who have demanded vector and matrix computation or parallel vectorization requirements will find the valarray class a welcome addition to the standard C++ class library. The valarray class is an important building block for many linear algebra applications. The complex class provides a complex number data type that is on par with the built-in numeric types in C++. The standardization of the complex class allows C++ programmers to use complex numbers as easily as floats, doubles, and ints are used. The numeric_limits, valarray, and complex classes can be used as building blocks for serious math, scientific, and engineering class libraries. Historically, the Fortran language has long been the staple of scientific and engineering applications. C++ is now a major contender for these types of applications.

The numeric_limits Class

Computer architectures come in many shapes and sizes, and it follows that the number of bytes in an integer or floating-point number differs from one computer to another. Integers have a different size on 64-bit computers than they do on 32-bit computers. The number of bytes in a character is not fixed by the C++ language. A character may have 1, 2, 4, 8 bytes, and so on. Besides differences in the number of bytes of particular data types, there are also differences with respect to how computers deal with floating-point round-off and truncation. Furthermore, how numeric overflow and underflow are dealt with varies from one hardware architecture to another. Professionals who do numeric programming often need to know what is the absolute largest or smallest number representable on a given computer. Quantities from the subatomic to the astronomical are represented in numerical applications. The numeric_limits class is designed to help the C++ programmer manage the differences in numeric and data type variations among computers.

The numeric_limits class is a template class, declared in the <limits> header file. Table 11.1 lists the core methods of this class and their meanings. The numeric_limits class is easy to use. A numeric_limits class can be declared accordingly:

```
numeric_limits<double>    X;
numeric_limits<int>       Y;
numeric_limits<char>      Z;
```

There are no method or operator prerequisites to use the numeric_limits class; it can be used as-is for the built-in data types. The class is provided by the compiler vendor. The numeric_limits class provides an object-oriented interface for many macros and constants found in <limits.h>, <climits>, and the <cfloat> header files. In general, the numeric_limits class is meant to be used with built-in data types, or user-defined data types that are numeric in nature. Although there are already template instantiations for most of the commonly used numeric data type, instantiations for other numeric data types are possible. For example, we could define a numeric_limits<rational> or numeric_limits<transfinite_number>. The program in Listing 11.1 uses a numeric_limits class instantiated to the float data type.

The numeric_limits class is called *Real*. Information returned by the accessor methods of the Real object is used to describe properties of floating-point numbers. We used the

Table 11.1 Core Methods of the numeric_limits Class

NUMERIC_LIMITS: METHODS	DESCRIPTION
min( )	Returns minimum finite value for the type.
max( )	Returns maximum finite value for the type.
epsilon( )	Returns the difference between 1 and the smallest value greater that 1 that is representable for the type.
round_error( )	Returns the maximum rounding error for the type.
infinity( )	Returns the representation of positive infinity if available.
quiet_NaN( )	Returns the representation of a quiet NaN ("Not a Number") for the type, if available.
signaling_NaN( )	Returns the representation of a signaling NaN ("Not A Number") for the type, if available.
denorm_min( )	Returns the minimum positive normalized value for the type.

Listing 11.1   Using the numeric_limits Class

```
1
2    // Listing 11.1
3    // This program uses numeric_limits::epsilon(), and
4    // numeric_limits::max() To build a test case vector.
5
6    #include <stdlib.h>
7    #include <iostream>
8    #include <limits>
9    #include <vector>
10   #include <algorithm>
11   #include <string>
12   #include <sstream>
13   #include <iomanip>
14
15   using namespace std;
16
17   void main(void)
18   {
19
20       int N;
21       vector<float> TestSet;
22       vector<float>::iterator I;
23       string R;
24       numeric_limits<float> Real;
25       stringstream Stream;
26       srand(Real.epsilon());
27       TestSet.push_back(Real.max());
28       TestSet.push_back(Real.epsilon());
29       for(N = 0;N < 40;N++)
30       {
31
32           TestSet.push_back(rand() * 0.10);
33       }
34       random_shuffle(TestSet.begin(),TestSet.end());
35       I = TestSet.begin();
36       cout.precision(10);
37       cout.setf(ios::showpoint | ios::fixed);
38       Stream << setiosflags(ios::showpoint | ios::fixed)
39               << Real.max() << ends;
40       Stream >> R;
41       while(I != TestSet.end())
42       {
43           cout << setw(R.length()) << *I << endl;
44           I++;
45       }
46
47   }
```

Real object to build a simple test-case vector. Building test cases can be as difficult as the programs the test cases are meant to test. It is a good idea to use the classes in the standard C++ library whenever possible to aid in generating test-case data. Many standard algorithms are useful in building test data, including:

- fill
- fill_n
- generate
- generate_n
- next_permutation
- random_shuffle

In Listing 11.1, we used the numeric_limits class and the random_shuffle( ) algorithm to generate a simple test data set. The TestSet vector contains a set of randomly generated numbers. The numeric_limits::epsilon( ) method is used to return a small number that will be the basis for the random number generator. The numeric_limits::max( ) method returns the largest float that can be used in the current execution environment. A list of randomly generated numbers is guaranteed to contain a very small number numeric_limits::epsilon( ) and a very large number numeric_limits::max( ). Numbers falling between these two values are randomly generated by the rand( ) function. Lists containing random sequences of integers or floating-point numbers are important parts of test data. Along with portability uses, the numeric_limits class is extremely useful in generating test data.

The valarray Class

The valarray class provides the C++ programmer with an object-oriented vector. It is the second vector class in the standard C++ class library. The first, a class named vector, is a general-purpose single-dimension array that can be used for many different types of applications, and it is designed to hold any kind of object, both user-defined and built-in data types. The valarray class is a single-dimension array optimized specifically for mathematical operations. The vector class is used as a container object, meant to provide direct and sequential access to collections of objects. The valarray class is designed to provide vector operations on numeric values. It defines vector addition, vector subtraction, scalar vector multiplication, and a host of transcendental mathematical functions. The standard vector class does not provide these mathematical operations.

The valarray Group of Classes

Used by itself, the valarray class presents the user with a single-dimension vector. However, there are four other classes that can be used with the valarray class, to build:

- Vector slices (subsets)
- N-dimensional matrices
- Vector-to-vector operations

- Vector-to-matrix operations
- Matrix-to-matrix operations

The slice_array, gslice_array, indirect_array, and mask_array classes are used in conjunction with the valarray class to build vector subsets or matrices from single-dimension vectors.

The valarray Subset Helper Classes

To use valarray for matrix processing, the standard C++ library includes four helper classes. Used with valarray, they give the programmer the building blocks for matrix processing. These classes work by providing a map from a single-dimension vector to a matrix containing two or more dimensions. For example, we can map a three-dimensional array from a vector by changing the index from element to element to increase from one to three. Figure 11.1 shows a mapping from a single-dimension array to a 3×4 matrix. This is done by using the concept of a *stride*.

A stride is the number of elements that will be counted from one index to another. Figure 11.1 shows that the index is incremented every fourth element to produce the 3×4 matrix. The rows of the matrix generated from the stride technique are called *slices*. The slice_array is used to represent the concept of a slice. Usually, the slice_array is used to build a two-dimensional matrix. The gslice_array is used to build an N-dimensional array. The mask_array and indirect_array are used to build a more general and flexible subset of the valarray. It is important to note that slice_array, gslice_array, mask_array, and indirect_array cannot be built standalone. The constructors for these arrays are not public.

In general, objects of these arrays are built through the [ ] subscript operator of the valarray class:

```
valarray<double>  X;
slice_array<double> V = X[slice(0,X.size(),3)];
```

These statements create a slice_array named V using the valarray X's subscript operator. Once the slice_array is created, the member functions can be called. Though the valarray class does define a number of arithmetic operations and mathematical functions for vectors, it does not define these operations for matrices. Matrices can be built using the slice_array, gslice_array, mask_array, and indirect_array classes, but these classes do not define any arithmetic operations or functions. Matrix multiplication, addition, scalar multiplication, and so on must be built! What the four helper arrays do

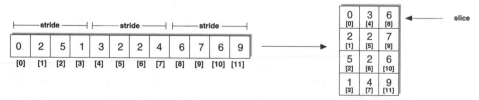

Figure 11.1 Mapping a vector to a 3×4 matrix.

Vector Toolkits and Math Libraries

Common applications requiring vectors and linear algebra include graphics programming, solid modeling, discrete simulation, scientific visualization, encryption, image processing, and digital sound processing. Among the more important toolkits available for these applications are the BLAS (Basic Linear Algebra Subprograms) and LAPACK (Linear Algebra Package) libraries. Made popular in Fortran environments, these libraries have since spread to other language environments, including C++. They provide important computations and data structures based on linear algebra.

The problem with the implementations of these libraries for C++, however, is that they are implemented in different ways by different library providers. Each provider has a unique approach to implementing these libraries, and sometimes different interfaces and APIs, as well. The introduction of the valarray class in the C++ standard library gives the library developer a set of standard building blocks that can be used to implement BLAS and LAPACK type functionality using a standard interface. The valarray, slice_array, glice_array, indirect_array, and mask_array classes combined can be used to build portable linear algebra class libraries and application frameworks based on vector and matrix operations.

is to enable the programmer to build matrices quickly. (For a comprehensive discussion of the helper arrays see Stroustrup 1997.)

Vector Operations and valarray

The standard valarray class defines standard vector addition and subtraction (see Figure 11.2). Vector addition and subtraction are done on a component-by-component basis. Given two vectors, A and B, then A + B or A − B is accomplished by adding A[1] + B[1], A[2] + B[2], . . . A[N] + B[N]. Keep in mind that when operations are performed on a vector, the operation usually has to be applied to each element of the vector, unless a particular element is selected using operator [ ], for example, X[N], where X refers to a valarray object and N refers to a particular element of the valarray. For instance, if we wanted to add 5 to each element of a valarray object called X, then we would write:

$$X = X + 5;$$

On the other hand, if we wanted to add 5 to a particular element in the valarray object X, we would have to specify the particular element using the subscript [ ] operator:

$$X[N] = X[N] + 5$$

where X is the valarray object and N is the position of the element in the valarray object.

The valarray class also supports scalar multiplication (see Figure 11.3) and vector multiplication (see Figure 11.4). In addition to the basic arithmetic operations, the valarray class supports some more common mathematical functions, such as sqrt( ), abs( ), sqrt( ),

$$A = \boxed{1 \mid 2 \mid 3 \mid 6 \mid 7}$$
[0] [1] [2] [3] [4]

$$B = \boxed{5 \mid 8 \mid 9 \mid 10 \mid 3}$$
[0] [1] [2] [3] [4]

Vector Addition: A + B = C

A[0] + B[0] = C[0]
 1 + 5 = 6
A[1] + B[1] = C[1]
 2 + 8 = 10
A[2] + B[2] = C[2]
 3 + 9 = 12
A[3] + B[3] = C[3]
 6 + 10 = 16
A[4] + B[4] = C[4]
 7 + 3 = 10

Vector Subtraction: A - B = D

A[0] - B[0] = C[0]
 1 - 5 = -4
A[1] - B[1] = C[1]
 2 - 8 = -6
A[2] - B[2] = C[2]
 3 - 9 = -6
A[3] - B[3] = C[3]
 6 - 10 = -4
A[4] - B[4] = C[4]
 7 - 3 = 4

$$C = \boxed{6 \mid 10 \mid 12 \mid 16 \mid 10}$$
[0] [1] [2] [3] [4]

$$D = \boxed{-4 \mid -6 \mid -6 \mid -4 \mid 4}$$
[0] [1] [2] [3] [4]

Figure 11.2 The method by which vectors are added and subtracted.

$$A = \boxed{1 \mid 2 \mid 3 \mid 6 \mid 7}$$
[0] [1] [2] [3] [4]

Scalar Vector Multiplication: 4 * A = C

4 * A[0] = C[0]
4 * 1 = 4
4 * A[1] = C[1]
4 * 2 = 8
4 * A[2] = C[2]
4 * 3 = 12
4 * A[3] = C[3]
4 * 6 = 24
4 * A[4] = C[4]
4 * 7 = 28

$$C = \boxed{4 \mid 8 \mid 12 \mid 24 \mid 28}$$
[0] [1] [2] [3] [4]

Figure 11.3 Vector A multiplied by a scalar C to demonstrate scalar multiplication.

$$A = \boxed{1 \mid 2 \mid 3 \mid 6 \mid 7}$$
[0] [1] [2] [3] [4]

$$B = \boxed{5 \mid 8 \mid 9 \mid 10 \mid 3}$$
[0] [1] [2] [3] [4]

Vector Multiplication: A * B = C

A[0] * B[0] = C[0]
 1 * 5 = 5
A[1] * B[1] = C[1]
 2 * 8 = 16
A[2] * B[2] = C[2]
 3 * 9 = 27
A[3] * B[3] = C[3]
 6 * 10 = 60
A[4] * B[4] = C[4]
 7 * 3 = 21

$$C = \boxed{5 \mid 16 \mid 27 \mid 60 \mid 21}$$
[0] [1] [2] [3] [4]

Figure 11.4 Vector multiplication.

and the transcendental (trigonometric) functions. Table 11.2 lists the mathematical operations and functions defined for the valarray class.

Constructing a valarray Object

The valarray object has several constructors:

```
valarray();
explicit valarray(size_t);
valarray(const T&, size_t);
valarray(const T*, size_t);
```

Table 11.2 Arithmetic and Mathematical Functions Defined for valarray

VALARRAY: ARITHMETIC OPERATIONS	DESCRIPTION
Computed Assignment	
+=	addition
−=	subtraction
%=	modulus
*=	multiplication
/=	division
Global Operations	
sin( )	sine
sinh( )	hyperbolic sine
asin( )	arcsine
cos( )	cosine
cosh( )	hyperbolic cosine
acos( )	arccosine
tan( )	tangent
tanh( )	hyperbolic tangent
atan( )	arctangent
atan2( )	arctangent of x[i] / y[i]
pow( )	raised to a power
exp( )	base e exponential
log( )	base e logarithm
log10( )	base 10 logarithm
abs( )	magnitude
sqrt( )	square root

There is a global nonassignment counterpart for all bolded member operators.

```
valarray(const valarray&);
valarray(const slice_array<T>&);
valarray(const gslice_array<T>&);
valarray(const mask_array<T>&);
valarray(const indirect_array<T>&);
```

The valarray object can be constructed as an empty vector or with a particular size, with each element initialized to a particular value. For instance:

```
valarray<float> X (3.14159,100000);
```

declares a valarray that will hold 100,000 floating-point numbers. Each element in the valarray is initialized to 3.14159. The valarray can also be constructed with one of the subset arrays:

slice_array

gslice_array

mask_array

indirect_array

Memory management for the valarray object is transparent to the user. However, the resize( ) method can be used to increase the number of elements that the valarray object can hold.

Important valarray Accessors

The elements of a valarray object are accessed by the [ ] subscript operator. In this sense, the valarray object can be accessed in the same fashion as a traditional C++ array. The size( ) method returns the number of elements in the valarray object; the min( ) method returns the smallest element in the valarray object; the max( ) function returns the largest element in the valarray object. The min( ) method is implemented using the operator <; the max( ) method is implemented using the operator>. The sum( ) method returns the arithmetical sum of the elements contained in the valarray object.

The program in Listing 11.2 demonstrates how valarray objects can be constructed and manipulated and how the sum( ) method is called.

The valarray Modifiers

The contents of a valarray object can be modified using the [ ] subscript operator, the shift method, and the resize( ) method. Unlike the standard vector class, which has erase( ) and clear( ) methods, the valarray class does not have these object-removal methods. Objects are easily put into a valarray but not easily taken out. The program in Listing 11.3 illustrates how a valarray is modified using the [ ] subscript operator and the assignment statement.

This program performs scalar vector multiplication. The vector is multiplied by the value stored in C. The valarray Y is modified by the multiplication.

Listing 11.2 Working with valarray Objects

```
1    // Listing 11.2
2    // This program uses vector addition
3    // and vector subtraction on valarray
4    // objects with the help of the numeric_limits
5    // class.
6
7    #include <valarray>
8    #include <iostream>
9    #include <limits>
10
11
12
13   using namespace std;
14
15   void main(void)
16   {
17       numeric_limits<double> Real;
18       valarray<double> X(Real.max(),100000);
19       valarray<double> Y(X);
20       valarray<double> Z(0.0,100000);
21       Y = Y - Real.epsilon();
22       Y = Y + Real.epsilon();
23       Z = X - Y;
24       if(Z.sum() == 0) {
25           cout << "The Math Stuff Worked!" << endl;
26       }
27       else{
28               cerr << "OH oh!" << endl;
29
30       }
31   }
```

The complex Class

Another building block in the numerics toolkit is the complex class, which is an object-oriented version of a complex number. The notion of a real + imaginary number and negative number under the radical sign is encapsulated in the complex class. Figure 11.5 shows the structure of the complex class.

Recall that a complex number is any number of the form:

$$a + bi$$

where a and b are any real numbers. The number a is called the real part and bi is called the imaginary part. The imaginary part of a complex number is that which allows us to deal with the square root of negative numbers. Some examples of complex numbers are:

Listing 11.3 Modifying valarray

```
1    // Listing 11.3
2    // This program demonstrates how to modify valarray and how
3    // scalar multiplication is done.
4
5    #include <valarray>
6    #include <iostream>
7    #include <stdlib.h>
8    #include <limits>
9
10   using namespace std;
11
12
13   void main(void)
14   {
15       valarray<float> X(10);
16       valarray<float> Y;
17       numeric_limits<float> Real;
18       int N;
19       float C = 15.5;
20       srand(Real.epsilon());
21       for(N = 0;N < 10;N++)
22       {
23           X[N] = rand() * 0.01;
24           cout << "Element: " << N << " " << X[N] << endl;
25       }
26
27       // Scalar Vector Multiplication
28       Y = X * C;
29       for(N = 0;N < 10;N++)
30       {
31           cout << "Element: " << N << " " << Y[N] << endl;
32       }
33
34   }
```

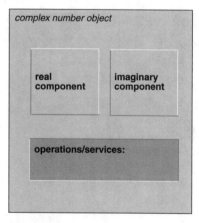

Figure 11.5 Structure of the complex class.

Table 11.3 Arithmetic Operations and Mathematical Functions of the complex Class

COMPLEX NUMBER: METHODS	DESCRIPTION
Arithmetic Operators	
+, +=	complex number addition
−, −=	complex number subtraction
/, /=	complex number division
*, *=	complex number multiplication
Value Operations	
real( )	Returns real component of complex number object
imag( )	Returns imaginary component of complex number object
GLOBAL FUNCTIONS AND OPERATIONS	
Trigonometric Functions	
sin( )	sine of complex number
sinh( )	hyperbolic sine of complex number
cos( )	cosine of complex number
cosh( )	hyperbolic cosine of complex number
tan( )	tangent of complex number
tanh( )	hyperbolic tangent of complex number
Exponentiation, Power, and Logarithmic Functions	
pow( )	complex number raised to a power
exp( )	base e exponential of complex number
log( )	base e logarithm of complex number
log10( )	base 10 logarithm of complex number
Other Mathematical Functions	
abs( )	magnitude of complex number
arg( )	phase angle of complex number
norm( )	squared magnitude of complex number
conj( )	conjugate of complex number
polar( )	value corresponding to a complex number
sqrt( )	square root of complex number

There is a global counterpart for all bolded member functions and operators.

Listing 11.4 Using the complex Class

```
1    // Listing 11.4
2    // This program demonstrates how
3    // easy it is to construct and use
4    // complex numbers with the standard
5    // complex class.
6
7
8
9    #include <complex>
10   #include <iostream>
11
12   using namespace std;
13
14   void main(void)
15   {
16       complex<double> Num1(-3,-1);
17       complex<double> Num2(4,-2);
18       complex<double> Num3(0,0);
19       Num3 = Num1 * Num2;
20       cout << " -3 - i * 4 - 2i = " << Num3 << endl;
21       complex<double> Num4(Num3.real(),Num3.imag());
22       cout << "cosine of " << Num4 << " is " << cos(Num4) << endl;
23   }
24
```

$$3 + 2i, 2 - i, 4i$$

The standard C++ complex class supports the complete range of complex number arithmetic. Table 11.3 lists the arithmetic operations and mathematical functions defined for the complex class. The operations defined for the complex class put it on par with the built-in data types double, float and int. The complex class is easy to construct and use. For instance, the program in Listing 11.4 multiplies the two complex numbers:

$$(-3,-i)(4 - 2i)$$

The complex class is easily constructed by supplying the real number and the coefficient of the imaginary number. Also, note that ostream << operator has already been defined for the complex class. The output from the program in Listing 11.4 is as follows:

$$-3 - i * 4 - 2i = (-14,2)$$

cosine of $(-14,2)$ is $(0.514432,3.59279)$

Summary

The numeric classes numeric_limits, valarray, and complex provide object-oriented versions of important components of a mathematical class library. Although the classes do not comprise a complete mathematical toolkit, they do supply the necessary building blocks to build one. Keep in mind that though the standard vector has not been designed to be used as a mathematical vector, the valarray class has. The full range of arithmetic operations and commonly used mathematical functions are defined for the complex and valarray classes. The numeric_limits class is little more than an object-oriented encapsulation of the constants and macros found in the <climits> and <limits.h> header files.

CHAPTER 12

Language Support

"Discovery is indeed much more appropriate than invention . . ."

—ROGER PENROSE
*THE EMPEROR'S NEW MIND:
CONCERNING COMPUTER MINDS
AND THE LAWS OF PHYSICS*

I f it is the goal of a software developer to produce software that will be used internationally, he or she must consider that users in different countries and regions will prefer to interact with the software using their local language and formatting customs. Therefore, the software should be flexible enough to translate messages, have customized formatting, and have a user interface that accommodates the language. For example, English is read horizontally from left to right; user interfaces accommodate this fact. Transforming the user interface could involve accommodating languages that are read vertically or from right to left.

Consider the user typing input data. With the English language, the cursor appears on the left and moves one character at a time to the right. There is also the issue of the characters of a language; certain languages may require a totally different character set. Formatting issues include dates, time, and currency. When marketing products over the Internet, Web pages will have to be flexible enough to allow for the change to the display of currency, to comply with the local conventions. Figure 12.1 shows some examples of time, date, and currency formatting issues. To deal with these formatting and translation issues, the software developer should not embed translated messages, prompts, customized formatting, or user-interface conversions in their code or have several versions of the same product, one for each locale.

Internationalization and Localization

Two processes can be used by developers to enhance software for worldwide use: *internationalization* and *localization*. Internationalization is the process of designing and

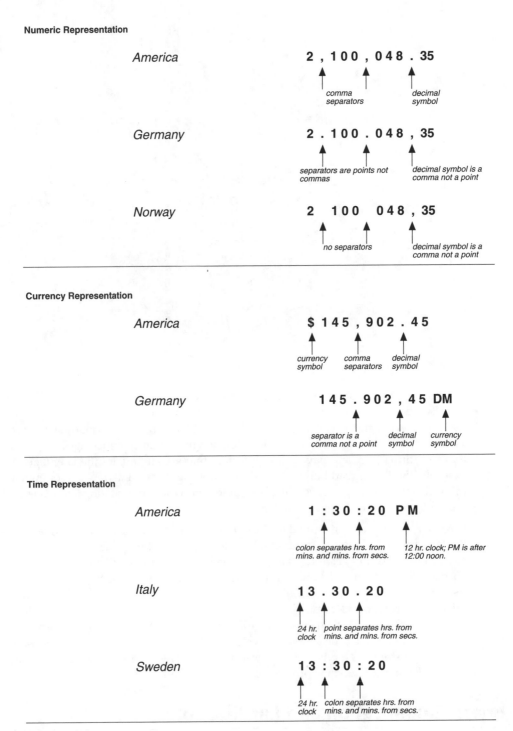

Figure 12.1 Examples of time, date, and currency formatting issues.

building software that has the potential to be used globally. This requires that the software developer consciously design and build software that has inherent flexibility for easy adaptation to different languages with their local conventions. The software developer must give the software the capability to:

- Read, write, and manipulate localized text.
- Conform to local conventions when displaying dates, times, numeric and currency formatting, string and character sorting.
- Display all user-visible text, messages, and prompts in the local language.

Other issues to consider in software development are:

- Language orientation
- Vertical writing and printing
- Keyboards of other languages
- Position and size of the screen displays

Localization is the process of adapting the internationalized software to a specific locale. This can include:

- Translating messages.
- Allowing the user to select the local conventions they prefer.
- Transforming the user interface to display the translated text.
- Modifying a user interface to accommodate user input.

A *locale* represents a geographical or cultural region and is frequently defined by a language and a country. For example, the United States English locale would be different from the British English locale. Although both countries speak English, there are differences in their local conventions. Therefore, the representation of the locales would have to make a distinction between the two. United States English locale would be represented as "En_US" and the British English locale would be represented as "En_GB." Another example: French is spoken in France and Canada. To make their locales distinct, Canada French locale would be represented as "Fr_CA" and France French locale would be represented as "Fr_FR."

Standard C++ Classes Internationalization Support

To create software that will be internationally acceptable, the developer must consider the differences in cultural conventions. These include but are not limited to:

- Language
- Numeric representation
- Display of currency
- Formatting of dates and times
- Rules for sorting characters and strings

The standard C++ class library has defined several classes to support the internationalization and localization of software. The locale class encapsulates a *locale*. The culture-specific information is represented in the *facets* of the locale class. A facet object encapsulates localization services representing the cultural and language conventions and dependencies, some of which have already been mentioned. Several predefined facets represent these conventions, and new facets can also be created.

The standard facet classes can be classified into six groups that describe the functions they perform:

Numeric

Monetary

Time

Ctype

Collate

Code conversions

Messages

As you can see, these groups reflect the internationalization issues mentioned earlier. Numeric facets handle numeric formatting and parsing. Monetary facets handle the formatting and parsing of monetary values. Time facets handle time and date formatting and parsing. Ctype facets are used for character classification. Collate facets handle collating sequences for strings. Code conversion facets are used to convert from one encoding scheme to another. Message facets are used to access and retrieve messages. Each facet group has a locale facet *category*. Table 12.1 associates a facet group with a category. The locale class has a type definition category value. The typedef is an integer that represents a locale category: none, collate, ctype, monetary, numeric, time, messages. These values are used to identify a facet type. Table 12.1 also lists the facet classes included in each facet category.

The Facet Classes

Each facet class is derived from the base class facet. The facet classes are template classes. As listed in Table 12.1, some facet classes require InputIterator or OutputIterator. The formal parameter InputIterator represents parameters that satisfy the requirements of an input iterator. The formal parameter OutputIterator represents parameters that satisfy the requirements of an output iterator. These iterators are used to read or write the characters from or to a stream. The wchar_t and char parameters represent the wide and narrow character types. The formal parameter C represents parameters that satisfy the requirements of a character. The formal parameter International is a bool parameter.

Facet Class Layout

The facet classes tend to follow this general layout:

- Base facet class
- Facet class

Table 12.1 Facet Groups, Categories, and Classes

FACET GROUPS	FACET CATEGORY	FACET CLASSES
numeric	numeric	numpunct
		numpunct_byname
		num_get
		num_put
monetary	monetary	money_get
		money_put
		moneypunct
		moneypunct_byname
time	time	time_get
		time_get_byname
		time_put
		time_put_byname
ctype	ctype	ctype
		ctype_byname
code conversions	ctype	codecvt
		codecvt_byname
collate	collate	collate
		collate_byname
messages	messages	messages
		messages_byname

- Specialization of the facet class
- A "byname" class

As just noted, all of the facet classes are derived from the base class facet, but many facet classes are also derived from a base class that has the facet name and the suffix "base":

```
facetname_base
```

These classes define structs, type definitions, and enumerator types. The facet class itself has this general format:

```
template<...>
class facetname : public locale::facet, public facetname_base{
public:

    // public methods

protected:

    // virtual methods of the form: do_publicmethodname
}
```

The public methods call the protected methods. There may be specialization of the facet class, which has a different template parameter from the original class. A facet class of the form:

```
facetname_byname
```

is a version of the facet class in which all of its services are protected. This class provides the same services as the facetname class but for a named locale passed to the con-

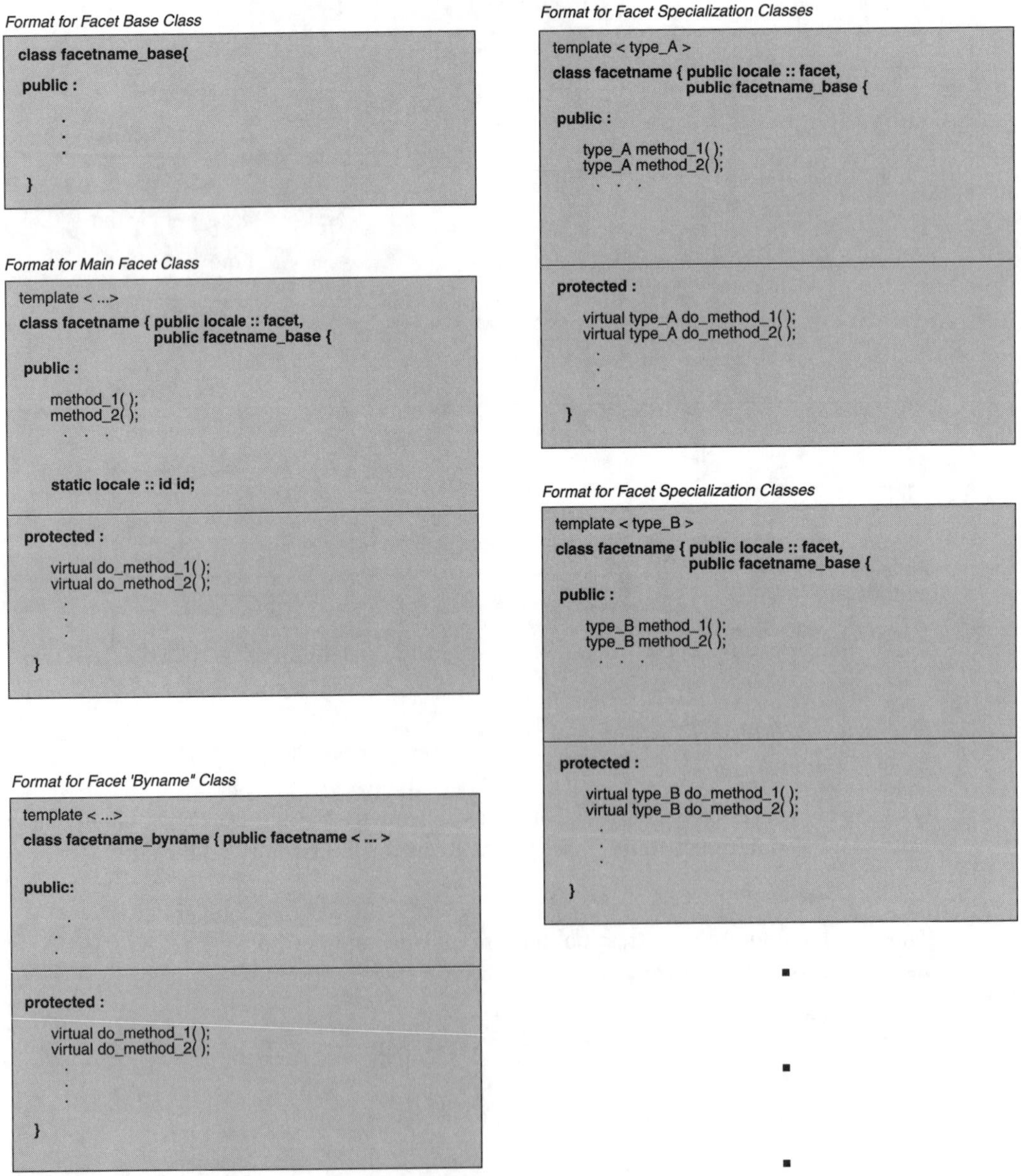

Format for Facet Base Class

```
class facetname_base{
public :

      .
      .
      .
}
```

Format for Main Facet Class

```
template < ...>
class facetname { public locale :: facet,
                  public facetname_base {

public :

      method_1( );
      method_2( );
       .   .   .


      static locale :: id id;

protected :

      virtual do_method_1( );
      virtual do_method_2( );
         .
         .
         .

}
```

Format for Facet 'Byname" Class

```
template < ...>
class facetname_byname { public facetname < ... >

public:

      .
      .
      .

protected :

      virtual do_method_1( );
      virtual do_method_2( );
         .
         .
         .

}
```

Format for Facet Specialization Classes

```
template < type_A >
class facetname { public locale :: facet,
                  public facetname_base {

public :

      type_A method_1( );
      type_A method_2( );
       .   .   .



protected :

      virtual type_A do_method_1( );
      virtual type_A do_method_2( );
         .
         .
         .

}
```

Format for Facet Specialization Classes

```
template < type_B >
class facetname { public locale :: facet,
                  public facetname_base {

public :

      type_B method_1( );
      type_B method_2( );
       .   .   .



protected :

      virtual type_B do_method_1( );
      virtual type_B do_method_2( );
         .
         .
         .

}
```

Figure 12.2 General layout of the facet class.

structor. Figure 12.2 shows the general layout of the facet class as described. This layout is a superset. Some facet classes conform to only one or two of these formats. Table 12.2 lists all of the facet classes by category and identifies the formats the class follows.

The facet name obeys a naming convention. The facets that contain *get* are classes that handle parsing, and facets that contain *put* handle formatting. For example, num_get and money_get provide services that handle the parsing of numbers and currency. The num_put and money_put provide services that handle formatting of numbers and currency. The facet classes that contain *punct* represent rules and symbols for punctuation. For example, the moneypunct facet class represents the symbols and punctuation rules for currency, and numpunct represents the symbols and punctuation rules for numeric representation.

Collate Facet Classes

The collate facet classes provide services concerning the rules for ordering or sorting characters and strings. Collating sequence is the order assigned to a set of items, which determines how items will be sorted. Languages may vary in the way characters or strings are sorted. When using the ASCII character set to define the collating sequence, in Table 12.3, numbers come before upper- and lowercase characters; uppercase characters come before lowercase characters. Table 12.4 shows examples of strings sorted according to the collating sequence defined by the ASCII table. This order is based on the numeric value of bytes mapped to each character and symbol in the table. This order is different from strings sorted according to the English alphabet. If we were to sort a list of strings of another language that could be represented by ASCII characters

Table 12.2　Facet Classes by Category and Their Formats

FACET CATEGORY	FACET CLASSES	FORMATS		
		BASE CLASS	SPECIALIZATION	BYNAME CLASS
numeric	numpunct			✔
	num_get			
	num_put			
monetary	money_get			
	money_put			
	moneypunct	✔		✔
time	time_get	✔		✔
	time_put			✔
ctype	ctype	✔	✔	✔
	codecvt	✔		✔
collate	collate			✔
messages	messages	✔		✔

Table 12.3 ASCII Character Set ISO 8859 Latin–1 with Control Characters

HEX	DEC	SCREEN	HEX	DEC	SCREEN
41h	65	A	73h	115	s
42h	66	B	74h	116	t
43h	67	C	75h	117	u
44h	68	D	76h	118	v
45h	69	E	77h	119	w
46h	70	F	78h	120	x
47h	71	G	79h	121	y
48h	72	H	7Ah	122	z
49h	73	I	.		
4Ah	74	J	.		
4Bh	75	K	.		
4Ch	76	L	80h	128	Ç
4Dh	77	M	81h	129	ü
4Eh	78	N	82h	130	é
4Fh	79	O	83h	131	â
50h	80	P	84h	132	ä
51h	81	Q	85h	133	à
52h	82	R	86h	134	å
53h	83	S	87h	135	ç
54h	84	T	88h	136	ê
55h	85	U	89h	137	ë
56h	86	V	8Ah	138	è
57h	87	W	8Bh	139	ï
58h	88	X	8Ch	140	î
59h	89	Y	8Dh	141	ì
5Ah	90	Z	8Eh	142	Ä
.			8Fh	143	Å
.			90h	144	É
.			91h	145	æ
61h	97	a	92h	146	Æ
62h	98	b	93h	147	ô
63h	99	c	94h	148	ö
64h	100	d	95h	149	ò

Table 12.3 (*Continued*)

HEX	DEC	SCREEN	HEX	DEC	SCREEN
65h	101	e	96h	150	û
66h	102	f	97h	151	ù
67h	103	g	98h	152	ÿ
68h	104	h	99h	153	ö
69h	105	i	9Ah	154	Ü
6Ah	106	j	.		
6Bh	107	k	.		
6Ch	108	l	.		
6Dh	109	m	E0h	224	α
6Eh	110	n	E1h	225	β
7Fh	111	o	E2h	226	Γ
70h	112	p	E3h	227	π
71h	113	q	E4h	228	Σ
72h	114	r	E5h	229	σ

(for example, German, which includes a–z A–Z and special characters ä ö ü Ä Ö Ü β) according the ASCII collation order, it would be sorted as shown in Table 12.4. The table also shows how that same list is sorted according to the German alphabet. Table 12.5 shows the German alphabet.

The collate class defines services used for the comparing and hashing strings. The collate classes consist of:

Table 12.4 Strings Sorted by the ASCII Table: English Alphabet and German Alphabet

ENGLISH			GERMAN		
Alphabetical Order			*Alphabetical Order*		
Android	external	pretty	Android	flüssig	Saturn
bad	flood	remark	außen	Flut	schön
bleak	liquid	Saturn	äußerlich	öde	übel
evil	outside	voyage	Äußerung	Reise	Übel
ASCII Rules			*ASCII Rules*		
Android	evil	outside	Android	außen	äußerlich
Saturn	external	pretty	Flut	flüssig	Äußerung
bad	flood	remark	Reise	schön	öde
bleak	liquid	voyage	Saturn	übel	Übel

Table 12.5 German Alphabet

GERMAN ALPHABET					
A a Ä ä	F f	K k	P p	T t	Y y
B b	G g	L l	Q q	U u Ü ü	Z z
C c	H h	M m	R r	V v	
D d	I i	N n	ß	W w	
E e	J j	O o Ö ö	S s	X x	

collate

collate_byname

Figure 12.3 shows the class relationship diagram of the collate family of facet classes, and Table 12.6 lists some services provided by the collate classes.

Ctype Facet Classes

The ctype family of facet classes consists of two groups of facet classes: ctype and code conversion. The code conversion classes are used to convert characters from one code set to another. For example, the ASCII character set is an 8-bit character-coding set of 256 characters in which the alphabets of Western and Eastern Europe, the Middle East, and Asia can be represented. Other languages cannot be represented by the ASCII character set. The Unicode character set is a 16-bit character-coding set of 65,536 characters representing the written languages of the Americas, Europe, India, Asia, the Middle East, Africa, and Pacifica. The Unicode is a superset of the ASCII code set.

Languages that consist of more than 256 characters require *multibyte* character codes. A multibyte character code set is a superset of ASCII code set (1 byte) and consists of a mixture of 1- and 2-byte characters. Multibyte character encoding can represent thousands of characters. This encoding scheme is used to represent characters outside a

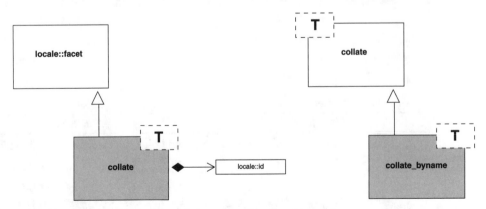

Figure 12.3 Class relationship of the collate family of facet classes.

Table 12.6 Services Provided by the Collate Classes

COLLATE: CORE VIRTUAL METHODS	DESCRIPTION
do_compare( )	Compares two strings; returns 1 if the first string is greater than the second string; returns −1 if the first string is less than the second string; returns 0 if the strings are equal.
do_transform( )	Returns a string object that compares lexicographically with the result of calling this method on another string; returns the same result as calling do_compare( ) on the same two strings.
do_hash( )	Returns an integer equal to the result of calling this method on any other string for which do_compare( ) would return 0.

program, in files for example. Once the characters are brought inside a program, they should be represented in a uniform format and size, called *wide characters*. Wide characters represent characters using 2 or more bytes. Unicode is an example of wide characters. For example, messages using an alphabet consisting of more than 256 characters are stored in a file using a multibyte encoding scheme. The characters are read into a program and converted to wide characters stored in an internal character buffer using the iostreams. Therefore, any multibyte characters that are 1 byte in length are converted to 2- or 4-byte wide characters. This is illustrated in Figure 12.4. A uniform representation of characters makes character manipulation easier and more efficient.

The code conversion group of ctype facet classes comprises:

codecvt

codecvt_byname

Figure 12.5 shows the class relationship diagram of these classes, and Table 12.7 lists some core services provided by the code conversion facet classes.

The ctype classes are concerned with the behavior of character-handling functions. The ctype classes are:

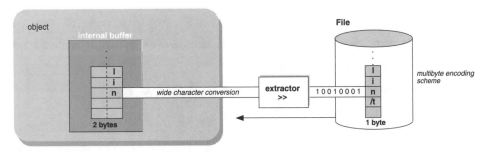

Figure 12.4 A character sequence that uses the multibyte encoding scheme. As the characters are read from the file using extractors, they are converted to wide characters stored in an internal buffer.

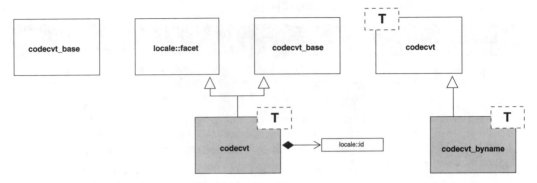

Figure 12.5 Class relationship of the codecvt facet classes.

ctype

ctype_byname

Figure 12.6 shows the class relationship diagram of these classes and Table 12.7 also lists some core services provided by the ctype facet classes.

Numeric Facet Classes

The numeric facet classes handle numeric formatting and parsing. Local conventions determine how numbers are represented. This can vary from one country or region to another. For example, the convention of grouping digits varies. In America, digits are grouped in threes; in other regions or countries, digit groupings are a mixture of two and three digits. Likewise, the character that separates the digit groupings varies. In America, a comma is used as a separator; in Germany, a period is used. The character that separates the fractional portion from the integer portion in America is a period or decimal point; in Europe, it is a comma. Here are some examples of the different conventions used for the same number:

America: 2,100,048.35

Germany: 2.100.048,35

Norway: 2 100 048,35

As you can see, Germany and Norway use a comma as the decimal point. Norway has no digit grouping separator, whereas Germany uses a period to separate digit groupings.

The numeric facet classes consist of:

numpunct

numpunct_byname

num_get

num_put

Figure 12.7 shows the class relationship diagram of these classes. The num_get and num_put classes provide services concerning the inputting and outputting of num-

Table 12.7 Core Services Provided by Code Conversion and Ctype Facet Classes

CTYPE: CORE VIRTUAL METHODS	DESCRIPTION
do_is( )	Classifies a character or sequence of characters. There are two versions of this method: the first identifies a value M of type ctype_base::mask for each character and returns the result of the expression (M & m) != 0; the second places M for all *p where: (low <= p && p < high) into vec[p – low] returns high.
do_scan_is( )	Locates a character in a buffer that conforms to a classification m; returns the smallest pointer p, such that do_is(*p) would return true.
do_scan_not( )	Locates a character in a buffer that does not conform to a classi-fication m; returns the smallest pointer p, such that do_is(*p) would return false.
do_toupper( ) do_tolower( )	Converts a character or characters to upper- or lowercase.
do_widen( ) do_narrow( )	Transforms a char value or sequence of char values to charT values, or transforms a charT or sequence of charT values to char values.

CODECVT: CORE VIRTUAL METHODS	DESCRIPTION
do_out( ) do_in( )	Translates characters in a range; the results are placed sequentially in another range; stops if it reaches a character it cannot convert.
do_encoding( )	Returns –1 if the encoding of sequences of type externT is state-dependent; returns the constant number of externT characters needed to produce an internal character; returns 0 if number is not a constant because the encoding involves sequences of vary-ing lengths.
do_always_noconv( )	Returns true if do_convert( ) returns noconv (no termination is needed for this state_type).
do_length( )	Returns from_next – from where from_next is the largest value in the range [from, from_end); this range represents max or fewer valid complete characters of type internT.
do_max_length( )	Returns the maximum value returned by do_length(state,from, from_end,1) of any valid range [from,from_end).

bers. These classes use an ios_base object to determine conversion and formatting of a number by using the format flags (refer to Chapter 3 for more information on format-ting flags in the ios_base class). The length can also be specified. The numpunct classes are concerned with the punctuation of numeric representation. They provide services that return the characters for the decimal point and thousands separator, and a string that contains the number of digits in a grouping starting at the rightmost group.

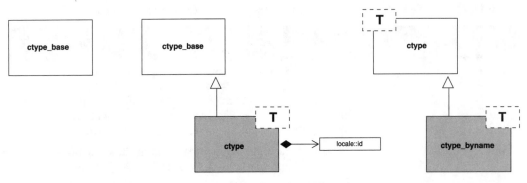

Figure 12.6 Class relationship of the ctype family of facet classes.

Input iterators are used to read the characters from an istreambuf. Each character is read from the input stream, then properly converted. The process is terminated when the iterator has reached the end of the stream. This process and its results are summarized in Table 12.8. The process of outputting numeric characters is similar. Output iterators are used to write characters to an ostreambuf. This process and the results of the processing are summarized in Table 12.9. Both processes use the num_punct object to determine the grouping of digits and the character for the decimal point and thousands separator.

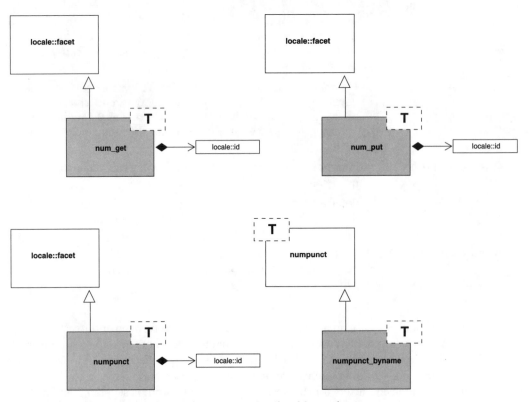

Figure 12.7 Class relationship of the numeric family of facet classes.

Table 12.8   Input of a Sequence of Characters That Represent Numbers

Stage 1: Determine a conversion specifier:
■ Initialize local variables using str.flags( ).
■ Convert to an integral type, floating-point, or void * using specifiers.
■ Determine length specifier, if needed.

Stage 2: Extract characters from input source and transform them into char according to conversion specification:
■ If the input iterator points to the end of the sequence, terminate this stage.
■ Determine if the character extracted is a decimal point.
■ Determine if the character is a thousands separator, and determine if digit grouping length != 0. If both are true, then the position of the character in the sequence is remembered.
■ If the character is allowed to be the next character in the sequence according to the conversion specification, then the character is accumulated.
■ Advance the input iterator to the next character and restart stage 2.

POSSIBLE RESULTS OF PROCESSING THE CHARACTERS
■ ios_base::goodbit is assigned to err: A sequence of characters has been accumulated and the value is stored in val.
■ ios_base::failbit is assigned to err: Digit grouping has been checked and the positions of discarded separators are not consistent, or scanf reports an input failure.
■ ios_base::eofbit is assigned to err: The end of the input sequence has been reached.

Monetary Facet Classes

There are many different ways the units of currency can be represented. Countries use different symbols to represent dollars, cents, and the currency symbol. Conventions also vary as to placement of that symbol. Here are some examples:

America: $145,902.45

Germany: 145.902,45 DM

Portugal: 145.902$45 Esc.

Sweden: 145 902,45 Kr

Italy: L.145.902

In America and Italy, the currency symbol is placed before the value.

The monetary facet classes consist of:

money_get

money_put

moneypunct

moneypunct_byname

Table 12.9 Output of a Sequence of Characters That Represent Numbers

Stage 1: If the current locale is the "C" locale, determine a printf conversion specifier (spec) and determine the characters that are to be printed:
■ Initialize local variables using this->flags( ).
■ Convert to an integral type, floating-point, or void * using specifiers.
■ Determine length specifier, if needed.
■ Representation would be chars printed by printf(s, val), where s is the conversion specifier.
Stage 2: Convert each char to charT using a conversion:
■ The conversion and the values are returned by members of: use_facet<numpunct<charT>> (str.getloc( )).
■ Any character other than the decimal point is converted.
■ Decimal point characters are replaced with punct.decimal_point( ).
■ Thousands separator characters are inserted into the sequence determined by the value returned by punct.do_grouping( ).
Stage 3: Determine the location of any padding:
■ If width( ) != 0 and the number of charTs in the sequence is less than width( ), then the fill characters are added at the position indicated for padding to bring the sequence equal to width( ).
Stage 4: Send the sequence to output:
■ The sequence is sent to output via: *out++ = c.
■ out is returned.
POSSIBLE RESULTS OF PROCESSING THE CHARACTERS
■ out.failed( ) becomes true during stage 4; output is terminated.

Figure 12.8 shows the relationship diagrams for these classes. The money_get facet class provides services that parse a sequence of characters representing currency. Each character is read from an istreambuf using an input iterator until the iterator reaches the end of the stream. All punctuation is removed; for example, the sequence $2,567.09 in the U.S. locale produces the 256709 units or the character sequence "256709." This is a sequence of digits representing a count of the smallest units of currency that can be represented. Groupings of digits are checked after all the elements have been read. If there is no grouping specified, the thousands separators are not considered part of the numeric formatting. The money_put facet class provides services that format a sequence of characters. The characters are written to an ostreambuf using an output iterator according to the format specified by the moneypunct object. Both the money_get and money_put facet classes use an ios_base object to determine formatting issues, such as determining whether the currency symbol is consumed when the character sequence is read or ignored when the currency is displayed or where fill characters will be placed.

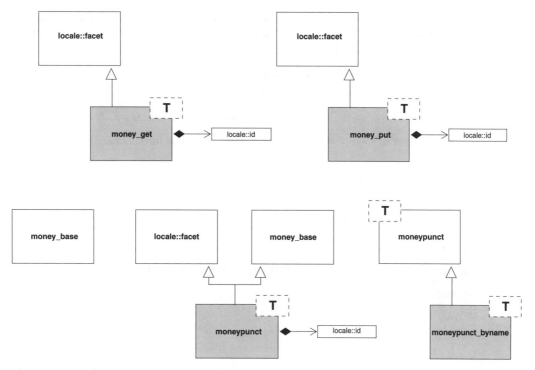

Figure 12.8 Class relationship for the monetary family of facet classes.

The moneypunct facet class encapsulates the currency punctuation. It contains the:

- Thousands separator
- Digit group separator
- Digit grouping pattern
- Currency symbol
- The string used to indicate the positive or negative monetary value
- Number of digits in the fractional part
- The order in which the elements appear

Currency can also be displayed and read as negative values.

Time Facet Classes

The time facet classes handle the formatting and parsing of time and dates, which vary by country. The names of months and days of the week and their abbreviations also vary. Local conventions will dictate the order that year, month, and day appear, along with any separators for their numeric short or long representations. Time measurement is also an issue. Some countries use a 12-hour clock, where others use a 24-hour clock, to measure the length of a day.

Some countries use the Western Gregorian calendar system to measure a year; others use historical events, astronomical, or seasonal criteria to measure a year. Consider the following long representation of a date:

America   Sunday, December 13, 1998

Germany   Sonntag, 13. Dezember 1998

This compares how a date is represented in America and Germany.

Countries differ in the order of and the separator used for the short representation of a date:

America   12/13/1998

Italy   13/12/98

Sweden   1998-12-13

Russia   13.12.98

Here are some examples of how time is represented in different countries:

America   1:30:20 PM

Italy   13.30.20

Sweden   13:30:20

Mexico   1:30:20 PM

Italy and Sweden use the 24-hour clock.

The time facet classes consist of:

time_get

time_get_byname

time_put

time_put_byname

Figure 12.9 shows the class relationship diagram for the time_get and time_put facet classes. The time_get facet classes provide services that parse a character sequence representing time. Input iterators are used to read the characters from the istreambuf. The components of time or date are extracted and stored in struct tm. For the time_get facet class, each method in the class reads the particular component it was designed to read. If the sequence is correct, the sequence is stored in the appropriate member of the struct tm. The members extract the time, the year identifier, the full name or abbreviation of the weekday or month name. It also stores the order of components for the date, year, and month date format. The time_put class provides services that format a character sequence. Output iterators are used to write the characters to an ostreambuf.

Messages Facet Classes

The messages facet class retrieves strings from a message catalog. A string name is mapped to a message catalog number. A particular string message can be retrieved from that catalog. The messages facet classes consist of:

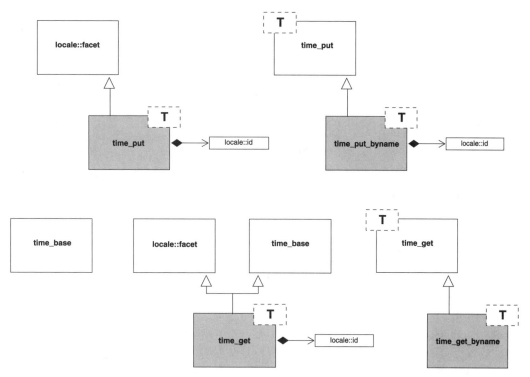

Figure 12.9 Class relationship for the time_get and time_put family of facet classes.

messages

messages_byname

Figure 12.10 shows the class relationship diagram for the messages facet classes.

Creating and Using Facet Objects

There are various ways to create facet objects. Facet classes can be bought as a facet library, which will contain facet classes and preconstructed and initialized facet objects. New facet classes can be built from scratch, say, a facet class that formats phone numbers and compares strings or numbers, or a facet class that creates user-interface components to accommodate messages. New facet classes can be derived from existing facet classes. Such facet classes would inherit the "byname" version of a facet. These facets utilize C locale. Constructing a new facet that is a locale-sensitive number comparison could look like this:

```
template<class charT>
class number_compare : public numpunct_byname<charT>{
public:
    number_compare(const char* name, size_t refs = 0)
    : numpunct_byname<charT>(name,refs) { }
```

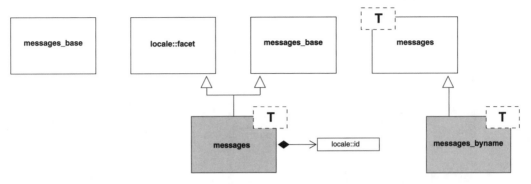

Figure 12.10 Class relationship diagram for the messages family of facet classes.

```
    ~number_compare { }
    bool compare(const charT* low1, const charT* high1,
              const charT* low2, const chart* high2) const;

    ...
};
string num1("1.234,22');
string num2("3.346,90");
number_compare<char> CompareNumber("De_DE");
if(Compare.compare(num1.begin(), num1.end(), num2.begin(), num2.end()) == 1)
{
    // 1 means num1 == num2
    ...
}
```

The facet object is constructed from a German C locale's external representation. Two numbers using German conventions are compared for equality using this single facet object.

The locale Class

The locale class encapsulates internationalization services by representing a number of particular cultural conventions. A locale object will contain facet objects in which each facet object represents a particular cultural convention for a specific region. Figure 12.11 shows the relationship between the locale object and its facets.

The locale object contains:

class facet

class id

The class facet is the base class for all the facet classes the locale will contain. The class id serves as an identification for a locale facet. The locale object can be considered an index of facets, and the ids are the indices. Each facet has a locale::id that can be initialized the first time a facet object is installed into the locale object.

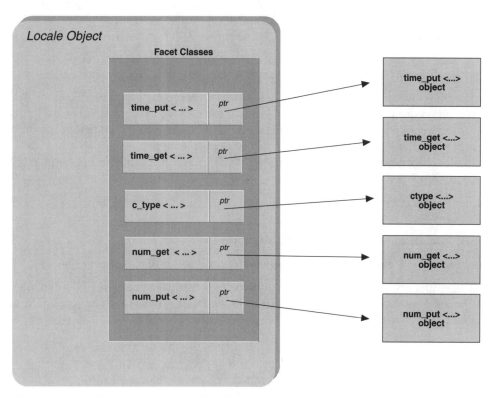

Figure 12.11 Relationship between the locale object and its facets.

Constructing Locale Objects

There are many ways to construct a locale object. It can be a copy of another locale object, including all or some facets. Some facets can be replaced with facets from a third locale object. The locale can also be named during construction.

The default constructor:

```
locale() throw();
```

creates a locale object that is a copy of the global locale. This would be the last locale passed to the function:

```
locale::global(locale&);
```

If this function is not called, then the default locale::classic( ) is used. The result is a new locale object that is a copy of locale::classic( ).

With this constructor:

```
explicit locale(const char* std_name);
```

a new locale object is created with the name std_name. This name has to be a standard C locale name. If the name is not valid, or null, a runtime_error exception is thrown.

These constructors create a locale object that is a copy of another locale object passed to the constructor:

```
locale(const locale& other) throw();
locale(const locale& other, const locale& one, category cats);
```

The first constructor creates a locale object that is a complete copy of locale other. The second constructor creates a locale object that is a copy of locale one. All of the facets are incorporated into the new locale, *except* the facet categories specified in the third argument. Remember, category is a typedef for an integer that represents any of the C locale categories or a group of local constants. The | and & operators can be applied to any two categories. For example:

```
monetary | numeric
time & collate
```

The locale member all is defined by this expression:

```
(collate | ctype | monetary | numeric | time | messages | all) == all
```

These category values can be passed to a locale constructor or any member function. The locale category can represent a set of locale facets. Those facets are copied from locale one. For example:

```
locale newloc (locale::classic(), locale("De_DE"), time);
```

A new locale object is constructed as a copy of locale::classic( ), with all the same facets except time. The facet time from the locale "De_DE" is assigned to the new locale newloc. The new locale has a name only if the other locale objects had a name.

Two constructors are template functions:

```
template<class Facet> locale(const locale& other, Facet* f);
template<class Facet> locale(const locale& other, const locale& one);
```

With both constructors, a locale object is created as a copy of locale other. All of the facets are incorporated, *except* the facet type specified in the template parameter. In the first constructor, the Facet f object is copied into the new object. In the second constructor, the facet is copied from locale one. If that locale object does not have a facet of that type, a runtime_error exception is thrown. The new locale object will not have a name. The destructor:

```
~locale() throw();
```

destroys a locale object.

Locale Operators

These operators are defined for the locale object:

```
const locale& operator=(const locale& other) throw();
bool operator==(const locale& other) const;
bool operator!=(const locale& other) const;
```

The assignment operator creates a copy of locale other. The equality operator will return true if:

- Both locale objects have the identical names.
- One locale object is a copy of the other locale object.
- Both are the same locale objects.

The inequality operator returns true if the locale objects are not equal.

The operator( ) is also defined for the locale object:

```
template<class charT, class Traits, class Allocator>
    bool operator() (const basic_string<charT, Traits, Allocator>& s1,
        const basic_string<charT, Traits, Allocator>& s2) const;
```

Two strings are compared. The comparison is according to the collate<charT> facet comparison method. A bool value is returned. If the first string is greater than the second string, 1 is returned. If the first string is less than the second string, –1 is returned. Otherwise, 0 is returned. Because the operator( ) is defined, a locale object can be passed as a predicate template argument for algorithms. For example, the collation rules for the locale object locx can be used to collate the vector of strings vect:

```
heap_sort(vect.begin(), vect.end(), locx);
```

Global and Classic Locales

This function sets the global locale:

```
static locale global(const locale& loc);
```

to the specified locale. Any calls to the default constructor will create a new locale that is a copy of this locale. This function actually calls the C's setlocale( ). The previous value of the global locale is returned. Internationalized components—for example, the iostreams—can use the global locale. Consider this:

```
...
locale::global(locale("De_DE"));
cout.imbue(locale());
cout << number;
```

The global locale is the locale "De_DE", a German locale. Any subsequent calls to cout will use this locale.

The classic locale is the C locale:

```
static const locale& classic();
```

This locale cannot be changed, new facets cannot be assigned to it, and the member function cannot be modified. This locale represents the U.S. English ASCII environment. The classic locale is also the default locale, meaning if programs do not use internationalization, this locale is used.

Accessing Locale Facets

These global templates allow facets of a locale to be accessed:

```
template<class Facet> const Facet& use_facet(const locale& loc);
template<class Facet> bool has_facet(const locale& loc) throw();
```

The use_facet template function returns a reference to the facet of the specified locale loc. The template argument determines the facet class. If the locale has that particular facet, a bad_cast exception is thrown.

The has_facet template function returns a bool value true if the locale has the specified facet. This function is called by use_facet to determine if the locale contains the facet.

Here is an example of how these template functions can be used:

```
charT decpoint;
...
if(has_facet<numpunct<char>>(xloc))
{
    decpoint = use_facet<<numpunct<char>>(xloc).decimal_point();
}
```

The has_facet< . . . > is called to determine if locale xloc has the facet class numpunct. If true is returned, then use_facet< . . . > is called. The reference to the facet numpunct of locale xloc is returned and the method decimal_point( ) is called. This method returns the decimal point character specified by the numeric punctuation of locale xloc.

The Stream's Facets

As mentioned earlier, the stream classes are internationalized. Each stream contains a locale object, which affects the parsing and formatting of numeric values. The global locale can be used to format all input and output of numeric values. If multiple locales are needed, insertion and extraction of numbers can be done using different locale objects. Each stream uses its own locale object. Locales can also be passed and used in various places in a program, as illustrated in Figure 12.12. For example, a number can be sent to output using different locale objects:

```
...
float number = 1345.90;
ostream cout1;
ostream cout2;
ostream cout3;

cout1.imbue(loc1);    // classic locale
cout2.imbue(loc2);    // French locale
cout3.imbue(loc3);    // German locale

cout1 << number << endl;    // 1,345.90
cout2 << number << endl;    // 1 345,90
cout3 << number << endl;    // 1.345,90
```

The member function imbue( ) assigns the specified locale to the locale object. The number is sent to the output stream formatted according to its respective locales.

The char_traits Class

The char_traits class is very important. It defines the characters used in a string, number, time, date, and so on. Therefore, any class that manipulates characters is dependent on this class. For example, when two strings are compared for equality, the

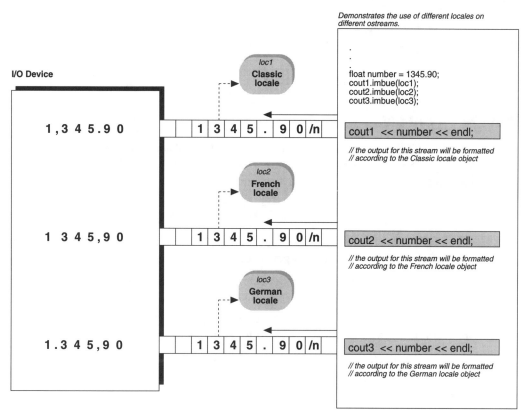

I/O Device

Demonstrates the use of different locales on different ostreams.

```
.
.
.
float number = 1345.90;
cout1.imbue(loc1);
cout2.imbue(loc2);
cout3.imbue(loc3);
```

loc1
Classic locale

`cout1 << number << endl;`

// the output for this stream will be formatted
// according to the Classic locale object

loc2
French locale

`cout2 << number << endl;`

// the output for this stream will be formatted
// according to the French locale object

loc3
German locale

`cout3 << number << endl;`

// the output for this stream will be formatted
// according to the German locale object

Figure 12.12   A program can use multiple facets.

characters of one string are compared with the characters of another string, character by character. This string comparison operation calls the comparison operation of the char_traits class defined for that particular character type. The char_traits class declares types and functions needed to manipulate the character type. The functions define comparisons, equality, assignment, and so on, between characters. The actual definition of the char_traits class is totally dependent on the character type in use. Each character type will have its own definition of the char_traits class. The character traits must be specialized for the specific character type in use.

Characters can be *narrow* or *wide*. A narrow character is a character represented by 8 bits; a wide character is a character represented by 2 or more bytes. The ASCII character set has 256 8-bit narrow characters. The Unicode character set consists of 65,536 16-bit wide characters. Narrow and wide characters are represented as:

```
char and wchar_T
```

respectively.

The header <string> declares two structs that are a specialization of char_traits. The struct char_traits<char> is the narrow character specialization, and the struct char_traits <wchar_t> is the wide character specialization. The struct char_traits<wchar_t> has type definitions as follows:

```
typedef wchar_T char_type;
typedef wint_type int_type;
typedef wstreamoff off_type;
...
```

Therefore, the interface of the class is not different.

The char_traits Methods

Character codes map characters to integer values. Therefore, obtaining an integer value, int_type, must be possible for a given character, and obtaining a character, char_type must be possible, for a given integer value:

```
static int_type to_int_type(const char_type& c);
static char_type to_char_type(const int_type& c);
```

When characters are to be compared, several member functions perform the task of comparing characters or their integer equivalents. These member functions:

```
static bool eq(const char_type& c1, const char_type& c2);
static bool eq_int_type(const int_type& c1, const int_type& c2);
```

determine if c1 == c2. In the first case, the char_types are compared for equivalence. In the second case, int_types are compared for equivalence.

The member function:

```
static bool lt(const char_type& c1, const char_type& c2);
```

determines if c1 < c2. And:

```
static int compare(const char_type* s1, const char_type* s2, size_t n);
```

for each char_type, i, in the range [0, n), this function returns 0 if s1[i] == s2[i] is true. A negative value is returned for each char_type j in the same range if s1[j] < s2[j] is true.

A negative value is also returned for each i in the range [0, j) if s1[i] == s2[i] is true. If these conditions are not met then a positive value is returned.

Both member functions:

```
static char_type* move(char_type* s1, const char_type* s2, size_t n);
static char_type* copy(char_type* s1, const char_type* s2, size_t n);
```

copies n characters from s2 to s1 using the assign(s[i],s2[i]). The move( ) member function will work correctly even if s2 is in the range of s1 + n.

The assignment operation is performed by:

```
static void assign(char_type& c1, const char_type& c2);
static char_type* assign(char_type* s, size_t n, char_type a);
```

The first assign( ) copies c2 to c1. The second assign( ) copies n copies of a into c1.

The member functions:

```
static int_type eof();
static int_type not_eof(const int_type& c);
```

return an int_type that is the end-of-file, and int_type c such that c is not the end-of-file. The multibyte conversion state of a character in pos is returned by:

```
static state_type get_state(pos_type pos);
```

The member function:

```
static const char_type* find(const char_type* s, int n,
                             const char_type& a);
```

finds the smallest char_type in the range s to s + n, where char_type is equal to a char_type.

Summary

Software that will be used internationally must be flexible enough to translate messages, have customized formatting, and have a user interface that accommodates the language of the user. The language may require a totally different character set; formatting issues include dates, time, and currency. To deal with these formatting and translation issues, software developers should not embed translated messages, customized formatting or user-interface conversion in their code or have several versions of the same product.

Two processes can be utilized to enhance global use of software: internationalization and localization. The standard C++ class library has defined several classes to support the internationalization and localization of software. The locale class encapsulates a locale, which encapsulates culture-specific information. This information is represented in facets classes contained in the locale class. A facet object encapsulates localization services representing the cultural and language conventions and dependencies. The standard facet classes can be classified into six groups that describe the functions they perform: numeric, monetary, time, Ctype, collate, code conversion, and messages. Each facet group belongs to a locale facet category: collate, ctype, monetary, numeric, time, and messages.

The locale class encapsulates internationalization services by representing a number of particular cultural conventions. A locale object contains facet objects in which each facet object represents a particular cultural convention for a specific region. The locale object also contains a class id, which serves as an identification for a locale facet. The locale object can be considered an index of facets and the ids the indices. Each facet has a locale::id that can be initialized the first time a facet object is installed into the locale object. There are several ways to construct a locale object: as a copy of another locale object with all of its facets or as a subset of facets where the missing facets are copied from yet another locale. The facets of a locale can be accessed by using a template function use_facet< >. The template function has_facet< > is used to determine if a locale actually contains a specific facet. The stream classes contain a locale object. Any locale can be assigned to the locale of a stream object by using imbue( ).

The char_traits class encapsulates the characteristics of a character type. It declares types and functions needed to manipulate the character type by defining functions that perform comparisons, equality, assignment, and so on between characters. Each character type will have its own definition of the char_traits class.

Characters can be narrow or wide. A narrow character is represented by 8 bits. The ASCII character set has 256 8-bit narrow characters. A wide character is a character represented by 2 or more bytes. The Unicode character set consists of 65,536 16-bit wide characters. There are two specializations of the char_traits class, one for narrow characters, char_traits<char>, and the other for wide characters, char_traits<wchar_T>.

CHAPTER 13

Interfacing C++ with Java

*"The essence of an effective rule for a game or a
law of physics is that it be stable in advance,
and that it apply to more than one case."*

—NORBERT WIENER
CYBERNETICS

Although the C++ language has a large and formidable class library covering areas from memory management to internationalization, the library does not address several areas: in particular, Internet programming and database programming. True, C++ components can be built to provide Internet and database functionality, but building complete Internet functionality and database frameworks in C++ from scratch can be a time-consuming task. Another option for C++ programmers who need Internet, user-interface, or database classes is to use some of the many third-party, vendor-specific, or proprietary class libraries available. But this approach often leads to software that is not platform-independent and to vendor lock-in.

If the goal is to provide platform-independent access to the Internet or to SQL-based or PC-based databases, then integrating C++ class libraries with Java class libraries is a good alternative to vendor-specific and proprietary libraries. Integration of C++ class libraries with Java class libraries can save the C++ programmer the work of developing Internet and database classes from scratch, and the integration of classes from these two languages is a good approach to developing platform-independent software. The Java Swing classes and AWT classes can also provide a platform-independent graphical user interface (GUI) to software written in C++.

Java is an object-oriented language (soon to have an ANSI/ISO standard!) that has a rich set of class libraries. Java is similar to C++, sharing much of the same syntax. Programmers comfortable with the object-oriented capabilities and features of C++ will find Java easy to learn and use. Among the more useful class libraries Java has to offer C++ users are Internet (TCP/IP) classes, database classes (JDBC), and user-interface classes (Swing and AWT). These classes can be used to supplement the standard C++

class library because the Java language has a built-in mechanism that allows it to interface with C++. Called the Java Native Interface (JNI), it enables C++ to access Java classes and methods, and vice versa. C++ programmers who need a vendor-independent and cross-platform solution for Internet programming, GUI, and database programming would do well to learn how to use the JNI. Similarly, Java programmers or C++ programmers who also use Java can take advantage of the functionality available in C++ that is not readily available in Java. For example, the Java I/O mechanism is no match for the C++ iostreams; the Java math classes cannot compete with the C++ valarray class or complex class. The containers in Java cannot compete with the rich containers and algorithms that are part of the standard C++ library. Through the JNI, Java can access C++ so that a Java program can take advantage of the expressive power of the C++ language. Likewise, a C++ class or application framework can take advantage of the strong Internet, database, and GUI features built into Java.

The Java API

As described earlier in this book, the C++ standard class library can be divided into 10 categories (see Table 13.1). The largest components in the standard C++ library are the iostreams, containers, and algorithms. The Java class libraries are divided into a collection of 22 Application Programmer Interfaces (APIs). Table 13.2 lists the major class categories in Java. The C++ programmer can access classes in these APIs through the JNI mechanism, which provides *class-to-class communication.*

C++ to Java Communication

There are several ways C++ can communicate with or use Java code. The simplest (perhaps crudest) method is through files. C++ writes a file and Java reads the file, or Java writes a file and C++ reads the file.

```
void main(void)
{
    java_object J_Object;
    ifstream InFile("JavaIn");
    Ofstream OutFile("JavaOut");
    InFile >> J_Object;
    J_Object.change();
```

Table 13.1 Standard C++ Class Library Functional Categories

■ numerics	■ algorithms
■ strings	■ containers
■ localization	■ iterators
■ input/output	■ language support

Table 13.2 Major Java Class Library APIs

■ Java Commerce	■ Java Management
■ Java Server	■ Personal Java
■ Java Security	■ Embedded Java
■ Java Enterprise	■ Java Media
JDBC	Java Speech
Java IDL	Java 3D
Java RMI	Java 2D (Animation)
JNDI (Java Naming and Directory Interface)	Java Telephony

```
        OutFile << J_Object;
        . . .
    }
```

Though this method may have performance problems for certain applications, it works just fine for other applications.

Another simple approach that allows C++ to use Java code is through the exec family of function calls. In this method, a C++ class uses one of the exec system calls to create a child process that will execute some Java program.

```
class use_java{
public:
    int callJava(void) {return(exe1("/bin/java",
                    "java","JavaProgram",NULL));}
    . . .
};
```

The Java program does its job, then control is returned to the C++ class that made the call to the exec function. Communication through files, pipes, and calls to the exec family of functions will allow C++ to use Java code and Java data.

Both the communication through files and the sharing through exec methods fall under the quick-and-dirty, or crude, category; nevertheless, they work. Fortunately, however, the JNI provides a cleaner interface between Java and C++.

Java Native Interface

Native code is any non-Java code that uses Java or is used by Java and has direct access to the operating system or hardware. The Java Native Interface (JNI) is a collection of function calls the Java environment implements that can be used to allow native code to interface with the Java runtime environment, also called the Java Virtual Machine (JVM). The JNI has two major functions. The first allows Java to call native code, and the second allows native code to call Java. For the purposes of this book, we are interested in the second major function of the JNI that allows native code (in this case C++)

to interface with the JVM. This second function is supported by a component called the Invocation Application Programmers Interface, or Invocation API. The Invocation API is a subset of the JNI that allows the C++ programmer to embed the JVM within a C++ program, thus giving the C++ program access to Java classes and Java methods. The Invocation API lets C++ classes call Java methods as if they were C++ methods. Through the use of the Invocation API, the C++ programmer can access Java's Internet, database, and GUI capabilities. Let's take a closer look at Java's Invocation API.

NOTE:
This chapter can only offer a brief introduction to the Invocation API. For a detailed tutorial or more information on the Java language, JNI, and Invocation API, visit www.sun.com.

The Invocation API

Two important pieces of the Invocation API are necessary to make the JNI work: the jni.h file and the javalib.so, javai.dll library files. The jni.h file declares the structures, data types, and function prototypes for the JNI; the library files contain implementations for the functions. The javalib.so file is used in Unix/Linux environments, and the javai.dll is used in the NT and OS/2 environments. The JVM is contained in the shared libraries, and is actually linked to the C++ program just like any other dynamically linked library. So, in the same fashion that the C++ programmer makes calls to shared or dynamic link libraries, the programmer can access the JVM through function calls in the javai library. The JNI declares 14 functional categories:

- String operations
- Exceptions
- Version information
- Global and local references
- Field access methods
- Object references
- Class operations
- Calling instance methods
- Static field access
- Static method access
- Array operations
- Monitor operations
- Java Virtual Interface
- Native method registrations

Functions from these categories can be used during calls to the JVM. Table 13.3 contains the core functions used when calling Java from C++. These functions are declared within the JNINativeInterface struct in the jni.h header file.

Table 13.3   Core Functions When Calling Java from C++

JAVA INVOCATION APIs	DESCRIPTION
JNI_CreateJavaVM( )	Loads and initializes a Java VM (Virtual Machine); returns a pointer to the JNI interface pointer.
DestroyJavaVM( )	Unloads a Java VM; all the resources are reclaimed.
JNI_GetCreatedJavaVMs( )	Returns all the Java VMs already created.
JNI_GetDefaultJavaVMInitArgs( )	Returns the default configuration for the Java VM.
AttachCurrentThread( )	Attaches the current thread to a Java VM.
DetachCurrentThread( )	Detaches the current thread from a Java VM.

Important JNI Structures

The jni.h file declares several important structs. The two structs accessed most often for those using the Invocation API are JNINativeInterface and JNIInvokeInterface. These structs declare the functions that make up the core of the interface to the JVM.

The JNINativeInterface has a typedef declared, and is accessed through a pointer of type JNIEnv:

```
JNIEnv *Env
```

The JNIInvokeInterface also has a typedef, and is usually accessed through a pointer of type:

```
JavaVM *Jvm
```

Through these two pointers most of the functionality of the JNI can be accessed. The JNIEnv* is used first in the call to create an instance of the JVM:

```
JNI_CreateJavaVM(&Jvm,&Env,&VmArgs);
```

If this function call returns successfully, Env will be used to access the majority of the functions in the JNI. Most functions that are not accessed through Env will generally be accessed through Jvm. However, a few important functions can be accessed without using JNIEnv* or JavaVM*. These functions are:

```
JNI_GetDefaultJavaVMInitArgs
JNI_CreateJavaVM
JNI_GetCreatedJavaVMs
```

The functions that require JNIEnv* pointers and JavaVm* pointers can be called using the C convention for calling JNI functions or using the C++ convention. When these functions are called with a C syntax, the call may be a little cryptic; for instance, to invoke a Java method, we have:

```
(*Env)->CallVoidMethod(Env,JavaObject,JavaMethod,Argument);
```

where CallVoidMethod( ) is the JNI function used to access a method called Java-Method that belongs to an object called JavaObject. When this CallVoidMethod( ) is called, it sends a message to JavaObject to execute JavaMethod, with the value stored in Argument as the method's parameter. This syntax can be cleaned up a little using the C++ syntax:

```
Env->CallVoidMethod(JavaObject,JavaMethod,Argument);
```

One method that will ensure the C++ syntax can be used is to make sure the function declaration that will ultimately invoke the JNI functions is declared as extern "C"; for instance:

```
extern "C" void useJava(void);
void useJava(void)
{
    // Get initial arguments
    // Create Java Virtual Machine instance
    // Find object

    // Find method
    Env->CallVoidMethod(JavaObject,JavaMethod,Argument);
    ...
}
```

Another method to ensure that the C++ syntax will be used is to call the JNI functions within C++ class methods. For instance:

```
class java_connection{
public:
    void useJava(void);
};

void java_connection::useJava(void)
{
    // Get initial arguments
    // Create Java Virtual Machine instance
    // Find object

    // Find method
    Env->CallVoidMethod(JavaObject,JavaMethod,Argument);
    ...
}
```

In both instances, we can use the nicer syntax when we invoke the JNI functions.

Java Data Types

The jni.h file declares a number of data types that should be used when interfacing with Java. Table 13.4 shows the Java data types, their C++ typedefs, and their C++ equivalents.

Calling the JVM

Six basic steps are required for a C++ method to call a Java method. The Java Runtime must be initialized; the necessary classes and methods must be found; and the Java Runtime must be destroyed when the interface is finished. Figure 13.1 shows a skeletal flowchart of these steps.

Table 13.4 Java Data Types and C++ Equivalents

JAVA TYPE	C++ DATA TYPE
jboolean	boolean
jbyte	byte
jchar	char
jshort	short
jint	int
jlong	long
jfloat	float
jdouble	double

Step 1: Initializing Structures

The first step is to set up the initial arguments to the JVM. These arguments will be in a structure with a name like:

```
JDKX_YInitArgs
```

where X and Y are stand-ins for the version of the VM you will use. In our case, this structure is declared as:

```
JDK1_1InitArgs VmArgs;
```

We need to set the version field of this structure. This is done accordingly:

```
VmArgs.version = 0x00010001;
```

We get the default arguments that will be passed to the JVM by calling the function:

```
JNI_GetDefaultJavaVMInitArgs(&VmArgs);
```

When this function returns, the variable VmArgs has some useful information filled in. Some values being filled are:

- Native stack size
- Java stack size
- Minimum heap size
- Maximum heap size
- Classpath

NOTE: It is a good idea to make sure the classpath is appended to include the directory where the Java class to be executed is located.

```
// append classpath
char TempPath[Size]
strcpy(TempPath,classPath);
strcat(TempPath,":");
strcat(TempPath,"PathOfJavaClass");
VmArgs.Path = TempPath;
```

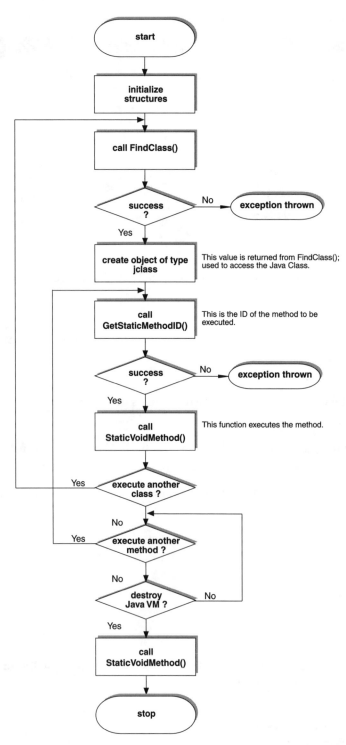

Figure 13.1 Charting the steps necessary to call the Java Virtual Machine from within a C++ class or program.

Step 2: Creating the Virtual Machine

Before creating an instance of the JVM, we need to declare at least three variables:

```
JNIEnv *Env;
JavaVM *Jvm;
JDK1_1InitArgs VmArgs;
```

Once these variables have been declared and step 1 has been executed, we can create a JVM instance by calling the JNI_CreateJavaVm( ) function as:

```
JNIEnv *Env;
JavaVM *Jvm;
JDK1_1InitArgs VmArgs;
VmArgs.version = 0x00010001;
JNI_GetDefaultJavaVMInitArgs(&VmArgs);
JNI_CreateJavaVM(&Jvm,&Env,&VmArgs);
```

This basically initializes and starts the JVM environment.

Step 3: Finding the Class

Once we have a "hook" into a JVM, we call the FindClass( ) function. This function will use the JNIEnv* returned from the JNI_CreateJavaVM( ) function call. This pointer will allow the C++ programmer to access most of the classes built into the Java environment. If successful, the FindClass( ) function returns a value that can be used to access JavaClass. FindClass( ) returns a value of jclass. We need to save this value, so we declare an object:

```
jclass JavaClass;
```

and the FindClass is called by:

```
JavaClass = Env->FindClass("SomeClass");
```

Step 4: Finding the Method

If the FindClass( ) function is successful in step 3, we can use the value of JavaClass to access the method in which we are interested. We do this by calling the function GetStaticMethodID( ), or GetMethodID( ) if the method is nonstatic. The GetStaticMethodID( ) returns a value of type jmethodID. Since we will use this value, we declare a variable:

```
jmethodID JavaMethod;
```

The GetStaticMethodID( ) is called by:

```
JavaMethod = Env->GetStaticMethodID(JavaClass,
                                    "SomeMethod",
                                    MethodSignature);
```

This calls the GetStaticMethod( ), which attempts to find a method called Some-Method( ) that belongs to a class called JavaClass. The value MethodSignature will contain Java shorthand for the method signature for which it is being searched. Table 13.5 shows the coding for the method signatures.

Let's take the Java method:

```
double add(double);
```

Table 13.5 Conventions for Creating Java Method Signatures

JAVA VM TYPE SIGNATURES	JAVA TYPES
I	int
J	long
F	float
D	double
L fully-qualified class;	fully-qualified-class
[type	type[]
(arg-types) ret-type	method type

The method signature using the Java shorthand would look like:

```
(D)D
```

If we had the Java method:

```
void count(double X[]);
```

The method signature using the Java shorthand would look like:

```
([D;)V
```

This signature is passed to the GetMethodID( ) functions as a string constant. For instance:

```
JavaMethod = Env->GetStaticMethodID(JavaClass,"count","([D;)V");
```

The GetStaticMethodID( ) function looks for the ID of the method count( ) that has the signature void count(double X[ ]) and belongs to a class called JavaClass.

Figuring out the method signatures can be tricky, so the Java environment comes with a utility that displays the method signatures for all the methods in a given class. It is invoked by:

```
javap -s -p JavaClassName
```

This utility will print the proper method signatures.

Step 5: Invoking the Method

If the GetMethodID( ) or GetStaticMethodID( ) function call is successful, it will return a value of type jmethodID. We can use this value to invoke the method we want to execute. The JNI contains several call functions; choosing which one to use depends on the kind of method being invoked. In our case, we are invoking a static void method, so our call function takes the form:

```
Env->CallStaticVoidMethod(JavaClass,JavaMethod,Argument);
```

This function call sends a message to a class called JavaClass to execute a method called JavaMethod( ) with a parameter of Argument.

Step 6: Destroying the Machine

Once the C++ program is done interfacing with the JVM, it is good practice to destroy the JVM by calling the DestroyJavaVm( ) method. This is done by using the JavaVM* returned in the JNI_CreateJavaVM( ) function call. This function is invoked as:

```
Jvm->DestroyJavaVM()
```

A JNI Example

We put all these JNI calls together in the program in Listing 13.2. This program has two components. The first is a Java class named resolved_address. This class represents an Internet address. It has one method, displayResolutions( ), which accepts a host string name address, such as:

www.ibm.com or www.microsoft.com

and returns all the IP addresses based on the host name. Listing 13.1 shows the declaration for the Java class resolved_address.

Listing 13.1 Resolving a Name with Java

```
1    // Listing 13.1
2    // This is a Java class that represents
3    // the resolution for a internet host name
4
5    import java.net.*;
6
7    public class resolved_address{
8        public static void displayResolutions(String args[]){
9            try{
10                   InetAddress Address = InetAddress.getLocalHost();
11                   System.out.println(Address);
12                   Address = InetAddress.getByName("www.ibm.com");
13                   System.out.println(Address);
14                   InetAddress X[] =
15                   InetAddress.getAllByName("www.microsoft.com");
16                   for (int i = 0; i < X.length;i++)
17                   {
18                       System.out.println(X[i]);
19                   }
20            }
21            catch (UnknownHostException e)
22            {
23                System.out.println("OH no!");
24            }
25        }
26    }
```

In our Java program, if we were to declare an object of type resolved_address, we could call the displayResolutions( ) method accordingly:

```
main
{
    resolved_address IPAddress;
    IPAddress.displayResolutions("www.ibm.com");
}
```

Invoking the displayResolutions( ) method for this class assumes that there is an active TCP/IP connection on the machine that is running the Java class. In the program in

Listing 13.2   Using the JNI from C++

```
1    // Listing 13.2
2    // This program demonstrates how to use the
3    // Java Native Interface (JNI) from C++.
4
5    #include <jni.h>
6    #include <iostream.h>
7    #include <string.h>
8
9    class addresses{
10   public:
11       void displayAddresses(void);
12   };
13
14
15   void addresses::displayAddresses(void)
16   {
17
18       JNIEnv *Env;
19       JavaVM *Jvm;
20       jclass JavaClass;
21       jint Result;
22       jmethodID JavaMethod;
23       char classpath[1024];
24       JDK1_1InitArgs VmArgs;
25       VmArgs.version = 0x00010001;
26       JNI_GetDefaultJavaVMInitArgs(&VmArgs);
27       strcpy(classpath,VmArgs.classpath);
28       strcat(classpath,";.");
29       VmArgs.classpath = classpath;
30       Result = JNI_CreateJavaVM(&Jvm,&Env,&VmArgs);
31       if(Result < 0){
32           cerr << "Could not creat Java VM " << endl;
33       }
34       JavaClass = Env->FindClass("resolved_address");
```

Listing 13.2 *(Continued)*

```
35        if(JavaClass == 0){
36            cerr << "Could not find resolved_address" << end1;
37        }
38        JavaMethod = Env->GetStaticMethodID(JavaClass,
39                    "displayResolutions","([Ljava/lang/String;)V" );
40         if(JavaMethod == 0){
41            cerr << "Could not get Id of displayResolutions" << end1;
42        }
43        Env->CallStaticVoidMethod(JavaClass,JavaMethod,"");
44        Jvm->DestroyJavaVM();
45    }
46
47    void main(void)
48    {
49        addresses X;
50        X.displayAddresses();
51        cin.get();
52
53    }
54
```

Table 13.6 Output from Listing 13.2

www.ibm.com/204.146.18.33
www.microsoft.com/207.46.130.14
www.microsoft.com/207.46.130.149
www.microsoft.com/207.46.130.150
www.microsoft.com/207.46.131.13
www.microsoft.com/207.46.131.137

Listing 13.2, a C++ class method is used to invoke this Java method. Listing 13.2 contains the C++ class addresses.

The C++ program calls the Java method to resolve one IP address for "www.ibm.com" and all the IP addresses for "www.microsoft.com." Table 13.6 shows the results of C++ calling the displayResolutions( ) method from the resolved_address Java class.

Comments

"These symbols may trigger each other all they want, but unless someone perceives the whole thing, there is no consciousness."

—DOUGLASS R. HOFSTADTER
GODEL ESCHER BACH

The New ANSI/ISO Standard

Finally, after about 10 years of debate, discussion, and changes in the language specification, there is an ANSI/ISO standard for the C++ language and C++ library. This standard is important because it means there is now a standard definition for commonly used classes, such as the string class. This class is so important in so many applications that nonstandard implementations have created many portability problems and have led to more than a few debugging nightmares. Also, there is now a single specification for important container classes such as stack, list, vector, and queue. Templates have been nailed down, localization and internationalization issues have been resolved, and the final set of keywords have been defined. All this is very good news for those government installations, educational institutions, and business and professional organizations of all shapes and sizes that require a stable and well-defined specification for C++. The many workshops and seminars on C++, as well as the university computer science and engineering curricula based on C++, now have a single specification to work from; there is no longer a need to depend on product- and version-specific information.

Keep in mind, however, that although a standard for the C++ language now exists, there are still hundreds of millions of lines of C++ in use, virtually none of which are 100 percent compliant with the ANSI/ISO standard and never will be. The C++ programmer and software developer will continue to encounter many incompatibilities between existing C++ code and the new ANSI/ISO standard. In this book, we focused on the new standard C++ library. Perhaps the greatest change to the C++ library is the addition of the Standard Template Library (STL), the "templatizing" of the iostreams class library and the string class. Using typedefs and macros, a great effort has been made to minimize the incompatibilities with current implementations of the C++ class library. But there will still be confusion and incompatibility issues. Changes in function arguments and return values have been made, too, as well as additions and removals of class methods. The iostreams have undergone a significant structural change. The point is, the C++ software engineer and developer must keep the architectural and structural changes in mind when mixing the old with the new.

Changes to the iostream Classes

The iostream classes are now templates. They now include components that support multibyte characters, localization, and internationalization. Through the addition of the char_traits template argument and the locale class accessed by the ios component and the streambuf component, the iostream classes are now extremely flexible and well suited to virtually any kind of input/output. On the other hand, implementations of the iostreams that depended on file descriptors for low-level Unix file I/O will not find file descriptor access built into the new iostreams. However, adding it where necessary is possible through inheritance.

The core public interface to the iostream classes remains the same, but the protected interfaces have undergone noticeable change. For those programmers, engineers, and software developers who implement new streams derived from the iostream classes, the addition of the sentry, char_traits, and locale classes will require some interface changes.

There are now 30 manipulators in the iostream classes, the counterparts to the ios component format methods. These manipulators include several brand new manipulators, such as boolalpha, noboolalpha, uppercase, and nouppercase. There are also a number of new manipulators that act as opposites for existing manipulators. For instance:

showbase noshowbase

showpoint noshowpoint

skipws noskipws

Beware—Narrow versus Wide

Once the new iostreams were templatized, something had to be done with current implementations of the iostream classes. The template versions of the iostream require the character type as an argument to the template, such as:

```
basic_istream<char>
basic_ostream<char>
```

The streams that instantiate the template classes with the char data type are called *narrow* streams. The streams that make declarations such as:

```
basic_istream<wchar_t>
basic_ostream<wchar_t>
```

are called *wide* streams. The narrow streams are meant to handle the traditional usage of the iostreams, whereas the wide streams can be used to handle multibyte character sets. Character sets such as Unicode, UTF, and UCS can be approached with the multibyte approach. These character sets require 2 or more bytes to represent a single character. The wide streams will be able to handle international character sets.

The iostream typedefs

Besides the wide versus narrow streams, there is also the issue of how to mix the old streams with the new template streams. The old streams have names like:

istream ostream iostream

ifstream ofstream fstream

and the new streams have names like:

basic_istream basic_ostreambasic_iostream

basic_ifstream basic_ofstream basic_ifstream

A standard implementation of the iostream classes will provide typedefs for the old and new streams. Table 14.1 lists the old narrow streams and the new wide streams.

New Default Stream Declarations

Besides cout, cin, cerr, and clog, standard implementations of iostreams will include wcout, wcin, wcerr, and wclog. These eight stream objects belong to the istream and ostream family of objects. They are predefined and can be used without any further definitions.

The iostreams and Exceptions

Under certain circumstances, the iostreams now can throw standard exceptions.

New Classes

Prior to the standard introduction of the basic_string<T> class, the only string classes that were available came from third-party compiler vendors, each of which had a different way of implementing the string class. Each string class had a different interface. The applications of text processing and parsing are so large that inconsistencies among the various string implementations have been the cause of many incompatibility headaches. The basic_string<T> (string and wstring) class solves this problem.

In addition to the string class, a standard specification for valarray and complex classes has been added. These classes are very important to those responsible for scientific, engineering, and math-intensive applications. Serious vector computations can be done with the new valarray class.

Table 14.1   Old Narrow and New Wide Streams

OLD STREAMS (NARROW STREAMS)	
typedef basic_streambuf<char>	streambuf;
typedef basic_istream<char>	istream;
typedef basic_ostream<char>	ostream;
typedef basic_iostream<char>	iostream;
typedef basic_stringbuf<char>	stringbuf;
typedef basic_istringstream<char>	istringstream;
typedef basic_ostringstream<char>	ostringstream;
typedef basic_stringstream<char>	stringstream;
typedef basic_filebuf<char>	filebuf;
typedef basic_ifstream<char>	ifstream;
typedef basic_ofstream<char>	ofstream;
typedef basic_fstream<char>	fstream;
NEW STREAMS (WIDE STREAMS)	
typedef basic_streambuf<wchar_t>	wstreambuf;
typedef basic_istream<wchar_t>	wistream;
typedef basic_ostream<wchar_t>	wostream;
typedef basic_iostream<wchar_t>	wiostream;
typedef basic_stringbuf<wchar_t>	wstringbuf;
typedef basic_istringstream<wchar_t>	wistringstream;
typedef basic_ostringstream<wchar_t>	wostringstream;
typedef basic_stringstream<wchar_t>	wstringstream;
typedef basic_filebuf<wchar_t>	wfilebuf;
typedef basic_ifstream<wchar_t>	wifstream;
typedef basic_ofstream<wchar_t>	wofstream;
typedef basic_fstream<wchar_t>	wfstream;

The addition of the valarray and complex classes finally gives the C++ community a push toward catching up with the Fortran math and engineering libraries.

Three Views of the Standard C++ Class Library

Keep in mind that there are three fundamental ways to approach or understand the standard C++ class library:

- Functional view
- Architectural view
- Interface view

The *functional view* shows how the classes are divided into different areas of functionality; that is, which classes are used for input/output, which classes are used for memory management, which classes are used for error handling, and so on. The *architectural view* shows how the classes fit together and their class relationships; for instance, showing which classes are related to which other classes and how, or how the memory management classes are used in conjunction with the error-handling classes. The architectural view also shows how object orientation and genericity are used to build the standard C++ class library, and how the standard C++ algorithms work with the iterators and containers to form generic object-oriented data structures. The *interface view* shows how the software designer and developer must design and develop software components if the components are to properly interface with the C++ standard class library. After all, the primary object in the game of sound parameterized programming and object-oriented programming is to achieve clean, meaningful, and well-designed software interfaces.

New Architectural View

Before the adoption of the STL into the C++ library, the objects defined in the C++ class library had a strict object-oriented architecture. Once the STL was added, the architecture of the entire C++ class library was revisited. The architecture is now a mix of object-oriented elements with a foundation of genericity and parameterized types. The iterators classes, container classes, and algorithms rely heavily upon parameterization and genericity. This is in contrast to polymorphism and object hierarchies. The new standard C++ class library finds a happy medium and uses the best of object orientation and parameterization to supply the C++ developer with an extremely flexible library structure.

The Interface View

The introduction of the iterators, allocators, and algorithms into the standard C++ library requires a different approach for those who develop class libraries. If a new class is considered some type of container, it will almost certainly be required that the class have iterator accessors. It will be assumed that the class supports an allocator class for memory model management. Any algorithms designed to work with the new class will be expected to accept iterator arguments and function objects. The way the C++ developer looks at interfacing his or her classes with the classes in the standard C++ library must account for iterators, allocators, char_traits, and algorithms.

Required Operators and Methods

Many container objects and function objects require that the user define the <, >, =, == operators, the << inserter, the >> extractor, and copy constructor. As a preemptive strike, it is a good idea to define the following operators and methods for any class that will be used with the standard C++ container classes, function objects, or algorithms:

- Constructor
- Copy constructor
- Destructor
- Assignment operator (=)
- Equality operator (==)
- Less than operator (<)
- Greater than operator (>)
- Inserter (>>)
- Extractor (<<)

If the class is considered a container class, the class should define:

- Iterators
- Allocators

If the component is to be used as a generic algorithm, the component should accept as arguments and use appropriately:

- Iterators
- Function objects
- Predicates

Although no set of operators and methods can be required for every class or every situation, the operators just listed make for easier integration into the standard C++ class library. If these operators and methods are defined for each class that will ultimately interact with the standard containers or algorithms, the programmer will save time in the end. When these operators and methods are designed as a part of the original class specification, the integration with the standard C++ containers and algorithms is usually clean. In short, these operators and methods form the basis for a minimal interface. In *Designing and Coding Reusable C++* (1995), Martin Carroll and Margaret Ellis refer to classes that implement a core set of basic operators and methods as "nice classes." Every class may not need to be a nice class, but most do.

Integrating Standard C++ Classes with Java Classes

Ordinarily, when we write about C++ our focus is strictly on C++. However, in this case we had to make an exception for the Java language. First, Java borrows a lot from C++ in syntax, semantics, and style. Second, Java provides many classes that can be helpful to the C++ programmer. Third, Java includes mechanisms called the Java Native Interface and the Invocation API designed to allow objects in C++ to use objects and methods implemented in Java.

Although the C++ language has a large and formidable class library covering areas from memory management to internationalization, the standard C++ class library does not address several areas. Internet programming and database programming are examples of two large areas that are not explicitly covered by the standard C++ library. It is true that C++ components can be built to provide Internet and database functionality, but building complete Internet functionality and database frameworks in C++ from scratch can be a time-consuming task. Another option for C++ programmers who need Internet, user-interface, or database classes is to use some of the many third-party, vendor-specific, or proprietary class libraries available. But this approach often leads to software that is not platform independent. This approach also leads to vendor lock in. If the goal is to provide platform-independent access to the Internet, SQL-based, or PC-based databases, then integrating C++ class libraries with Java class libraries is a good alternative to vendor-specific and proprietary libraries. Integration of C++ class libraries with Java class libraries can save the C++ programmer the work of developing Internet and database classes from scratch. The integration of classes from these two languages is a good approach toward developing platform-independent software. The Java Swing classes and AWT classes can also provide a platform-independent graphical user interface (GUI) to software written in C++.

Diagramming C++ Classes and Object Hierarchies

Though there are many different class and object diagraming schemes, we chose to use the UML, a combination of several of the most tried-and-true object modeling and diagramming languages, for diagramming class relationship diagrams. The diagrams in which inheritance relationships, aggregation relationships, and containment relationships were important are based on UML. UML has been adopted by the Object Management Group (OMG) as a standard for notation, and it is widely recognized as the de facto standard for depicting object-oriented systems and object-oriented relationships.

Compiler Compatibility, Portability, and Wishful Thinking

Many techniques and code examples used in this book rely on compiler implementations that comply with the new ANSI/ISO standard for C++. The C++ implementations we worked with were Gnu C++ 2.8, KAI C++, IBM's Visual Age C++ 4.0, Inprise's (formerly Borland) C++ Builder 3.0 and 4.0, Microsoft's Visual C++ 6.0, and Sun's C++ Workshop. There was a wide variance in compatibility with the new ANSI/ISO standard, but the latest compilers from IBM, Microsoft, and Inprise were very close to the standard. There were a few minor anomalies, possibly a difference of opinion between their compilers and the new ANSI/ISO standard. Most of the suspicious deviation was due to template implementation. Nevertheless, all but the most strict and demanding interpretations of the ANSI/ISO standard will compile successfully under IBM's

Visual Age C++ 4.0 or greater, Microsoft's Visual C++ 6.0 or greater, and Inprise's C++ Builder 4.0 and greater. The other compilers offered about 90 percent compatibility. Ideally, each vendor's next upgrade will supply complete ANSI/ISO compliance. Gnu C++ 3.0 should be very close.

Once all the compiler vendors have caught up to the new ANSI/ISO standard, portability of core components between systems should be a snap. Until then, when portability, cross-platform execution, and robustness are concerns, it is recommended that the C++ software developer build any new classes upon the standard C++ components. If the standard C++ class library is used as the foundation of new classes, the new classes will be portable in all environments that have a standard implementation of the language.

Just a Start . . .

This book is intended as only an introductory tutorial and reference to the essential standard C++ classes. Many topics in the standard C++ class library deserve books in their own right; for instance, a thorough discussion of internationalization and the locale class; in-depth coverage of valarray and its supercomputing applications; or a complete treatment of the complex class. We did, however, try to include the vocabulary and architecture of the most commonly used classes and their most commonly used methods. The truth is, the only real way to get to know the standard C++ classes is to use them thoroughly and extend them in your programming.

T he source code for all the examples contained in this book can be found on this disk in a directory named listings. In addition to the source for each example there is an HTML document that can be used as a class quick reference. The quick reference has information on the important C++ classes and objects. Information about protected methods, public methods, and member classes can be found in the HTML document. The HTML document also contains UML class relationship diagrams for every class in the C++ standard class library.

Software Requirements

An ANSI/ISO C++ compiler is required to compile the examples in this book. Most examples in this book can also be compiled with GNU C++ 2.7.2 and above. A HTML browser or Web browser is required to view the HTML document contained on the disk accompanying this book. The HTML document is compatible with Netscape 2.02 and above, Microsoft Internet Explorer 3.0 and above and the HTML 3.2 specification.

Using the Software

The C++ examples can be compiled as is. There are no special include files or modules. Each example can be compiled as a standalone program. The HTML document can be opened using any HTML or Web browser. To access the HTML document use your browser to open the file named index.htm contained in root directory of the disk. For more information about the HTML document see the readme.doc file contained on the disk.

User Assistance and Information

The software accompanying this book is being provided as is without warranty or support of any kind. Should you require basic installation assistance, or if your media is defective, please call our product support number at (212) 850-6194 weekdays between 9 AM and 4 PM Eastern Standard Time. Or, we can be reached via e-mail at: **wprtusw@wiley.com**.

To place additional orders or to request information about other Wiley products, please call (800) 879-4539.}

Aho, Alfred V., Ravi Sethi, and Jeffrey D. Ullman. 1986. *Compilers, Principles, Techniques, and Tools.* Reading, MA: Addison-Wesley.

Andleigh, Prabhat K., and Michael R. Gretzinger. 1992. *Distributed Object-Oriented Data System Design.* Englewood Cliffs, NJ: Prentice-Hall.

ANSI Committee Document, 1994. Doc No.X3JI6/94-0027 W621/NO414.

Baase, Sara. 1988. *Computer Algorithms: Introduction to Design and Analysis,* 2nd ed. Reading, MA: Addison-Wesley.

Baker, Louis. 1992. *C Mathematical Function Handbook.* New York: McGraw-Hill.

Barr, Avron, and Edward A. Feigenbaum. 1982. *The Handbook of Artificial Intelligence.* vols. I–II. Los Altos, CA: William Kaufman.

Behforooz, Ali, and Onkar P. Sharma. 1986. *An Introduction to Computer Science: A Structured Problem-Solving Approach.* Englewood Cliffs, NJ: Prentice-Hall.

Benedikt, Michael, ed. 1982. *Cyberspace: First Steps.* 4th ed. Cambridge, MA: MITT Press.

Blum, Adam. 1992. *Neural Networks In C++: An Object-Oriented Framework for Building Connectionist Systems.* New York: John Wiley & Sons, Inc.

Booch, Grady. 1994. *Object-Oriented Analysis and Design with Applications,* 2nd ed. Redwood City, CA: Benjamin/Cummings.

Borg, A. "Fault Tolerance by Design," UNIX Review, April 1987, pp. 46–53.

Borger, Egon. 1988. *Trends in Theoretical Computer Science.* Rockville, MD: Computer Science Press.

Bruce, Phillip, and Sam M. Pederson. 1982. *The Software Development Project Planning and Management.* New York: John Wiley & Sons, Inc.

Budd, Timothy A. 1994. *Classic Data Structures In C++.* Reading, MA: Addison-Wesley.

Campbell, Joe. 1987. *C Programmer's Guide to Serial Communications.* Indianapolis: SAMS.

Carroll, Martin D., and Margaret A. Ellis. 1995. *Designing and Coding Reusable C++.* Reading, MA: Addison-Wesley.

Chaitin, G. J. 1987. *Algorithmic Information Theory.* New York: Cambridge University Press.

Clocksin, W. F., and C. S. Mellish. 1981. *Programming in Prolog,* 3d ed. Heidelberg, Berlin: Springer-Verlag.

Covington, Michael A., Donald Nute, and André Vellino. *Prolog Programming in Depth.* Glenview, IL: Scott, Foresman.

Cox, Brad J. 1986. *Object-Oriented Programming: An Evolutionary Approach.* Reading, MA: Addison-Wesley.

Davis, Phillip J., and Reuben Hersh. 1981. *The Mathematical Experience.* Boston, MA: Houghton Mifflin.

Davis, William S. 1987. *Operating Systems: A Systematic View,* 3rd ed. Reading, MA: Addison-Wesley.

Deitel, H. M. 1990. *Operating Systems,* 2nd ed. Reading, MA: Addison-Wesley.

Eckel, Bruce. 1993. *C++ Inside and Out.* Berkeley, CA: Osborne McGraw-Hill.

Ellis, Margaret A., and Bjarne Stroustrup. 1990. *The Annotated C++ Reference Manual.* Reading, MA: Addison-Wesley.

Ellzey, Roy S. 1987. *Computer System Software: The Programmer/Machine Interface.* Chicago: SRA.

Ellzey, Roy S. 1982. *Data Structures for Computer Information Systems.* Chicago: Science Research Associates.

Elson, Mark. 1975. *Data Structures.* Chicago: Science Research Associates.

Englemore, Robert, and Tony Morgan. 1988. *Blackboard Systems.* Workingam, England: Addison-Wesley.

Ezzel, Ben. 1990. *Graphics Programming in C++: An Object-Oriented Approach.* Reading, MA: Addison-Wesley.

Finkbeiner, Daniel T., and Wendell D. Lindstrom. 1987. *A Primer of Discrete Mathematics.* New York: W.H. Freeman and Company.

Fischler, Martin A., and Oscar Firschein. 1987. *Intelligence, the Eye, the Brain, and the Computer.* Reading, MA: Addison-Wesley.

Fowler, Martin, and Kendall Scott. 1997. *UML Distilled: Applying the Standard Object Modeling Language.* Reading, MA: Addison-Wesley.

Gibbons, Alan. 1987. *Algorithmic Graph Theory.* New York: Cambridge University Press.

Goodheart, Berny, and James Cox. 1994. *The Magic Garden Explained: The Internals of UNIX System V Release 4.* New York: Prentice-Hall.

Goodman, S. E., and S. T. Hedetniemi. 1977. *Introduction to the Design and Analysis of Algorithms.* New York: McGraw-Hill.

Gonnet, G. H. 1984. *Handbook of Algorithms and Data Structures.* London: Addison-Wesley.

Gordon, Geoffrey. 1969. *System Simulation.* Englewood Cliffs, NJ: Prentice-Hall.

Gorlen, Keith E., Sanford M. Orlow, and Perry Plexico. 1990. *Data Abstraction and Object-Oriented Programming in C++.* New York: John Wiley & Sons, Inc.

Harbison, Samuel P., and Guy Steele L. Jr. 1991. *C Reference Manual,* 3d ed. Englewood Cliffs, NJ: Prentice-Hall.

Harmon, Paul, and David King. 1985. *Expert Systems.* New York: John Wiley & Sons, Inc.

Hashim, Safaa A. 1990. *Exploring Hypertext Programming: Writing Knowledge Representation and Problem-Solving Programs.* Blue Ridge Summit, PA: Windcrest Books.

Haviland, Keith, and Ben Salama. 1987. UNIX System Programming. Workingham, England: Addison-Wesley.

Holub, Allen I. 1990. *Compiler Design in C.* Englewood Cliffs, NJ: Prentice-Hall.

Hughes, Cameron, Thomas Hamilton, and Tracey Hughes. 1995. *Object-Oriented I/O Using C++ Iostreams.* New York: John Wiley & Sons, Inc.

Hughes, Cameron, and Tracey Hughes. 1997. *Object-Oriented Multithreading Using C++.* New York: John Wiley & Sons.

Hughes, Cameron, and Tracey Hughes. 1996. *Collection and Container Classes in C++.* New York: John Wiley & Sons.

IBM. 1989. *Object-Oriented Interface Design: IBM Common User Access Guidelines.* Carmel, IN: Que.

IBM. 1992. *OS/2 2.0 Presentation Manager Graphics Programming Guide.* Carmel, IN: Que.

Irvine, Kip R. 1997. *C++ and Object-Oriented Programming.* Upper Saddle River, NJ: Prentice-Hall.

Jacobson, Ivar, Magnus Christerson, Patrik Jonsson, and Gunar Overgaard. 1992. *Object-Oriented Software Engineering: A Use Case-Driven Approach.* Workingham, England: Addison-Wesley.

Kan, Stephen H. 1995. *Metrics and Models in Software Quality Engineering.* Reading, MA: Addison-Wesley.

Kaner, Cem. 1988. *Testing Computer Software.* Blue Ridge Summit, PA: Tab Books.

Kerninghan, Brian W., and Dennis M. Ritchie. 1978. *Programming in C.* Englewood Cliffs, NJ: Prentice-Hall.

Knuth, Donald E. 1973. *Sorting and Searching: The Art of Computer Programming,* vol. 3. Reading, MA: Addison-Wesley.

Kolatis, Maria Shopay. 1985. *Mathematics for Data Processing and Computing.* Reading, MA: Addison-Wesley.

Korsh, James F., and Leonard J. Garret. 1988. *Data Structures, Algorithms, and Program Style Using C.* Boston, MA: PWS-Kent.

Kowalski, Robert. 1979. *Logic for Problem Solving.* New York: Elsevier Science.

Lehnert, Wendy G., and Martin Ringle. 1982. *Strategies for Natural Language Processing.* Hillsdale, NJ: Lawrence Erlbaum Associates.

Liebowitz, Jay, and Daniel A. De Salvo. 1989. *Structuring Expert Systems Domain, Design, and Development.* Englewood Cliffs, NJ: Prentice-Hall.

Linden, Peter van der. 1998. *Just Java 1.1 and Beyond,* 3rd ed. Palo Alto, CA: Sun Microsoft Systems Press.

Lindley, Craig A. 1991. *Practical Image Processing in C: Acquisition, Manipulation, and Storage.* New York: John Wiley & Sons, Inc.

Luse, Marv. 1993. *Bitmapped Graphics Programming in C++.* Reading, MA: Addison-Wesley.

Mandrioli, Dino, and Carlo Ghezzi. 1987. *Theoretical Foundations of Computer Science.* New York: John Wiley & Sons, Inc.

Manning, Michell M. 1997. *Teach Yourself JBuilder in 14 Days.* Indianapolis, IN: Sams Net.

Matsumoto, Yoshihiro, and Yutaka Ohno. 1989. *Japanese Perspective in Software Engineering.* Singapore: Addison-Wesley.

Meyer, Bertrand. 1988. *Object-Oriented Software Construction.* New York: Prentice-Hall.

Mowbray, Thomas J., and Ron Zahavi. 1995. *The Essential Cobra: Systems Integration Using Distributed Objects.* New York: John Wiley & Sons, Inc.

Murray, William D. 1990. *Computer and Digital System Architecture.* Englewood Cliffs, NJ: Prentice-Hall.

Musa, John D., Anthony Iannino, and Kazuhira Okumoto. 1987. *Software Reliability Measurement, Prediction, Application.* New York: McGraw-Hill Books.

Musciano, Chuck, and Bill Kennedy. 1996. *HTML: The Definite Guide,* 2nd ed. Cambridge: O'Reilly.

Nance, Barry. 1990. *Network Programming in C.* Carmel, IN: Que.

Naughton, Patrick, and Herberts Schildt. 1998. *The Complete Reference: Java 1.1,* 2d ed. Berkley, NY: Osborne McGraw-Hill.

Oram, Andrew, and Steve Talbott. 1986. *Managing Projects with make.* Sebastopol, CA: O'Reilly & Associates.

Pagan, Frank G. 1991. *Partial Computation and the Construction of Language Processors.* Englewood Cliffs, NJ: Prentice-Hall.

Patterson, David A., and John L. Henessy. 1994. *Computer Organization & Design: The Hardware/Software Interface.* San Mateo, CA: Morgan Kaufmann.

Peng, Yun, and James A. Reggia. 1990. *Abductive Inference Models for Diagnostic Problem-Solving.* New York: Springer Verlag.

Plauger, P. J. 1995. *The Draft Standard C++ Library.* Englewood Cliffs, NJ: Prentice-Hall PTR.

Plauger, P. J. 1992. *The Standard C Library.* Englewood Cliffs, NJ: Prentice-Hall.

Plauger, P. J., and Jim Brodie. 1992. *ANSI and ISO Standard C Programmer's Reference.* Redmond, WA: Microsoft Press.

Prata, Stephen. 1998. *C++ Primer Plus,* 3rd ed. Indianapolis, IN: SAMS.

Purdin, Jack. 1992. *C Programmer's Toolkit*, 2d ed. Carmel, IN: Que.

Reynolds, John C. 1981. *The Craft of Programming.* Englewood Cliffs, NJ: Prentice-Hall International.

Rimmer, Steve. 1992. *Supercharged Bitmapped Graphics.* Blue Ridge Summit, PA: Windcrest/McGraw-Hill Books.

Robbins, Kay A., and Steve Robbins. 1996. *Practical UNIX Programming: A Guide to Communication and Multithreading.* Upper Saddle River, NJ: Prentice-Hall PTR.

Rubin, Tony. 1988. *User-Interface Design for Computer Systems.* New York: John Wiley & Sons, Inc.

Schildt, Herbert. 1987. *Artificial Intelligence Using C.* Berkeley, CA: Osborne McGraw-Hill.

Schulmeyer, Gordon G., and James McManus. 1987. *Handbook Software Quality Assurance.* New York: Van Nostrand Reinhold.

Sedgewick, Robert. 1983. *Algorithms.* Reading, MA: Addison-Wesley.

Seyer, Martin D. 1991. *RS–232 Made Easy: Connecting Computers, Printers, Terminals, and Modems,* 2d ed. Englewood Cliffs, NJ: Prentice-Hall.

Sippl, Charles J. 1985. *Computer Dictionary.* 4th ed. Indianapolis, IN: Sams.

Smith, James T. 1991. *C++ for Scientists and Engineers.* New York: McGraw-Hill.

Soukup, Jiri. 1994. *Taming C++ Pattern Classes and Persistence for Large Projects.* Reading, MA: Addison-Wesley.

Staugaard, Andrew C. Jr. 1994. *Structuring Techniques: An Introduction Using C++.* Englewood Cliffs, NJ: Prentice Hall.

Stitt, Martin. 1995. *Building Custom Software Tools and Libraries.* New York: John Wiley & Sons, Inc.

Stroustrup, Bjarne. 1997. C++ *Programming Language,* 3d ed. Reading, MA: Addison-Wesley.

Stroustrup, Bjarne. 1994. *The Design and Evolution of C++.* Reading, MA: Addison-Wesley.

Stroustrup, Bjarne. 1991. *The C++ Programming Language,* 2d ed. Reading, MA: Addison-Wesley.

Swartz, Ray. 1990. *UNIX Application Programming: Mastering the Shell.* Carmel, IN: SAMS.

Teale, Steve. 1993. *C++ IOSTREAMS Handbook.* Reading, MA: Addison-Wesley.

Tenenbaum, Aaron M., Yedidyah Langsam, and Moshe J. Augenstein. 1992. *Data Structures Using C.* Englewood Cliffs, NJ: Prentice-Hall.

Tenenbaum, Andrew S. 1987. *Operating Systems Design and Implementation.* Englewood Cliffs, NJ: Prentice-Hall.

Thompson, William J. 1992. *Computing for Scientist and Engineers: A Workbook of Analysis, Numerics, and Applications.* New York: John Wiley & Sons, Inc.

Watt, Alan. 1989. *Fundamentals of Three-Dimensional Computer Graphics.* Workingham, England: Addison-Wesley.

Winston, Patrick Henry, Berthold Klaus, and Paul Horn. *LISP.* Reading, MA: Addison-Wesley.